‘Everyone must choose
his own way, and mine will
be the way of colour’

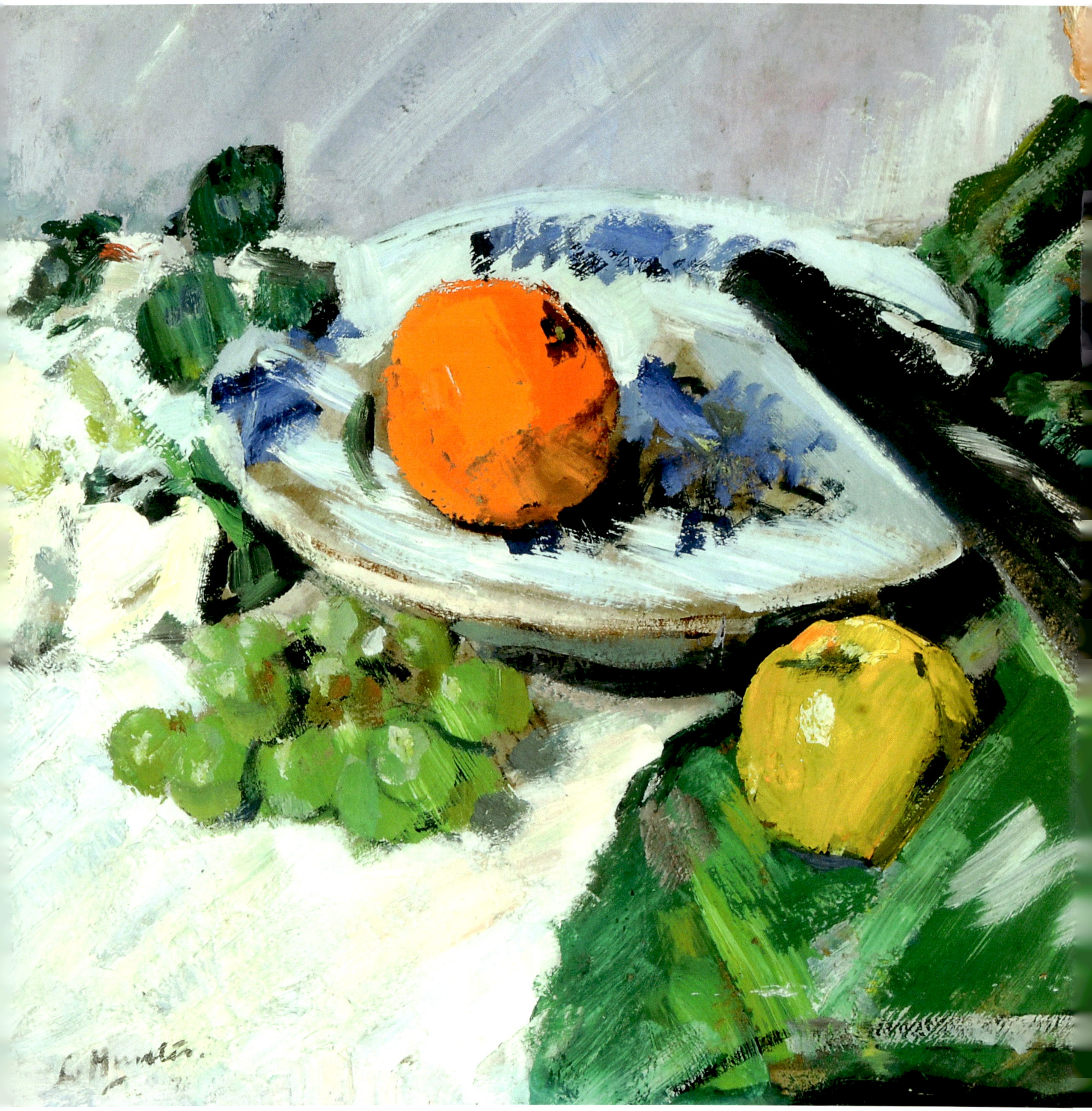

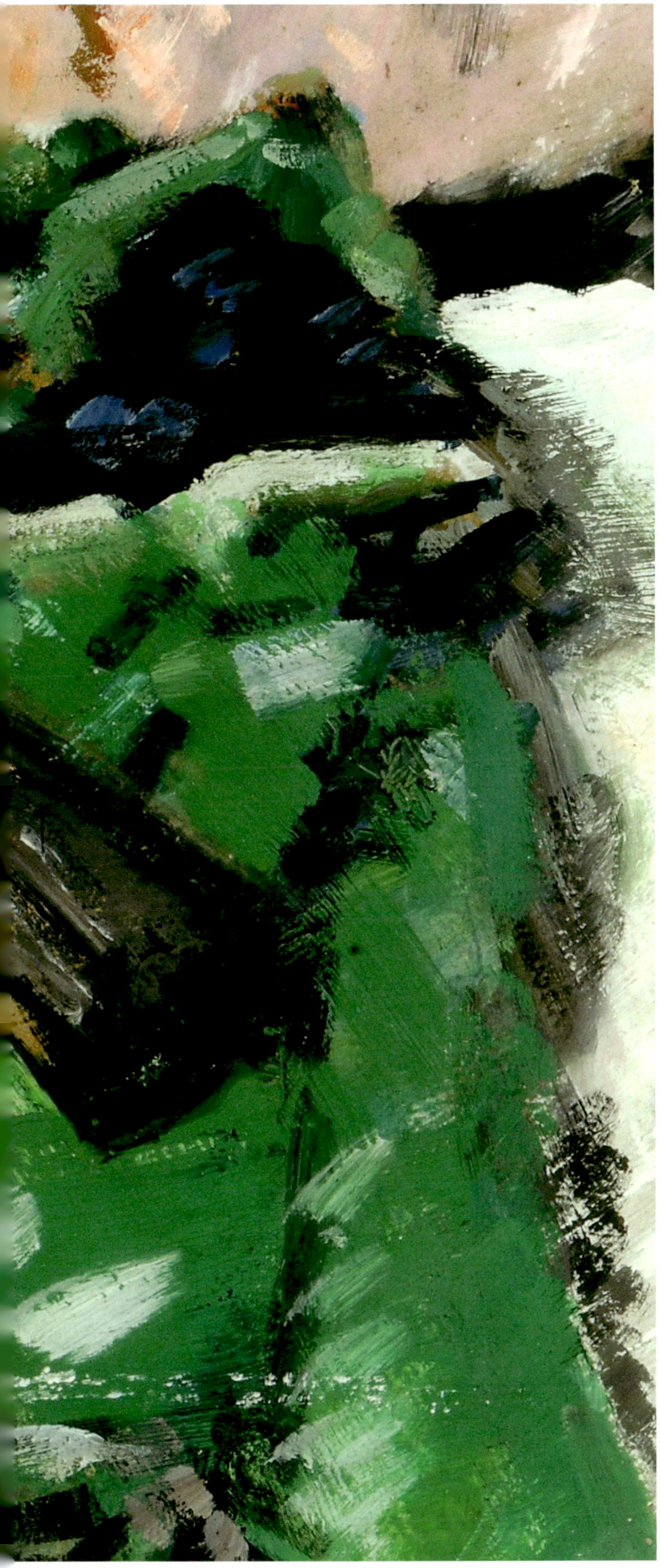

Bill Smith & Jill Marriner

HUNTER REVISITED

The life and art of Leslie Hunter

Atelier Books · Edinburgh

First published in Great Britain in 2012
by Atelier Books Limited, 6 Dundas Street,
Edinburgh EH3 6HZ
an imprint of The Fine Art Society, London

ISBN 978 1 873830 23 9

Frontispiece: *Still Life with Fruit and Black Fan*, 1921
(Museums Sheffield)

Designed and typeset in Dante by Dalrymple
Printed in Belgium by DeckersSnoeck

*Unless stated otherwise, all works illustrated
are by Leslie Hunter*

Contents

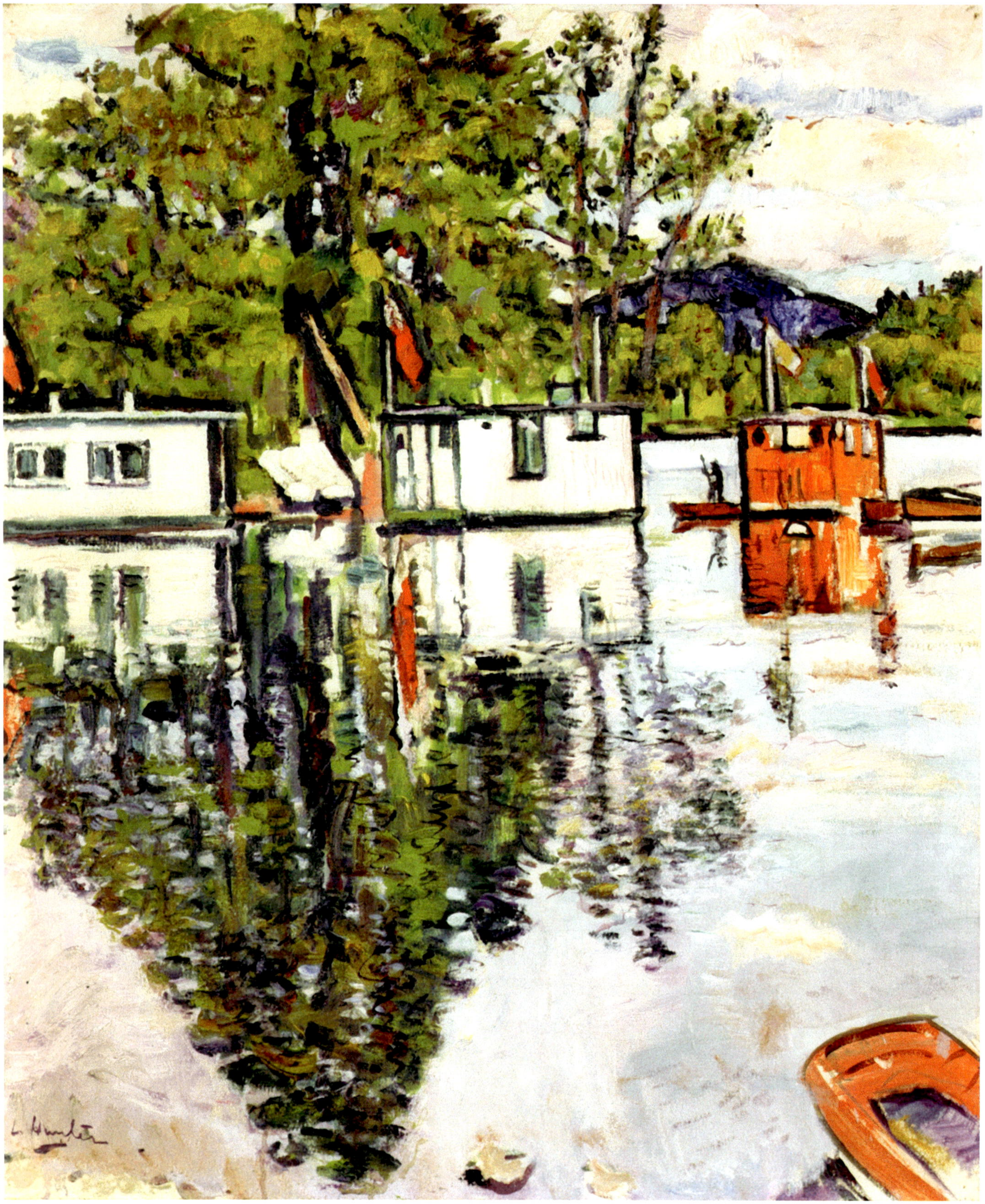
L. Hunter

Preface and Acknowledgements

INTRODUCING LESLIE HUNTER, the first biography of the artist, written by his friend, Tom Honeyman, was published seventy-five years ago. Except for two good, but slender volumes written by Derek Ogston in 2002 and 2004, Honeyman's biography has remained the only work devoted to Hunter himself. Then he was relatively unknown except by a small band of dedicated collectors. His vision for art and his painting were frequently misunderstood by those who considered themselves well-versed in such matters. This included many of his fellow painters. Writing in 1950 about the 'Three Scottish Colourists', Ion Harrison, one of the Colourists' most loyal patrons, stated that 'during their lifetime their work aroused intense jealousy among their contemporaries. It is only now that they are dead that they have come into favour and are esteemed by those who were their competitors. They professed to admire Peploe; they disdained Cadell, and they frankly detested Leslie Hunter, and all swore that he could not draw, because he was an Impressionist. However, this, of course, was utter nonsense for he was a very fine draughtsman.'[1]

Today the work of the group now known as the Scottish Colourists – Peploe, Fergusson, Hunter and Cadell – is recognized and collected internationally. Prices at auction have soared beyond the wildest dreams of the four painters, even allowing for inflation. However to an extent Hunter is still misunderstood and underrated compared with the other three. Yet at his best he has few equals in Scottish, if not British painting. Peploe's comment: 'That is Hunter at his best, and it is as fine as any Matisse', referring to *Houseboats, Loch Lomond* (pl.1), the painting acquired by the French Government in 1931, can equally be applied to many works by Hunter.[2] It is also true that, for a number of reasons, his work can be uneven, but that can be said of most artists. Hunter was an intelligent, sensitive, driven man, who lived for his art to the exclusion of almost everything else. He was much more attuned to what was happening in artistic circles in France at the time than the vast majority of his contemporaries in Britain. Colour was unequivocally the guiding principle throughout his life.

The occasion of a major exhibition of Hunter's work at the City Art Centre in Edinburgh in 2012 seemed to the authors an ideal time to make an in-depth reassessment of Hunter's life and work. In particular we have addressed the key question, left largely unanswered by Honeyman, as to how Hunter progressed from his feeling of profound shock, when he viewed the *avant-garde* paintings by Picasso and Matisse in the Paris apartment of Leo and Gertrude Stein in 1908, to his whole-hearted admiration for Matisse and his work, which inspired Hunter to produce bold, exciting 'modern' paintings during the last twelve years of his life. Inevitably a body of rumour and innuendo builds up around any prominent person and Hunter is no exception; we have tried as far as possible to distinguish between fact and myth. Substantial new research has been undertaken, building on the published work of both Honeyman and Ogston, as well as correcting a

1 | Houseboats, Loch Lomond
Oil on canvas, 1924
Musée national d'art moderne, Centre Pompidou, Paris

number of factual errors by Honeyman. We are very grateful to Derek Ogston for sharing his research with us. Access was generously granted to the unpublished research of Douglas Harrison, carried out in the 1980s and '90s, for which we warmly thank him. Martin Hopkinson kindly allowed his research on Hunter's printmaking, first published in *Print Quarterly* in 1999, to be included in this book.

No biography can be prepared without the kindness and ready assistance of many people, to all of whom the authors are most grateful. Jean Barnard, the great niece of Leslie Hunter, has been most helpful in furnishing family information about his years in California, where she lives. Individuals who shared their personal memories and family memories of Hunter include Margaret Wilson, daughter of Dr T.J.Honeyman, Christine Kelly, Emily Newall, Hylda Patton, Hylda Smith, and Yvonne Roux of *La Colombe d'Or*, St Paul de Vence (sadly all no longer with us). Other individuals who assisted in a variety of ways include Douglas Annan of T. & R. Annan, Colin Clark, Mervyn Donnelly, Bill Hardie and Fiona Robertson, Christine Holley, Gilly Kinloch, Cordelia Lingard of The Fine Art Society, Alison McGill of The Scottish Gallery, Alex Maclean, Lynda McLeod of Christie's Archives, Jean McMillan of Bute Museum in Rothesay, Penny Marks and Susan Morris of Richard Green, Mark Medcalf, Sidonie Metherell of Portland Gallery, Rosie Micklewright of Lefevre Gallery, Duncan Miller and Sue Palmer of Duncan R. Miller Fine Arts, Eileen Moran of the Local History Centre of Dundee Central Library, Ewan Mundy, Jean Read of Larkhall Heritage Society, Corrymella Scott, Peter Shaw, the late Professor Frederick Stone and Mrs Zelda Stone, and Clara Young.

Staff in libraries and art galleries have been very generous with their time, including the Archives & Accessions Department of the National Library of Scotland, the British Library, Glasgow University Library's Special Collections Department, the London Library, the Tate Library & Archive Collections, Patrick Elliott, Alice Strang, Hannah Brocklehurst and Lauren Rigby at the National Galleries of Scotland, Hugh Stevenson and Jean Walsh (alas both now retired) at Glasgow Art Gallery, Anne Dulau, Sarah Skinner and Graham Nisbet at the Hunterian Art Gallery, Ann Steed and Jennifer Melville at Aberdeen Art Gallery, Anna Robertson at Dundee Art Gallery, David Patterson at Edinburgh's City Art Centre, Jane Freel at Kirkcaldy Art Gallery, and Selina Skipwith and Briony Anderson at The Fleming Collection.

In the search for images Bonhams, Christie's, Sotheby's and The Bridgeman Art Library have been very helpful. John McKenzie was responsible for the photography of many pictures in Edinburgh, London and the west of Scotland.

Sincere thanks are due also to numerous private collectors, many of whom wish to remain anonymous, who have allowed the authors into their homes to view their prized paintings and drawings, and in many instances have permitted the works to be photographed for this book. The authors are particularly grateful to Professor Henry Walton, who read the text at an early stage and made a number of beneficial suggestions, to Athina Athanasiadou, who so efficiently handled the sourcing of images, to Emily Walsh for editing the final text, and to Patrick Bourne for his encouragement and support.

Last and not least, the authors owe a great debt of gratitude to their respective families for their patience and understanding. Without the support of Bill Smith's wife, Audrey, and Jill Marriner's husband, Dave, and her children Chris, Jenny and Andy, the preparation of this book would have been well-nigh impossible.

BILL SMITH
JILL MARRINER
April 2012

A NOTE ON DATING HUNTER'S PAINTINGS

Leslie Hunter very rarely dated his work. Exhibition catalogues, Hunter's letters – which frequently he did not date although usually he mentioned the address from which he was writing – and the development of his painting style have allowed the authors to be fairly precise in dating the majority of the pictures illustrated or mentioned in this book.

In the case of dated works, the fact that it is dated by Hunter is noted specifically. Where a year is given for a work, this indicates that the authors are reasonably certain that the work was executed in that year. In cases where the authors have doubts about the precise year, the date is preceded by *circa*. In several cases a range of years has been stated.

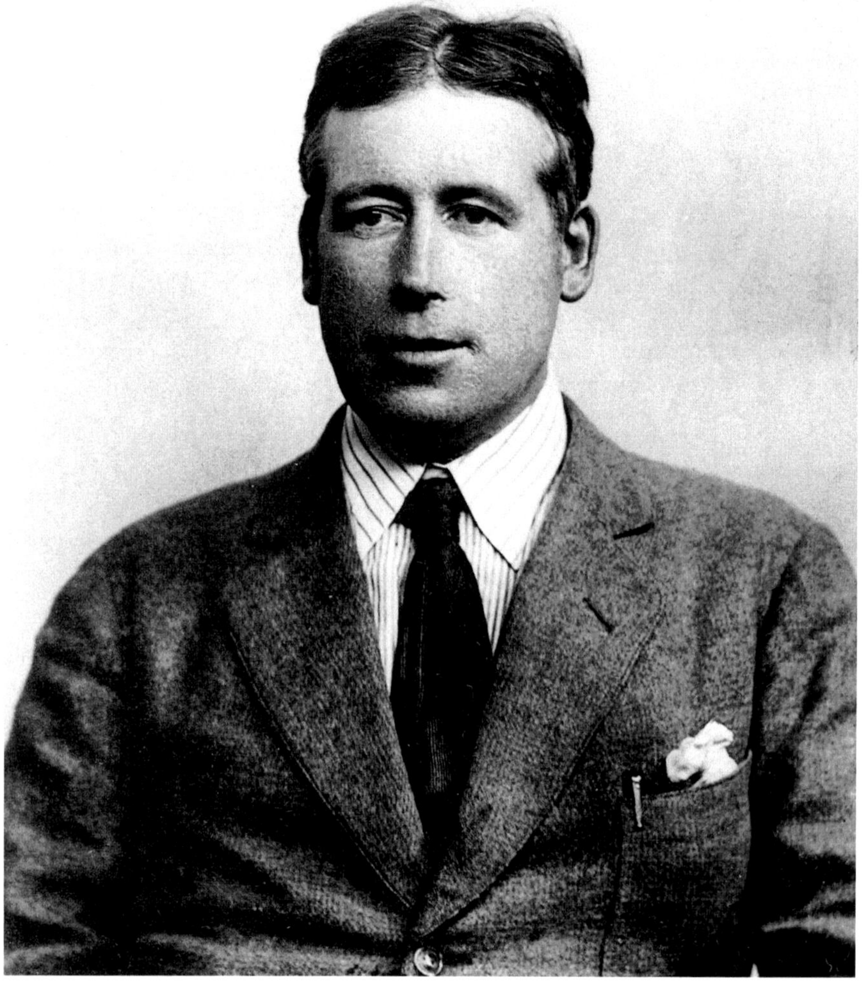

2 | Hunter as a young man
National Library of Scotland

1 A Passage to the 'New World'

SAN FRANCISCO was an ideal place for a young, aspiring artist like Leslie Hunter to live and work during the first few years of the twentieth century. The city had a unique character, forged in the Gold Rush of 1848–49 and moulded by a number of special factors, including its splendid setting on the Pacific coast, its climate of perpetual spring, its relative isolation, a certain lack of inhibition in sections of society – 'visitors never seemed able to make up their minds whether or not San Francisco was respectable'[1] and a freedom of thought. The presence of many artists and writers, and the fact that significant numbers of San Franciscans continued to live in hotels and boarding houses and eat in cafés and restaurants, a product of the transient nature of the *forty-niners*, engendered a bohemian approach to life and living. Literature and the arts flourished in such fertile soil.

Hunter had emigrated from Scotland to California in 1892 with his parents and two older siblings. The family settled just to the east of Los Angeles with the intention of establishing a ranch to farm oranges. Perhaps it was not as easy as his father had imagined, because two or three years later they moved to the city, leaving the orange ranch in the hands of a manager. In 1899 the family returned to Scotland, but Leslie made the bold decision to stay on in California and move to San Francisco.

From the time he was a young boy Leslie had had a passion for drawing. Now aged 22, he thought that he should allow himself the chance of becoming an artist, and that San Francisco offered significant advantages in this respect. There he quickly became a member of the lively bohemian community, mixing with artists, writers and poets. Initially life must have been tough for him, but through his friendship with journalists and writers he obtained commissions for magazine and book illustrations, which provided some income to sustain him whilst he worked at his painting. He made reasonable progress and somehow managed to finance an extended visit to Europe. He spent a time in Paris, then the centre of the art world. Having heard so much about Paris and her painters from some of his friends who had been there, it must have been truly exhilarating for Leslie to experience the vibrant life and art of the French capital for himself. It further strengthened his resolve to become a painter. In San Francisco he was showing his work in various group exhibitions and was beginning to be noticed by the critics. He had made plans to hold his first solo exhibition. It was an exciting time and, although Leslie did not have much money, life for him was good. He had high hopes for the future.

But the Fates were about to deal a cruel blow to his artistic endeavours.

Leslie Hunter was born on 7 August 1877 to William Hunter, a chemist and druggist, and his wife, Jeanie Stewart, at 7 Tower Street, Rothesay, the principal town on the Isle of Bute. He was the youngest of five children: two brothers, James and William, and two sisters, Catherine and Jeanie. His father came of farming stock, born at Chapel Farm, Carluke, Lanarkshire. William Hunter trained as a chemist in Glasgow, where he married Jeanie in 1867, before moving to Rothesay.[2] Leslie was christened 'George Hunter' and he was always known as George within the family. However he adopted the forename 'Leslie' when he was living in San Francisco. Why he did so, and why 'Leslie', is unknown. He may have felt the need to give himself a new identity – to reinvent himself as an artist. Today he is known as George Leslie Hunter or, more commonly, Leslie Hunter.

In Hunter's day Rothesay was a pleasant town with a population of around 8,500. It was the quintessential Clyde coast resort, first discovered by the moneyed classes and then populated by Glasgow's mercantile élite, who stayed in increasingly grand summer residences. It went on to become one of the most popular holiday destinations for Glasgow's working classes, who, during the Glasgow Fair holiday, boarded steamers at the Broomielaw in their thousands to sail 'doon the watter' to Dunoon and Rothesay, escaping the crowded tenements and polluted air of industrial Glasgow for a brief period. During the months of July and August the population of Rothesay could triple, thousands thronging the town's main pier and esplanade all day long, until it was time to return to hotels, boarding houses and the houses or flats of families who took in paying guests in the summer. From the late 1800s to the First World War more than one hundred steamers from Glasgow and other Clyde coast ports could call at Rothesay daily during the height of the holiday season. Such was the demand that around the time George was born a second pier was built at Craigmore on the outskirts of Rothesay to take exclusively passenger traffic.[3]

William Hunter had a chemist's shop at 64 Montague Street, one of the principal shopping streets in Rothesay. The family lived in a flat above the shop. There were another three chemists in the town, two of them further along Montague Street.[4] In Hunter's day chemists made up their own pills and potions to a doctor's prescription, there being few proprietary medicines then. Later Hunter was to take on an additional role as the town's first dentist.[5] Whether he had any formal training in dentistry is unknown.

Hunter was a pillar of the community: upright, courteous, straightforward.[6] Cultured and well-read, he was a 'man of ideas that carried him beyond the compounding and dispensing of drugs'. He was very interested in natural history. He collected ferns as a hobby, installing a fernery in the window in the back room of his chemist's shop. He had a good friend in James Cameron, a watchmaker and jeweller with a shop at 82 Montague Street, just along from Hunter's premises. The two men were kindred spirits and, as their shop doors were always open, they conversed with other Rothesay citizens with similar interests, including Rev. William Ross, David Fraser, mathematics master at Rothesay Academy, and Peter Whyte, a local doctor. The five were all young men and would meet at Ross's manse for conversation and debate on a variety of subjects. On one of those occasions in 1872 the five men established the Physical and Archaeological Society of Bute, which still flourishes today as the Buteshire Natural History Society.[7]

Having two older brothers and two older sisters, there was no lack of children to play with George – and look after him – as he grew up. When he was born, James was nine, Catherine seven, William almost five and Jeanie three. However this did not prevent an incident that could have proved fatal when George was four, whilst the family were on holiday at Carluke, probably staying with relatives. George, later described by his sister, Jeanie, as a 'pretty child with a beautiful head of golden curls', was playing with other boys like himself when he fell into a stonemason's barrel with water in it. A mason heard a gurgling sound and turned to see a pair of little feet sticking out of the barrel. He rushed to the barrel and pulled George out, dripping wet and no doubt very shaken by the experience.[8]

The Hunter children were fortunate that their father was an enlightened man, who also could afford to give them a good education.

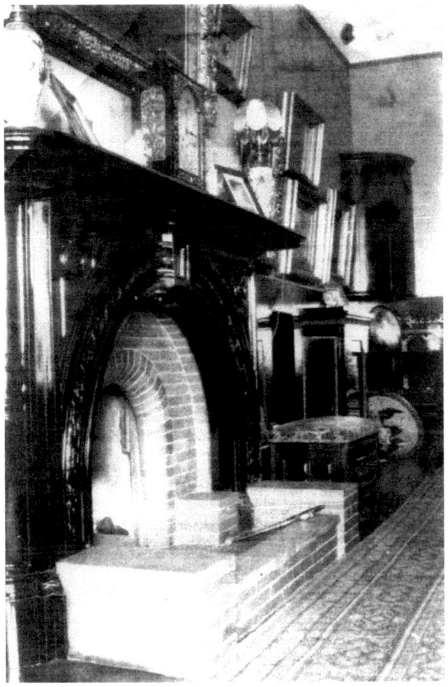

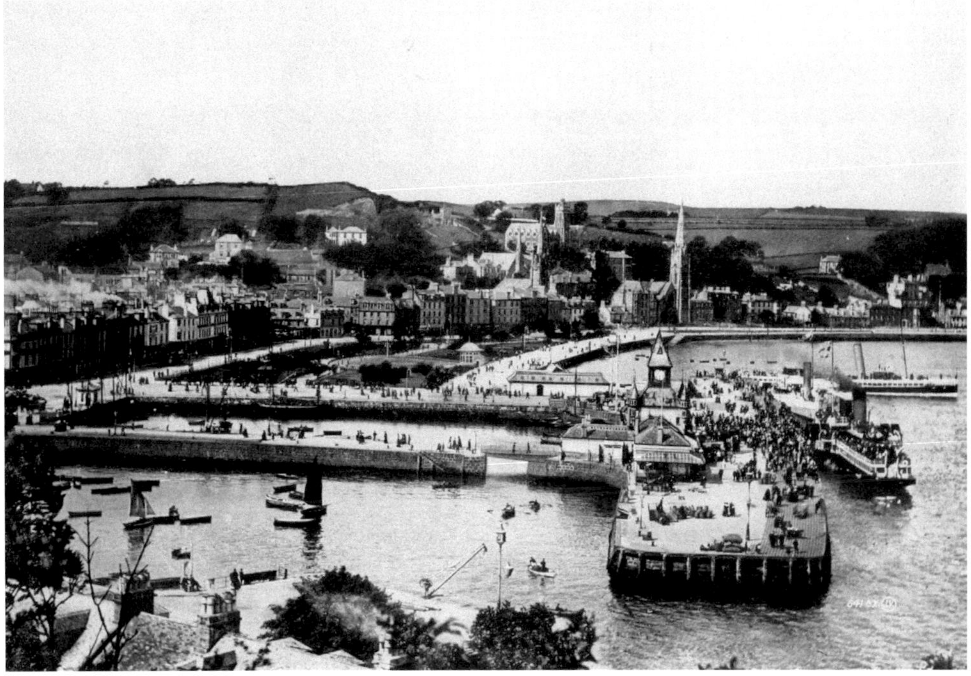

3 | Interior of family home in Rothesay in 1890
Mrs Jean Barnard

4 | The town of Rothesay around 1900
National Library of Scotland

James studied medicine and William trained as a chemist like his father. There were two schools in the town that provided a good education from primary to university entrance, the larger Public School and Rothesay Academy. The latter had its origins in the two Free Church schools and specialised in higher education.[9] It seems likely that George received his education at Rothesay Academy, but all records were lost when the school was destroyed by fire in 1954.

It is not known when George started to show an aptitude for drawing, but Jeanie thought that it was when he was very young. In a manuscript she prepared after George's death in 1931 for Dr Tom Honeyman, her brother's first biographer, she recalls that one evening when he was eight or nine he began drawing from memory a moonlight scene he had seen in a stationer's window nearby. A visitor to the family home at the time was amused by his disappearance every few minutes while he ran outside to take another look at the picture in the window and then back to add several touches to his sketch. Finally the boy presented the drawing to the visitor, who jokingly remarked "I'll keep this until you are a famous artist', which she did![10]

George's ability to capture a likeness was remarkable. William Hunter was a committed Christian, and acted as Session-Clerk at the West Free Church in Rothesay. The family were required to attend church every Sunday. Jeanie recalled that George always made for the head of the pew and during the sermon busied himself drawing portraits of people in adjacent pews. When the Minister's wife called at the family home and saw the drawings she immediately recognised and named the members of the congregation depicted in George's sketches.[11] Whether George's talent for art was encouraged by his parents is not recorded; it was not the sort of career that the vast majority of parents would have viewed with equanimity. However when he was about thirteen George was very keen to have painting lessons and his parents agreed that he should take instruction from a local lady artist. One of his first attempts was to paint a portrait of the family dog. It turned out a very good likeness, remarkable for someone who had not painted before.[12] Later in life he would express the opinion that he had not gained much from the lessons, the only instruction he ever had. However the lessons did not last more than three months, possibly due to the consequences of two tragedies in the family.

On 20 February 1892 Catherine, the older daughter, died. This was followed within three weeks by the death on 9 March of James, the eldest son, who was a medical student. It seems likely that both were victims of the influenza pandemic of January 1892.[13] The parents were devastated. It also must have been traumatic for the three surviving siblings. Within a matter of months the family had emigrated to California. Whether they had been contemplating this move for some time, or they felt there and then that they just had to get away, will never be known. The previous year the family had moved home to 'Newark', a large house in Serpentine Road, Rothesay. It was owned by Mrs Hunter's brother, James Stewart, a house painter, who lived there with his wife, eight children and four nieces.[14] It seems likely that Hunter had sold his own home in Montague Street in preparation for a move to America, perhaps to ensure a cleaner environment and more equitable climate for his children, and the family were lodging with the Stewarts in the interim. Recently the young State of California had mounted a publicity campaign to attract 'well-disposed, industrious people, who desire to better their conditions in life, to come to California and help to settle her vast territory and make for themselves comfortable and happy homes – to dwell under their own vines and fig trees – not only in the land of promise, but in the land of real fruition'. [15] The appeal resulted in a second massive migration to the state, on this occasion not to prospect for gold, but to be given land on which to produce fruit on a significant scale.

William Hunter sold his chemist's business in Montague Street to a Mr Jamieson. At the close of the prayer meeting on 17 August at the West Free Church, of which William Hunter had been a tireless supporter and worker, a presentation of a silver tea and coffee service, silver salver and a purse of sovereigns was made to Mr and Mrs Hunter, the minister remarking that "as individuals and as a congregation they would be the poorer by the removal of Mr Hunter and his family from amongst them'.[16] On 1 September 1892, almost exactly twenty-five years after William Hunter and his bride had arrived in Rothesay, he and his wife and three surviving children – William, Jeanie and George – boarded the *S.S. Ethiopia* at Glasgow bound for New York and a land of endless opportunity.[17]

The Anchor Line's *Ethiopia* was an emigrant ship of some 4,000 tons with a single screw, three masts rigged for sail, and a top speed of 13 knots. It made a regular crossing of the Atlantic between Glasgow, Moville in County Donegal on the north-west tip of Ireland, and New York. That September 262 passengers embarked at Glasgow or Greenock – Scots, English, a score or so of Scandinavians and a handful of other nationalities – with a further 180, all Irish, boarding at Moville.[18]

In the early 1890s travelling to California was a daunting and, even then, somewhat risky venture, taking five or six weeks. In *The Amateur Emigrant* written in 1879, Robert Louis Stevenson graphically describes the trials and tribulation experienced on his journey across the Atlantic on an emigrant ship and thence by train to California. Stevenson travelled second class on the ship. Although this meant taking a berth in a communal cabin in which one's meals were served, in the company of men he did not know and with whom he had little in common, and offering little privacy, it was far preferable to the primitive, cramped conditions, poor food and fetid air in steerage. The thin partition between second class and steerage was no barrier to the hubbub in the latter: chattering, children crying, the rattle of knives and forks on tin plates and the coughing and retching of those afflicted with sea sickness. Added to this was the roar of the sea, buffeting waves against the hull, flapping sails and the difficulty of keeping one's feet when the ship pitched and rolled in even a moderate swell. It was wonderful to get up on deck in reasonable weather and have a walk, breathing in the clean, fresh sea air. Each class had a separate area of deck; movement downwards was permitted, but upward movement was forbidden. The monotony of the journey was broken in second class and steerage by impromptu concerts; fiddles and accordions were brought out and most joined in the singing of songs of all nations. There was some dancing, although many of the passengers were rather reticent about taking part, preferring to watch instead. Games, puzzles and competitions were organized for the children.[19]

Admittedly it was fourteen years later that the Hunters embarked on their travels, when facilities for first and second class passengers might have improved, but the hardship experienced by the majority of emigrants had not got any less. The Hunters travelled first class, which would have allowed them a measure of privacy and comfort. In his first letter to Hilda Davidson, the girl he left behind in Scotland and whom he later married, William, George's brother, wrote: 'There is a very nice company on board. I have spoken to half of them already. I have a very comfortable berth and expect to be comfortable here.'[20] For George, then aged 15, it would have been an adventure once he had gained his sea legs, offering plenty opportunity to indulge his passion for making sketches of the passengers and the ship. However the voyage soon turned into a nightmare. All went well for two days, but early on the morning of 4 September the coupling bolts of the ship's after-crank shaft broke and the engines had to be stopped. The ship lay to until 8.30am the following morning, when following repairs she got underway again. Over the next seven days the coupling bolts gave way on a further three occasions, one involving wallowing without power in the Atlantic for three and a half days, before the ship was able to proceed at half speed for the rest of the voyage. Finally, almost three weeks after setting out from the Clyde and with her supply of fresh provisions exhausted, *S.S. Ethiopia* reached New York:[21]

Cheer after cheer went up. We thought it the most pleasant sight we had seen in years. We went in pretty near the shore and really it was beautiful. The sun was shining on Coney Island ... About 4 hours sail brought us to Sandy Hook. We lay in quarantine two days. We were landed in New York on Thursday night and stayed in a hotel. We started at 9am the next morning for Mich [Michigan]*. And what was my surprise when boarding the train to see some of the fellows on the steamer.*[22]

The family had decided to break the journey across America and stay for an extended period with John Hunter, William's eldest brother, and his wife, Sarah, at Fairgrove in Tuscola County, Michigan, some 60 miles north of Detroit.[23] John was about 17 years older than William. He had emigrated from Scotland with his wife in 1882 and now farmed close to the small township of Fairgrove.[24] William and the family probably took the train from New York to Detroit and thence to Vassar, a small town not far from Fairgrove, a journey that would have taken two or three days and involved several changes of train.

After a break of several weeks the Hunters embarked on the second leg of their journey to Los Angeles.[25] Refreshed by their stay with John and his family, they were much better placed to withstand the inconveniences and tedium of a long train journey. Travelling by regular services, possibly having to change train a number of times, the journey would have taken three days or so, perhaps longer. Stevenson, travelling on emigrant trains fourteen years earlier, had taken a full week to get from Chicago to San Francisco; he expresses frustration when his emigrant train is left in a siding, sometimes for what seemed an age, to allow an express to pass. Undoubtedly travel conditions had improved considerably in the intervening fourteen years, but the Hunters could not escape the same feelings of monotony and tedium experienced by Stevenson as they travelled across the vast open plains of the Mid-West, through the Rockies – truly splendid though they are for the first couple of hours or so – and thence to Los Angeles.[26]

On arrival in California the family settled near the town of Riverside some fifty miles east of Los Angeles. In a letter to Hilda written in November 1892 George's brother describes Riverside as:

... one of the loveliest spots on earth. Entering the town, it is a continuous line of avenues – pepper, eucalyptus and palms. The town is a busy little place. After passing through town, we suddenly whirled into an avenue which for beauty I have never seen the likes. On one side enormous palms, 20 feet high, in the middle magnolias and peppers and on the other side enormous eucalyptus. Throw upon this scene the rays of the western sun and you have the picture. While along the side are orange groves, yellow with fruit and this is for 7 miles ... [27]

By February the following year William was able to report to Hilda:

Father has bought an orange grove up near San Bernardino, so we are building a house on it. What a change it will be for us. But after taking everything into consideration we thought outdoor life to be healthier than business. It is quite a large house with a porch and veranda in front ...

The other night I was riding home late with George. I do love horses. We have two at home now. George and I rode up to Rialto on Sunday. He was on Bendigo and I was on my mare, Mabel. We tried a race. For a while I kept up with him but he beat me as he had the biggest and fastest horse.[28]

The orange grove was close to Colton, a small, relatively new town between Riverside and San Bernardino. Whether the grove was virgin land or had a number of existing orange trees is unknown. It can take up to seven years before the trees bear fruit for sale, a fact that no doubt the publicity campaign of the State of California played down and of which William Hunter appears to have been unaware.[29] Until the trees matured, income had to be found by other means, as is obvious from another of William's letters, in which he states 'Pa is working for a druggist in Colton. George, the kid will be able to do the light work on the grove and for the other we will hire. It costs about $2 a day for each man.'[30] George might have been able, but apparently he was far from willing! Jeanie recounts that George had been set to plough some of the land, a task that he abandoned after about two lengths and then returned to the house, where he was found 'sitting drawing & had entirely forgotten the poor horse standing with the plough, waiting patiently for him to return'.[31] Apparently George 'hated it'; he much preferred drawing. Jeanie recalls that in his spare time 'he was always drawing. He used to go to the library in Los Angeles & sketch the people he saw there. A lady who saw his drawings, thought them so good she wrote to my father asking him to give Leslie a chance.'[32] George must have been overjoyed. Here was someone totally impartial who recognised his talent for art: a gift that the family should encourage rather than side-line.

Sometime in 1894 or the following year William acquired a fruit and grocery business in Los Angeles at 323 W Fourth Street and was joined by the family late in 1895, a man being hired to work the ranch. By July the following year he was working as a chemist in Azusa, a town twenty-seven miles north-east of Los Angeles. The orange trees appear to be doing well, William writing to Hilda on 30 July 1896 'The ranch is looking first rate. I believe there will be a fair crop next year.'[33] It was not all hard work, however, William telling Hilda: 'We are all

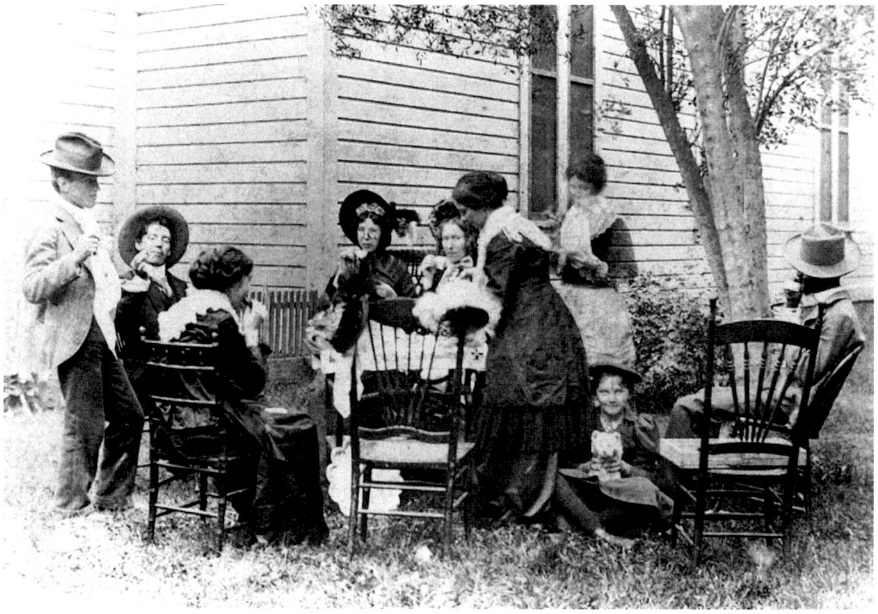

5 | Tea party at Hunter orange ranch at Colton, California *c.*1894. It is thought that the seated young man second from left is Leslie Hunter
Mrs Jean Barnard

going up in the mountains camping for a month. We live in a tent all the time. Most people go in the hot months. It is enjoyable and healthy. There is plenty of shooting and fishing …'[34]

George was in his late teens when the family moved to Los Angeles in 1895 and was beginning to make his own way in life. He was a handsome, well-built youth, who had an eye for the girls, as his brother attests in a letter to Hilda:

I saw Mother and the rest in Los Angeles. Father and I drove to Westlake Park. I saw George there with two girls but Pa did not catch on. George is a good-looking boy and seems to be a favourite with the girls. When I was leaving him last night he said, 'Adios Kid, I've got a date with a little girl in blue.'[35]

However he had difficulty in finding employment that would make use of his skill in drawing. At that time such jobs were hard to come by. In 1893, shortly after they arrived in California, a major financial crisis had hit America. It was followed by an economic depression that lasted almost to the end of the century. In May 1896 William reports in a letter to Hilda that his brother 'has been promised a job in a Frisco painting business'. The job duly materialised, William writing in September 'George is working in a Frisco painting house which is exactly to his taste. He has been pulling for this for a long time and has succeeded at last.'[36] It was a bitter blow for him when he was laid off in October 1896, no doubt due to the poor economic outlook. From then until 1898 George switched between Colton and Los Angeles. In April 1898 William writes:

George is still in Los Angeles. He is trying to get on one of the papers as a sketch artist. They are greatly taken with his work and told him to come round the next day but their regular artist kicked so much they told George they could not employ him. I do hope he will get something to do.[37]

However nothing turned up, William reporting:

George is coming home from Los Angeles as he cannot get anything to do. He is a smart boy but there seems to be no opportunity for him. He wants to be a newspaper artist but has no chance to get experience.[38]

In 1897 the business in Los Angeles was sold and the family returned to the Colton ranch. The ranch itself was sold in December the following year and the family went to live in the nearby town of Riverside.[39] They had taken the decision to return to Scotland. George on the other hand resolved to stay on in California and move to San Francisco. Probably California had not lived up to the family's expectations. Undoubtedly the economic climate had taken a turn for the worse just after their arrival. It is possible that George's father, who was then 58, may have felt homesick for Scotland; perhaps he had left the move to California too late. Certainly George's brother, William, would have been anxious to be reunited with Hilda, his intended bride.

In Spring the following year George's parents, brother and sister embarked on the long train journey to Michigan, to stay for a period with John Hunter in Fairgrove. From there the family travelled to Montreal, where on 13 May they embarked on the Dominion Line's *S.S. Scotsman* for Britain. The ship docked at Liverpool on 30 May.[40] On 12 July, six weeks after returning from America, George's brother, William, was married to Hilda Davidson in Glasgow.[41] Irene, their first daughter, was born on 11 June the following year.[42] On their return William and his father had cast around for a business to acquire. A number of possibilities were considered before they decided to buy a bakery business in Pitlochry, which they styled 'William Hunter & Son'.[43] However the joint enterprise did not last long – William Hunter died on 20 December 1900 aged 60.[44] Jeanie and her mother stayed on in Pitlochry for a brief period until the bakery was sold and then moved to Glasgow. William joined the Glasgow firm of Robert Neil, flour importers in Hope Street, and Hilda, Irene and he also moved to Glasgow. A second daughter, Hilda, was born on 17 April 1904.[45] William later became a partner in Robert Neil.[46]

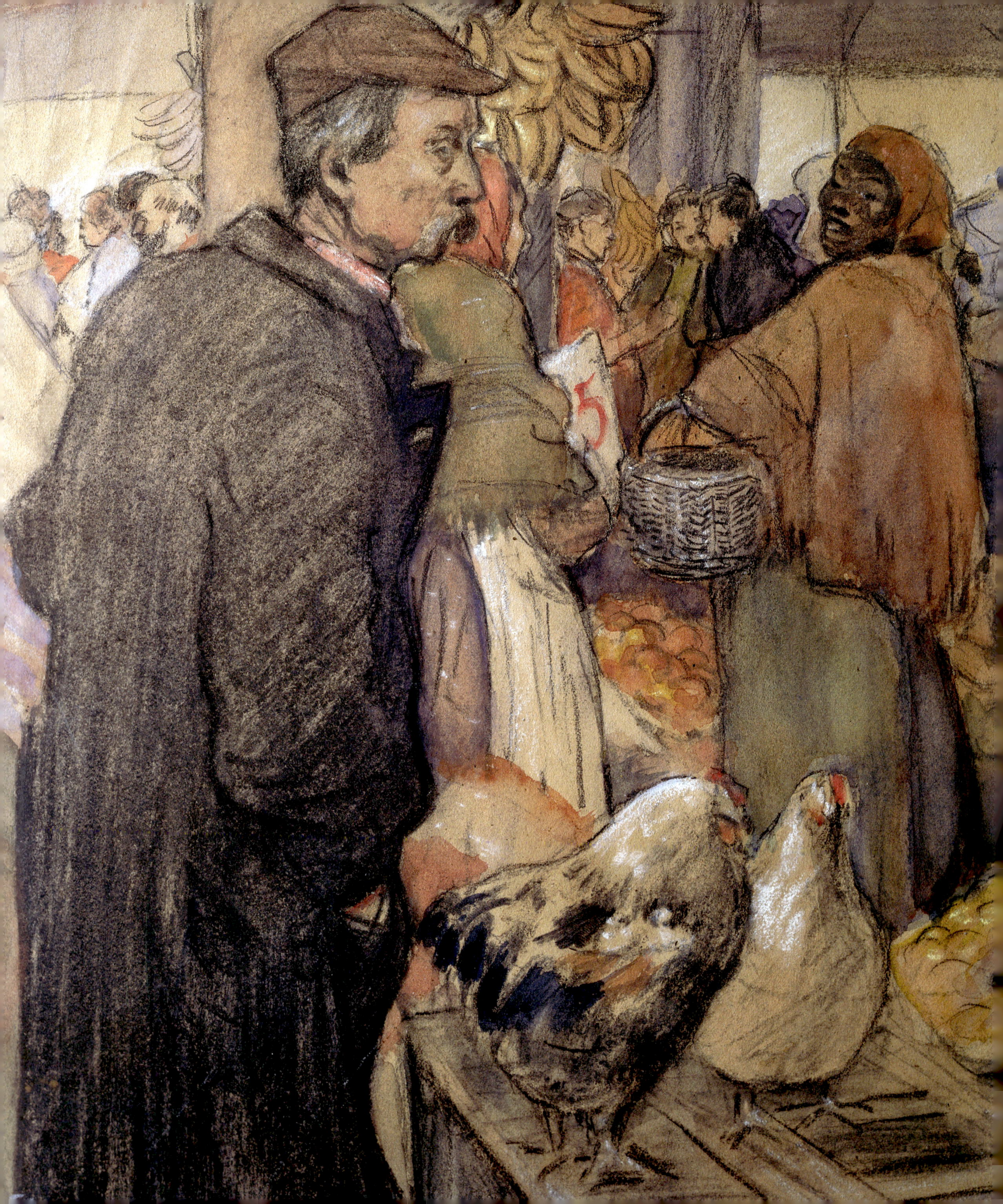
5

2 The Bohemian Life

George Hunter moved to San Francisco in the second half of January 1899, leaving his family in Riverside to prepare for the journey back to Scotland.[1] He was 21 and full of hope and optimism. His outlook is best described in the words of Gelett Burgess, magazine editor, artist, poet and humorist, who coined the term 'blurb': 'One finds in San Francisco whatever one looks for. I was young and ardent. I found Romance. I found Adventure. I found Bohemia.'[2] Hunter and Burgess would become good friends.

Of course Hunter had lived in San Francisco for a brief period in 1896, when he worked in a painting business in the city. No doubt he had made a number of friends, some of whom may have encouraged him in his decision to come and live there. It was the perfect place for an aspiring painter. San Francisco 'called Americans to pleasure and to the enhancement of life through the enjoyment of art'.[3] A close friend, the journalist and writer Will Irwin, described the city then as the 'gayest, lightest hearted, most pleasure loving city of the western continent, and in many ways the most interesting and romantic …'[4]

San Francisco lies on a series of hills at the north end of the Coast Range of mountains in northern California. In Hunter's day the city was limited to a peninsula bounded on the west by the Pacific, on the east by the enclosed expanse of water known as San Francisco Bay, and, to the north, the narrows of 'Golden Gate' (though the famous suspension bridge would not be built for another 38 years). The city had recovered well from the depression of the mid-1890s, and optimism coloured most aspects of city life. Along Market Street and in the commercial district the first skyscrapers had appeared, including the 18 storeys high 'Call Building' built by the owner of the *San Francisco Call*, one of the city's daily newspapers. More skyscrapers were planned. A number of plush hotels also had been built, including the Fairmont in Greek Revival style and The Palace Hotel, known for decades as the world's finest.[5]

Apart from these modern buildings, however, the city 'presented at first sight a disreputable appearance'.[6] Most of the houses and commercial premises were low and made of wood. On the waterfront, described by Stevenson as the 'smelting pot of the races', vestiges of the frontier town remained, including the 'Barbary Coast': 'a loud bit of hell … simply three blocks of solid dance halls, there for the delight of the sailors of the world'.[7] Up to 30,000 Chinese – many brought across the Pacific in the 1860s to labour on the construction of the Central Pacific Railroad – populated Chinatown, an area only six blocks long and two wide. The dwellings were old business blocks from an earlier era, but the Chinese had:

… added to them, had rebuilt them, had run out their own balconies and entrances, and had given the quarter that feeling of huddled irregularity which makes all Chinese built dwellings fall naturally into pictures. Not only this; they had burrowed to a depth of a story or two under the ground, and through this ran passages in which the Chinese transacted their dark and devious affairs – as the smuggling of opium,

6 | The French Market, New Orleans (detail)
Charcoal, watercolour and bodycolour, 1902
Private collection

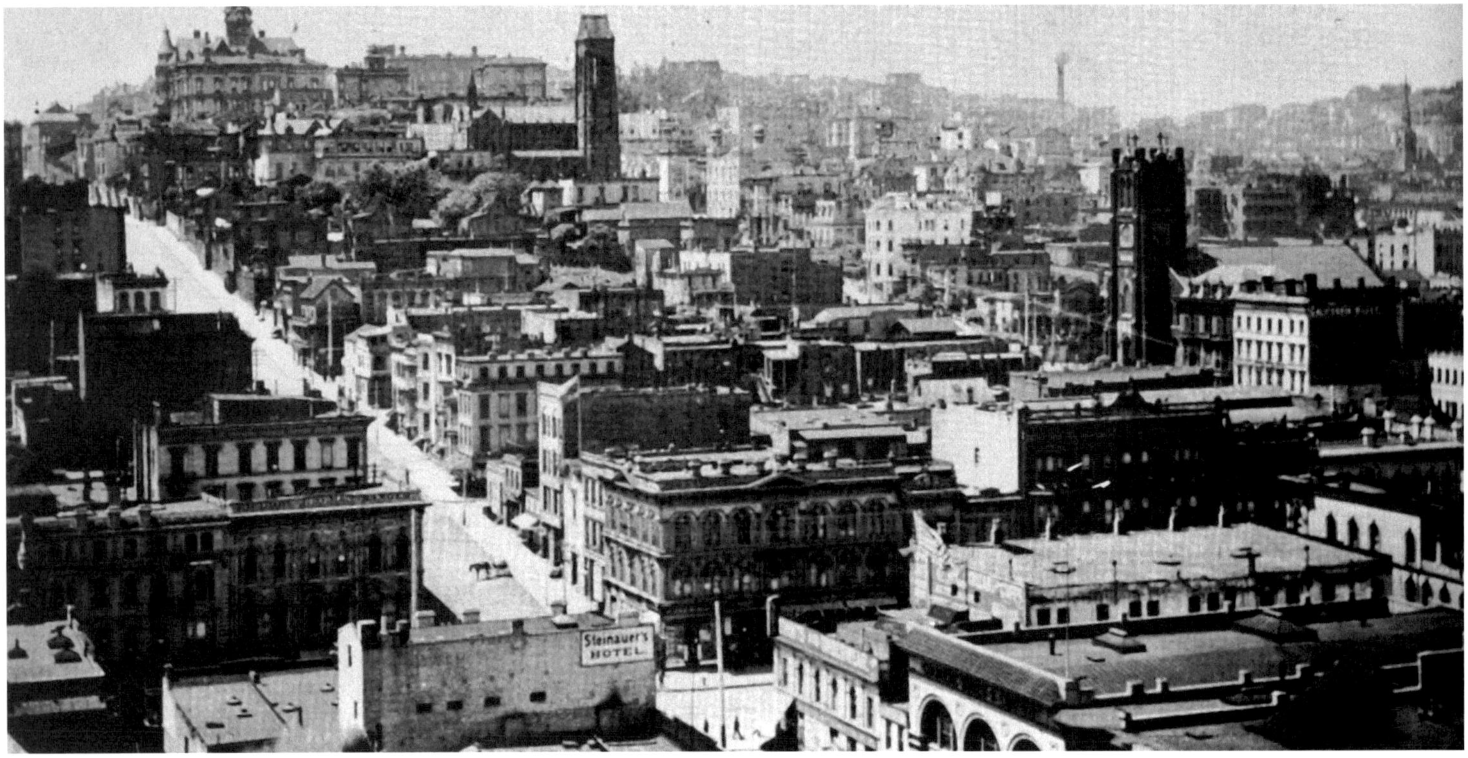

7 | The City of San Francisco pre-1906
California Historical Society

the traffic in slave girls and the settlement of their difficulties.[8]

Chinatown was a haunt of artists, writers and the photographer, Arnold Genthe. The area would become a favourite painting ground for Hunter too. He executed hundreds of drawings of the area and its inhabitants. Honeyman notes that all his life Hunter was impressed by 'the friendliness, the deep humanity, and the gaiety of the Chinese'.[9] Chinese theatre, with its decoration and dramatic spectacle and almost complete absence of scenery, held a particular fascination for him. There were two theatres in Chinatown, and it was the colour, the beauty and ancient symbolism of costume, the laughter, the frequent representation of violence, and even the music that Hunter sought to convey in the numerous sketches he executed on the spot. What he thought of the plays themselves, chosen from a repertoire of thousands dating back many centuries, is another matter! All traditional Chinese plays illustrate a moral or virtuous aim, but the plot is so grounded in symbolism that it must have been difficult for someone from the West to decipher it. Hunter's love of the theatre continued throughout his life. Over the years he executed numerous sketches of shows that caught his attention from the seaside *Pierrots* in Fife and the distinctly *avant-garde* in the south of France to acclaimed revues in London and Glasgow.

At the other end of the social spectrum, the very wealthy lived on Nob Hill, crowned with the castle-like mansion of Mark Hopkins, one of the four promoters of the Central Pacific Railroad. Described as 'painfully penurious', Hopkins had been against the mansion from the outset. It was his wife, Mary Frances Hopkins – reputedly the wealthiest woman in the world following her husband's death – who wanted a splendid house and personally directed its building. After her death the mansion was eventually gifted by her second husband to the University of California for the specific use of the San Francisco Art Association. The California School of Design moved there in 1893, later becoming the Mark Hopkins Institute of Art.[10] The San Francisco periodical *Overland*

Monthly described the school in 1897 as a 'thoroughly modern institution, fully equipped in all its many branches'. Around the time Hunter arrived in San Francisco the Institute had around 100 art students, taught largely by European-trained teachers led by Arthur Mathews, who took the life class. However there is no evidence to suggest that Hunter attended any classes (but, as discussed later in the chapter, every reason to believe that he would not have wished to do so!).

San Francisco attracted many artists, both established and aspiring, as well as writers and journalists. An artistic and literary revival coincided with James Duval Phelan's tenure as mayor between 1897 and 1902. The son of an Irish-born *forty-niner* who had become a millionaire, Phelan responded to the artistic side of San Francisco. Well-educated and cultured, he did all he could – frequently using his own fortune – to encourage the arts and letters. As mayor he did much to root out civic corruption and streamline city government. A Catholic upbringing and two years travelling around Europe after taking a degree in classics and philosophy engendered in him a love for the cities of southern Europe, particularly Rome. Phelan 'dreamed of San Francisco as a city of art and sound governance, the Florence of the Pacific … of California as a sunny land of artists, an American Italy in the surge of new creativity'.[11]

The city's Bohemian Club assumed a new vitality around this time. Established in 1872 by a group of journalists who were accustomed to getting together on Sundays for conversation, the club soon admitted to membership anyone who had an interest in the arts, whether practising or not. It was a place for creative personalities to come together in the evening for conversation and conviviality. Members mounted theatrical entertainments. There were exhibitions of the work of artist members. Excursions into the beautiful redwood forests north of the city were organised, which eventually developed into extended summer encampments. Older members included the artists, William Keith (1838–1911), born in Oldmeldrum, Aberdeenshire, who was reputed to earn $60,000 a year from his Californian landscapes, and Charles Rollo Peters (1862–1928), a landscape and naval painter, and the notable naturalist, John Muir (1838–1914), who was born in Dunbar, moved with his family to America as a boy and later founded in San Francisco the conservationist Sierra Club. The younger Bohemian members – many of whom Hunter would come to know well – included journalists Frank Norris (1870–1902) and Will Irwin (1873–1948), the writer Jack London (1876–1916), poets Gelett Burgess (1866–1951) and George Sterling (1869–1926), the photographer Arnold Genthe (1869–1942), artists Gottardo Piazzoni (1872–1945), Xavier Martinez (1869–1943) and Maynard Dixon (1875–1946), and the sculptor Arthur Putnam (1873–1930).[12] It seems very unlikely that Hunter himself was a member of the Bohemian Club, which by then was dominated by the San Francisco Establishment, and Hunter was not – and never would be – an Establishment man.

San Francisco was a welcoming, friendly place. As has been noted already, a significant proportion of the population still lived in hotels and boarding houses and ate in restaurants. This, together with the city's relatively small scale and equitable climate, made making and meeting friends an inevitable product of the daily round. Conversation, particularly when eating and drinking, was a way of life; the reserve of the eastern cities of the United States was notably absent in San Francisco. Hospitality 'was nearly a vice'.[13]

The city never slept. Most of the cafés were open until at least two in the morning. The saloons remained open all night and on Sundays if they wished. San Francisco was famous for its cafés and restaurants. Writing in 1906, Will Irwin noted:

Probably they were lacking at the top; probably the very best, for people who do not care how they spend their money, was not to be had. But they gave the best fare on earth, for the price, at a dollar, seventy-five cents, a half a dollar, or even fifteen cents … The eating was usually better than the surroundings.

Meals that were marvels were served in tumbledown little hotels.

Irwin went on to describe a meal served up by Louis at the *Hotel de France*, which catered for 'Frenchman of the poorer class, or young and poor clerks and journalists who had discovered the delights of his hostelry' (he could have added impoverished artists):

First on the bill of fare was the [peasant] *soup … thick and clean and good. Next, one of Louis' three cherubic little sons brought on a course of fish – sole, rock cod, flounders or smelt – with a good French sauce. The third course was meat. This came on en bloc; the waiter dropped in the centre of each table a big roast or boiled joint together with a mustard pot and two big dishes of vegetables. Each guest manned the carving knife in turn and helped himself to his satisfaction. After that, Louis, with an air of ceremony, brought on a big bowl of mixed salad which he had mixed himself. For beverage, there stood by each plate a perfectly cylindrical pint glass filled with new, watered claret. The meal closed with 'fruit in season' – all that the guest cared to eat. I have saved a startling fact to close the paragraph – the price was fifteen cents!*[14]

Not surprisingly, Hunter frequented the *Hotel de France*. T.J.Honeyman, a friend and confidant for many years prior to the artist's death in 1931, recounts that Hunter 'often talked of this and other feeding places, also remembering one where the charge was "ten cents – including nut-crackers".'[15]

Hunter appears to have settled in very quickly, according to a letter dated March 1899 from his brother, William, to Hilda Davidson in Scotland, whom William would shortly marry:

George is getting along first rate and likes San Francisco very well. I had a letter from him the other day and he raved about the pretty girls up there but says they are very fast and dress extravagantly. He goes sketching in Chinatown and he says there is always a crowd of loafers round him watching him work. He is protected by a friendly 'cop' who keeps the 'boys' off. They make remarks to one another about this artist from the Examiner. George is in his element there, wears his hair long and is perfectly enthused with his work. I think he will make something of it someday and may be famous. He gets lots of encouragement from other artists.[16]

Shortly after arriving in San Francisco, George had landed a job as an artist with the *San Francisco Examiner*.[17] Owned by William Randolph Hearst, the *Examiner* was one of the city's three morning newspapers, the others being the *San Francisco Call* and the *San Francisco Chronicle*. Until Hunter's work became better known to dealers and collectors, virtually the only way to earn money to pay for food and lodging was by providing illustrations for newspapers and magazines. It appears from a letter Hunter wrote to Hilda at the end of June that he occasionally hired himself out to ranches in the surrounding countryside as an agricultural labourer in order to earn extra money:

Heavens how hot it is. But tis but a few more days of this and I lay down my palette for the sickle (or some such implement) for I expect to hie off myself to some secluded spot far from the madding crowd, exchanging the sunlit sidewalks of the city for the shade of the orchard, the clanging of [cable] *car bells for the lowing of fat kine, the scent of Havanas for the odour of new mown hay. A few weeks later I will return to the metropolis sun burnt and happy with money to throw at birds.*[18]

In the same letter he wrote:

On this blistering hot summer morning with the thermometer climbing up into the 90's, I lift my pen and commence this little 'billet' to you [Hilda]*. The windows of the big studio are open to catch the first breeze of the afternoon trades and through them I have a glimpse of Telegraph Hill and the Barbary Coast simmering in the sunlight.*

Inside the atelier my fellow students are lounging lazily, work being out of the question until the hours are cooler. Our old Portuguese model Manuel, dozes in the corner. Everything and everyone is saturated with the languor of a summer day. And now to our ears come the rustling of skirts. The door opens to the visitors, two girl students who have come for a few moments of chatter. They ask us to join a small party that will spend the warm hours of Sunday sketching in some cool canyon across the Bay, and when they leave, the studio drops into its former drowsiness and only the faint odor of perfume in the air recalls our fair visitors. This is as it is all that happens in the 'Rivivez vous' on this the 30th of June.

The letter is fascinating not only for the light it casts on Hunter's life in San Francisco relating to his art – and to his interest in girls – but also for its eloquent style, the product of a good Scottish education up to age fifteen and a keen appetite for reading. The atélier to which he refers is not named. In San Francisco the only known academy along the lines of a Paris atélier was Gottardo Piazzoni's Atelier d'Art at 609 Sacramento Street, but that was not established until 1901, when Piazzoni returned to the city after a period in Paris.[19] Hunter may have been using the term loosely to describe an arrangement whereby several young artists club together to hire a model. He always maintained that the only formal lessons he had were the few he received in Rothesay in the months before the family left for America.

The *San Francisco Directory for 1900–1901* records 'G.Leslie Hunter, designer and illustrator' working at 611 Clay Street,[20] close to the intersection with famed Montgomery Street and not far from Chinatown in one direction and the waterfront in the other. This would be Hunter's studio for the next three years or so. It was in the heart of that area of the city where the majority of writers and artists lived. Although the address he gave in his letter to Hilda dated 30 June is 258 Tenth Street (a considerable distance from Clay Street), that was possibly temporary lodgings on his arrival in the city. In all probability he would have lived in his Clay Street studio, as many aspiring artists did. It must have been a good size, not the traditional artist's garret, because the *San Francisco Call* carried a report in its *Society* page that on 12 April 1900 a party was held in Hunter's studio for the author, Dr C.W. Doyle, by 'a number of his friends in art and literary circles'. The studio had been:

... gaily decorated for the occasion with lanterns and evergreens. Dr Doyle and Herman Scheffauer gave the company readings from their recent contributions to fiction and poetry, and music and dancing served most pleasantly to pass the remainder of the evening.[21]

Hunter was never the tidiest of people. No doubt he – and probably some of his friends – would have had to do a fair amount of work to ensure that the studio looked as attractive as it appears to have done!

Will Irwin mentions in his autobiography another 'memorable party' that Hunter threw in his studio several years later:

Leslie Hunter ... gave in his studio one of those parties from which people date time. I was enjoying myself hugely, when I passed a man wearing a flannel shirt and a belt, who sat in a corner with a pair of remarkably bright eyes fixed on vacancy. He had strong shoulders, a fine head, features of the chiselled type. Impertinently, I asked:
'Having a good time, old man?'
He fixed those brilliant eyes on me.
'I can't enjoy this kind of thing. I was never young!' he said.

So I dropped down beside him and engaged him in mature conversation. I can't remember the topic, but he talked brilliantly. Suddenly, something he said made me realize that he was Jack London. His fame then rested solely on his vital Klondike stories, but he was already a professed and militant socialist, defiant of the bourgeois and delighting to shock them.[22]

Honeyman also mentions this party:

Everybody who was anybody in Bohemia was there. I have gathered accounts of it from several angles. A list of those who were known to be present would certainly include many who have since made their mark ... I suspect that May Griswold had a big share in the running of the party. She certainly roped in the 'gang' with a complete disregard of the host's capacity to entertain.[23]

Will Irwin and Edith May Griswold were journalists and good friends of Hunter. Griswold was later to marry the New York war correspondent, Edwin Emmerson, noted for his German bias. The only other woman at the party was Isabel Fraser, another journalist, about whom more shall be said in chapter four.

Many years later one of Hunter's friends

from those days, the artist and illustrator Blendon Campbell (1872–1969), described him to Honeyman as 'a solitary sort of chap, popular, well liked, but shy because he was so often hard up'.[24] Campbell's description of Hunter as 'a solitary sort of chap … shy' seems rather wide of the mark, judging from the company at both parties. Campbell also described him as 'popular, well liked' and that certainly is true. It is clear that within a comparatively short time Hunter had built up a circle of friends that included many of the leading lights of 'Bohemia'. As well as Will Irwin and May Griswold, Hunter's close friends included Gottardo Piazzoni and Xavier Martinez, the elders of the younger generation of painters, and the poet, Herman Scheffauer. His wider circle included Gelett Burgess, Arnold Genthe, the graphic artist Rea Irvin, the illustrator Stanley Armstrong, Jack London and George Sterling. Hunter was well-read, particularly in philosophy. He was very interested in the German philosophers, Arthur Schopenhauer (1788–1860) and Friedrich Nietzsche (1844–1900), whose writings were keenly discussed in such circles at that time. In talking about how to first approach a work of art, Hunter would paraphrase Schopenhauer: 'You must treat a work of art as you do a great man; stand before it and wait patiently until it deigns to speak.'[25]

When Honeyman's biography of Hunter was published in 1937, his brother, William, took issue with Honeyman over his portrayal of Hunter as invariably 'hard up', pointing out that Hunter had the use of family money.[26] Undoubtedly it must have been difficult at times for Hunter, on his own in a large city trying to make a living as an artist. Occasionally he would take casual paid employment to get by, such as as an agricultural labourer or a ticket-taker at one of San Francisco's dance halls.[27] Judging from his letter to Hilda it did not seem to bother him unduly. He was going to get as much out of life as he could.

All the while he worked away feverishly at his art. Campbell told Honeyman of Hunter's 'enormous energy and industry':

His passion for making sketches, many of which were intended to serve as notes for more complete pictures, made the others look like playboys. None of them felt that Hunter was wasting his energy, for they sensed something big in his work as well as in his personality. They might have thought some of his work untidy, and unlikely to appeal to their Art School professors, but they knew in their hearts that he enjoyed a freedom which gave his art vitality.[28]

He had a very good memory. In a quick drawing he would record a scene or an experience with greater clarity than most people could convey in words. By selecting only the essentials, he captured 'the entire spirit of the subject, while lesser minds were obsessed with the need for accuracy'.[29]

Hunter's skill in drawing and his sheer tenacity paid off towards the end of 1899, when he landed a commission to provide three illustrations for a short story in the San Francisco magazine, *Overland Monthly*.[30] Established in 1868, its first editor was Bret Harte (1836–1902), the author and poet, who quickly established it as one of America's leading literary journals. By the turn of the century it had developed into a magazine of more general interest, encompassing the life and environment of California and covering subjects as diverse as the infant automobile industry and California's Lick Observatory and astronomy. By this time much use was being made of photographs; nevertheless the magazine continued to publish stories and poems, many illustrated with artists' drawings. Some of Jack London's short stories appeared for the first time in *Overland Monthly*.

Two of the black and white drawings are signed 'Hunter' and the third, a full-page portrayal of a poor, elderly couple in their prairie homestead, their figures illuminated by the light of a single oil lamp on the floor in front of them, is signed 'G. Leslie Hunter' and dated '*99*'. This is the first recorded occasion that Hunter uses the middle name 'Leslie'. As mentioned in the first chapter, he was christened plain George Hunter. 'Leslie' does not appear to have been a family name, and its adoption by Hunter is

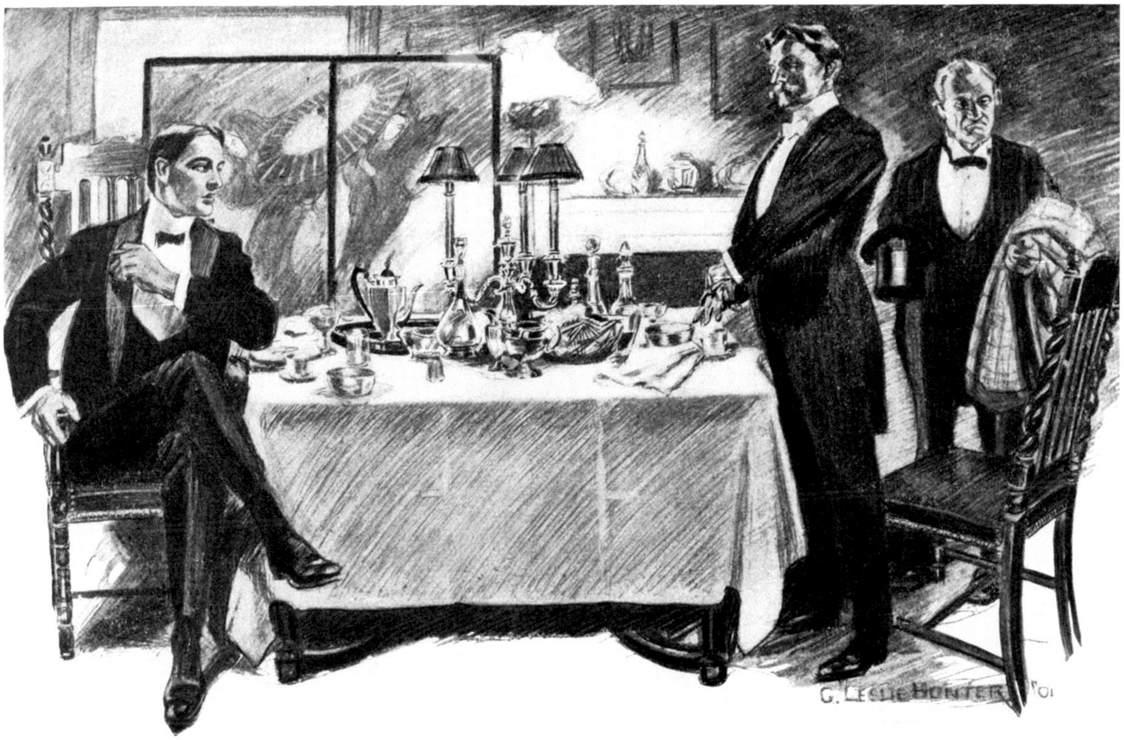

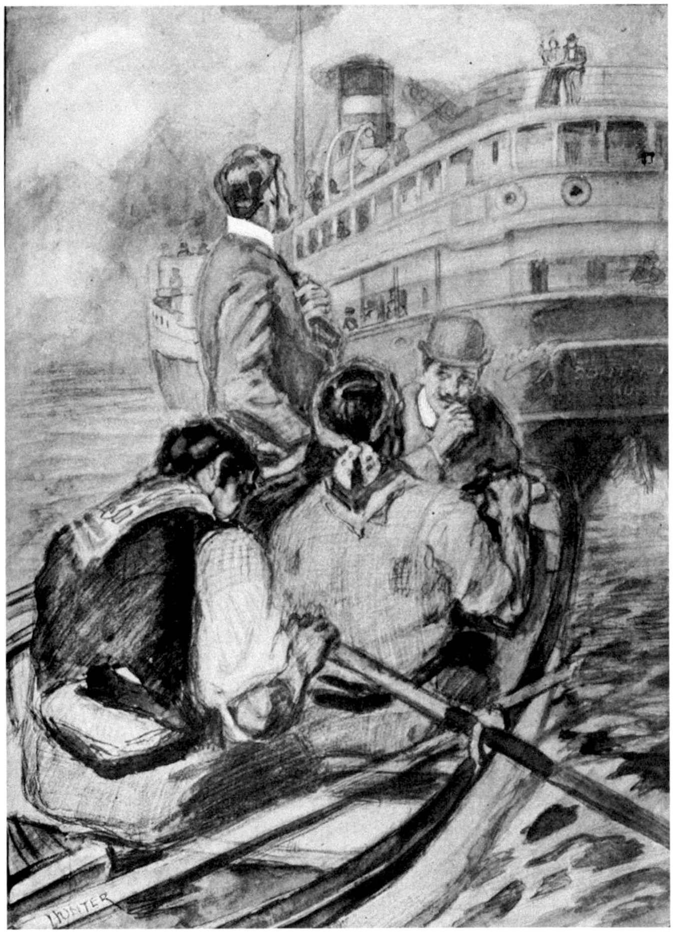

8 | *'He had risen to his feet while speaking'* Illustration in *Overland Monthly* for 'The Free Trader' by A.J. Brown, September 1901
The British Library

9 | *'Au revoir' she laughed. 'Call this time tomorrow.'* Illustration in *Overland Monthly* for 'The Girl from Noumea' by J.F. Rose-Soley, April 1901
The British Library

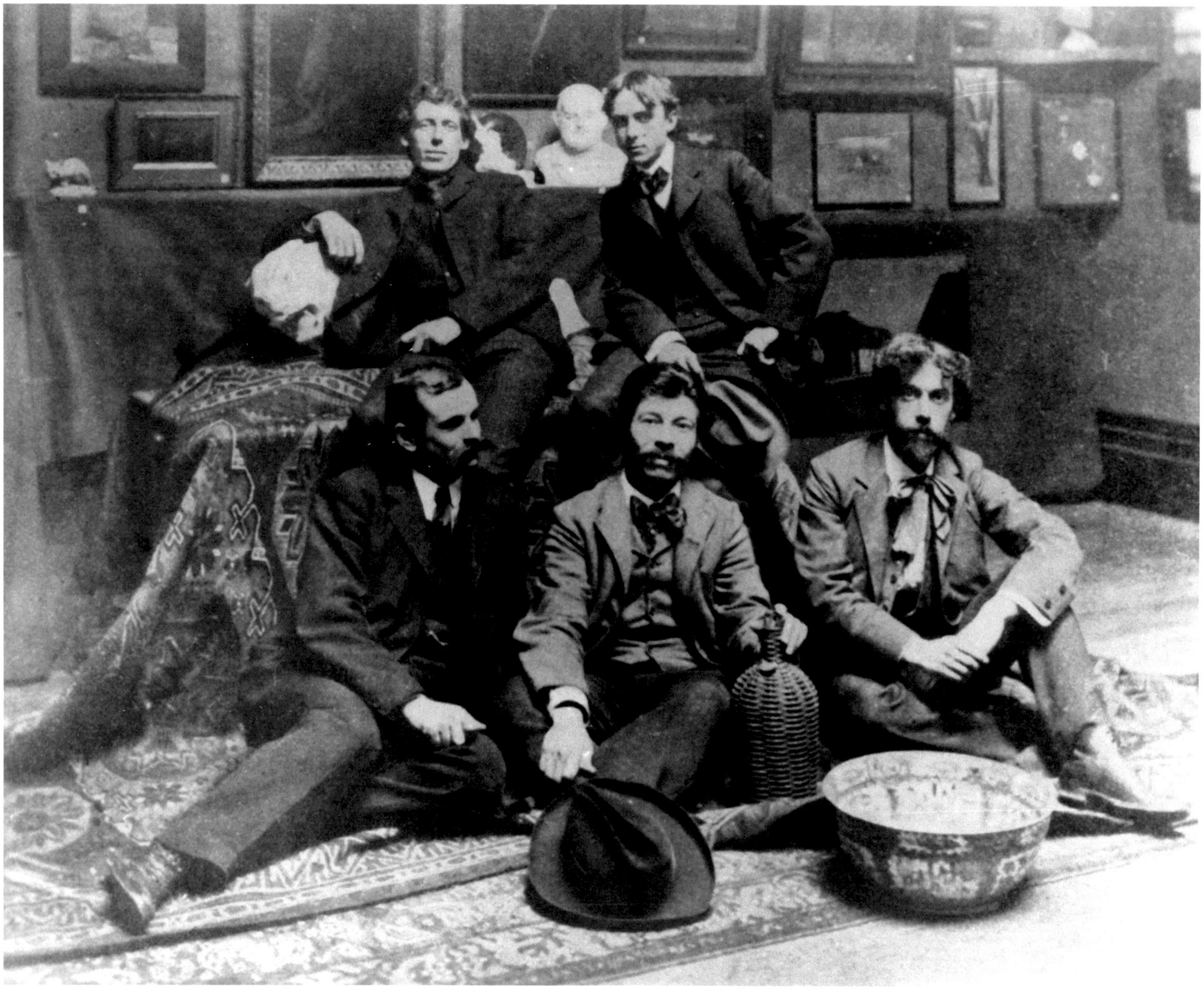

unexplained. In California he signed his work 'G. Leslie Hunter' or 'Hunter' and occasionally 'G.L.H.' In the 1920s he would drop the name 'George' completely. From this point Hunter will be referred to as 'Leslie' rather than 'George'.

The editor of *Overland Monthly* must have been impressed by Hunter's work, because the following year he was entrusted with the cover of the magazine's *Christmas Number*, a sketch in black ink and white bodycolour of a mounted cowboy with a guitar. This was followed by a full-length profile of a monk in contemplation holding a small cross, with two other monks and monastic buildings in the middle distance, on the cover of the issue for January 1901. Hunter was to provide the magazine with some sixty illustrations over the next two years or so.[31] The work brought him some much-needed income; like the majority of artists, he executed illustrations for magazines out of necessity, rather than by choice. Unlike his cover pieces, which by design are sketches, the majority of his story illustrations are finely-executed drawings in black ink and wash, often on card. Many are full page

10 | Exhibition Hanging Committee of the California Society of Artists *c.*1902. Clockwise from top left: Leslie Hunter, Blendon Campbell, Peter Neilson, Xavier Martinez, Gottardo Piazzoni
National Library of Scotland

and all are in black and white. They exemplify Hunter's skill as a draughtsman and his ability to evoke atmosphere in a scene and character in a face. At the beginning of 1901 he supplied six drawings for a short story, *Francesca, a Tale of Fisherman's Wharf*, based on his sketches of life at the city's Fisherman's Wharf, which led the *San Francisco Call* to comment in its *Literary Notes*:

The Overland Monthly for February has rather a departure from its usual illustrations in some impressionistic washes by G. Leslie Hunter. One of these, depicting the fishermen at work mending their nets on the wharf, is an excellent composition ...[32]

He executed three illustrations for a new story by Jack London that appeared in the May issue of *Overland Monthly* that year.

In 1902 Hunter was one of two artists asked to illustrate two of Bret Harte's early and most notable stories, reprinted as a tribute in the *Bret Harte Memorial Number* of *Overland Monthly* in the September issue. Harte, who left California in the early 1870s, had died in England earlier that year. Stanley Armstrong, a friend of Hunter and a regular contributor of images to *Overland Monthly*, illustrated *The Luck of Roaring Camp*, and Hunter provided a title piece and five illustrations for *The Outcasts of Poker Flat*, both published for the first time in *Overland Monthly* in 1868 and 1869 respectively. Tales of life and death in the lawless rough-and-tumble of the California Gold Rush in 1848–49 brought Harte instant fame; within two years he was the highest-paid writer in America. *The Outcasts of Poker Flat* tells the story of the demise of John Oakhurst, a professional gambler who has 'cleaned-out' several of the citizens of Poker Flat and is forced at gunpoint to leave town, together with three other 'undesirables' – two women of dubious reputation and a drunkard. The four make for the next mining camp over a mountain pass, but they are caught in a heavy snowstorm and face a lingering death. In his story Harte makes the point that, even in such terrible circumstances, some apparently heartless individuals have a conscience and sacrifice themselves for the sake of others, though, as it turns out in this case, it was to be in vain.[33] Even today, despite the standard of reproduction and the quality of paper and print, the illustrations have considerable impact on the page.

Fifteen drawings by Hunter appeared in six consecutive issues of the monthly periodical *Sunset*, beginning in September 1902. Established by the Passenger Division of the Southern Pacific Railroad in 1898, the magazine was first and foremost a promotional venture, publicizing the delights of California and the railroad's premier train, the *Sunset Limited*, which ran between New Orleans, Los Angeles and San Francisco. However the magazine also carried stories and poems, many illustrated by artists. His friend, May Griswold, was assistant editor of *Sunset* for a number of years and probably was instrumental in Hunter getting the job. His principal commission was to provide illustrations for a story in four parts by Flora Haines Loughead, *Mine Eyes unto the Hills*, which appeared in successive issues of the magazine. Despite the biblical allusion in the title, it was a romance.

Honeyman asserts that in illustration Hunter 'swore allegiance to Forain and Steinlen'.[34] Although it is likely that he had seen the work of both artists – there was a constant flow of painters between San Francisco and Paris, bringing news of what was happening in European art movements, and European magazines such as *Gil Blas illustré* were to be had in San Francisco – there is little sign in Hunter's illustrative work for *Overland Monthly* and *Sunset* of the influence of either Jean-Louis Forain (1852–1931) or Theophile Steinlen (1859–1923).

During his first three years in San Francisco Hunter must have earned at least enough from magazine illustrations to cover his basic living expenses. At the same time he was building up a body of work that he could sell to collectors. He exhibited for the first time in 1901, when he showed three watercolours of local scenes at the San Francisco Art Association.[35] Towards the end of that year, or early the following year, Hunter was one of a group of young artists who founded the California Society of

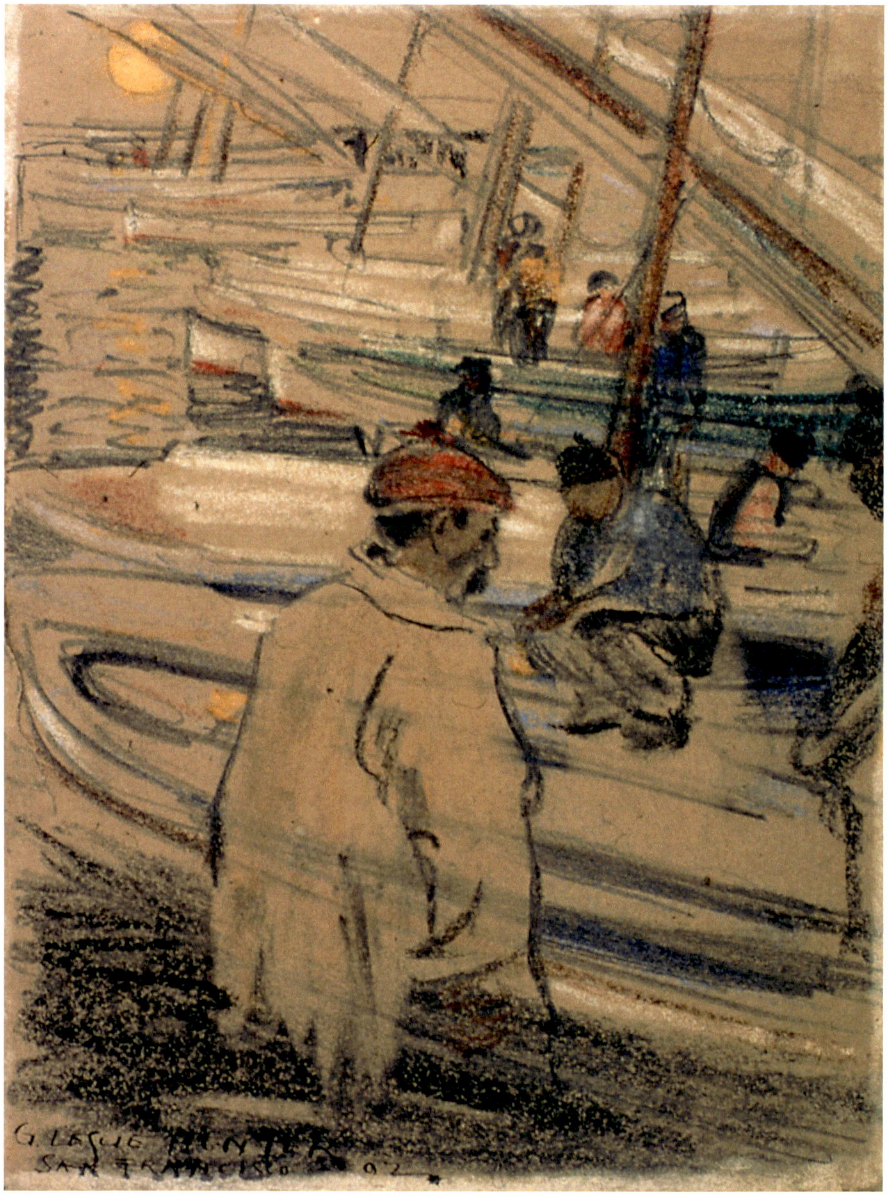

11 | Fisherman's Wharf, San Francisco
Coloured chalks on grey paper, dated 1902
University of Glasgow, Hunterian Art Gallery

Artists. The others included Maynard Dixon, another illustrator for *Overland Monthly* and *Sunset* who is noted today for his paintings of the landscape, settlers, cowboys and Indians of the American West, Gottardo Piazzoni, who had recently returned from Paris full of admiration for the work of Cézanne and the other Post-Impressionists, Xavier Martinez, born at Guadalajara in Mexico, a colourful bohemian who was to become Professor of Painting at the California College of Arts and Crafts for over 30 years, the sculptor Arthur Putnam, Matteo Sandona (1883–1964), born in Italy and known today for his portraiture, Charles Peter Neilson (1866–1937), a fellow Scot from Pitlessie in Fife, William Howell Bull (1861–1940) and Blendon Campbell.[36] There had been a growing sense of unease among younger artists about the prevailing reactionary stance of the San Francisco Art Association and the somewhat imperious attitude of Arthur Mathews, the head of the Mark Hopkins Institute of Art. The California Society of Artists was intended to be an alternative art organization – Honeyman describes it as a *Salon des Refusés*[37] – that would encourage contact with progressive art movements and provide younger, less established artists with an opportunity to exhibit their work on the same terms as the society's members.

An inaugural exhibition was held in the studio of Charles Neilson at 207 Sutter Street from 26 April to 3 May 1902, to which twenty-three artists sent work.[38] Hunter served on the hanging committee along with Piazzoni, Martinez, Neilson and Campbell.[39] Maynard Dixon designed the cover for the catalogue and submitted fourteen watercolours and drawings.[40] Hunter exhibited fifteen works, executed in San Francisco and Monterey and priced from \$8 to \$20, except for no.47 *Old Fisherman's Wharf* which may have been an oil painting because it was priced at \$50 (at this time both Britain and the United States were on the Gold Standard and the exchange rate was fixed at five dollars to the pound).[41] The coloured chalk drawing, *Fisherman's Wharf, San Francisco* (pl.11), may be a sketch for the oil painting. The exhibition was so well received that it was extended several days beyond its intended closing date. Under the headline 'Big Crowds Delight in Painters' Exhibition' the critic of the *San Francisco Call* wrote:

Piazzoni's fantastic ideals are much liked for the daring of the treatment and originality and Charles P. Neilson, Xavier T. Martinez, C. Chapel Judson, G. Leslie Hunter and Sandona have each won a multitude of admirers for their admirable works which adorn the gallery's walls.[42]

The *San Francisco Newsletter* commented:

Mr G. Hunter has struck a new note in some very strong black and white drawings portraying life in the more sordid quarters of the town, among Chinatown and Barbary Coast wrecks and outcasts. He also has several vivid tinted Monterey sketches.[43]

Hunter told Honeyman that he did not sell anything, which is puzzling in view of the enthusiastic review in the *Call*.[44] However, as artists know, admiration for a painting is one thing, parting with money for it can be another thing entirely. As to the society itself, it did not last long and no further exhibitions were held. The younger members of San Francisco's artistic community were constantly on the move and consequently the initial momentum was lost.

As well as appearing on the arts pages of San Francisco's newspapers, Hunter's name crops up occasionally in the society columns. For instance in its issue of 29 December 1901 the *San Francisco Call* reported that Hunter was one of twenty-five guests at a party given at their home by Wallace Irwin, the younger brother of Will, and his wife. Other guests included the sculptor, Arthur Putnam, and literary luminaries Gelett Burgess, Porter Garnett and Charles Field.[45] As mentioned earlier, Hunter was an intelligent, well-read, personable young man. He was good company, both within his immediate circle and the higher echelons of San Francisco society. An article in the *San Francisco Newsletter* in May 1902 reveals that by then Hunter was a well-known artistic character in the city, with a wit comparable to that of Whistler, no mean compliment as Whistler was famous for his wit.[46]

Since arriving in San Francisco in 1899 Hunter had worked hard at his art. His passion for making sketches was admired by his artist friends. None of his friends felt that he was wasting his time thereby, 'for they sensed something big in his work …'[47] Hunter sensed something of the same, and he had to make it a reality. But how? Many of his friends had trained in Paris or had lived and worked there for a time. Hunter determined that he too must go to Paris.

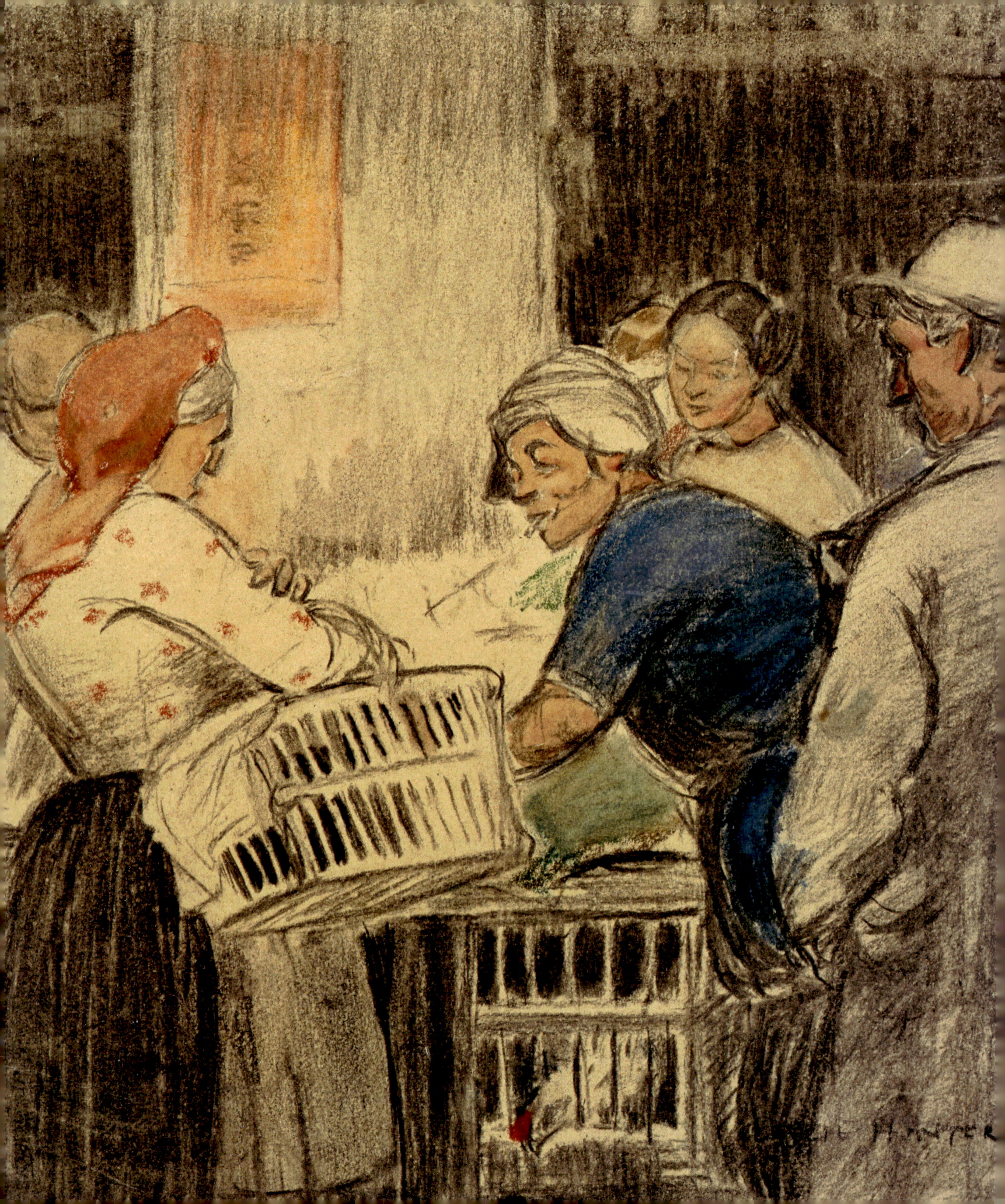

3 Scotland and Paris

TOWARDS THE END of 1902 or early the following year Hunter left San Francisco for Europe. It was over three years since he had seen his family, who had returned to Scotland in May 1899. In the intervening period his father had died and his mother and sister, Jeanie, as well as his brother, William, and his family had moved to Glasgow.

Hunter was also anxious to visit Paris. Then universally acknowledged as the centre of the art world, Paris was an exciting and stimulating city for an aspiring painter. The focus of interest had moved from the French Impressionists to Cézanne and the Post-Impressionists (although that term had not yet been invented). Matisse, Derain and other *fauves* were to startle the enlightened and open-minded, confound the mass of the art-loving public and be ignored by the majority of other artists. What was going on in Paris at the time would have been well known even in San Francisco from the flow of artists between San Francisco and Paris. In 1901 Gottardo Piazzoni, the 'spiritual advisor and father confessor to two generations of local painters',[1] returned to San Francisco after an extended stay in Paris. No doubt he would have recounted all that was happening there, enthusing Hunter and other young artists. Hunter's friend, the sculptor Ralph Stackpole later recalled Piazzoni 'used to tell us about the masters, about Giotto, about Dante, about Europe and art life in Paris and we listened with amazement'.[2]

Hunter had saved money for his fare across the Atlantic from the fees he received for providing illustrations to *Overland Monthly*. Possibly he got a return rail ticket to his port of embarkation – Montreal or New York – free of charge from the Southern Pacific Railroad in part payment for his illustrative work for *Sunset*, which then was owned by the railroad. The exact sequence of events is uncertain. He may have gone to Paris first, perhaps in the company of several other young San Francisco artists, stayed there for a time, and then travelled on to Glasgow. Alternatively he may have travelled direct to Glasgow.[3] What is certain is that Hunter was in Scotland by March 1903 at the latest, because he secured a commission to execute a series of drawings for the Glasgow weekly magazine *Society Pictorial* (later called *Lady's Illustrated Weekly* and then *Scots Pictorial*), which provided him with much-needed funds for an extended trip to Paris the following year.

His first illustration, *Street Flowers*, appeared in *Society Pictorial* on 4 April. Edward VII and Queen Alexandra visited Edinburgh and Glasgow in May 1903, not long after their coronation, and two drawings by Hunter, *Welcoming Their Majesties to Edinburgh* and *Welcoming Their Majesties to Glasgow*, appeared in the issue of 23 May. Another twelve drawings appeared at intervals up to 17 December 1904. In addition *Society Pictorial* repeated four of the drawings during the period mid-1905 to August 1906, when Hunter was back in San Francisco.[4] The illustrations are not sketches, but substantial, fully worked-up drawings in black ink with wash or bodycolour (it is difficult to be precise as only one of the original drawings, *A Garden Party*

12 | Poultry Market, Paris
Coloured chalks on paper, 1904
University of Glasgow, Hunterian Art Gallery

(pl.14), appears to have survived). The majority are full-page; one, *Samaritan Fancy Dress Ball*, is a two-page spread, depicting a fancy dress ball held in aid of Glasgow Samaritan Hospital in November 1903, which raised £1,300.[5] All but two of the illustrations portray contemporary events in Scotland, involving mainly the middle and upper classes – not surprising in the case of a society journal – and incorporating numerous figures. In terms of both composition and draughtsmanship Hunter's handling of a crowd of individuals is very good. His appreciation of the work of Steinlen is apparent in this series of illustrations.

As well as enjoying being with his mother, sister and brother again, Hunter would have spent many fruitful hours studying the paintings in Kelvingrove Art Gallery and Glasgow University's Hunterian Museum. He went out into the Scottish countryside, executing as usual numerous drawings and paintings. Possibly around the beginning of 1904 he left Glasgow for London, before going on to Paris.[6] Further work was done in and around London. No doubt he spent many hours in the National Gallery looking at the Old Masters. Honeyman reports that Hunter had begun to do this in San Francisco through the medium of 'very indifferent reproductions':

> *... his first album of postcards and magazine cuttings and catalogues still exists although it is much the worse for wear. From it one can surmise the line of approach and make a fair guess at his heroes. Chardin and Manet competed with the Dutch in his early essays in still-life painting.*[7]

It is easy to imagine Hunter's sheer joy at seeing some of those works hanging on the walls. Founded in 1807 and named after Dr William Hunter,[8] a former student of Glasgow University, the Hunterian holds three superb works by Chardin, bequeathed to the University by William Hunter in 1783.

Hunter was always on the lookout for illustration work as a source of income. Shortly after he arrived in London, he got a commission from *The Idler*, the London monthly magazine. It was a relatively small piece of work – twelve illustrations over two years – but the money was welcome nonetheless.[9] From London Hunter crossed over to the Continent. There is very little evidence available today to indicate where he went, what he saw and what he did. Apart from an extended stay in Paris, it is known that he visited Holland, because three works executed in that country were included in the thirty works he exhibited at the San Francisco Artists' Society in December 1905.[10]

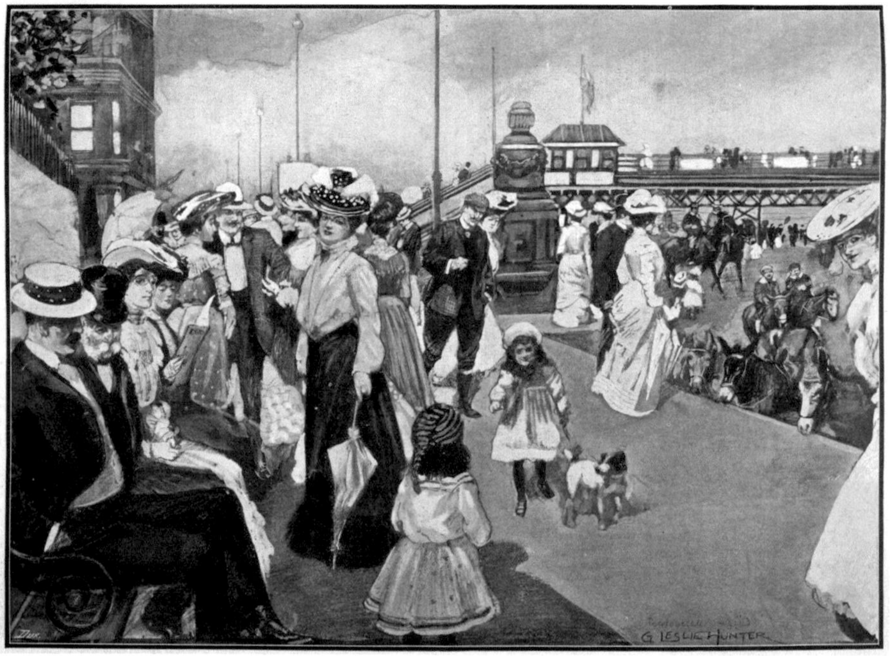

13 | *By the Sea – A Sketch at Portobello*, illustration in *Society Pictorial*, 12 September 1903 (repeated in the issue of 2 September 1905 and in *Lady's Illustrated Weekly*, 4 August 1906)
The British Library

In Paris the lifestyle of an artist was very similar to that in San Francisco. Montmartre and Montparnasse were full of artists and writers, and it was this company that Hunter kept during his extended stay in the French capital. He was by nature a gregarious person. He would have found a cheap hotel or an artists' commune where he could sleep. Meals were to be had in a vast number of cafés and restaurants at prices to suit all pockets. He could sketch from life anywhere he cared. In the Louvre he could study the work of the Dutch and French masters, Italian Renaissance and painters such as Velázquez. Paintings by the French Impressionists and artists such as Cézanne,

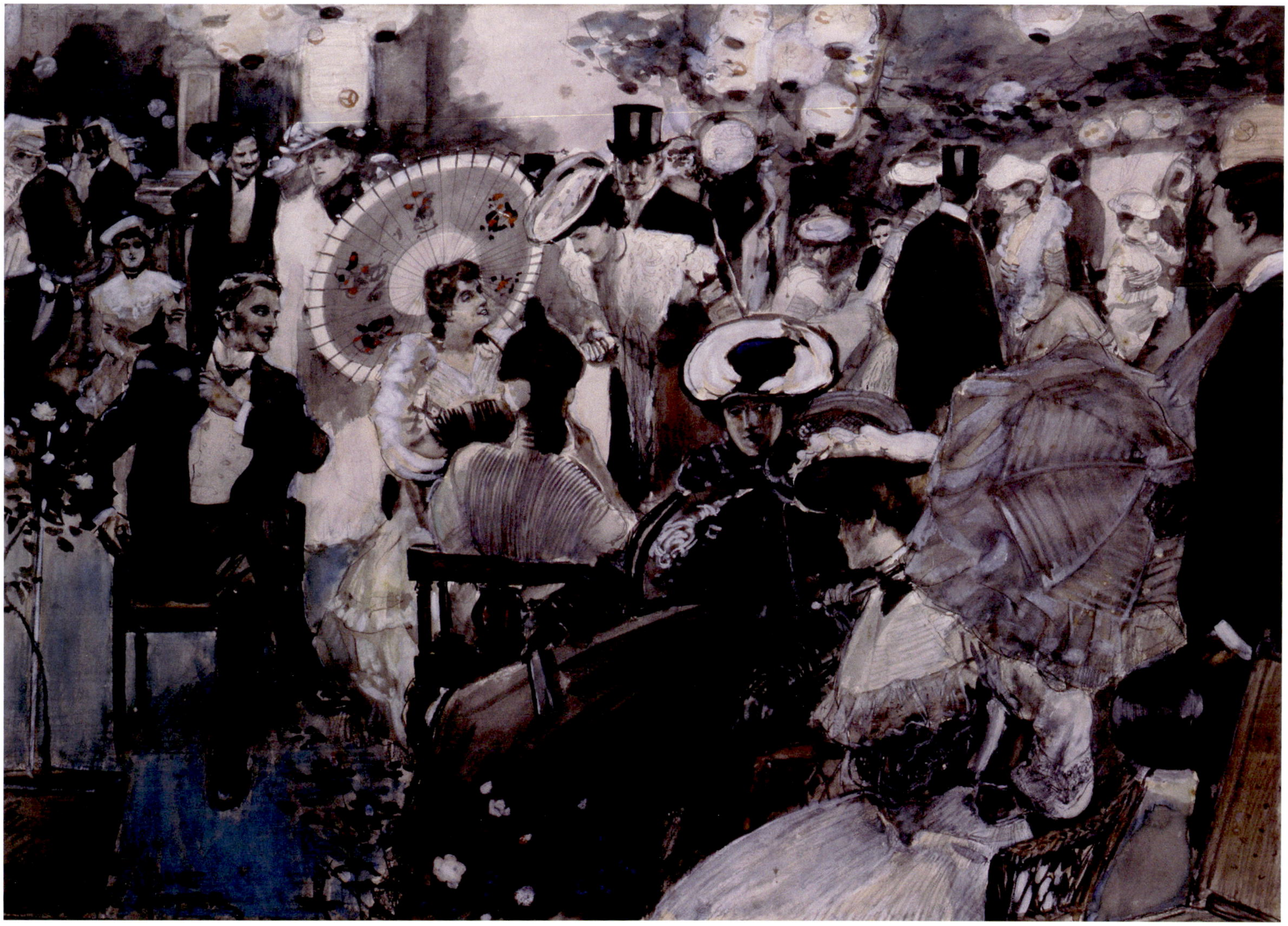

14 | *A Garden Party*
Drawing for *Society Pictorial*, 11 July 1903
(repeated in the issue of 29 July 1905)
Ink, watercolour and bodycolour
Private collection

Gauguin and Van Gogh could be seen in the galleries of dealers such as Boussod-Valadon, Durand-Ruel, Georges Petit and Vollard. There were the Paris Salons to view; Cézanne had been given an entire room at the Salon d'Automne in 1904. However his friend, Tom Hunt, later told Honeyman that although Hunter returned 'with the gossip of Montparnasse concerning Cézanne, Van Gogh and Gauguin, he did not appear to have any great appreciation of the post-impressionists'. Manet, Degas, Steinlen and Forain were Hunter's heroes then.[11]

A small window on Hunter's life in Paris is provided by a wealthy American from Philadelphia. Almost the same age as Hunter, Samuel Stockton White III was a muscular young man, a gymnast and award-winning bodybuilder who had studied at Princeton and Cambridge University. On a visit to Paris in 1901 he posed as a model for Rodin, resulting in the sculpture *Athlete*. He sat for the sculptor in Paris a second time in 1904, when he met Hunter.[12] In a conversation with Honeyman in Philadelphia many years later, White recalled Hunter as 'a young man, ill clad, under-nourished, but with a restless activity. He would sit there in the front of the café, always sketching on scraps of paper any head or figure which attracted him.' It was the rapidity with which Hunter executed the drawings that amazed White, something which 'he had never seen equalled'. White told Honeyman that the café was either the *Café du Dôme* or the *Café de la Rotonde*, both very popular gathering spots in Montparnasse for well-known painters, writers and intellectuals as well as a multitude of would-be artists and writers. White, who was to become a noted art collector, wanted to encourage and help Hunter, whom he considered a promising artist, and purchased several sketches from him on that occasion, together with two colour monotypes, *Two Labourers* (*c.*1904) and *A Woman with a Basket* (*c.*1904, pl.19). Subsequently all were acquired from White by Honeyman and are now in the Hunterian Art Gallery in Glasgow.[13] Another four monotypes by Hunter are known, three held by the Hunterian and one by the National Galleries of Scotland.[14] A monotype is a unique print, made by painting with ink on an untreated metal plate and then transferring it to paper using a printing press, when a reverse image of the original is obtained. At that time it was an unusual process for a British artist to employ.[15] Invented in the 1640s, the monotype was taken up in the nineteenth century, notably by Degas.[16] Hunter may have learned the technique in San Francisco from Piazzoni on the latter's return in 1901 from Paris, where he had discovered the medium. However it is equally likely that Hunter acquired the skill during his stay in Paris. Why Hunter took up the process is unclear, unless it was merely experimentation. Martin Hopkinson has suggested that Hunter may have employed monotypes as the basis for some of his magazine illustrations.[17] However only three examples of his original work for books and magazines (out of almost 200 known illustrations) have come to light so far and all are ink, watercolour and bodycolour on card.

Weighed down by a large number of sketches and wash drawings, Hunter returned to Glasgow, probably in the autumn of 1904, to spend a further period with his family before returning to California. He saw his niece, Hilda, for the first time, born on 17 April that year to his brother, William, and wife Hilda. Towards the end of November Hunter said goodbye to his mother, sister Jeanie, and William and his family at Glasgow's Central Station and took the train to Liverpool. On 28 November he sailed for America on board *S.S.Etruria*, landing in New York six days later.[18]

Hunter decided to remain in New York for a few months before returning to San Francisco. No doubt he was keen to find out what was going on in the art world in the American east, and perhaps investigate the opportunities in New York for newspaper and magazine illustration in order to replenish his funds. Another reason to stay on was that some of his San Francisco friends, such as Will Irwin and Gelett Burgess, had moved to New York very recently and he would have wanted to meet up with them again. His arrival coincided with the emergence of Greenwich Village in lower Manhattan as a bohemian enclave for artists, writers, musicians and the like, the equivalent in New York of Montparnasse in Paris. Hunter discovered that there was a lot going on. In the first decade of the twentieth century some of the younger artists in New York were following the example of their Californian brothers and rebelling against the art establishment, particularly the National Academy of Design and its restrictive exhibition policies. They were led by Robert Henri (1865–1929), born in Cincinnati and trained in Philadelphia and Paris. Henri settled in New York in 1899 and went on to teach at the New York School of Art before establishing his own school. Hunter would have empathised with the fears of those artists and understood their aims, not only because their frustration was the very reason that had prompted Piazzoni, Hunter and their friends to establish the California Society of Artists in 1902, but also because, like Hunter himself, a number of Henri's followers were newspaper illustrators whom he had encouraged to become painters. In 1908 Henri would help organize an independent exhibition in New York of work by a group of those artists, who came to be known as the 'Eight'.[19] At the same time Henri was challenging such artists to adopt an 'art for life' approach in their painting, rather than 'art for art's sake', insisting that the painter had a moral obligation to give artistic expression to contemporary life.[20] At the beginning of the twentieth century immigration was continuing at a very high rate and, despite rapid urban development, living conditions in New York for the poor and disenfranchised were bad. Henri urged his followers to eschew academic subject matter and portray everyday life on the streets, truthfully and with vitality and sensitivity. These artists formed the core of a group dubbed the 'Ashcan' school (though the term was not coined until 1934); they were joined later by painters such as George Bellows and Edward Hopper.[21]

In photography Alfred Stieglitz (1864–1946), often called the father of modern photography, and his friend, Edward Steichen, had founded Photo Secession, an association of modern photographers, in 1902. About the time Hunter was in New York Stieglitz opened the Photo Secession Gallery at 291 Fifth Avenue with the intention of holding exhibitions of modern photography. Stieglitz, interested in everything new and revolutionary, kept in touch with developments in Paris through Leo and Gertrude Stein, and went on to show art and sculpture in his gallery.[22] The gallery quickly became a focus for home-grown American *avant-garde* art.

In New York Hunter met Tom Hunt,[23] another young artist, and the two spent some time together. It is possible that Hunt may have given Hunter the use of his studio, perhaps even offered him a bed. They must have sketched together, because Hunt later recalled to Honeyman that 'Hunter's industry was amazing, and if he had had any commercial aptitude he would have made a great deal of money'! According to Hunt, Hunter was:

... utterly independent of time, place and materials. Night or day suited him for work – a café or a park for location – a scrap of paper – a bit of cardboard – cheap crayons or a wash of ink would serve as material. He had plenty of work with him. Hundreds of drawings of places he had visited and sketches of almost everybody he had met comprised his stock in trade. There were no buyers, but he was able to use some of his work as an introduction to magazine editors ... [24]

Hunter was totally immersed in his art; to him mundane everyday tasks were of little consequence. Throughout his life he was a rather untidy, disorganised person. This is illustrated by an anecdote from Hunter's time in New York, related by Hunt to Honeyman in the 1930s:

One day Hunter had a special bit of luck. He received two cheques, amounting to about 250 dollars [the equivalent of £50]*, in payment of some illustrations. Here was the wherewithal to take him home to his beloved California. But there must be a celebration first. The studio was cleared and made more presentable for a party. Down they marched to* *the nearest delicatessen for food and drink. When the eatables were assembled on the counter of the store, Hunter could not find the cheques which the proprietor had arranged to cash. The food was left while they all rushed back to the studio. After an agonising search, the two envelopes containing the cheques were found in a heap of rubbish which had been consigned to the garbage can.*[25]

Whether the cheques were in settlement of illustrations he had produced while in New York is unclear. It is not known whether Hunter did manage to get any commissions in New York; none have come to light so far. It is more likely that the dollar payments resulted from work he had done for the *Society Pictorial* in Glasgow the preceding year. His illustrations appeared in that magazine up to August 1906.[26] According to his friend, Hunter had little commercial nous and was fairly pessimistic about the future for illustration, because by then newspapers and most magazines were to a very large extent using photographs. Hunter frequently remarked to Hunt:

This illustration business is finished. It is changing in character and style, and we are going to be left behind. I want to be doing something else. And I'll find out very soon what it is.[27]

By May 1905 he was back in San Francisco, the *Call* announcing, alongside a sketch by him titled *In the Latin Quarter, Paris*, that Hunter 'goes to Monterey to do some local work. He will soon hold an exhibition.'[28] Two days later the newspaper reported in its *Smart Set* column:

J. [*sic*] *Leslie Hunter, who has recently returned from Europe, where he travelled extensively, has joined the throng that will make Del Monte its abiding place for the next month.*[29]

Del Monte was a resort established by the Southern Pacific Railroad on the Pacific coast near Monterey. Some fifty miles south of San Francisco, Monterey and Carmel were favoured spots for artists and writers to work; a number had made their permanent home in the area. Hunter frequently sketched in and around Monterey.

Probably the *San Francisco Call* was alluding to a first solo exhibition by Hunter.[30] He now had a substantial body of work from which to select drawings and paintings that could form an exhibition and produce much needed cash. In the interim, however, he had to eat, and turned again to magazine work, providing further illustrations for both *Overland Monthly* and *Sunset* from a new studio at 610 Montgomery Street.[31] The studio was just across the street from his former one, and a short distance from the Montgomery Block, affectionately called the 'Monkey Block' because of the bohemian lifestyle of its residents – largely artists, musicians, poets and writers. When it was built in 1853, the four-storey building was the largest structure on the West Coast and the first fire-proof building in a city that was plagued by fires. Constructed of granite and brick, it fronted Washington and Montgomery Streets, providing luxurious business space. However, as time went by and newer buildings sprang up, the Block's wealthy occupants gradually left and a bohemian crowd of literary and artistic people took advantage of the much lower rents then on offer and moved in to the Block's spacious rooms on the three upper floors, taking them as studios or living accommodation.

At the end of 1903 Guiseppe 'Papa' Coppa, a Turinese chef, opened a ground-floor restaurant in the Block, located on the corner almost opposite the studio Hunter moved into some sixteen months later on his return from Europe. Coppa was generous with his portions, and generous with his credit if a diner temporarily was unable to meet the thirty-five cents cost of a meal. From the outset the restaurant was very popular with the bohemian crowd and quickly became the favourite gathering place for artists and writers. On his return Hunter became one of that crowd. The attraction was not just the food; conversation and discussion were just as important, if not more so. The far-ranging nature of the latter can be deduced from a series of murals and texts scrawled around the walls by the 'Coppans', the artists and others who gathered round the restaurant's central table. Alongside the caricatures and other images executed by the likes of Gelett

Burgess, the sculptor Robert Aitken, Maynard Dixon and Xavier Martinez, Porter Garnett had added a decorative border of the names of philosophers, writers and painters who inspired the Coppans – Aristotle, Sappho, Dante, Goethe, Nietzsche, Kant, Rabelais, Verlaine, Velázquez, Villon and Whistler – along with the names of a number of prominent local personalities from the bohemian community.[32]

Hunter exhibited thirty works at the *Annual Loan and Sale Exhibition of Paintings and Sketches by Painters and Illustrators of San Francisco,* organised by the San Francisco Artists' Society and held in the Maple Room of The Palace Hotel from 18 to 20 December 1905. They were paintings and sketches he had done in Scotland, Holland, London and Paris, as well as locally in San Francisco and Monterey. Two were loaned works, which probably indicates that he *did* sell work in San Francisco, despite his protestations to the contrary recorded by Honeyman.[33] Laura Bride Powers, the art critic of the *San Francisco Call*, described the exhibition as 'far and away the best of its kind that has been held'. She continued:

... and a happy lot they were on Wednesday night, when Neilson had ten sales to his credit, Cadenasso five, and Joseph Greenbaum, John M. Gamble, Henry Raschen, Maurice del Mue, G. Leslie Hunter, Maynard Dixon, Gordon Ross and L.P.Latimer sharing in the wondrous luck.

... G. Leslie Hunter gave a good account of himself, the 'Dutch Luggers', 'The Windmill' and 'A California Landscape' capturing a lot of attention.[34]

In April the following year the *San Francisco Call* announced the formation of a new artists' society:

On Tuesday night the Society of California Artists will open its first exhibition at 723 Sutter Street ...

... By Tuesday night, when the artists will welcome their friends in their dress togs – poor chaps! – everything will be in ship-shape for a good show.

The following painters have joined the society, which is, by the way, all the name implies – with a president, a secretary, a board of directors and all the other trimmings of a well ordered society: C.P.Neilson, C. Chapel Judson, Henry Raschen, Joseph Greenbaum, Maynard Dixon, Walker Francis, Alice B. Chittenden, Sophie Marston Brannan, M. del Mue, Gordon Coutts, Maren M. Froelich, Sarah Bender de Wolfe, R.F.Thomson, G. Leslie Hunter, Will Sparks and W.S.Hansen.

Manager Leggit has worked up a splendid clientele for his 'Permanent Exhibition', which has, for a starter, a good location and excellent rooms.

The artists themselves must do their part and a discriminating public should do the rest.[35]

Since the California Society of Artists had quietly 'withered on the vine' after its inaugural exhibition four years earlier, there had been no association to represent the interests of younger artists. This new society – its title a transposition of the earlier one – was a bold venture in that vein. Although the *Call* trumpeted 'Some stunning pictures at the new artrooms', its critic admitted that it was 'quite a presentable lot of pictures in the aggregate – some good, some bad and some indifferent'. Hunter exhibited 'illustrative work',[36] probably because his first solo exhibition was due to open shortly at the Mark Hopkins Institute of Art and he was saving his best for that; the paintings and drawings Hunter had selected were ready in his studio or with the framers. He also had four oils – *On the Seine at Paris* and three Scottish scenes – hanging in the Spring Exhibition of the San Francisco Art Association, which had opened at the Mark Hopkins Institute on 16 March.[37]

On one of the walls of Coppa's restaurant Porter Garnett had scrawled a line from Oscar Wilde's *Salome*: 'Something terribble [sic] is going to happen'.[38] The words would prove prophetic. Having done as much as he could in preparation for his forthcoming one-man show, Hunter and the sculptor, Ralph Stackpole, accepted an invitation from Heinz Springer, an 'ardent admirer and patron of young artists', to spend a few weeks on his ranch in Lake County, to the north of San Francisco.[39] Then almost twenty-one, Stackpole was some eight years younger than Hunter. The two artists probably knew each other already; certainly they became good friends, later travelling together in France and Italy.

Back in San Francisco, New York's Metropolitan Opera had just arrived in San Francisco. On the evening of Tuesday, 17 April Enrico Caruso, singing the role of Don Juan in Bizet's opera *Carmen*, sent the audience at the Grand Opera House into raptures. Early next morning the blue sky and imperceptible breeze heralded a beautiful day. At 5.12am a very loud rumbling noise was followed almost immediately by a violent shaking of the ground and the thud of falling masonry. The earthquake lasted for over a minute. The terrified population rushed into the streets, most in their night-clothes. At 5.26am the first of many aftershocks rocked the city. Fires had started immediately, but many were put out that morning. However some fires could not be checked, despite the dynamiting of numerous buildings by the city authorities in futile attempts to create fire breaks. For three days the fires raged across thousands of acres, destroying San Francisco's business district and almost two-thirds of its homes and lodgings. The earthquake and fire claimed over 450 lives. Some 30,000 structures were destroyed and a quarter of a million people made homeless, most of whom were able to save only what they could carry. All the grandiose buildings constructed over the last decade and all the plush hotels were gutted by fire. Only the Montgomery Block and one other building were left intact. The Mark Hopkins Institute of Art was gutted, and the pictures that had been carried out of the building carefully by volunteers and laid on the lawn were also lost to the fire. Surprisingly, however, more of San Francisco was left comparatively unscathed than was destroyed.[40]

The severity of the earthquake was such that it must have been felt by Hunter and Stackpole in Lake County to the north. Certainly they would have seen the night sky aglow from the flames; people living fifty miles to the north or south recalled a sky so luminous '... you could read a newspaper at midnight'.[41] California's veteran poet, Joaquin Miller (1839–1913), captured the living nightmare in his poem, *San Francisco*, published in *Sunset's* June-July issue:

... Three days, three nights, three fearful days
Of death. Of flame, of dynamite,
Of God's house thrown a thousand ways;
Blown east by day, blown west by night –
By night? There was no night. Nay, Nay.
The ghoulish flame lit nights that lay
Crouched down between this first, last day!
I say those nights were burned away! ... [42]

Hunter and Stackpole would have been anxious to get back to the city as soon as possible to see for themselves the extent of the damage, and rescue what they could. It must have been difficult, because transport and communications

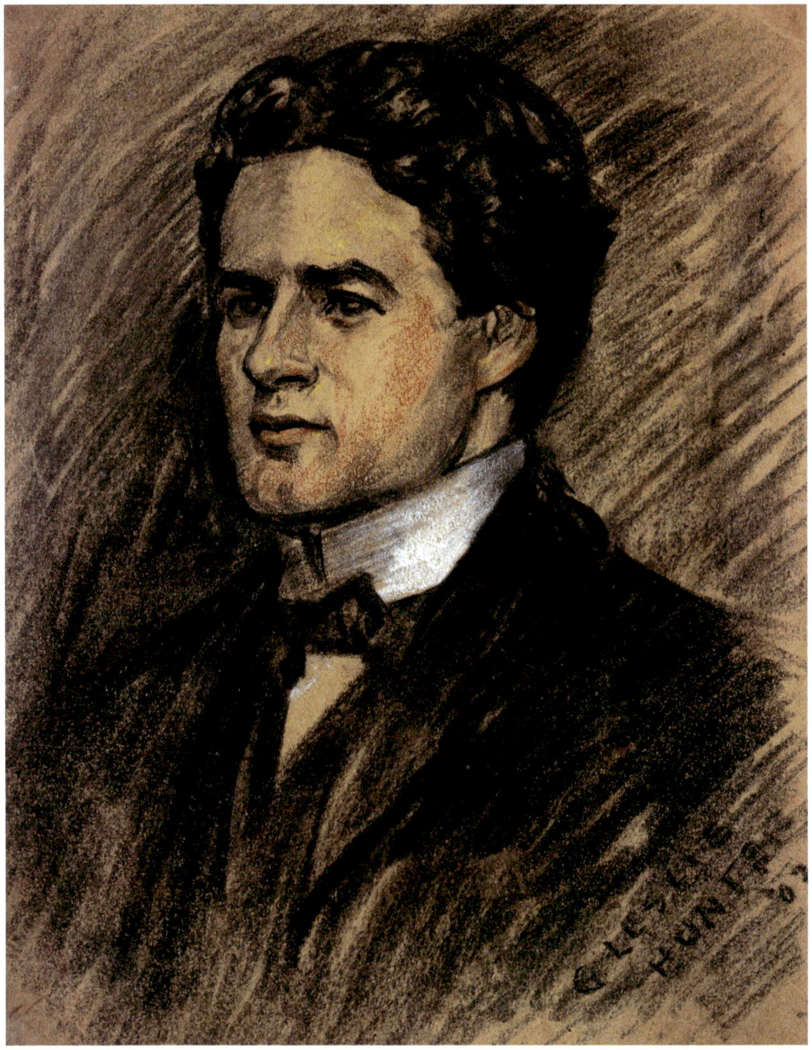

15 | Herman Scheffauer
Pastel, dated 1902
Private collection

were severely disrupted in the days immediately after the earthquake. When eventually they managed to reach Montgomery Street, they found to their utter despair that both studios had been gutted by fire. There was nothing left to be saved. All the work Hunter had done in California, Scotland and on the Continent had been lost. He had nothing but the clothes he stood up in, as the *San Francisco Call* confirmed on 10 June under the heading 'The Social Shake Up':

Leslie Hunter, whose studio was located in the building next to Coppa's, and went both down and up on the 18th, is foraging for material up in Lake County. The poor chap lost every one of the beautiful studies he brought back from abroad, notably the things from his bonny Scotland – a loss that only a fellow-painter can know.[43]

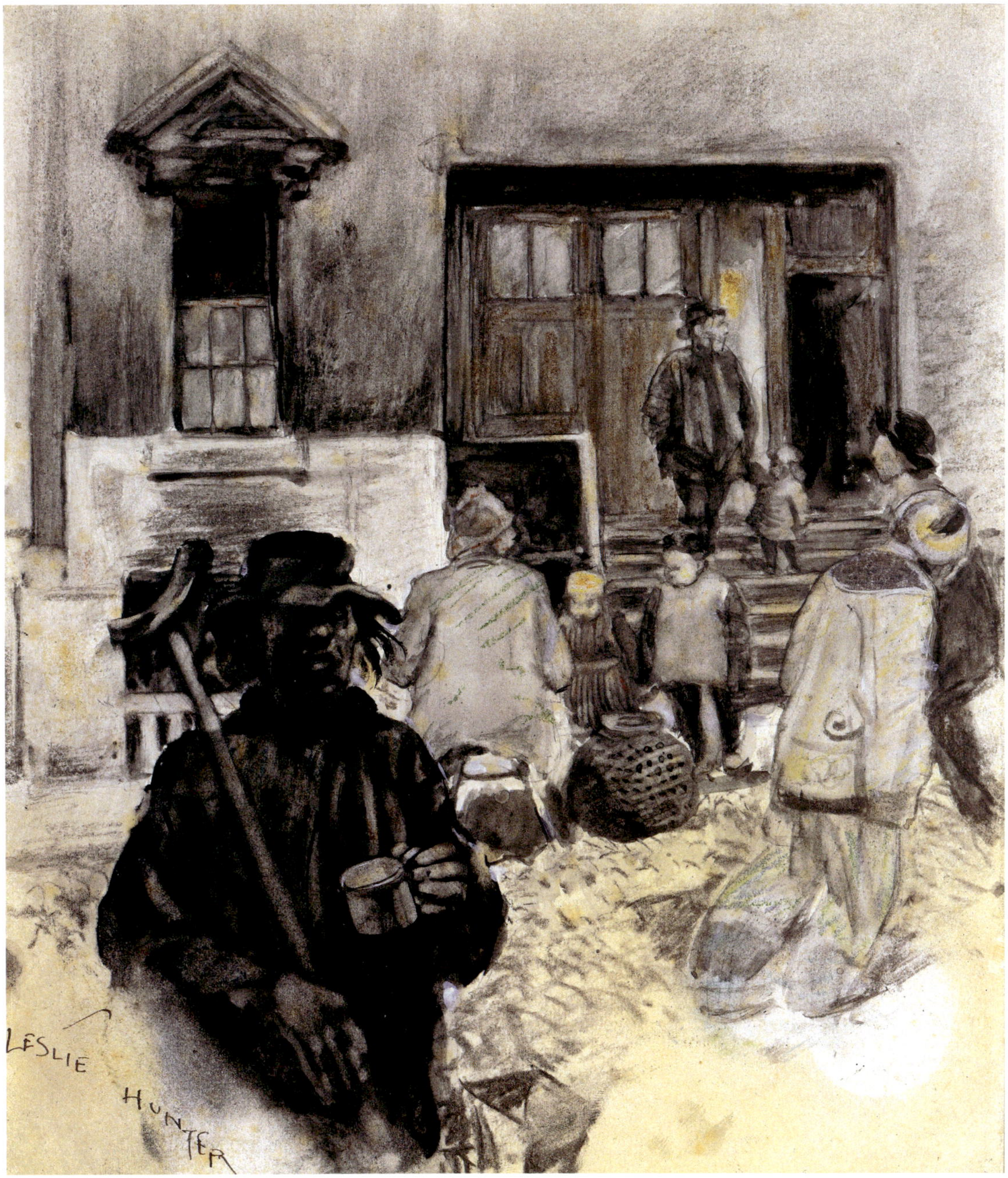

16 | Chinatown, San Francisco
Pencil, ink, crayon and wash, 1902
Aberdeen Art Gallery & Museums Collections

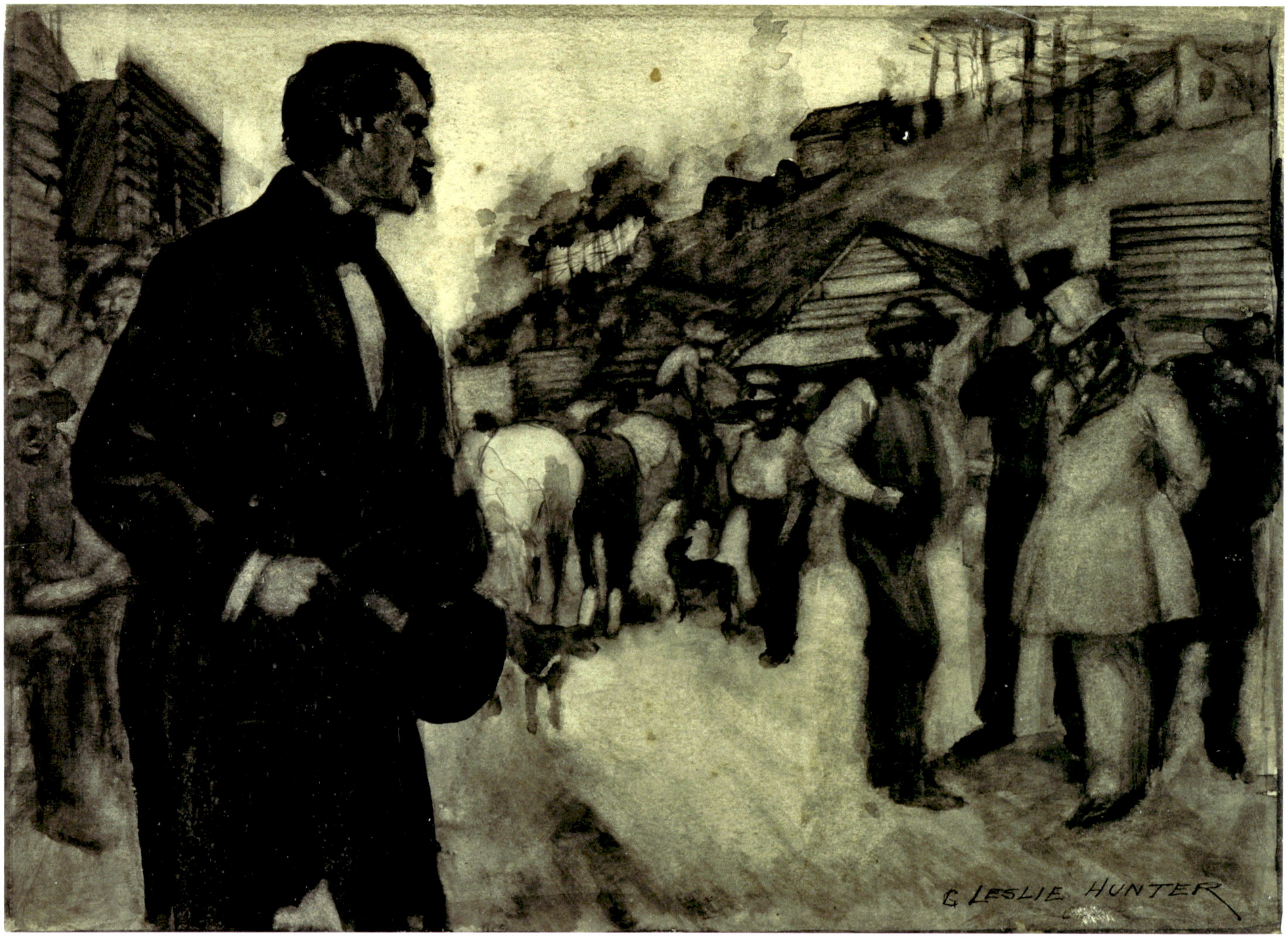

It was a disaster for Hunter. He was in total despair. Years later, Honeyman relates, Hunter frequently referred 'with profound regret to the irreparable loss of the work he had done in San Francisco'.[44]

Of course Hunter and Stackpole were not the only artists to lose everything by any means. Numerous painters were in the same boat, including Piazzoni and Martinez. William Keith, the grand old man of California painting, had hundreds of valuable canvases destroyed, the product of four decades of work.[45] For Hunter, however, the situation was particularly devastating, because his first solo exhibition was due to open in a room at the Mark Hopkins Institute several days after the earthquake struck. All the arrangements had been finalised, the framing of the pictures had been completed and the works were in his studio awaiting collection in due course.[46] When the full extent of the disaster was known in the American east, numerous organisations came to the rescue of those who had lost everything. One such source of assistance was the artists of New York, who sent a substantial sum of money to help their brothers in San Francisco. Stackpole received $200, which appears to have been the standard handout, and there is no reason to doubt that Hunter got a similar sum.[47]

Hunter must have been in a quandary about what to do. Was there any future for him in California now? Several of his friends and acquaintances had left San Francisco for the American east even before the earthquake.

17 | *'I reckon they're after somebody', he said*, illustration in *Overland Monthly*, September 1902, for Bret Harte's short story *The Outcasts of Poker Flat*
Pencil, ink and wash on card, 1902
University of Glasgow, Hunterian Art Gallery

Subsequently, many more left for Monterey, Carmel or further afield. Perhaps Hunter had gone to Lake County to seek advice from Heinz Springer, rather than to find subjects to paint as the *San Francisco Call* had reported. Finally, however, he decided to return to Scotland, despite having become a naturalised US citizen in July the preceding year.[48] In its issue of 4 July the *Call* reported that 'Leslie Hunter leaves for New York within a few weeks'.[49]

Stackpole too must have wondered what the future held for him. He was only twenty-one. His mentors, Arthur Putnam and Gottardo Piazzoni, were both in Paris. Stackpole decided to join them there.[50] It seems fairly certain that Hunter and Stackpole travelled to Paris together, probably spending time in New York with Hunter's friend, Tom Hunt, before boarding a steamer for France.[51] Putnam, Piazzoni and their wives had rented a two-storey house with a garret in the Paris suburb of Neuilly sur Seine. They allowed Stackpole – and presumably Hunter – the use of the garret.[52] Hunter probably remained in France for several weeks before going on to Scotland.

Hunter was well liked by his San Francisco friends, who would miss him. One of them, the poet Herman Scheffauer, whom Hunter had sketched in pastel in 1902 (pl.15), penned several verses as a farewell tribute to their friend, which Hunter was to treasure all his life:[53]

Here's to you, Leslie Hunter, here's to you!
Soon the West Wind blowing o'er you
From the fair Pacific shores
Bears you to the land that bore you –
All our wishes go before you –
Wishes that could be no more –
Here's to you, Leslie Hunter, here's to you! ...
... Fare you well, Leslie Hunter, fare you well.
Lo, the friends around you meeting,
Find a hope in parting's pain,
And their hearts still warmly beating
Shall await to give you greeting
When our Leslie's home again –
Fare you well, Leslie Hunter, fare you well![54]

Not surprisingly, the paintings and drawings that survive from Hunter's first eight years as an artist are relatively few in number. Most of them eventually came into the hands of Honeyman, some acquired from the American, Samuel Stockton White, who had purchased them from Hunter in Paris in 1904. Nevertheless an indication of Hunter's early talent can be seen in the interesting harmony of figures and pattern of

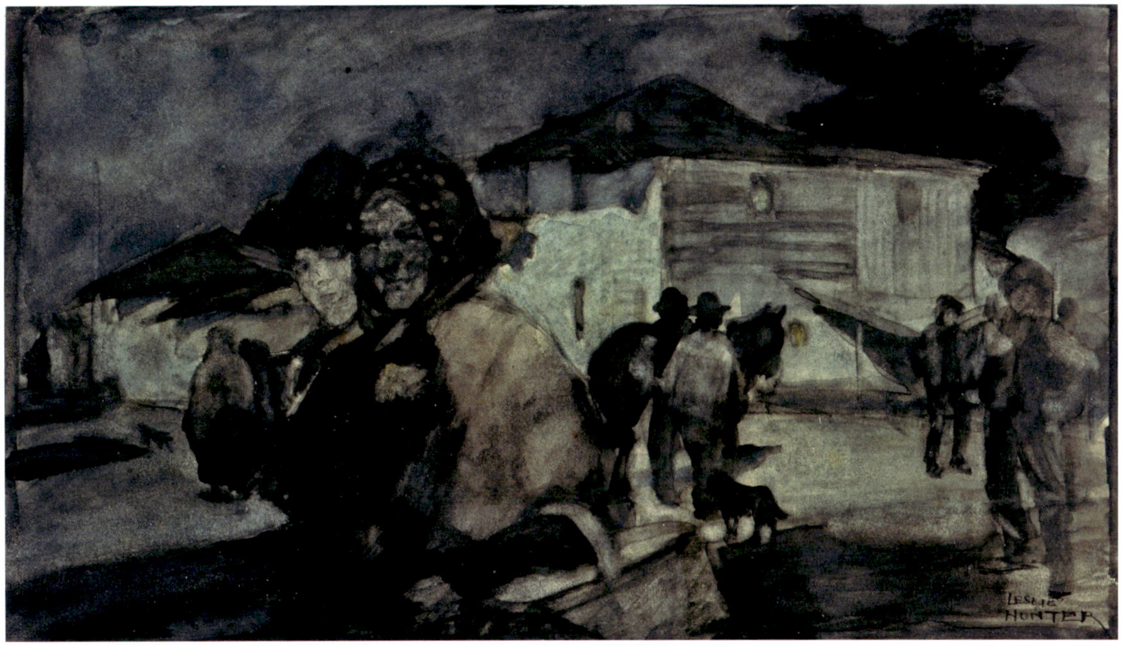

18 | Drawing for *Overland Monthly*. Untraced or unused illustration, possibly for Bret Harte's short story 'The Outcasts of Poker Flat'
Pencil, ink and wash on card, 1902
University of Glasgow, Hunterian Art Gallery

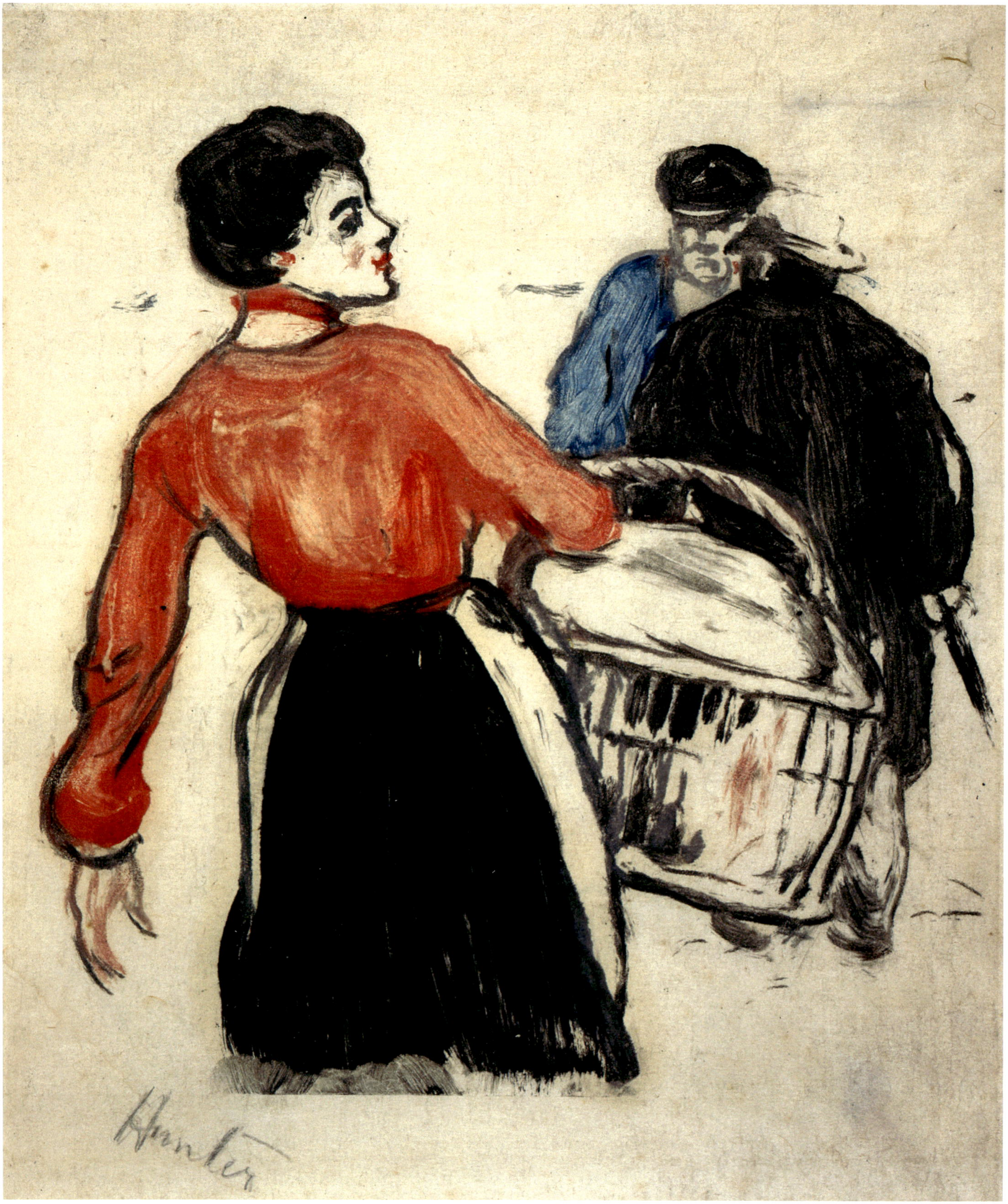

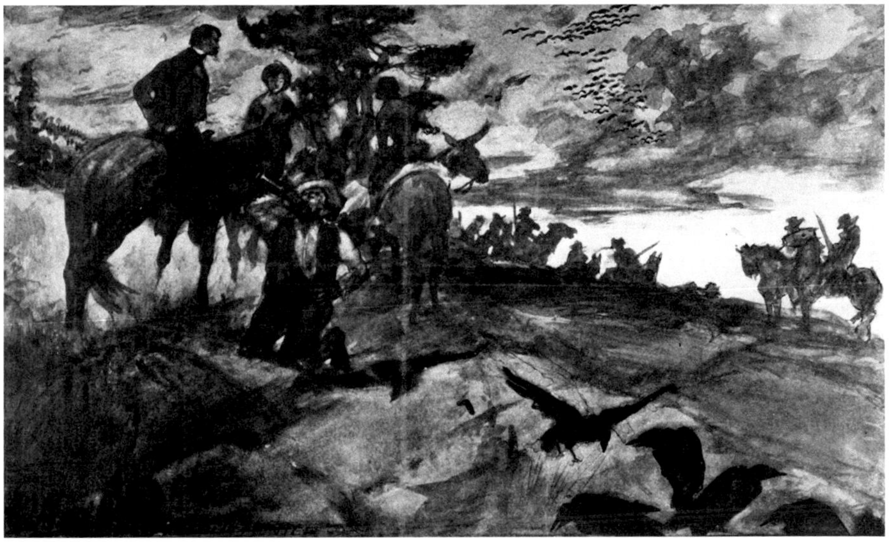

19 | Woman with a Basket
Colour monotype, 1904
University of Glasgow, Hunterian Art Gallery

20 | *The exiles were forbidden to return*, illustration in *Overland Monthly*, September 1902 for Bret Harte's short story 'The Outcasts of Poker Flat'
The British Library

boats, brought alive by vibrant use of crayon, in *Fisherman's Wharf, San Francisco* (1902), in the confident, well-balanced *Chinatown, San Francisco* (*c.*1902, pl.16) and in *The French Market, New Orleans* (pl.6). Instinctively Hunter knew what to select from a view and how to capture it on paper. Early in his career he demonstrated his natural feel for time, place and atmosphere.

Judging from the style of the signature, *Chinatown, San Francisco* and *The French Market, New Orleans* were intended as magazine illustrations (as yet untraced). New Orleans is a considerable distance from San Francisco, but Hunter had relatives there and, as it was the southern terminus of the Southern Pacific Railroad's crack *Sunset* express, he may have received a free return ticket in payment for illustrations he executed for the railroad's magazine, also called *Sunset*. Sadly, very few of the original drawings for Hunter's magazine illustrations have surfaced so far. *'I reckon they're after somebody,' he said* (1902, pl.17) is a fine ink, wash and pencil drawing for the lead illustration in Bret Harte's short story *The Outcasts of Poker Flat* in the *Bret Harte Memorial Number* of *Overland Monthly*. Plate 18 (*c.*1902) is a similar drawing for an unidentified illustration. It may be one that Hunter prepared for *The Outcasts of Poker Flat*, but was not used by the magazine, or it may relate to another story in *Overland Monthly*, or some other magazine, that has not yet come to light.

The earthquake and fire had left Hunter down, but not out. The San Francisco he had known was no more. His friends had scattered or were on the point of leaving the city. He too had taken the decision to move on.

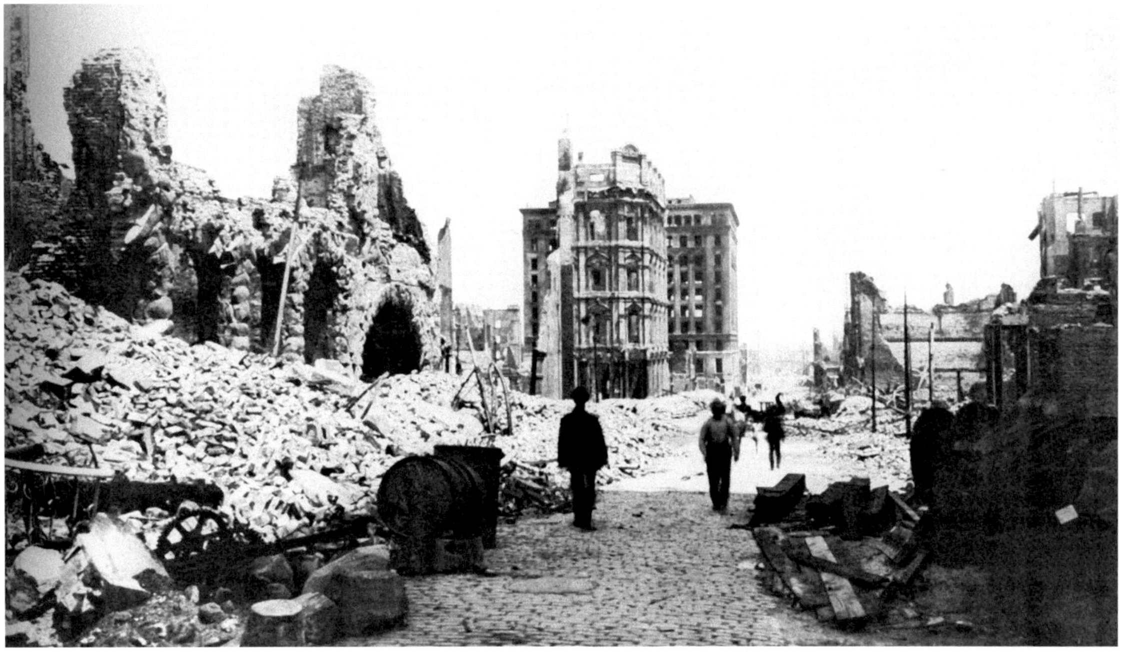

21 | San Francisco after the 1906 earthquake and fire. The fires that followed the earthquake were intense and attempts to make fire breaks by dynamiting buildings proved futile. Even modern buildings, like the one in the middle distance, were totally gutted
California Historical Society

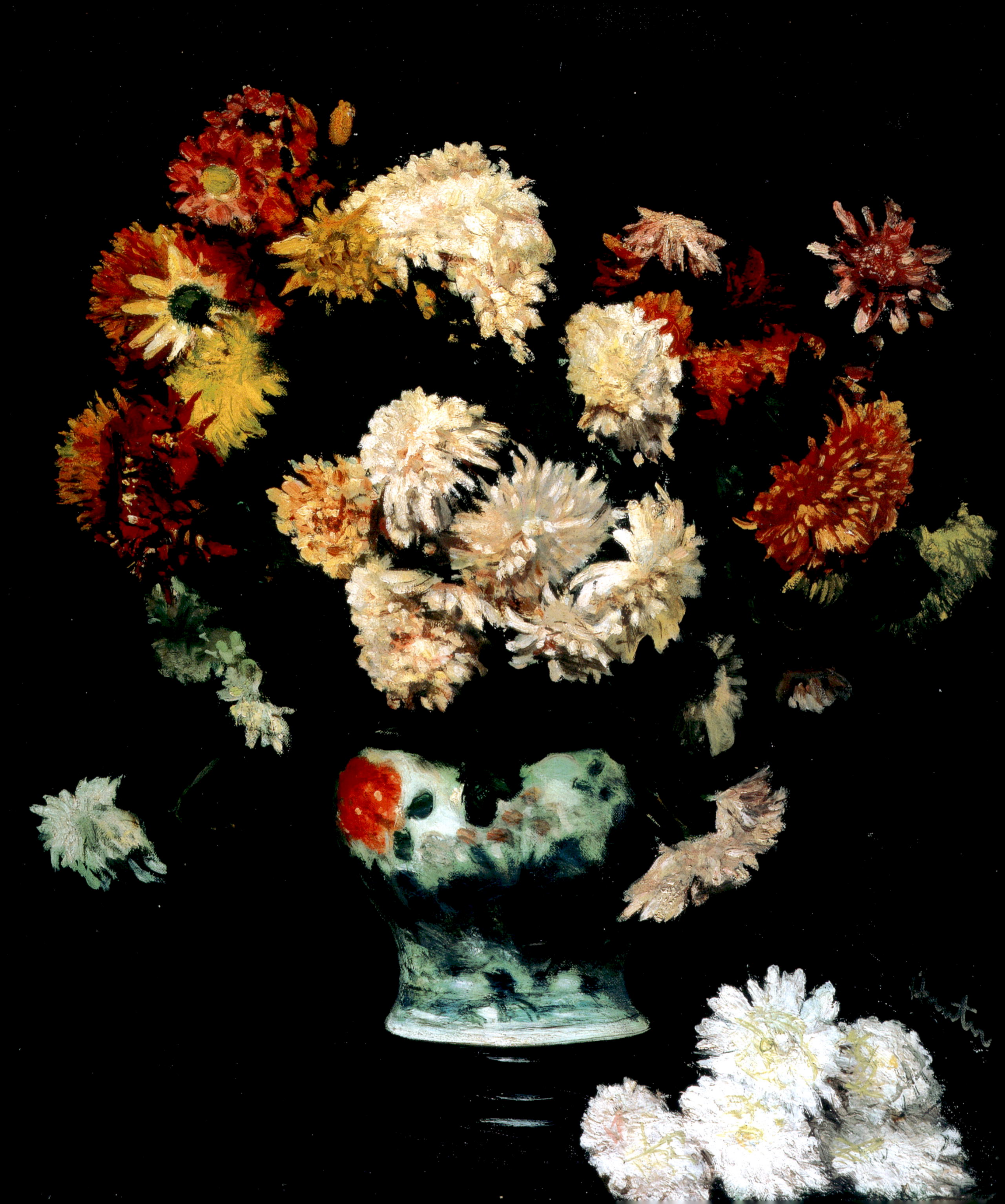

4 Renewal

LESLIE HUNTER returned to Glasgow in the autumn of 1906 to a joyful reunion with his mother, sister Jeanie, and brother William and his family, whom he had not seen for three years. His mother's home at 279 Byres Road, not very far from Kelvingrove Art Gallery and Museum, became Hunter's permanent address until her death in 1913. Hunter was devoted to his mother. He had great respect for her intelligence and courage.[1] In turn her faith and encouragement supported him through thick and thin. It must have been difficult at times, because Hunter was not an easy man to live with, and, as demonstrated later in the chapter, his behaviour could be somewhat erratic and unpredictable. Hunter executed several sketches of his mother and in 1908 a portrait in oil in the manner of Whistler, in which she is wearing a coat with a large fur collar or wrap and a rather ornate hat. On his mother's death her role in Hunter's life was assumed by Jeanie, soon to be married to James McFarlane, a marine engineer. Then it was to Jeanie's home at 147 Crow Road in Partick, and to her ever-present affection and care, that Hunter would return 'in times of depression, fatigue of mind or of body'.[2]

Now Hunter had to face the fact that he had lost everything in the fire that followed the San Francisco earthquake. He had little to show for seven years' hard work. Almost all his watercolours, drawings and innumerable sketches had been destroyed. He had left behind many good friends in San Francisco, almost all of whom had lost everything too; many followed Hunter's example and abandoned the city. Almost as important, he had left behind a way of life that he loved.

Still only 29, Hunter had to start all over again, something that initially may have been difficult for him even to contemplate. However he had a hunger for painting that could not be extinguished. He *had* to pursue his dream of becoming a successful painter. With financial support from his mother, he did not need to return to hack illustrative work. He had told Tom Hunt in New York that for him illustration was dead and he meant it. The following year (1907) he was back in Paris, a letter from Gottardo Piazzoni in Neuilly-sur-Seine to Arthur Putnam in California reporting that 'Hunter is in Paris for the summer, very romantic.'[3] If Piazzoni was alluding to the presence of a female companion with Hunter, there is no clue as to the identity of the lady in question. Undoubtedly Hunter was attractive to women. He had not been short of female company in California. In San Francisco he had fallen in love with the beautiful Isabel Fraser,[4] a feature writer for the *San Francisco Examiner* and the 'official darling' of the Coppans, the artists and writers who frequented Coppa's restaurant in the 'Monkey Block', just opposite Hunter's studio in Montgomery Street. At one memorable party at Maynard Dixon's studio on Telegraph Hill Isabel Fraser had 'mounted a ladder and was acclaimed Queen of Bohemia'. The writer Gelett Burgess used her as a model for one of his characters having 'that free, fearless gaiety, the almost abandoned good nature of San Francisco girls'.[5] However

22 | Chrysanthemums
Oil on canvas, 1913
Private collection

Hunter was only one of many to fall under the spell of this beguiling creature (Hunter's friend, Scheffauer, being another),[6] and the romance did not blossom.[7] Later her passion for the mystic took Isabel Fraser to Persia, where she became a priestess in a Bahai temple.[8]

Also in Paris that summer of 1907 was Hunter's sculptor friend, Ralph Stackpole, the protégé of Arthur Putnam. Stackpole and Hunter must have spent some time together then, or possibly the year before, travelling to places outside Paris, because in a letter written from San Francisco in 1912 Stackpole reminds Hunter of 'our very happy days in Paris', telling him:

I was glad to hear that you had been to Paris twice lately [post-1907]. *That sounds fine and I congratulate you as I know how hard it is to get back there. I wish you would write and tell me how you are and some of the impressions in these last trips to Paris, and also if I might impose on your past friendship. What class did you travel, & did you refuse to be British? I was showing my wife a reproduction of the Cathedrale Notre Dame of Rouen the other day. I showed her the door on the extreme left and said there's where Leslie Hunter and I went in. It seems a long way from there out here but I hope one day to see those great Gothic monuments again with you. I think they would mean a great deal more to me now. They naturally would.*[9]

Stackpole's question about whether or not Hunter refused 'to be British' relates to his dual nationality. Hunter had been granted American citizenship, but switched nationalities when it suited him. Hunter liked Stackpole, later writing to his friend, Matthew Justice:

... besides having the most amiable personal qualities, [he] *has the broadest appreciation possible on art and nature alike, so that it is a pleasure to go to see anything with him. He paints not badly and has made immense strides in his sculpture, though he is modesty itself.*[10]

However it was to be over ten years before they met again, when Stackpole was Hunter's companion on a visit to Florence and the surrounding Tuscan countryside in 1923.

Paris was not merely the artistic centre of Europe, it was also the cultural centre. The city remained a constant source of inspiration throughout Hunter's life. He loved living and working there. At times he did not have much money, but that does not appear to have caused him any great concern. He relished the city's rich and varied artistic life, its museums and galleries and the bohemian life style that reminded him of San Francisco before the earthquake. There is little evidence of where he went and what he did during the period from 1907 to the outbreak of the First World War, and much of what does exist is anecdotal in nature. However an insight may be gained from the experiences in Paris of Hunter's friends, and of other artists and writers, particularly those of fellow Americans.

In 1903 Gertrude Stein had moved from San Francisco to join her brother, Leo, in Paris. In her book, *Paris France*, written in 1940, Stein sums up the attraction of the city: '... really what they [the French] do do is to respect art and letters, if you are a writer you have privileges, if you are a painter you have privileges and it is pleasant to have these privileges'.[11] The police and other authorities tended to treat artists

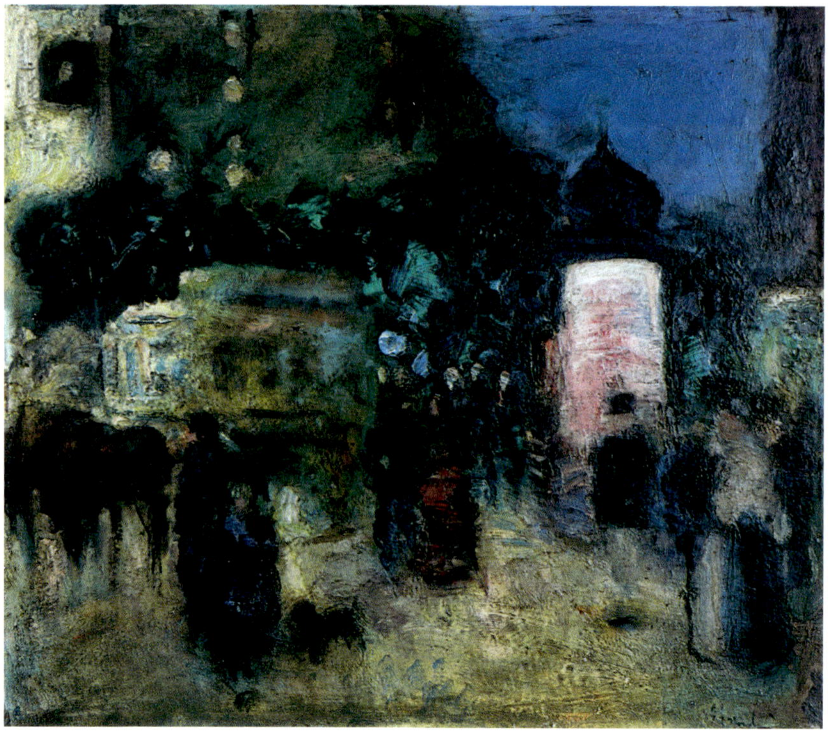

23 | Paris Boulevard by Night
Oil on board, 1907–10
Private collection

and writers deferentially, regarding them as useful members of the commonwealth, not as 'oddities or parasites'. The French took it for granted that the arts had a place in the national well-being.[12] Stein considered that Paris was the right place to be from 1900 to 1939, because Britain refused to leave the nineteenth century, America was overwhelmed by the technology of the twentieth century, and only France remained relatively unaffected.[13] She concluded: '... Paris was the place that suited those of us that were to create the twentieth century art and literature, naturally enough.'[14]

Another important factor, Stein suggests, is that at the beginning of the twentieth century most of the creativity was effected by foreign artists and writers, for example, Picasso in painting, Stravinsky in music and Joyce in literature. She had a theory that a writer must live abroad to be fully alive to his inner feelings and able to express himself, saying 'that is why writers have to have two countries, the one where they belong and the one in which they live'. [15] Her view helps in understanding the value of Paris to Hunter; living in Paris made

24 | Sunlit Avenue, Northern France
Oil on canvas, 1907–10
Private collection

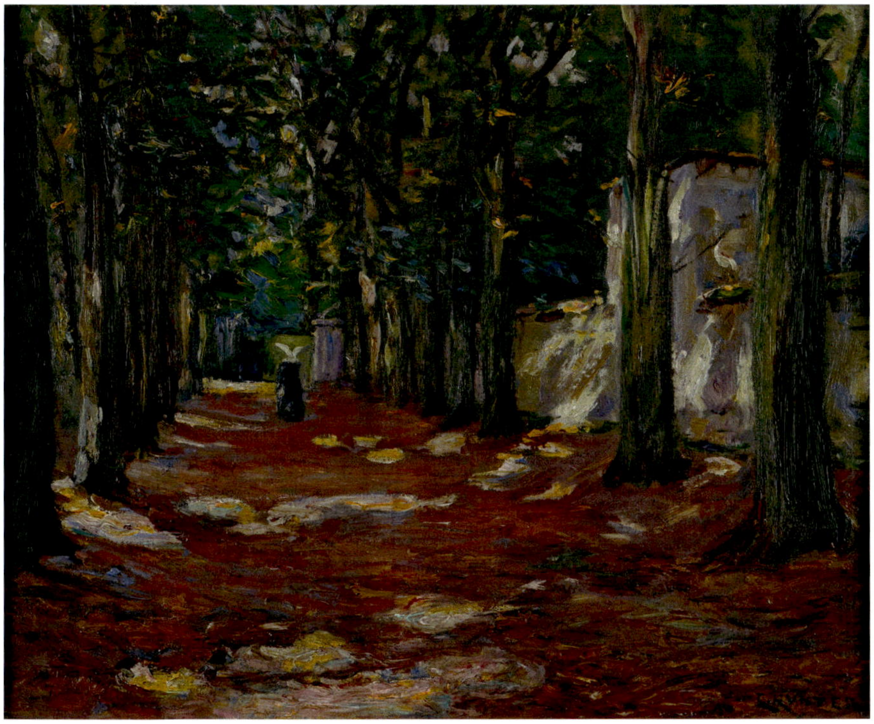

him more aware of Scotland. Based in the compact quarter around the Luxembourg Palace and Gardens and the cafés of Montparnasse, the bohemian way of life suited Hunter well, but for him Bohemia was much more than that – it was where the *avant-garde* was. Experiment was the keynote of the arts of Paris; all manner of new movements and styles proliferated there. Hunter was entirely self-taught. Like fellow artist, J.D.Fergusson, he never would have submitted to the regimentation and constraints of a formal art education. Instead he was eager to extend his knowledge of the art and technique of the Old Masters and embrace current developments by means of observation, analysis and experimentation. Paris provided wonderful opportunities for that.

One significant event for Hunter is recorded by Stein's lover, Alice Toklas, which opens up hitherto missing connections and possibilities of Hunter's pre-First World War experiences in Paris, and helps to explain why his artistic development changed so dramatically from an accomplished traditional painting style to astonishingly vibrant colour in the space of ten years. Alice, who was the same age as Hunter, arrived in Paris from San Francisco in 1907, met Gertrude Stein on her first evening and remained with her until the latter's death in 1949. She recounts:

Crossing the Luxembourg one day I ran into Leslie Hunter, a San Francisco painter, a large burly Scotchman. He came to see me and took me on long, cold, winter walks and I took him to see the pictures at the rue de Fleurus, which shocked him profoundly. He wished he had never gone to see them. His painting was under the influence of Sir Thomas Lawrence.[16]

It is very likely that Hunter and Alice had met in San Francisco and were well-acquainted by the time they came across each other in Paris.

Leo and Gertrude Stein lived at 27 rue de Fleurus, adjacent to the Luxembourg Gardens and a short walk from the Boulevard Montparnasse. As well as pictures by Renoir and Cézanne, the Steins had a formidable *avant-garde* collection of paintings by Matisse and Picasso. Leo was the first real patron of Matisse, and

Gertrude of Picasso. As an indication of how far-reaching Matisse and Picasso's art was from the mainstream, there are various contemporary recollections, including Hunter's friend, Gelett Burgess. Writing of a visit to the Salon des Independents in 1910, Burgess remarks:

I had scarcely entered the Salon des Independants when I hear shrieks of laughter coming from an adjoining wing. I hurried along ... until I came upon a party of well-dressed Parisians in a paroxysm of merriment, gazing, through weeping eyes, at a picture ... If this example of the new art was shocking, there were other paintings that were as dire.[17]

The Steins held weekly Salons, a peculiarly French social event at which artists and writers mixed with patrons to discuss the arts and, according to Mabel Dodge, after viewing the pictures 'people giggled and scoffed after they left'.[18]

Hunter's encounter with Alice Toklas suggests that probably he viewed the Steins' paintings during the day, while Gertrude was out, most likely during the winter of 1908–1909.[19] Visitors to the apartment entered a cluttered space with pictures at times skied four high, books everywhere and portfolios of prints and drawings stacked against the wall.[20] Alice recalled that pictures adorned the walls 'from *cimaise* to ceiling'.[21] It is likely that Hunter went to see the Cézannes; perhaps he was even curious about the Matisse and Picasso paintings from Alice's conversation with him. Nothing could have prepared him for the assault on his senses! Whether it was Matisse's wildly-coloured *Woman in a Hat* of 1905,[22] or Picasso's monumental primitive *Boy Leading a Horse*, also 1905,[23] or other equally bold pictures, Hunter's consciousness would have been jolted. There is every reason to suppose their extreme effect set him thinking, as had been the case for others.[24]

At this point another facet of Hunter's artistic development was activated, one that

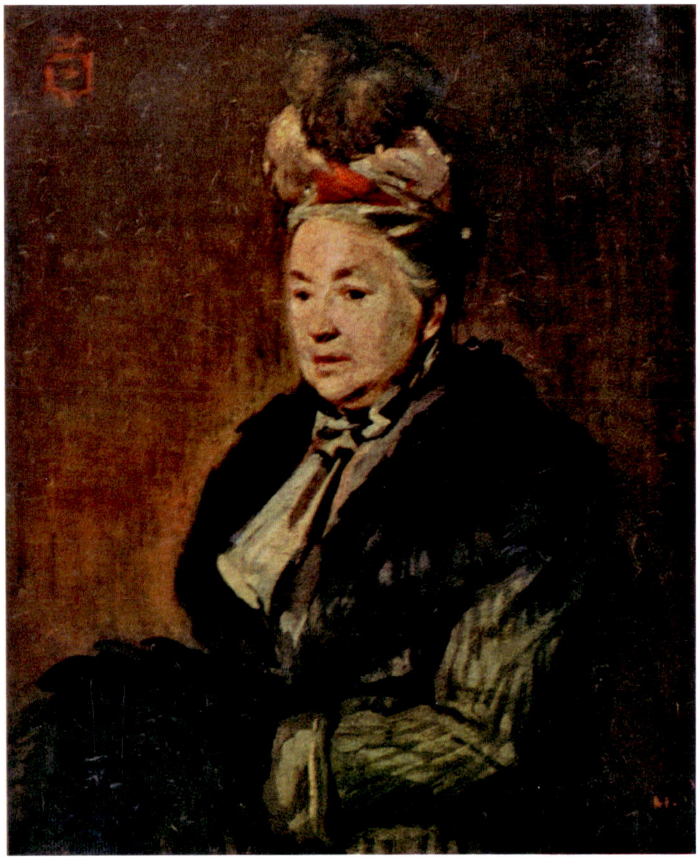

25 | Jeanie Hunter, Leslie Hunter's Mother
Oil, *c.*1908
Hunter Family, California

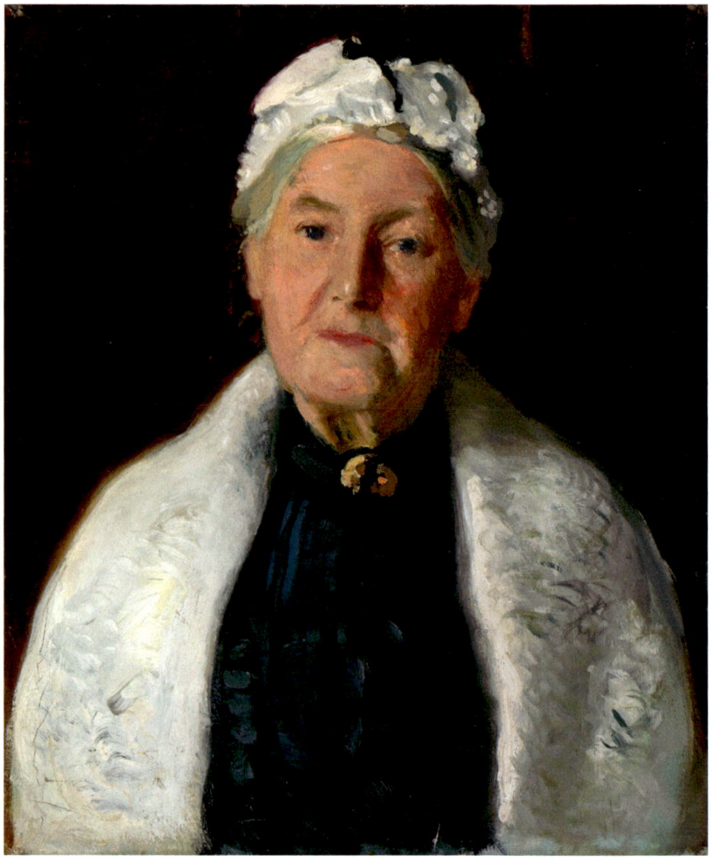

26 | Mrs Helen Meldrum
Oil on canvas, *c.*1917
Glasgow Museums

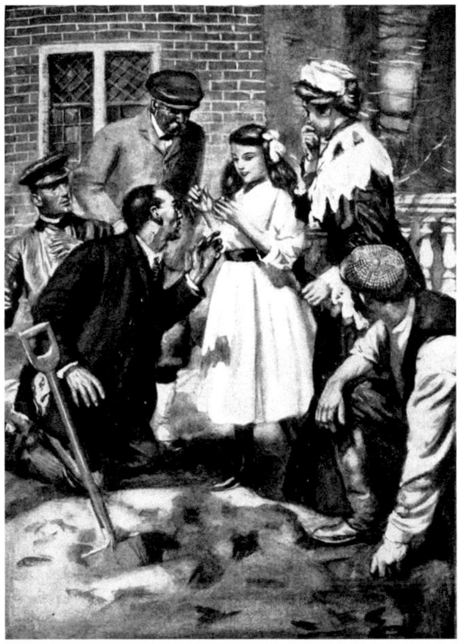

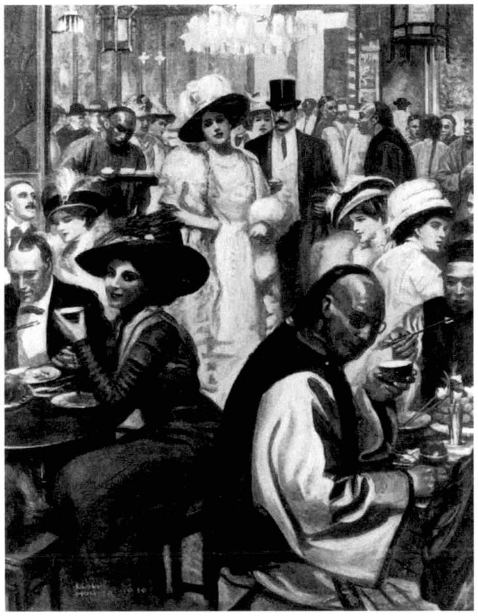

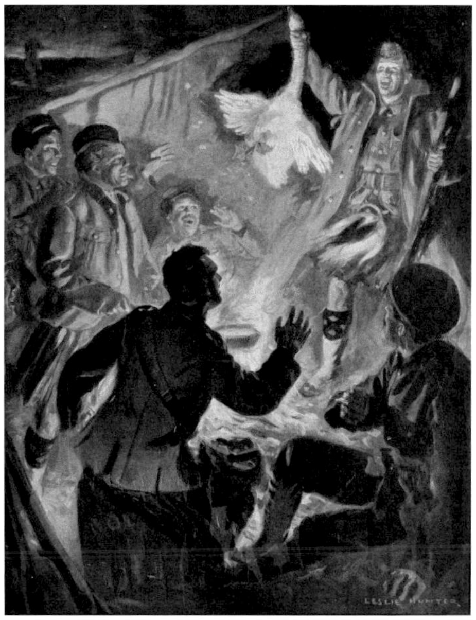

27 | *She held up a round whitish stone, and Jack held out his hand for it,* illustration in *The Strand Magazine*, February 1911, for 'Clever Mr Painter' by Morley Roberts
The British Library

28 | *The Latest Craze of American Society: New Yorkers dining in a Chinese Restaurant*, illustration in *The Graphic*, 25 November 1911
National Library of Scotland

29 | *The Christmas Goose in the Trenches,* illustration in *The Graphic*, 26 December 1914
Mervyn Donnelly

had its origins in the lively discussions on the philosophy of Kant, Schopenhauer and Nietzsche in which Hunter and his friends had engaged in San Francisco some years before. He was shocked by the Steins' pictures, but the natural subjective approach to their motif would not have been lost on him. This subjective approach was something that a year or two later Gelett Burgess commented on in his 1910 article with particular reference to Matisse:

[Matisse] *chats thoughtfully of the 'Harmony and volume' and 'architectural values' … Maitre Matisse, if I understand him … stands quite primarily for the solid existence of things. He paints weight, volume, roundness, colour and all the intrinsic physical attributes of the thing itself, and then imbues the whole with sentiment … you turn from his pictures, which have so shockingly defied you, and you demand of other artists at least as much vitality and originality – and don't find it! He paints with emotion, and inspires you with it … But fearful as it is, it is alive – awfully alive! … It is a revolt against 'mere charm', against accidental aspects of illumination; a return to simplicity, directness, pure colour and decorative qualities.*

Hunter's exploration of colour was under way, and there would be no turning back.

Although it is unlikely that Hunter knew Gertrude particularly well – she was known not to engage in conversation except with her intimate friends[25] – it is clear that Hunter knew Leo Stein sufficiently well to visit him in Italy fifteen years later. From 1904 Leo had a studio on the ground floor of rue de Fleurus, which became an informal gallery in which he displayed works by Cézanne, Gauguin, Renoir, Manguin and Vallotton that he had purchased recently, and which Americans often visited.[26]

Alice's reference in her book to Sir Thomas Lawrence being an influence on Hunter is puzzling. She is the only source that has been uncovered of Hunter's interest in Lawrence's work. At that time the portrait painter was not represented in either Glasgow Art Gallery or in the National Gallery of Scotland, but Hunter may have seen paintings by him in the National Gallery in London, or indeed in Paris or the United States where he was popular then. A biography of Lawrence by Lord Ronald Gower appeared in 1900; with his appetite for reading, this may have prompted Hunter to obtain a copy somehow and to take a closer look at Lawrence and his technique.

Although Hunter and Toklas were only friends, Hunter did have a number of amorous relationships throughout his life. In February

1910 a daughter, Katherine, was born to Hunter and Margaret Munro. Nothing is known about the mother, apart from her name. Katherine was adopted and her name changed to Kathleen Fairgrieve.[27] The same year Hunter decided to move to London. Whether the move was connected in any way to the birth of the child is not known. In those days the birth of an illegitimate child scandalized the mother's family and often brought down opprobrium on the father and his family. Hunter's mother, a devout churchgoer, would have been hurt and affronted by the whole affair.

According to Honeyman, Hunter was accompanied to London by Reid Kelly, an illustrator and distant relative of his.[28] Hunter must have been hard up, because immediately he got there he looked around for illustrative work, even though he had vowed not to touch it again. Perhaps to express her displeasure his mother may have cut off the financial support she must have been giving her son. Hunter did obtain a small amount of work, producing four large drawings for the weekly periodical, *The Graphic*, one of which was reproduced in a German periodical, *Buch für Alle*, in 1912, and five drawings to illustrate a short story in *The Strand Magazine*. In addition he executed drawings for the American magazine, *Harper's Weekly*, to illustrate two short stories by his friend from San Francisco, Herman Scheffauer, which appeared in the second half of 1911.[29] Probably it was on the instigation of Scheffauer that Hunter landed the commission.

In a letter to Honeyman written in 1936, the artist, E.A.Taylor, sheds some light on what Hunter was doing during the three years up to the outbreak of the First World War. In 1908 Taylor had married the artist, Jessie M. King, and the couple moved to Paris two years later, when Taylor was appointed Paris correspondent of *The Studio*. He met Hunter several times in Paris, initially introduced to Taylor by an American artist, Harry DeMaine, three years younger than Hunter, confirming yet again Hunter's preference for being with Americans.

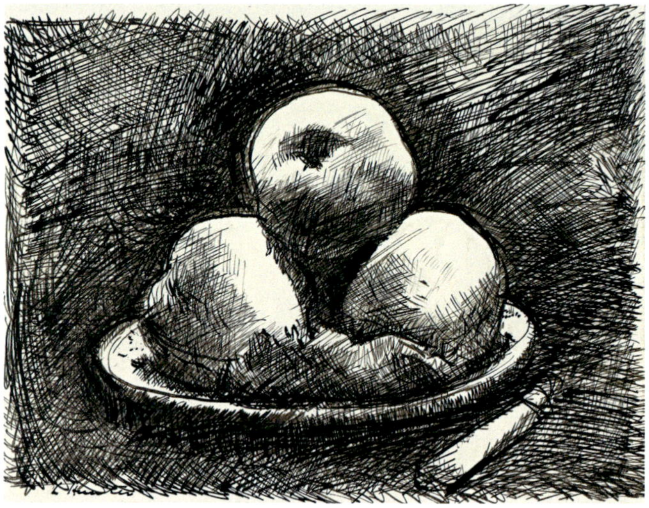

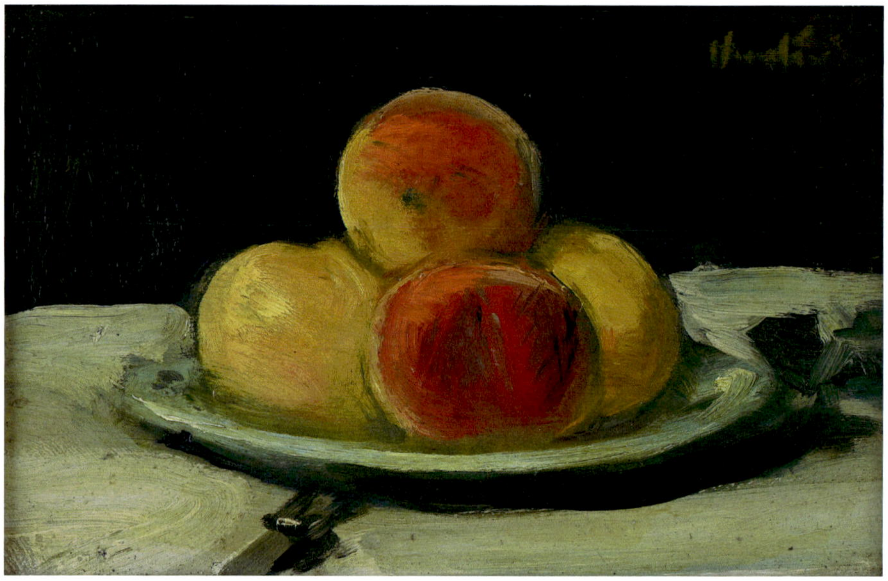

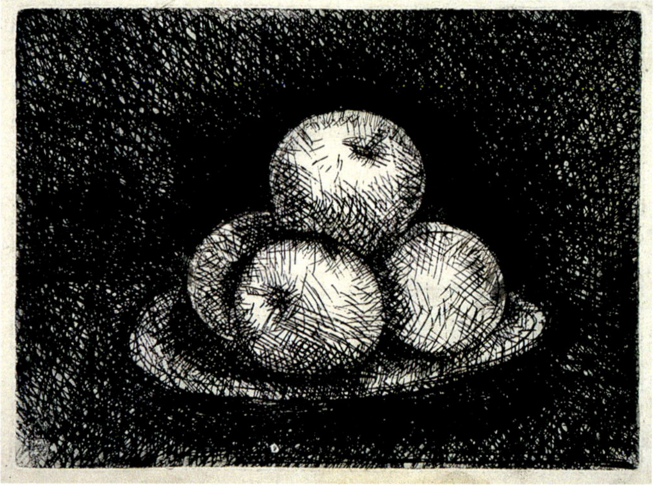

DeMaine and Hunter were staying in a cheap hotel in the rue Delambre near the Café Dôme in Montparnasse.[30]

The American artist, Marsden Hartley, also provides revealing accounts of Montparnasse, and remarks how close an artist can be to the cultural life in the city:

One has a sense somehow of the mere timeliness of the Cubistes and the Futuristes here. I see them often and have met several ... They all talk so glibly but what do they produce ... I only know there is a terrific deal of talking and I avoid it whenever possible. The charming fact is that one can shut one's door and be as far as one wishes from it – right here in Paris, and the real value is in being close to the great things and in such quantity ... Here one finds more cliques and groups than could be imagined – such groups as for instance the Fergusson-Estelle Rice Group which exploits itself in Rhythm.[31]

Hunter's experience is likely to have been similar. Living near the Luxembourg Gardens and Montparnasse it was impossible not to meet the same people every day in the gardens or in the cafés, which were located almost in a line from the Closerie de Lilas to the Café Dôme. Although it does not appear to be documented, it is very likely that Hunter came across J.D.Fergusson and his circle in Paris at this time.

In spring 1912 Hunter had been painting at Étaples in the Pas de Calais, a region on the French Channel coast popular with many Scottish painters, including Fergusson, Peploe and, later, Anne Redpath. Taylor takes up the story:

Hunter asked me up to have a look at his pictures & was very anxious to get a little publicity in 'The Studio'. I remember getting rather a surprise at that time perhaps his talking to me before I went to see his things. I may have expected something great. However he showed me a number of small panels ... all very much in the style & manner of Eugène Boudin, the French landscape and sea painter. Little figures sketchy – pretty & sort of lyrical on sandy dunes & glimpse of sea – some of them after the style of an artist who was then in Étaples, named Fred Mayor – & Hunter I understand rather admired his work also that of Boudin (& Monet slightly) ... The work was dainty but rather ordinary & thin, & I knew it would not in any way appeal to 'The Studio' – & he mentioned he would do something better in the country during the summer. So I said we'll wait & have a look at what you do.[32]

Taylor's observation that he was expecting something great, after Hunter had talked up his art at some length, may well confirm that Hunter's intellectual consciousness was far more advanced than his ability to transfer it to canvas at that time. The art did not match the talk. Hunter was well-informed on modern art, but his painting was still at the development stage. Equally, it is possible that Hunter's passion for talking about modern art may have been on a different level to that of Taylor. In his published articles in *The Studio* in 1912 and 1913 it is noticeable that Taylor appears to seek out and evaluate *mainstream* art, which of course was abundant in Paris.

The next contact that Taylor had with Hunter was in London a couple of months or so later, when Taylor came to his studio:

I found him in a little room (I could not call it a studio) in a street off the Tottenham Court Road. A most awful-looking landlady came to the door, and with her naked arms directed me up a flight of narrow stairs to the very top of the house, and there was Hunter. There was hardly room for both of us in the room, which was very untidy. He told me he was busy doing illustrations and covers for Pearson's Magazine, but I never saw the illustrations and rather fancy he had no commission to do them but was just doing them on chance ... [33]

In fact Hunter did get a commission from *Pearson's Magazine*, providing three illustrations for a short story by P.G.Wodehouse, which appeared in 1915.[34] Shortly after Taylor and Hunter met in such grubby circumstances, his fortunes must have improved, because he moved to rather more gentile accommodation at 97 Shepherd's Bush Road, possibly following a reconciliation with his mother.[35]

In 1913 Hunter was producing illustrations for the monthly *Pall Mall Magazine*, including

30 | Still Life with Apples, Plate and Knife
Pen and black ink on paper, *c.*1913
Scottish National Gallery of Modern Art

31 | Dish of Peaches
Oil on panel, 1907–10
Private collection

32 | Still Life with Apples
Etching touched with ink, *c.*1913
University of Glasgow, Hunterian Art Gallery

26 drawings for two articles by his San Francisco friend, Herman Scheffauer.[36] Hunter met Scheffauer in Berlin, and it was in that city that Hunter had what can only be described as a quite extraordinary amorous 'adventure', an account of which the artist later gave to Honeyman:

[Hunter] *was in Paris when he received telegraphic instructions to proceed immediately to Berlin. Further instructions and money would be awaiting him at Cook's Berlin office. Hunter had used all his available cash in buying his railway ticket, and arrived in Germany with a few sous in his pocket. Much to his annoyance, not to say alarm, there was no letter at Cook's. He was in a quandary. Well, the small change would at least get him a drink. As he sat in the corner of a café, trying to find a way out of his awkward predicament, an elegant and beautiful lady engaged him in conversation. The reason of her interest and the nature of her usual occupation soon became apparent, but Hunter's financial status appeared to be of no account. She offered him the hospitality of bed and board, as a gesture from one 'artist' to another in distress. Three days elapsed before the letter at Cook's made its appearance, but not a breath of doubt or of impatience marred the enjoyment of 'three most perfect days'.*[37]

1913 was a year of great sadness and of success for Hunter. On 15 March his mother died at home in Glasgow aged 73.[38] Hunter loved his mother dearly. His sister, Jeanie, assumed the mantle of friend and counsellor and, in the 1920s, guardian and nurse. In November Hunter held his first one-man exhibition at La Société des Beaux-Arts, Alexander Reid's prestigious galleries in Glasgow's West George Street.

Reid has been described as 'an instinctive dealer, who developed a passion for certain artists'. He championed the work of the French painter, Eugène Boudin, and William McTaggart in the 1900s, and the artists who were to become known as the Scottish Colourists – particularly Hunter – from about 1912 onwards. [39] Until then Hunter had managed to sell the occasional painting. Around 1912 he executed a commission for a church friend of his mother, involving a 'large still life in which Hunter was required to incorporate some family treasures and harmonise the whole with the dining-room scheme of decoration'. The picture aroused considerable interest and 'was seen by a number of people, among whom were several who ultimately claimed that they had 'discovered' a young artist of such promise as to justify calling Reid's attention to his work'.[40] Indeed Reid did acquire a couple of Hunter's paintings and promised him an exhibition when he had completed a sufficient number of pictures to justify mounting a one-man show.[41]

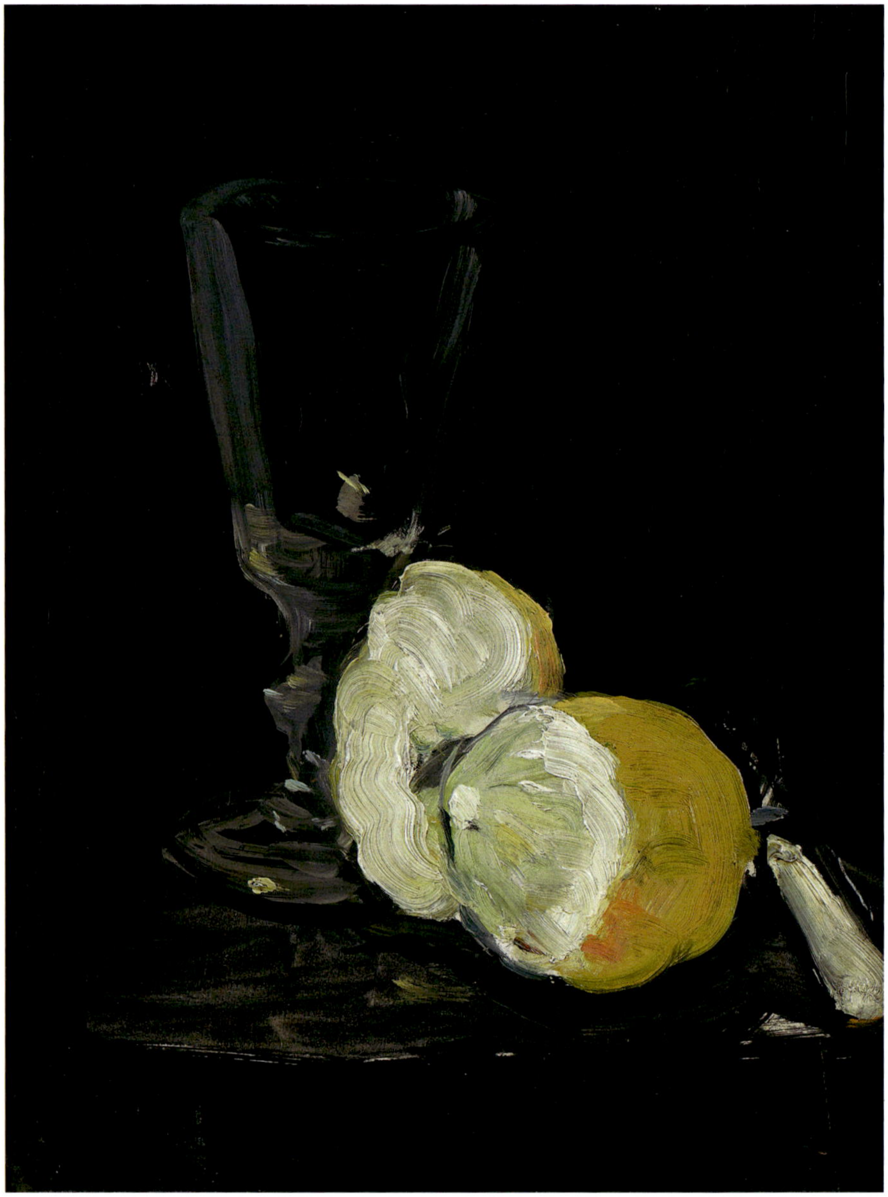

33 | Lemon and Knife
Oil on board, 1913
Private collection

34 | Chrysanthemums in a Chinese Vase with Phoenix
Oil on canvas, 1913
Private collection

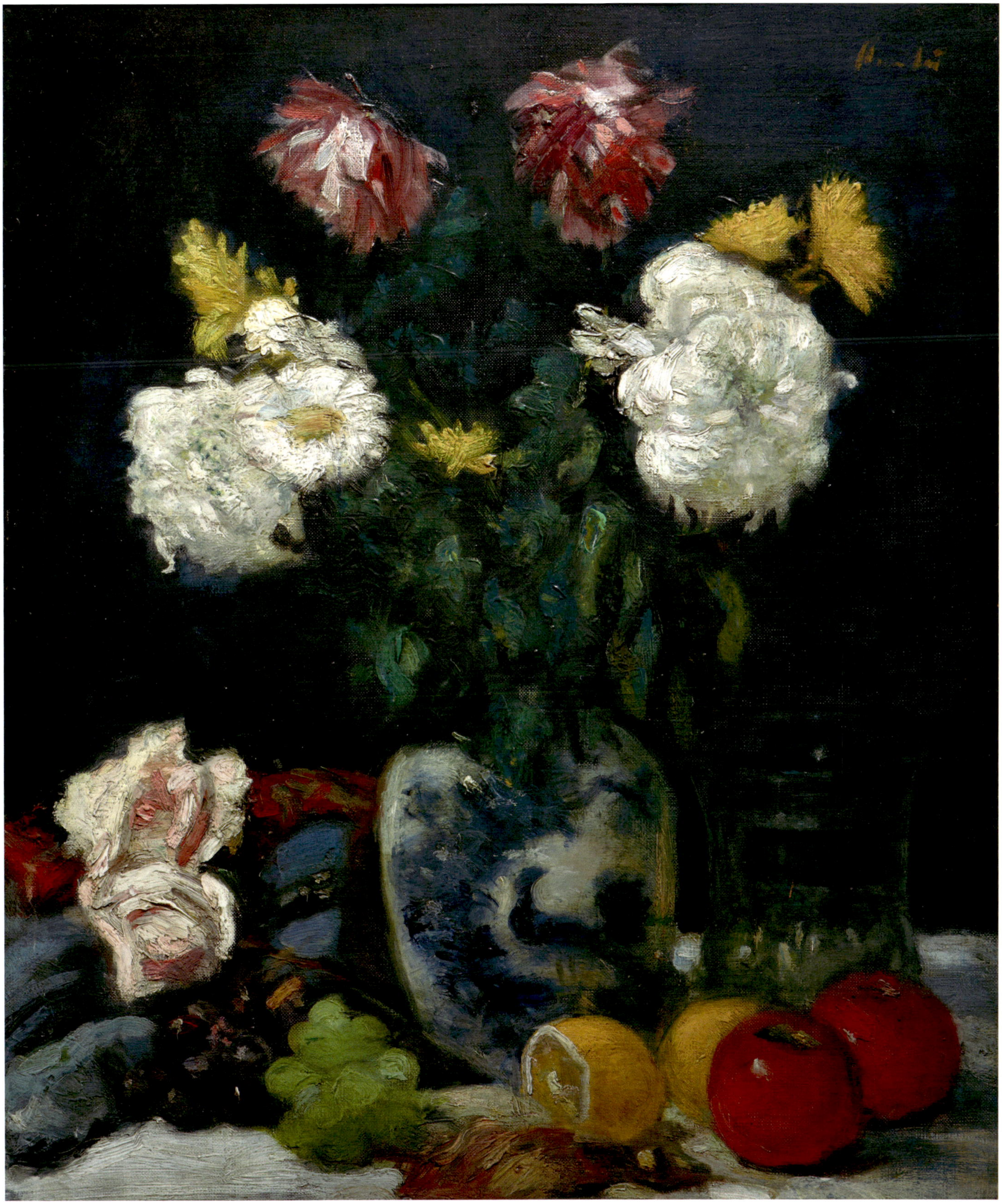

That exhibition, comprising mainly still life paintings, opened in November 1913. The critic of the *Glasgow Herald* described Hunter as 'a vigorous and confident painter with a fine sense of colour' and praised him for his 'punctilious regard for actuality', though he considered that Hunter had overcrowded his larger works with too much detail. The newspaper felt that the still life was a 'form of artistic expression which perhaps makes limited appeal' (an opinion that was soon to be proved well wide of the mark by the Scottish Colourists, especially Peploe and Hunter). The critic concluded: 'This modest and attractive show should serve as a favourable introduction of Mr. Hunter's work among local collectors.'[42] And so it proved; a total of seventeen pictures were sold,[43] which must have pleased Reid and delighted Hunter.

The key to an understanding of Hunter's work during the period from his return from San Francisco right up to the end of the First World War is that his artistic development must be seen against the background of European art, rather than that of Scotland or indeed Britain. Hunter had a great admiration for the paintings of Dutch seventeenth-century artists, such as Jan Vermeer, Frans Hals and Willem Kalf. Equally, Schopenhauer, the German philosopher whose views influenced Hunter, considered Dutch still life to be the best type of painting, because it was able to help the viewer see beauty in ordinary, everyday objects.[44] In trying to render his impressions on canvas, Hunter may have connected with Dutch still life as a good starting point in the development of his subjective approach and feeling for strong colour.

An arrangement of objects against a dark background to accentuate a structured perspective, combined with sumptuous, often jewel-like richness, are elements that captivated Hunter. His affection for Kalf, with his bright-coloured fruit amid blue and white porcelain dishes and his complex contrasts with jewel-like glass vessels in the middle to far background,

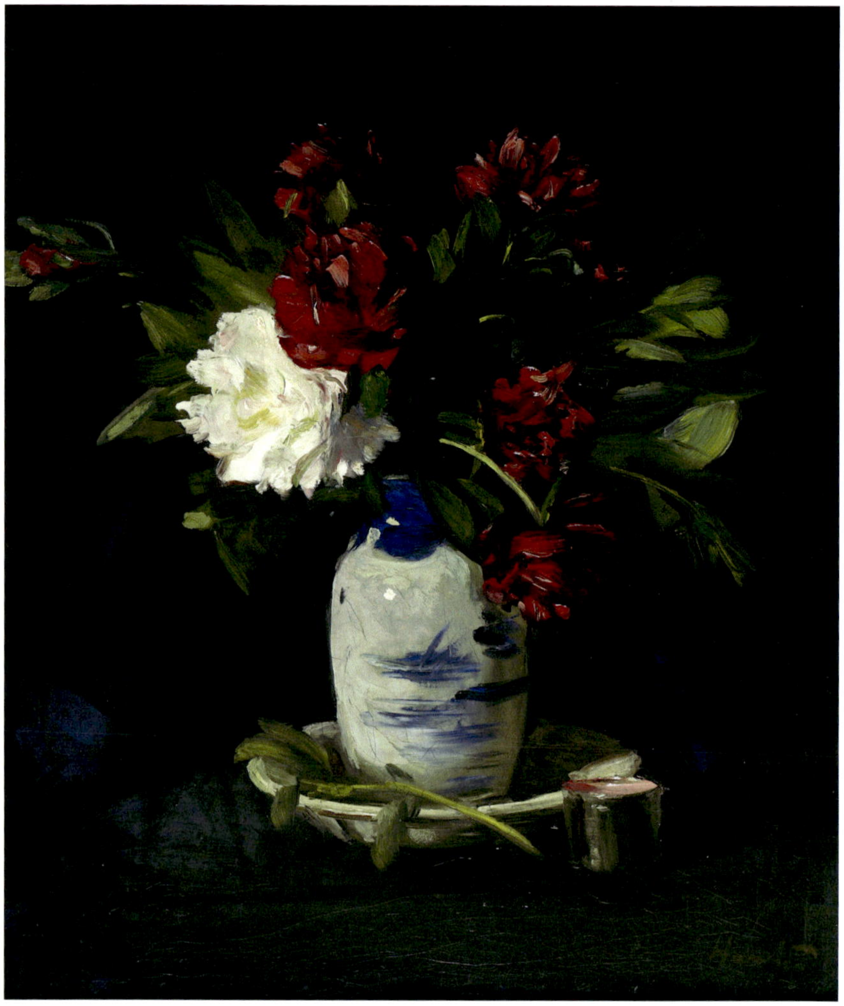

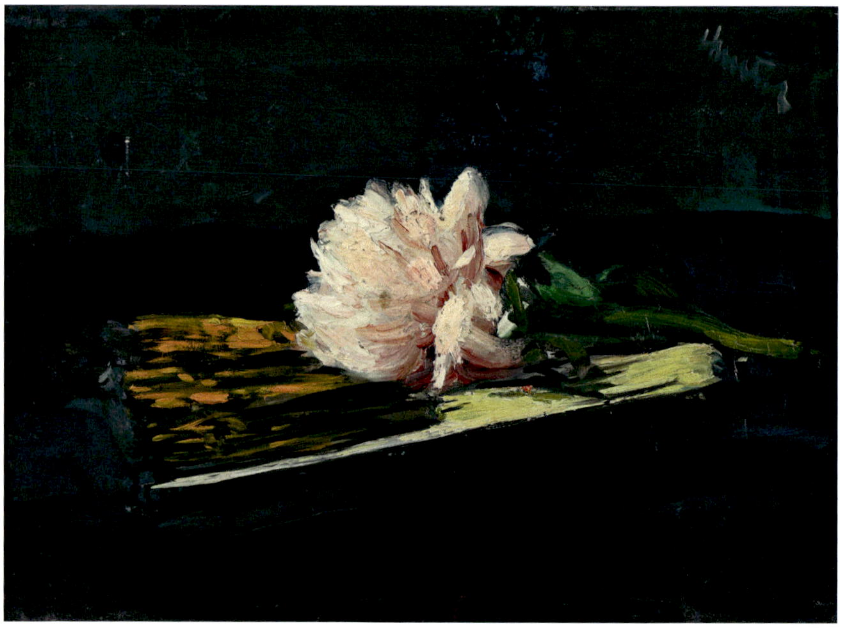

35 | Peony Roses
Oil on canvas, 1913
The Glenmore Collection

36 | Still Life with Flower and Fan
Oil on board, 1913
Private collection

is very evident in a series of paintings by Hunter himself, of which *Chrysanthemums in a Chinese Vase with Phoenix* (pl.34) is a fine example.

The direct simplicity and heightened reality of still life objects juxtaposed against plain backgrounds are features that Hunter admired in paintings by the French eighteenth-century artist, Jean-Baptiste-Siméon Chardin. He would have been able to study three superb examples in the collection of Glasgow University. The work of the modern French masters was studied assiduously as well. In Manet's early flower pieces Hunter delighted in the fluid brushwork that created softness in tone and texture, giving the blooms a vitality all their own. Thus, using a variety of sources, Hunter experimented with specific elements and techniques, blending them in the search for *his* way forward.

Unlike the French Impressionists, Hunter's main focus was not on the strength or effect of light, but the simple shape and direct presence of certain objects, a characteristic that has an affinity with the work of Chardin. In *Lemon and Knife* (pl.33) Hunter attempts to achieve this concept by applying heavy brushstrokes to model the form he so admired in Manet's work. The painting was included in the 1913 exhibition and singled out by the *Glasgow Herald* for its 'simplicity, refinement of colour and arrangement'. Commending 'a vase of blossoms in creamy white and luscious red' (possibly *Peony Roses*, pl.35) the critic goes on to say: 'the vase itself, a delicate harmony in blue and white, is beautifully painted'.[45] This still life owes little to the Dutch masters; its arrangement and fluid brushwork once again demonstrates the influence of Manet.

Whilst paying homage to the Dutch masters, *Chrysanthemums* (*c.*1913, pl.22) has a delicacy more akin to the nineteenth-century flower painter, Henri Fantin-Latour, whose work was very popular in Glasgow for many years around the turn of the century thanks to the efforts of Reid, who was very keen on the artist and was able to get a regular supply of his paintings through his friend, the Paris dealer Jean Tempelaere.[46] Hunter would have been able to see many examples of Fantin-Latour's work in Glasgow. *Chrysanthemums* is one of the most complete and satisfying of Hunter's early works, testifying to a more confident handling of oils. Hunter so enjoyed the motif of chrysanthemums in this vase that it reappears at regular intervals throughout his life, albeit in very different styles that provide interesting points of reference for identifying key shifts in his artistic development.

His exhibition at Reid's gallery raised Hunter's profile considerably. He met a number of local art collectors, many of whom became friends. Two of those were John Tattersall, a Dundee dentist, and Matthew Justice of Justice & Sons, the Dundee cabinet and furniture makers, who accompanied Hunter to Paris early the following year [1914], as E.A.Taylor recounted to Honeyman:

[Hunter] *turned up at the Café du Dôme – with two friends & took me aside telling me they were very important people (one I think was a dealer or collector from Dundee. I forget the names) & that they had paid his fare over etc. & he was their guest. To help them buy pictures & show them around – I saw little of him during that time – I think he went off to the country with them or with any little money he had made.*[47]

Later both Tattersall and Justice would prove crucial to Hunter's survival as an artist.

Taylor's next encounter with Hunter was not long after, when he turned up at Taylor's Paris flat unannounced:

[He was] *in a terrible state. He evidently had some little spot on the inside of his nose & had scratched it – & his nose was really awful, quite the size of three & red & raw. I took him in & washed it* [with] *hot water & some disinfectants etc. but he did not like being seen, so he used to come up of an evening. Then again he disappeared. Away to the country.*[48]

This anecdote illustrates a particular facet of Hunter's character. Always preoccupied with his work, he cared little about his health or his general welfare. It was a trait that intensified as he grew older.

Hunter had 'disappeared' to Étaples to paint. He had planned a sketching holiday there in the company of his cousin from New York, Arthur Leyden. As it happened, the trip coincided with the outbreak of the First World War. Any sensible person would have cancelled, and his cousin did. Hunter on the other hand was not going to allow a war to disrupt his painting plans and arrived in Étaples and began work. The local gendarmes, ever alert to the possibility of an enemy plot so close to the border with Belgium, promptly arrested Hunter and escorted him to the local gendarmerie. After all the 'artist' with the fresh complexion and fair, sun-bleached hair 'sketching' on the coast *must* be a German spy! Pure farce followed. While details were being taken, Hunter panicked, made a bolt for the gendarmerie's front door and got clean away![49] He resurfaced later at Taylor's flat in Paris.

By this time Hunter was subjecting the work of the Post-Impressionists to intense scrutiny and analysis. In addition to what was readily accessible in Paris, it seems likely that he would have seen Roger Fry's ground-breaking exhibition, *Manet and the Post-Impressionists*, at the Grafton Galleries in London in 1910, in which the work of Gauguin, Van Gogh and Cézanne was well represented. He must have viewed Fry's *Second Post-Impressionist Exhibition* in 1912, which was dominated by the work of Picasso and Matisse. Hunter's initial exposure to the work of Gauguin, Van Gogh and Cézanne dates from the early years of the previous decade. Now Van Gogh's use of colour enthralled Hunter, his renewed interest in the painter perhaps prompted by the publication that year of 'Lettres de Van Gogh', which the Parisian art dealer, Ambroise Vollard, was selling.[50] Hunter strove to understand what made it so exciting. However the most lasting influence on him was Cézanne. Taylor told Honeyman:

... later [he] *turned up. The nose better & he was full of Cézanne – he had been where Cezanne had worked etc.* [almost certainly in the vicinity of Paris, rather than in Provence] *– & he ... showed me a number of chalk drawings in colour he had done, quite a departure from the things he had originally shown me.*[51]

Taylor does not elaborate on the meaning or extent of 'departure', but Hunter's understanding of Cézanne was focused on line, form and design. Peploe was in Paris at the time and Hunter told Taylor that he would like to meet him. However 'at the time Peploe was not awfully happy in his health & work – & was ... not anxious to meet Hunter – In fact it was not until Hunter had settled in Glasgow [i.e. after the war had ended] that he met Peploe.'[52]

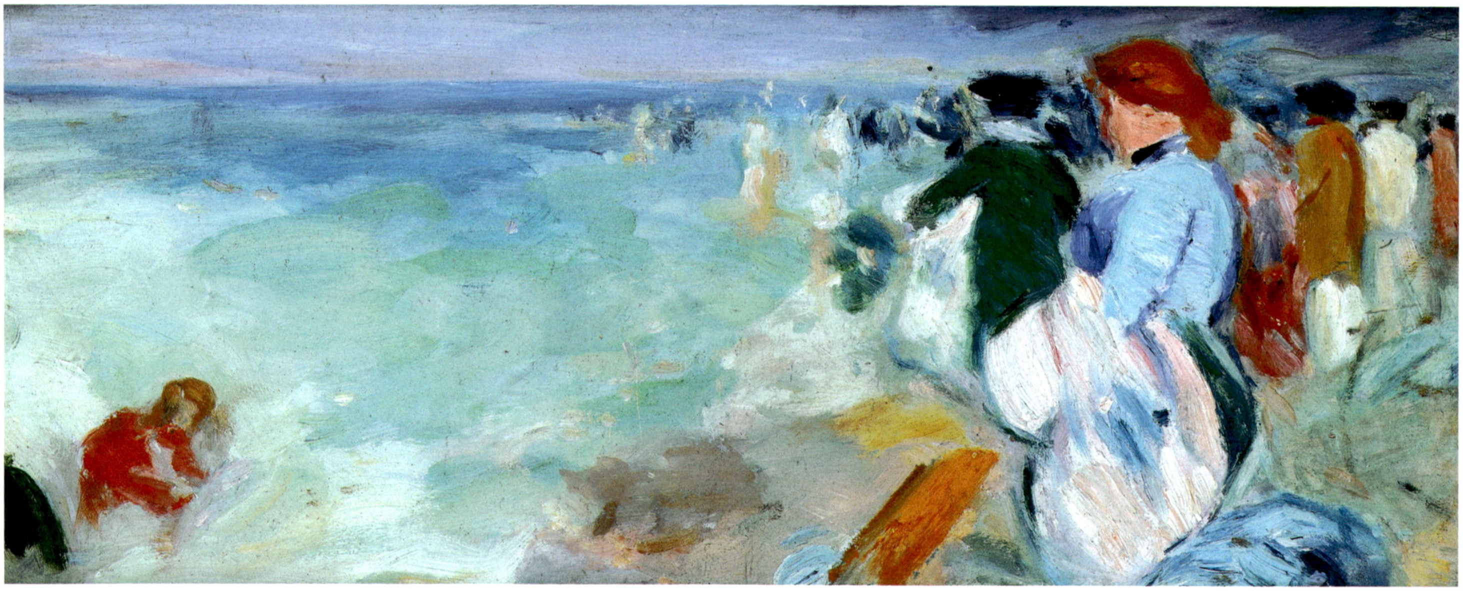

37 | On the Beach
Oil on panel, 1913
Private collection

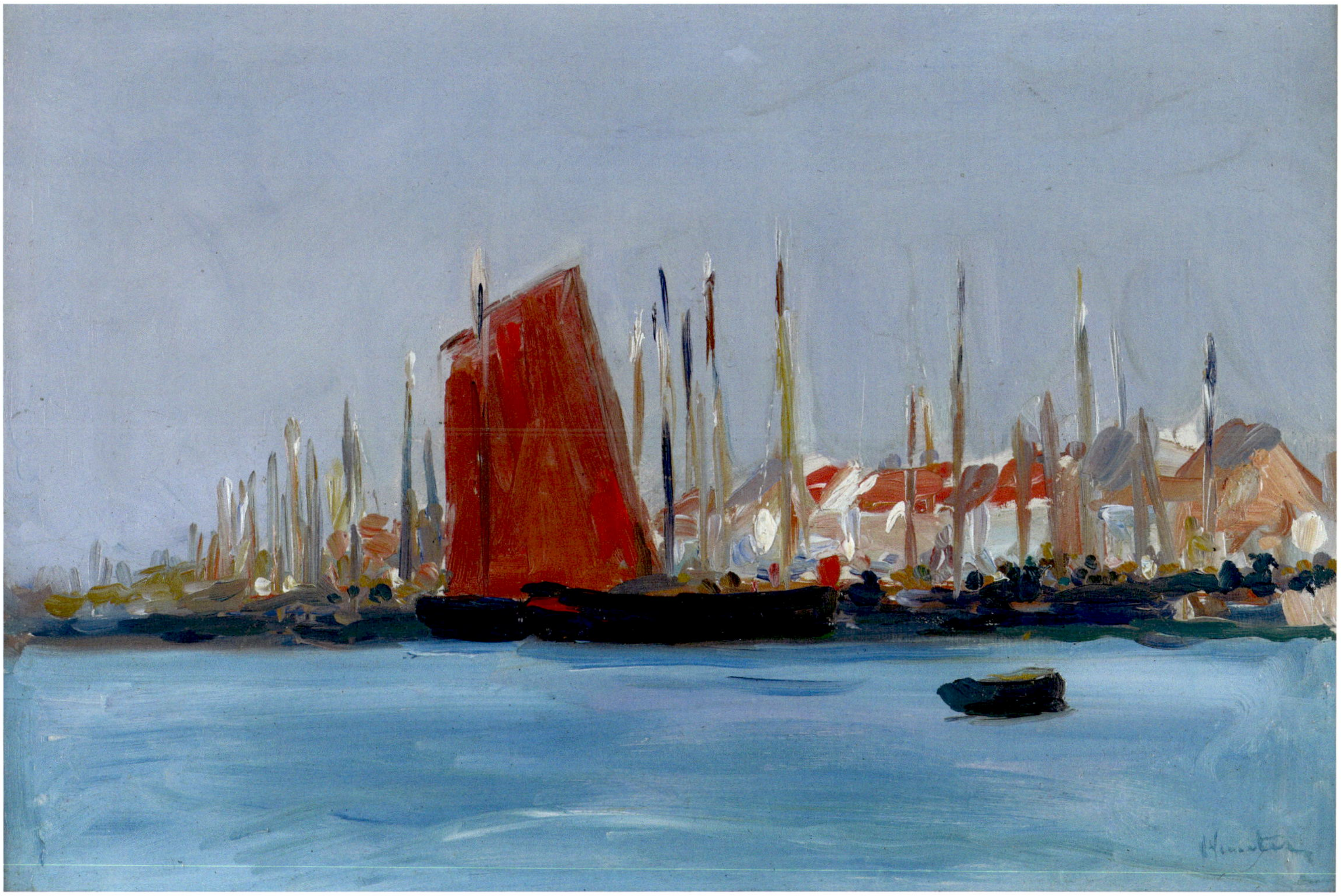

38 | Fishing Boats, Étaples
Oil on panel, 1913
Private collection

The work Hunter did manage to execute at Étaples on this occasion demonstrates a close study of Cézanne's paintings of the countryside near Paris. In its handling of paint, texture and feeling *Sunlit Avenue, Northern France* (pl.24) captures the same sense of animation that Cézanne displays in his views of the villages and the surrounding landscape executed around 1873. Hunter produced a series of beach and harbour scenes at Étaples that clearly shows a lightening of his palette and a concentrated attempt at working with a broader and more loaded brush. *On the Beach* (pl.37) captures the freshness of the sea breeze and, in a bare minimum of strong brushstrokes, brings the figures alive with a sense of bustling movement. The bold blocks of strong colour and flattened perspective are post-impressionist in conception, marking a fundamental shift in Hunter's treatment of nature. *The Beach Party* (pl.39) confirms Hunter's attempt to reduce form to a minimum by flattening perspective and employing basic blocks of colour. Despite the absence of detail, Hunter evokes well the pleasure and warmth of an intimate scene. *Fishing Boats, Étaples* (pl.38) has the same ingredients as *The Beach Party*, but Hunter's eye has responded with inspired sensitivity to the random decorative pattern effected by a group of boats floating listlessly, awakening the romantic notion of impending adventure beyond the safety of the harbour. These paintings herald Hunter's passion for nature and colour.

The Germans did not get near Paris during the First World War and Hunter stayed on in the capital for a short time. Soon after showing Taylor his new drawings, Hunter turned up

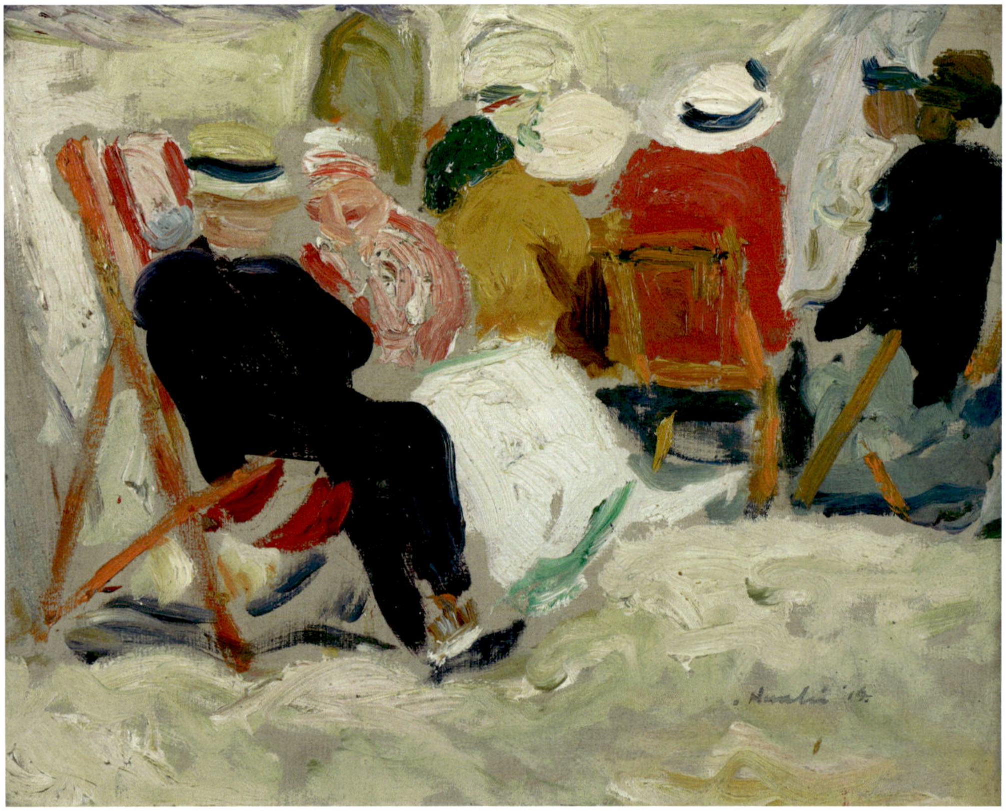

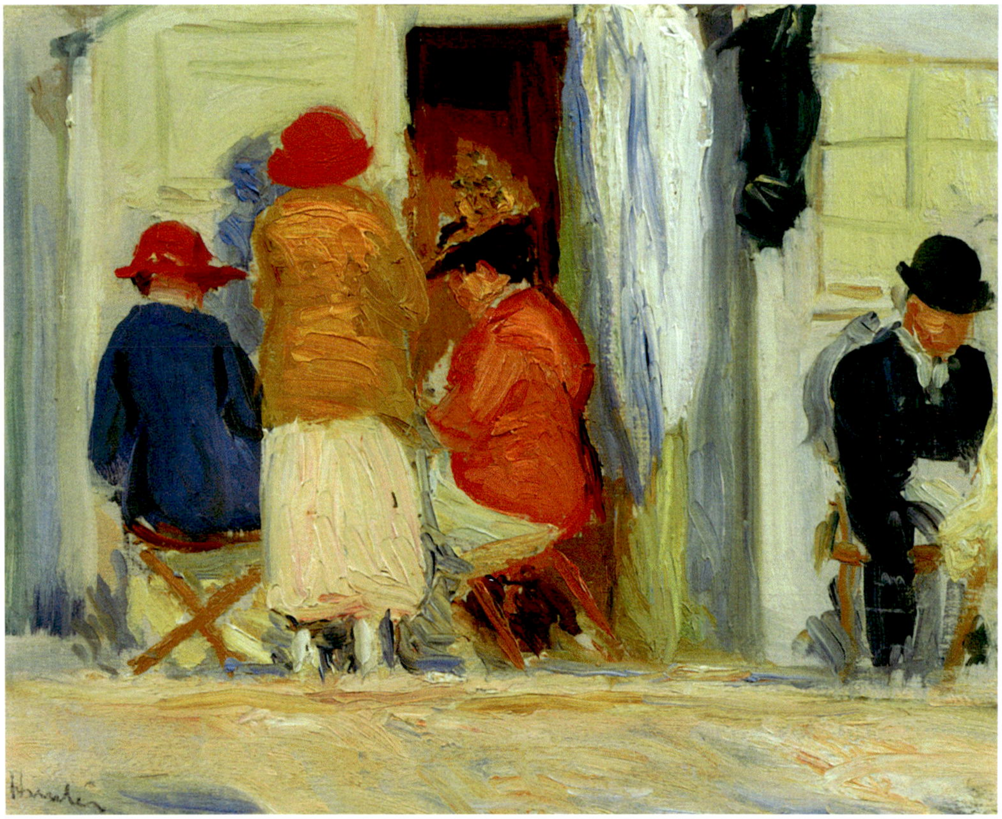

39 | The Beach Party, Étaples
Oil on panel, dated 1914
Private collection

40 | Après-midi, Beau Rivage, Étaples
Oil on board, 1914
Private collection

again at Taylor's flat accompanied by Tom Hunt, Hunter's artist friend from New York. Hunter had heard that the finest collection of Cézanne's work in France was in the home of the Swedish Consul in Paris, a Monsieur Pellerin. Eager to view the collection, Hunter persuaded Taylor and Hunt to accompany him to the Swedish Embassy, where they were told that to gain access to view the paintings foreign visitors required a card of introduction from their respective country's ambassador, which seemed to Taylor not unreasonable. The three of them set off for the British Embassy, where Taylor gave his details to an embassy official and then proceeded to introduce Tom Hunt as American and Hunter as Scottish. Reluctantly Hunter gave his particulars, but both Taylor and Hunt noticed that he was becoming increasingly agitated. All the details having been recorded, the official asked them to return in the evening when the papers necessary for admission to the collection would be ready. By then Hunter was visibly distressed and desperate to leave. To the amazement of Taylor and Hunt, just as they reached the foot of a long flight of stone stairs on their exit from the embassy, Hunter abruptly dashed off without a word of explanation. They searched for him in the street, but he was nowhere to be found. Neither Taylor nor Hunt was to see him again for several years. Taylor was shaken; he told Honeyman that he was 'expecting a visit from the police or something of the kind – but nothing in that way happened'.[53]

Throughout his life Hunter had a tendency to 'cut and run' if trouble threatened or he was unable to cope with a particular situation. He was not alone in this among his California friends and acquaintances, several of whom eventually committed suicide, including his good friend, Herman Scheffauer. The reason behind this particular incident is unexplained. It seems unlikely that it was connected with the war and that by giving his details he might be conscripted. It might have been an irrational fear regarding his dual nationality; he seemed unsure whether in fact he had American citizenship or not, though this was put beyond doubt in 1918 when he received conscription papers from the American authorities that had been sent to his last known address in San Francisco – 101 Montgomery Street – and he had to contact the US Vice Consul in Glasgow.[54] It is more likely, however, that he did not like giving his personal details to any public authority.

After his hurried exit from the embassy, Hunter left Paris immediately and returned to the family home in Glasgow and his sister, Jeanie. In March the following year (1915) Jeanie married James McFarlane and moved to his house at 147 Crow Road in Partick; Hunter and his niece, Irene, the fourteen-year old daughter of William Hunter, were the witnesses. To all intents and purposes Crow Road became Hunter's home base for the rest of his life.

That same year Hunter exhibited a still life at the Royal Scottish Academy in Edinburgh, the first of only twelve works to be shown at the academy over the sixteen years to Hunter's death in 1931. He exhibited *Fruit, Flower and Vase* at the Royal Glasgow Institute of the Fine Arts in 1916, the first of twenty-eight works. 1916 was also the first occasion that he exhibited at Glasgow Art Club. Proposed by George Henry and seconded by David Gauld, he was elected an artist-member of the club the following year.[55]

However the principal event for Hunter around this time was the opening of his second one-man show at Alexander Reid's gallery in Glasgow in 1916. It marked a watershed in his development as a painter, a fact acknowledged by the critic of *The Bailie*, a Glasgow weekly newssheet, who wrote:

Leslie Hunter's pictures in Reid's Gallery, West George Street, are great. Perhaps that is not the adjective the artist himself would like, but 'The Bailie' is quite an impressionable person, and when he finds a wallful of pictures that are arranged in such a way as these, he feels the influence at once of a man of courage, individuality, and ability. Pioneers are brave men who hew their way through the thickets and jungle of convention and conservatism. They let

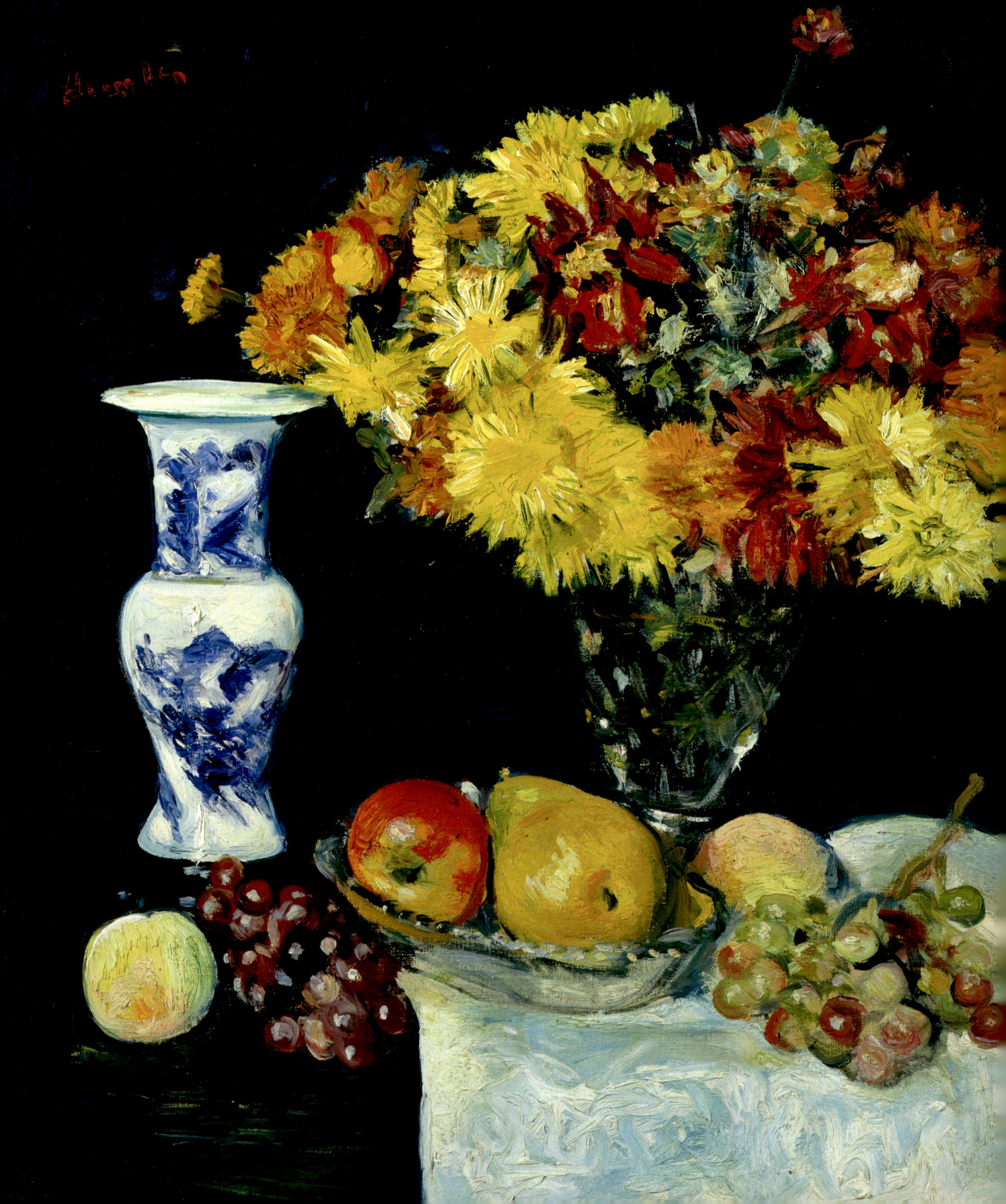

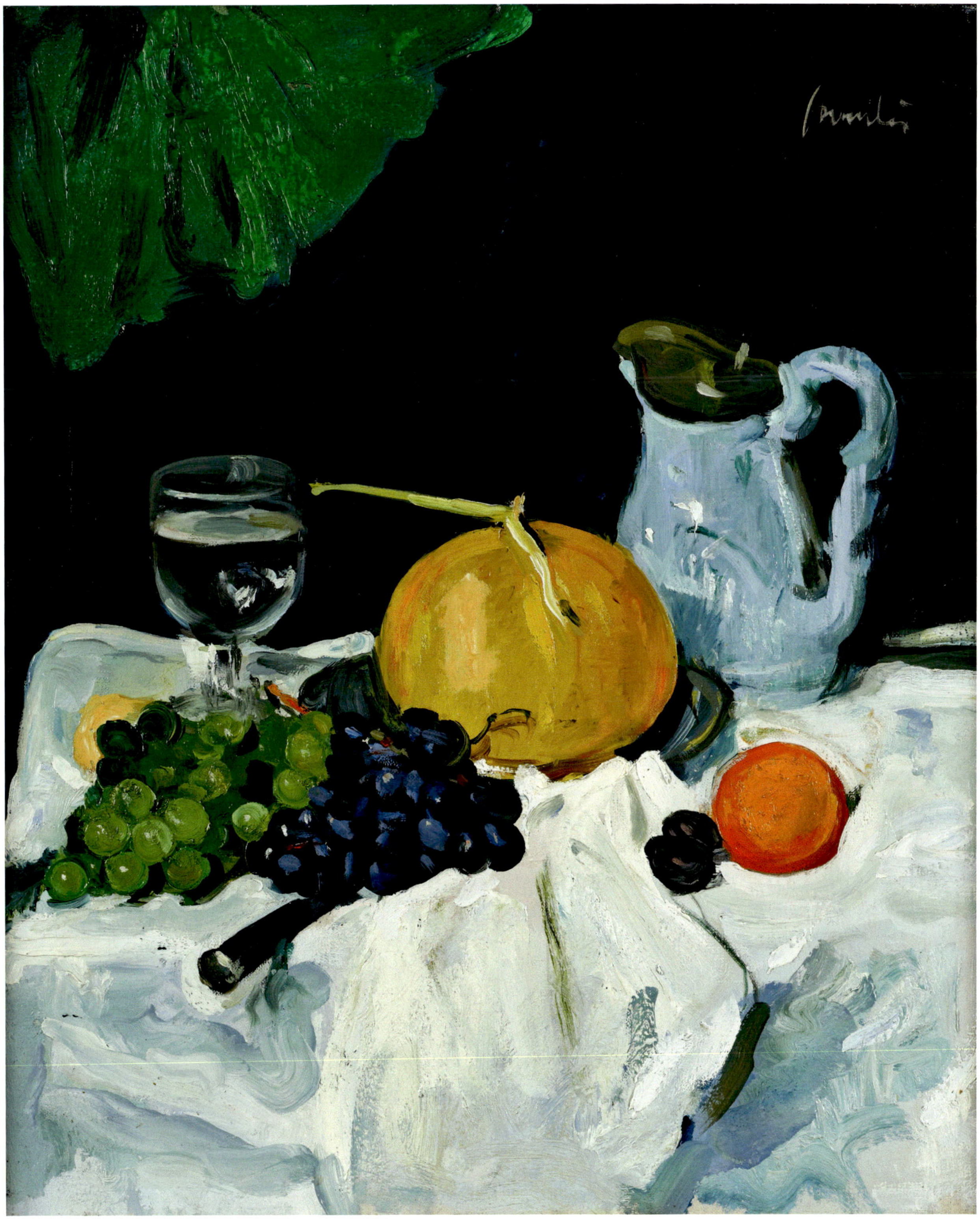

41 | Flowers in a Vase and Fruit
Oil on canvas, 1915
Glasgow Museums

42 | Still Life with Fruit, Wine Jug and Glass on a Table
Oil on canvas, 1916
Private collection

in the light. Sometimes it is so bright and dazzling that those who have fattened and dozed in the undergrowth are startled and blinded. Why should their easy-moving methods be disturbed? They resent the intrusion, and the pioneer is often made a martyr. But his soul goes marching along! Leslie Hunter is not likely to be a martyr in a town like Glasgow, which has been fond of breaking old conventions, but he has made certain affirmations in paint that will be disputed by those who do not get right into his atmosphere. He has three or four examples of still life that are superlatively strong. Such work is bound to live, for they show a mastery of form and colour that takes one back to the triumphs of the Dutchmen. It

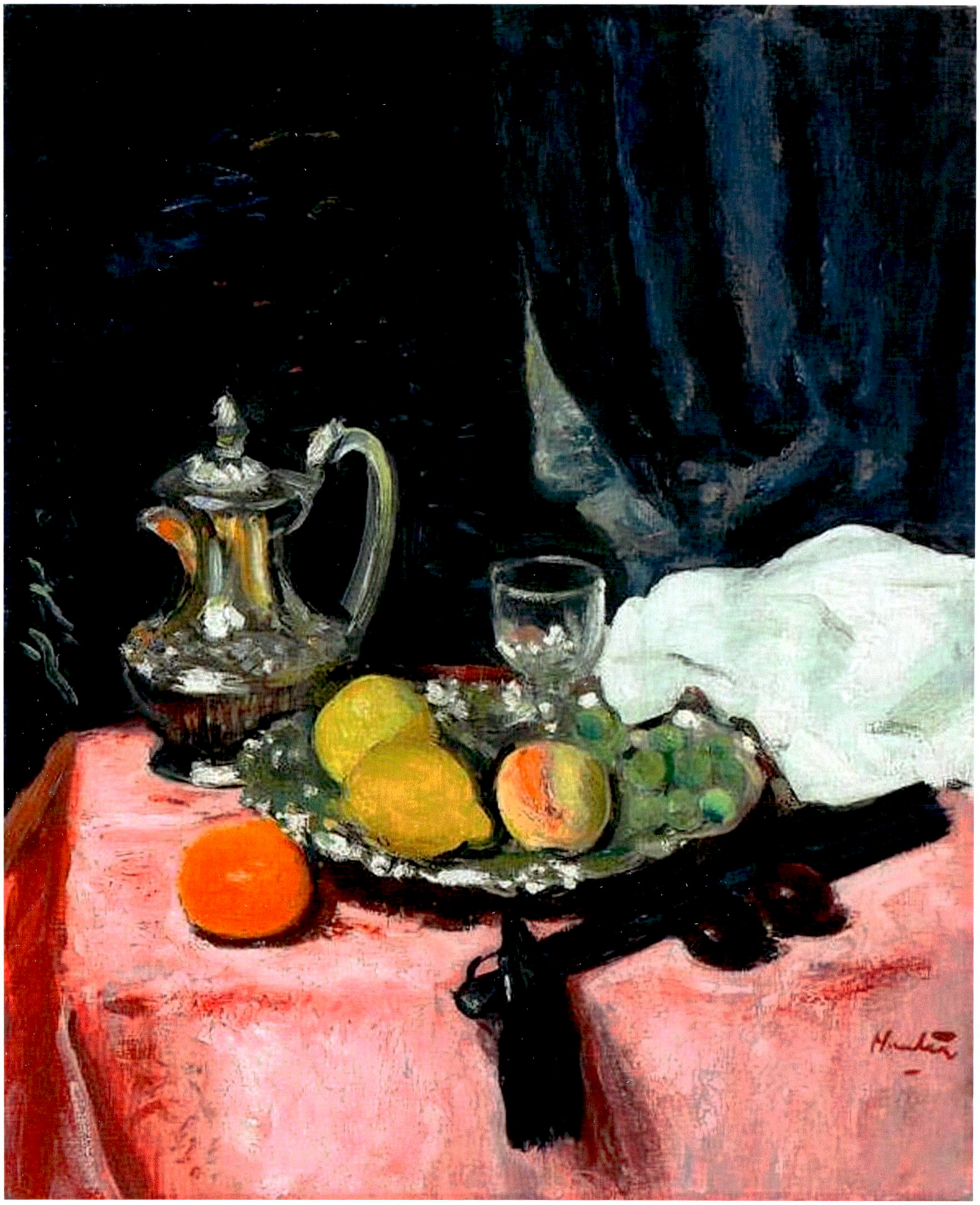

43 | The Pink Tablecloth
Oil on canvas, 1916
Private collection

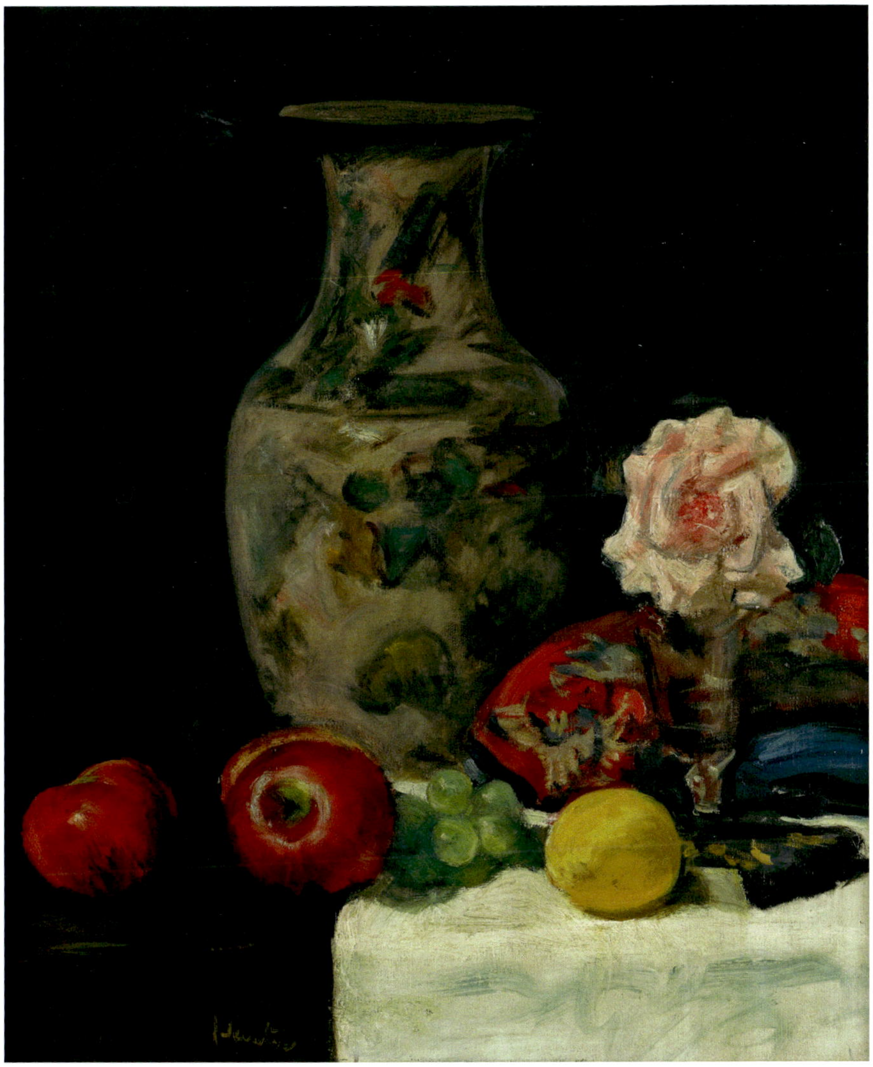

44 | Red Apples, Oriental Vase and Pink Roses in a Glass Vase
Oil on canvas, 1916
Private collection

is with his later works that he has taken his courage in both hands. He has pictures titled 'Sur la plage'. They are dabs of colour, one may say, but the artist knows what he is doing, and his arrangement is never at fault. He knows what to leave out, which is the true test. The man who tries to put in all he sees is up against the camera, and starts handicapped. We have to respect Leslie Hunter, as we respect the strong man who is cutting a path for us and leading us through the forest.

Mr Hunter has studied deep and travelled far. He knows California, and something of the colour of the orange grove is the persistent note in all his work. He knows and loves Paris, and he confesses to the influence on himself of some of the masters of impressionism. This influence is seen in some of the pictures now on view. It is to be hoped that Hunter will make his home permanently here.[56]

The exhibition included a number of still lifes with dark backgrounds, as well as the 'dabs of colour' executed at Étaples in 1914. According to Honeyman, Hunter and Reid had disagreed over the choice of frames. Apparently Reid preferred glossy black 'Dutch' frames for the still lifes and gilt 'Whistler' frames for everything else, whereas Hunter wanted a 'French' frame toned in harmony with the picture.[57] Reid got his way, as he usually did. The art dealer was very strong-minded, and regularly imposed his own will over that of an artist he was promoting.[58] Only ten sales are recorded in Reid's stockbook, which may reflect the psychology of wartime and the government's exhortation to help the war effort by saving money and investing in war bonds. Alexander Duncan, a Dundee boot manufacturer, bought four works from the exhibition, two still lifes and two landscapes costing a total of £50. A still life was acquired for £31 10s by Andrew Reid, an emerging collector and one of the sons of James Reid of Auchterarder, who was the head of Neilson, Reid & Co, the railway locomotive builders in Glasgow's Springburn, which later merged with two other companies to form the world-renowned North British Locomotive Company. Alexander Reid was to introduce Hunter's work to a growing number of art collectors, many of whom were to become staunch friends of Hunter. For example, in July 1917 William Burrell acquired his first Hunter from Reid – *Peaches*, a still life, for £10 10s – and several months later bought another still life for £38.[59]

The government also exhorted able-bodied men and women to do something to help the war effort, if they were not already doing so; conscription was not introduced until the beginning of 1916. It may be for that reason that Hunter decided to leave Glasgow about this time to go and stay with his cousin, Robert Hunter, and his wife, Mary, at Millburn Farm on the Dalserf Estate in Lanarkshire, about seventeen miles south-east of the city. He was to remain there for the rest of the war, though he made periodic visits to Glasgow by train from nearby Larkhall.

Millburn was a mixed farm of approximately 170 acres. Robert and his wife, who came from the neighbouring farm of Swinhill, had no children. Robert managed the farm and his elder bachelor brother, James, lived with them and worked on the farm.[60] Robert was noticeably better off than most of the farmers in the locality. He had one of the first cars in the district and his wife had 'fur coats and jewellery' and two live-in maids. The source of Robert's money was a mystery to the locals. He was fond of socialising, and organised dances and musical evenings in one of the barns on the farm. He had a collection of violins and played the double bass.[61]

Whether Hunter considered his move to a farm as a contribution to the war effort is unclear. Honeyman reports that Hunter 'did all that was required of him to the complete satisfaction of man and animals', which is probably true as far as it goes, but he did not 'do a full day's work on the farm' as Honeyman asserts.[62] Robert would have got the measure of his cousin soon after his arrival and concluded that he was not a natural farmhand! In reality Hunter did very little on the farm apart from helping with haymaking and the occasional skirmish with a dairy cow and a milk pail according to research carried out by Douglas Harrison in the early 1980s.[63] He spent his time much more fruitfully in sketching and painting, while being well looked after by his understanding cousin and his wife.

The war years afforded Hunter time and opportunity to experiment in his painting. At first he found it difficult to move away from the format of the Dutch still life, but in time he began to free himself from its constraints. He was acquiring a deeper understanding and appreciation of contemporary French painting. His pictures of Étaples are evidence of a lightening of his palette. He began to use bright colour in his still life. The contents

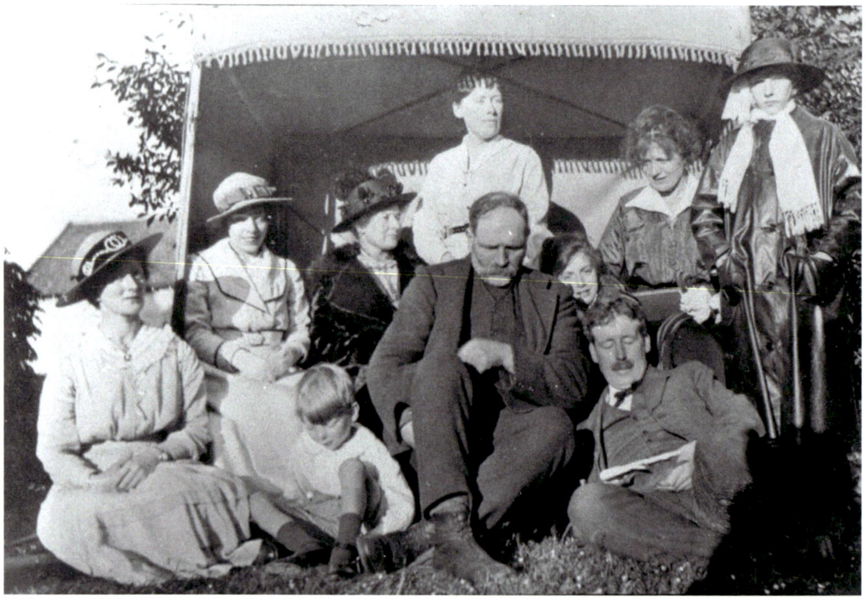

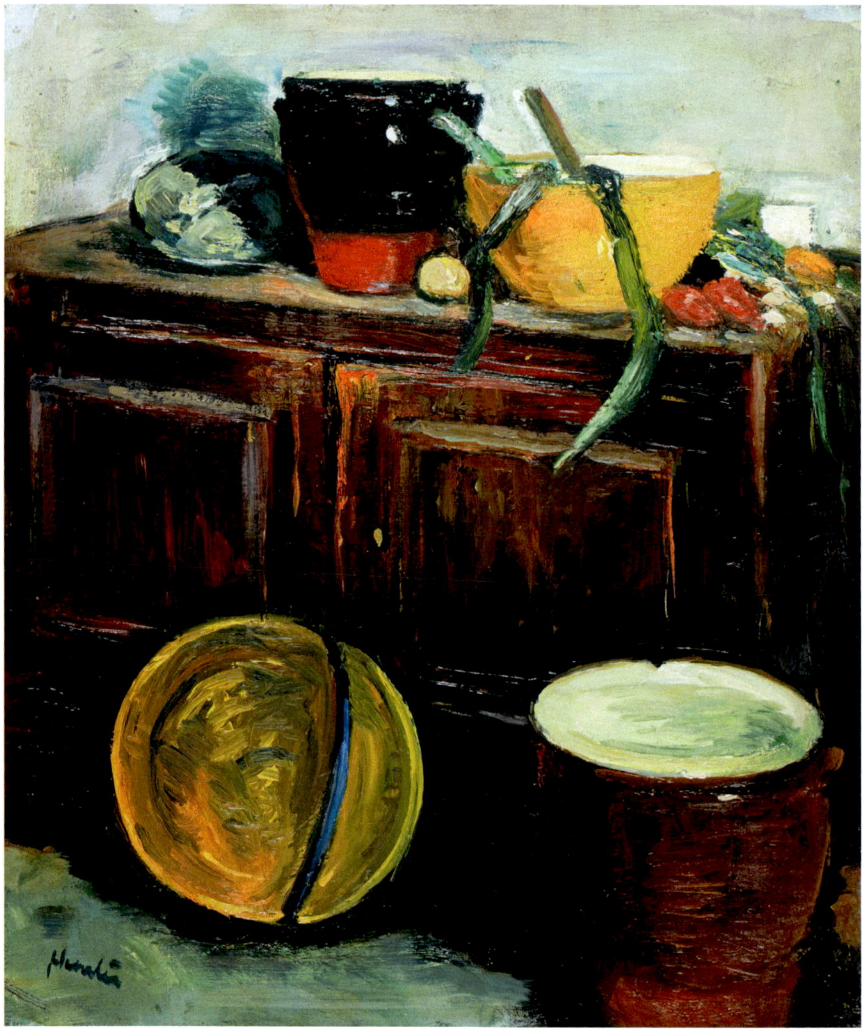

of a notebook dating from around the end of the decade clearly demonstrate that Hunter was striving to apply the fundamentals of post-impressionism. Following an initial two neat pages of current receipts and payments, the notebook descends into a rather haphazard mixture of sundry precepts and aphorisms, quotations from articles on art and artists and Hunter's own observations thereon. Commenting on Van Gogh, Hunter notes:

Everyone, he [Van Gogh] *says, must choose their own way and mine will be the way of colour. Colour, he writes, says something of itself, something over and above its other significance as the colour of some definite thing – one must not overlook that – one must use that.*[64]

For Hunter, colour was to become the central unifying element in his painting. In his notebook Hunter is stating his commitment to the modern use of colour, in other words the *sensation* of colour the eye perceives when looking at an object, rather than the prevailing Newtonian theory that colour is the object itself. It is a significant difference that has been missing in any appreciation of Hunter's art to date, and places him among the pioneers of modern art.

Hunter was fascinated by Van Gogh's ability to set primary colours uncompromisingly next to one another. He notes that in the later work:

... there commences an intensification of the colour scale ... I guess decorative principle is his main impulse. A principle which he did not bring from Holland but learned from his young French associates. His colour sense drove him to study the most intense decorative problems ... he sought a decorative style in which strong colour chords vibrate against each other ... his colour was bound in following his decorative idea to be heightened many degrees above reality.

Hunter concludes that for him Van Gogh's paintings 'miss, becoming too two-dimensional'. His notes on Gauguin are in the form of advice attributed to the master: 'Seek harmony not contrast. Go from light to dark not from dark to light. Your work is never light enough. The eye seeks refreshment in painting, give it joy not mourning.'[65]

However it is Cézanne's views on form and colour that engage Hunter most:

Forms are for their volumes. Form is not separated from colour. They condition one another. They are indissolubly united. All nature must be modelled after the sphere, the cone and the cylinder. As for colour, the more the colours harmonise, the more the design will take place itself. Painting is the registration of one's colour sensations. There is no such thing as line. No such thing as modelling. There are only contrasts. When colour attains its richness – form attains its plenitude.[66]

Hunter understood Cézanne's logic, but acknowledges that he is having difficulty putting it into practice, lamenting: ' It is because I cannot render my sensations at once! Hence I put on colour again. I put it on as best I can but when I begin I endeavour always to paint with a full impasto like Manet giving the form with the brush.'[67] Cézanne replaced light with colour (in its modern sense) and that approach is central to Hunter's subsequent development.

He also carefully records in his notebook the colours Van Gogh, Gauguin and Cézanne arranged on their respective palettes, as well as the outdoor and indoor palettes of William McTaggart and the palette of Whistler. Under his sketch of the latter's palette Hunter has written:

The palette from first to last should be orderly, measured, rational ... The palette is the instrument on which the painter plays his harmony. It must be beautiful always as the tenderly cared for violin of the great musician is kept in condition worthy of his music.[68]

Such counsel of perfection is unlikely to have been followed by Hunter, who was somewhat shambolic in his approach to most things! When his palette became heavy with the encrustation of dried paint, he reached for a new one. Honeyman considered that Hunter was 'quite incapable of carrying through any project on methodical lines. He would adhere to the main scheme of his plans, but his good intentions would dissolve in the flood of fresh ideas.'[69]

The extent to which Hunter was

45 | A picnic at Millburn Farm. The man seated in the centre is farmer Robert Hunter, Leslie Hunter's cousin, with Leslie lounging on the right
National Library of Scotland

46 | Cupboard and Kitchen Utensils
Oil on plywood, *c.*1917
Tate Britain

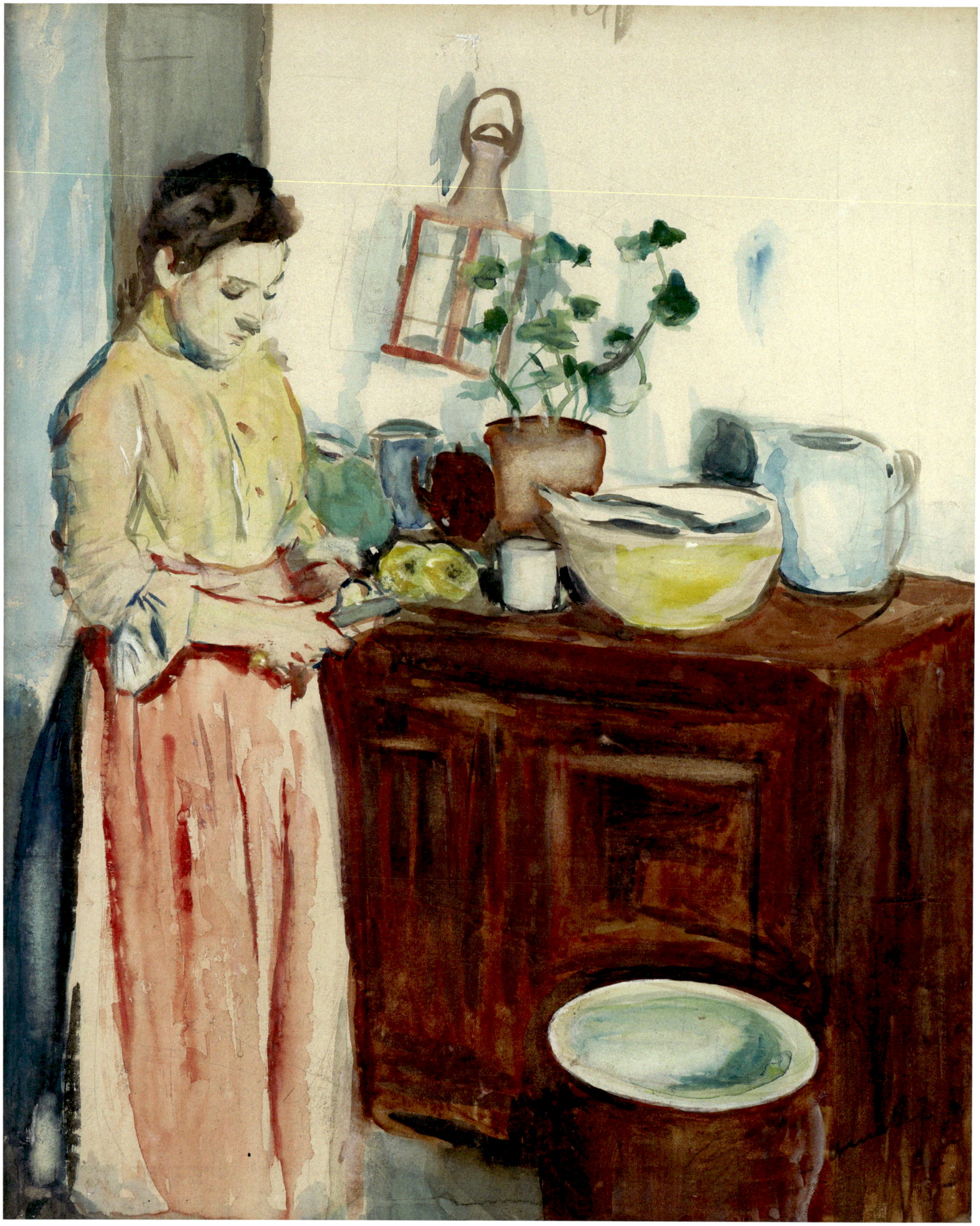

47 | Woman Peeling Potatoes
Pencil and watercolour, 1917
Private collection

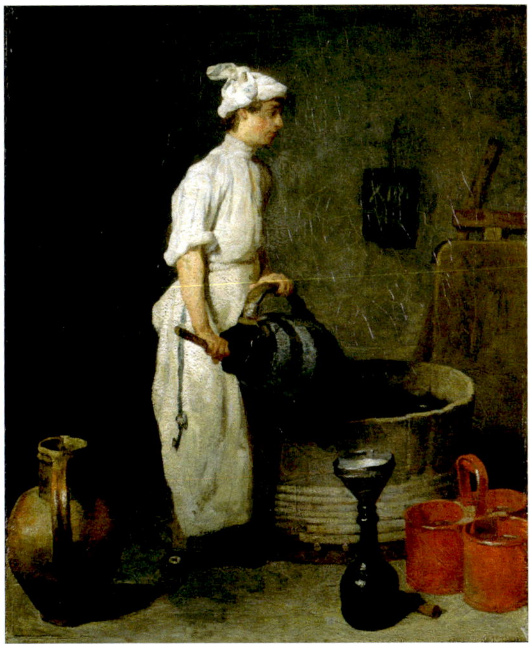

48 | Jean-Baptiste-Siméon Chardin, *The Cellar Boy*
Oil on canvas, 1738
University of Glasgow, Hunterian Art Gallery

experimenting with colour can be seen in a comparison of *Chrysanthemums in a Chinese Vase with Phoenix*, a superb example of his Manet phase of circa 1913, and work executed three or four years later. In *Flowers in a Vase and Fruit* (pl.41) he has retained the Dutch-inspired dark background and solid ledge, but uses the colour in the flowers and fruit, juxtaposed against the static blue and white of the oriental vase, to create a feeling of more tangible form and vitality. The use of blue and white oriental porcelain alongside areas of bright colour is a theme he develops well into the 1920s. In *Still Life with Fruit, Wine Jug and Glass on a Table* (pl.42) and *The Pink Tablecloth* (pl.43) the choice and arrangement of objects are derivative of Kalf, but Hunter uses blocks of bright colour instead of detail or light to striking effect,

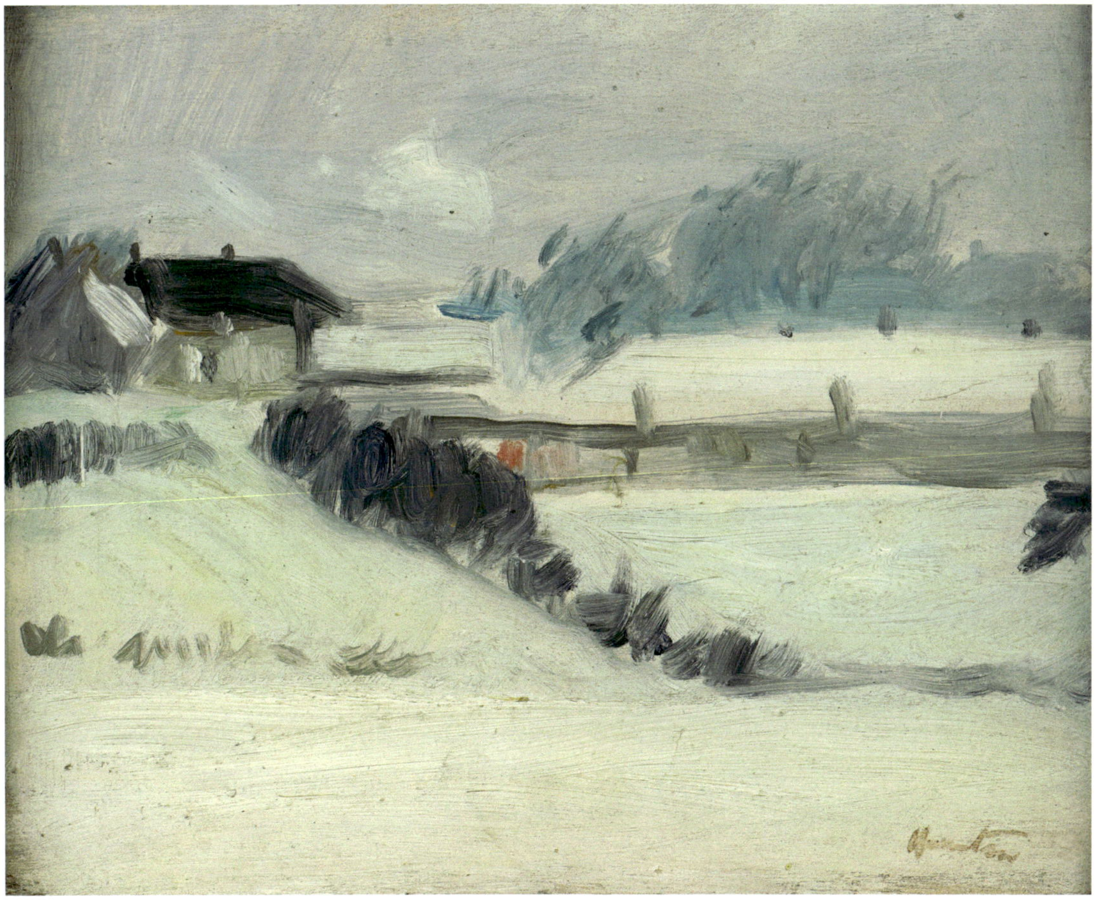

49 | Winter
Oil on board, 1917 · Private collection

which also serve to harmonise the structure of the composition.

Life at Millburn Farm must have been relatively pleasant for Hunter. He was treated as one of the family, and joined in many family activities, such as picnics and the regular – and rather lively – musical evenings and dances. For most of the time, however, he was left to get on with his painting. He had the use of a large room on the first floor of the farmhouse and a huge walk-in cupboard in which to store his easel, canvases, brushes and paints. He spent a lot of his time painting in the farm kitchen. It was a large, old-fashioned kitchen with a flag-stone floor, a window at each end, an old dresser in a corner and in the middle of the room a table complete with a tasselled velvet cover. In the boiler house there was a small cupboard used by Hunter to set up farm utensils and food for still life; the white-washed walls made everything appear more colourful.[70]

The wonderful *Cupboard and Kitchen Utensils* (pl.46) affirms Hunter's desire to place strong colours against each other without disrupting the overall harmony of a painting. The work has a strong affinity with W.Y.Macgregor's *The Vegetable Stall* (1883–84, National Galleries of Scotland), but it is doubtful whether Hunter ever saw that picture. Hunter's treatment of the shining jelly pan is akin to that in Chardin's *The Scullery Maid*, which he so admired. In Hunter's case the handle of the pan is picked out in strong blue in glorious contrast to the golden-yellow of the pan itself; he has used Van Gogh's blue and yellow opposing colours. *Woman Peeling Potatoes* (pl.47) is another good example in the series of paintings based on the cupboard in the boiler house, in which Hunter retains the composition, balance and quiet contemplation of Chardin's *The Cellar Boy* (pl.48), updating it to a modern setting without losing the essence of a timeless scene.

The farm itself presented an attractive aspect of gently-rolling fields and the occasional isolated farm building. In landscape Hunter retained the confidence of his work at Étaples, reducing form with lively, fluid brushwork and conveying the essence of the scene with a minimum of detail, as in *Winter* (pl.49). Equally he embraces Van Gogh's style of strong colour chords vibrating against each other, such as in his watercolour, *Lanarkshire Landscape* (pl.50). The latter demonstrates his keen eye for exploiting the natural pattern of a landscape. This would become a key feature in uniting colour, form and texture in his later landscapes.

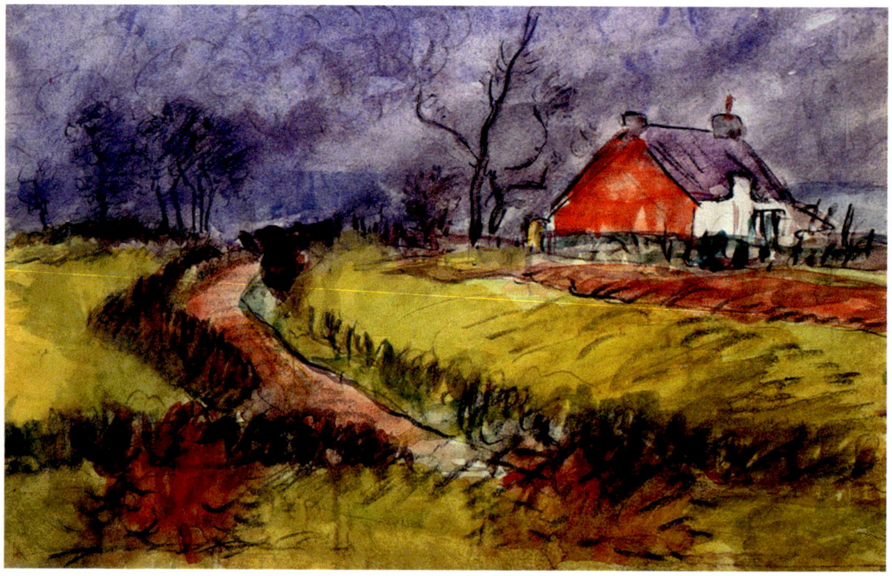

50 | Lanarkshire Landscape
Charcoal and watercolour, 1917
Private collection

It is a misconception that Hunter did not execute portraits (as opposed to sketches) until the last two years of his life. In fact he had painted portraits as early as 1907, and continued to do so throughout his career. The early examples are similar to his illustrative style, but by 1908 the portraits of his mother (pl.25) and of Mrs Meldrum (pl.26), a friend of his mother, display a painterly quality hitherto absent. Most of his sitters were family; these can be thematic as well as likenesses. He passed through a phase of historical themes, dressing a cousin, John Leyden, in a tunic and ruff and placing him against a light background, and portraying his niece, Hilda, then aged 16, in purple with a large black Regency-style hat with cascading feathers on her long Titian-coloured hair. Another cousin, Arthur Leyden, is painted almost monochromatically in his dinner suit with hat and gloves, resulting in the sitter's opinion that he had been made to look uncharacteristically melancholic. As has been mentioned earlier, Hunter had several romantic attachments (though he was always very uncommunicative on the subject) and on different occasions he left at least two ladies under the impression that they were engaged to him.[71] Around 1916 one of those ladies, Minnie Cowan, was the subject of a portrait. Often Hunter would ask a person on the farm to pose for him, as in *Boy Eating Apple: Jamie* (pl.51), in which Hunter reduces overall form to areas of colour, bringing the portrait to life with inspired, fluid brushstrokes.

It is unfortunate that little of Hunter's work from the period between 1906 and 1918 appears to have survived, apart, of course, from pictures sold to private collectors following Reid's exhibitions in 1913 and 1916. When Hunter moved to Millburn Farm, it seems likely that he took with him the majority of his sketchbooks and other work. However, when the war ended and he moved back to Glasgow, he left almost everything behind at the farm, including virtually all his work and painting materials. For reasons that remain a mystery, Hunter never returned to the farm. He never contacted his cousins again, which understandably left them very hurt in view of the kindness and consideration they had bestowed on him. His cousin, Robert Hunter, died in 1920 and the latter's elder brother, James, took over the running of the farm. There are conflicting reports of what happened to his work thereafter. It is said that in 1924, during an enforced period of quarantine following an outbreak of foot and mouth disease in the district and having heard nothing from Hunter in the interim, all his belongings and all his work, except a few of his paintings that James decided to keep, were burned on a bonfire at the farm.[72] On the other hand John McCrimmon, who knew Hunter when he was at Millburn Farm and was married to a niece of Mary Hunter, Robert Hunter's wife, told Honeyman in 1936 that 'we in this family circle had a great respect for the quiet and unassuming artist. We have a great amount of his pictures and black and white drawings [perhaps some of the original work for his magazine illustrations] which are greatly prized by the proud possessors.'[73]

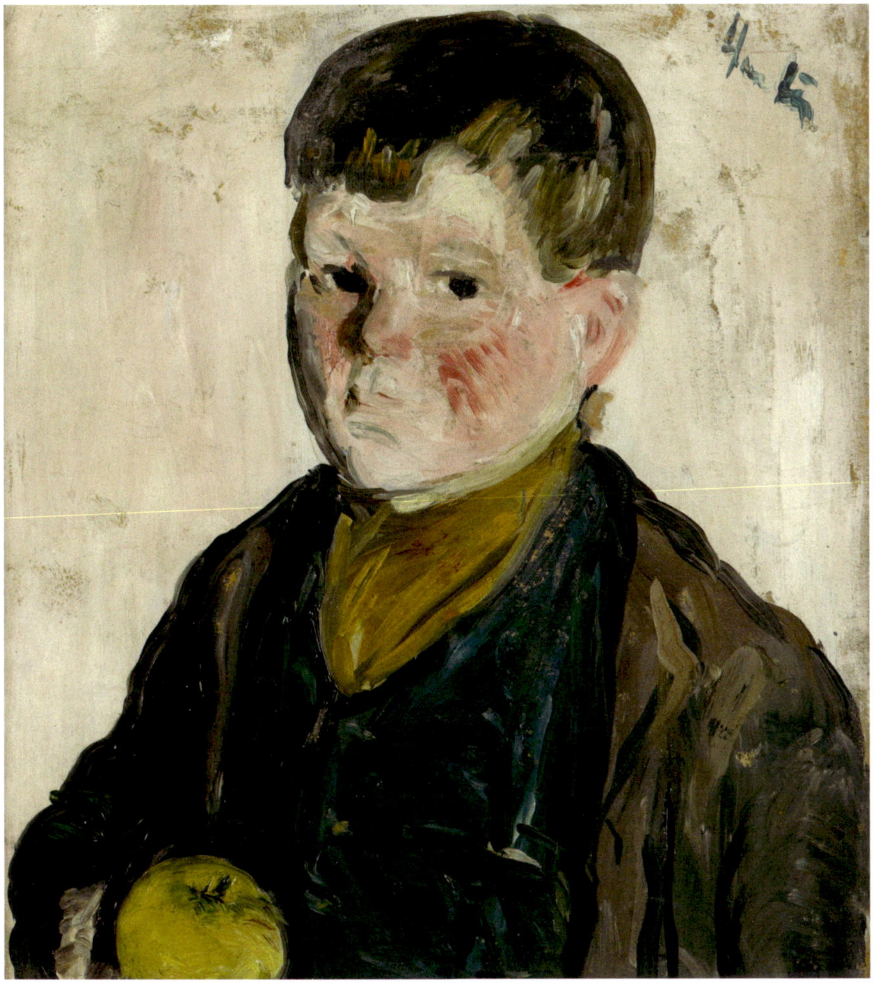

51 | Boy Eating Apple (Jamie)
Oil on board, *c.*1917
Private collection

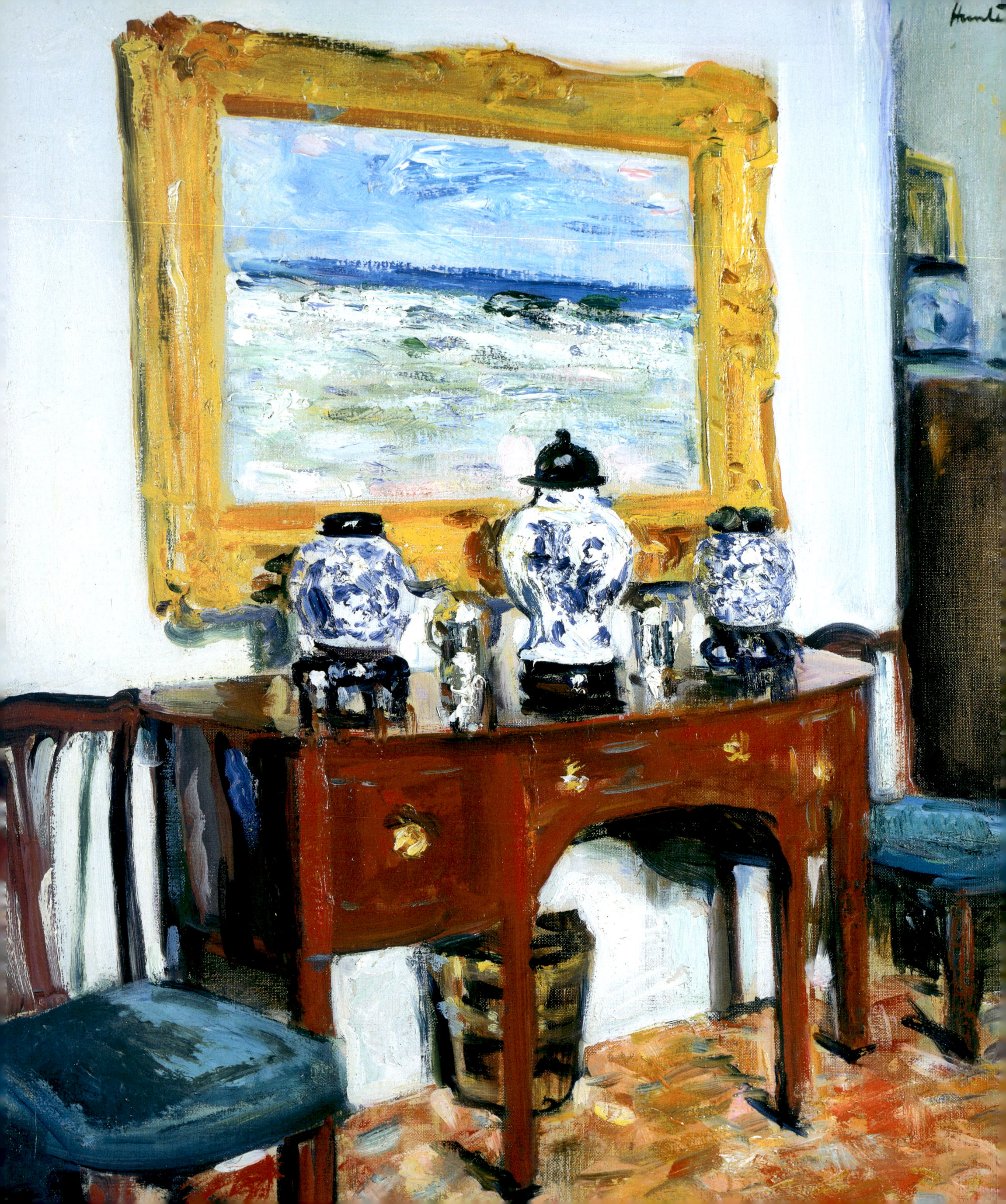

5 Seeking the Way Forward

THE END OF THE First World War in November 1918 and Hunter's return to Glasgow from Millburn Farm early the following year meant that once again he was free to devote himself solely to his art.[1] He had been looked after very well at the farm by his cousin and his wife – far better than if he had had to rely on his own resources – but he was eager to move on to new challenges. During the war he had been able to go the short distance to and from Glasgow, but there were various restrictions in force on journeys further afield, and travel to Paris was simply impossible. Now he felt that he had got back his freedom; he was optimistic about the future. He took encouragement from the impact that Peploe, Fergusson and Cadell were making on the Scottish art scene.

In his painting Hunter was moving steadily towards a deeper understanding of Cézanne's principles. He was finding expression through a distinctive application of colour and a more thoughtful creation of form. Over the next few years his active and enquiring mind would respond to a wealth of stimuli. His art would develop through new-found sources of inspiration, in particular the landscape of Fife. There would be trips to London, Paris, Florence and Venice. There would be opportunities for regular study of post-impressionist work by Cézanne, Van Gogh, Édouard Vuillard, Othon Friesz and Jean Marchand. This interaction of stimulation and inspiration would result in a period rich in vibrant, strongly-coloured still lifes and landscapes.

From now on Hunter's most significant source of stimulation – and support – would be a small band of friends and acquaintances with a common interest deeply rooted in the visual arts, some of whom Hunter had met before the war through Alexander Reid. This was one aspect of Hunter's life that remained constant till the end. One group of friends lived on the east coast of Scotland, comprising Matthew Justice, John Tattersall, William Boyd and Alexander Duncan. Another extraordinary group was based in Glasgow; William Mclnnes, William McNair and Major Ion Harrison were all partners in the Glasgow shipping company of Gow, Harrison & Co. Through these men, whose common link was the art dealer, Alexander Reid, others such as Percy Moore Turner, Archibald Hyslop, T.J. Honeyman, John Ressich, R.C. Roy and D.W.T. Cargill were brought into Hunter's immediate circle of followers. Together these men exerted a crucial influence on contemporary Scottish art. Not only did they admire and buy modern French art, but they also believed in and actively encouraged Scottish artists. It is no exaggeration to state that without their foresight a whole generation of Scottish painters would have been seriously disadvantaged. Most importantly for Hunter, they understood his art and appreciated what he was striving to achieve.

Based in Dundee, Matthew Justice was probably the most influential figure. Hunter is likely to have met Justice through Reid in 1913. The two men must have become friends almost immediately, because shortly afterwards they were in Paris together, where they came across

52 | Dining Room Interior
Oil on canvas, 1919
Private collection

E.A.Taylor. Two years older than Hunter, Justice was a fascinating man. A skilled and practising cabinetmaker, he managed the family business, the renowned Dundee furniture company of Thomas Justice & Sons, originally founded by his father. His passion for modern paintings was a recreational activity. Business trips to Europe, primarily to purchase raw materials such as marble from Italy, provided Justice with regular access to all that was happening in contemporary European art. It was on one of his visits to the gallery of a Parisian art dealer that Justice met the dealer and connoisseur, Percy Moore Turner; they became firm friends. Turner frequently recounted his good fortune in finding a man of Justice's advanced taste and enthusiasm. Justice's affection for France was apparent not only in his painting collection, but also in his family life, employing a French governess for his two sons. Characteristic modesty, and the fact that Justice spent the last six years of his life in ill health isolated in Switzerland, has resulted in his important contribution to Scottish art in the 1920s being overlooked. The years of friendship he shared with Hunter were lively and challenging. Hunter relied greatly on Justice's constructive criticism, relishing the resultant debate in the knowledge that his friend's advice was sincere, fair and based on a wealth of experience. Hunter wrote numerous letters to Justice, many of which are still in the possession of the Justice family.[2] These letters are an invaluable source of information, not only about Hunter the artist, but also about Hunter the man. Where appropriate, Hunter's own words and thoughts, as revealed in his letters to friends such as Justice, are used throughout this biography to illustrate aspects of his personality, attitudes, objectives and artistic methods.

Justice shared his passion for modern art with friends such as John Tattersall, William Boyd of Broughty Ferry and Alexander Duncan of Carnoustie. Little is known about Tattersall other than that he was a Dundee dentist and art collector. For a brief spell in 1916 he was a silent partner in Alexander Reid's Glasgow gallery, and for a time a director of Thomas Justice & Sons.[3] Less still is known about Duncan except that he had a boot factory in Dundee. It is evident from Hunter's letters to Justice that Tattersall was a close friend of both Justice and Hunter. There were occasions when Tattersall generously offered refuge to Hunter during the bouts of overwork and depression from which he began to suffer. Hunter highly valued Tattersall's opinion and advice on his work.

It was through Justice that William Boyd of Broughty Ferry was brought into the Dundee circle. His patronage and hospitality, as well as his art collection, was invaluable to Hunter during this period. Boyd was managing director of Keiller & Son, the renowned Dundee marmalade and jam manufacturers. Justice frequently acted as adviser to Boyd on purchasing paintings, eventually becoming a dealer in his own right and taking a number of clients from Reid.[4] At least twenty of Boyd's finest French paintings came directly from Justice.[5] A regular visitor to Boyd's home, Hunter's appreciation of his support prompted him on one occasion to say 'I'm sorry Boyd did not get the other picture he desired as appreciation counts more than doubloons'.[6]

In this group of people centred on Matthew Justice, Percy Moore Turner was in some respects the outsider. In common with his Scottish friends, his considerable contribution to the arts in Britain has never been fully recognised. The prevailing attitude at the time was one of art appreciation being confined to the 'privileged few', who perpetuated the belief that true art could spring only from the traditions of the Italian Renaissance. An enlightened, generous man, Turner held the opposing view that art should be made more accessible to the public, and spent his life trying to realise that aim. A Yorkshireman by birth and the same age as Hunter, Turner was brought up in Norfolk. He had a long, active association with the Castle Museum in Norwich. His exceptional services to art were recognised – typically not by Britain, but by France – when in 1927 the rank of Officier de la Legion d'Honneur was conferred on him. True to his principle, Turner left his collection of paintings to the nation, notably enriching the collections of the National Gallery, the Tate, the Ashmolean at Oxford and the Fitzwilliam at Cambridge.[7]

Turner's passion for French art dates from before the First World War, when he was in partnership with 'a well-known art dealer in Paris [as yet unidentified] and became closely associated with famous artists of the modern French art movement.'[8] It was shortly after the war that Turner and Justice met in Paris. Discovering a mutual desire to share their appreciation and passion for modern art more widely, they became friends immediately. In common with Hunter, they were horrified by the narrow-minded, stubborn perpetuation of past tradition as practised by the art establishment, be it academy, art school or museum trustees. The highly-motivated Turner owned and ran the Independent Gallery in London's Grafton Street, noted for its high standards and ambitious exhibitions of French Impressionist, Post-Impressionist and Modern painting and its unerring commitment to supporting progressive British art. In 1920 *The Burlington Magazine* described the gallery as '... a breath of fresh air in the stiff, unadventurous, staid London art market'.[9]

In Glasgow, Hunter's circle of friends centred on William McInnes and his two business colleagues, William McNair and Ion Harrison. McInnes was a modest man, who spent what little money he had to spare on building up a collection of French and Scottish modern art for his own enjoyment. Hunter played an important part in advising and encouraging McInnes on his purchases, particularly in relation to *The Pink Tablecloth* by Matisse (pl.139). Through the direct influence of T.J.Honeyman, then Director of Glasgow Art Gallery, McInnes's collection was gifted upon his death in 1944 to the City of Glasgow. Included in the gift of over seventy paintings were works by Monet, Degas, Renoir, Van Gogh, Cézanne, Picasso and Matisse, as well as a number by Hunter.

William McNair was a quiet man of whom little is known except that he was a solicitor and lived in Troon in Ayrshire. He shared with his colleagues a passion for art. Ion Harrison, then the most recent partner in Gow, Harrison & Co., was younger than McInnes and McNair, but no less enthusiastic about art. He also was particularly friendly with artists James McBey and F.C.B.Cadell. To find three business partners so ready to spend their leisure-time enjoying the same pursuit is rare indeed. Often Hunter would arrive at the company's offices, bringing with him sketch books and all manner of other things to show to and discuss with his friends. On other occasions he would join them for morning coffee and conversation in nearby Craig's in Gordon Street.

Surrounded by such stimulating and altruistic individuals, Hunter genuinely felt part of a forward-looking, innovative movement in Scottish art. Thus encouraged, he was able to push forward in his art and, to a greater or lesser extent, ignore the pressures and criticisms of the Scottish art world regarding his use of strong colour and perceived 'eccentric' views.

The main thrust of Hunter's development post-war was a fuller understanding of Cézanne's principles and an exploration of their application to his own painting. By the beginning of the twentieth century Cézanne was the acknowledged pioneer in what is today referred to as 'Modern Art', which represented a radical departure from the prevailing view that in general a painting should be a close likeness of the subject. The invention of the camera had changed that and at the same time signalled the slow death of illustrative art in newspapers and magazines. Cézanne posed the question: how does one paint the 'weight' in an object? Grasping that concept, the pictorial representation of weight led a number of painters to approach art from a totally new angle. One of those approaches was the sensation of colour on the eye, opening up a different and joyous interpretation of Nature, which was what engaged Hunter.

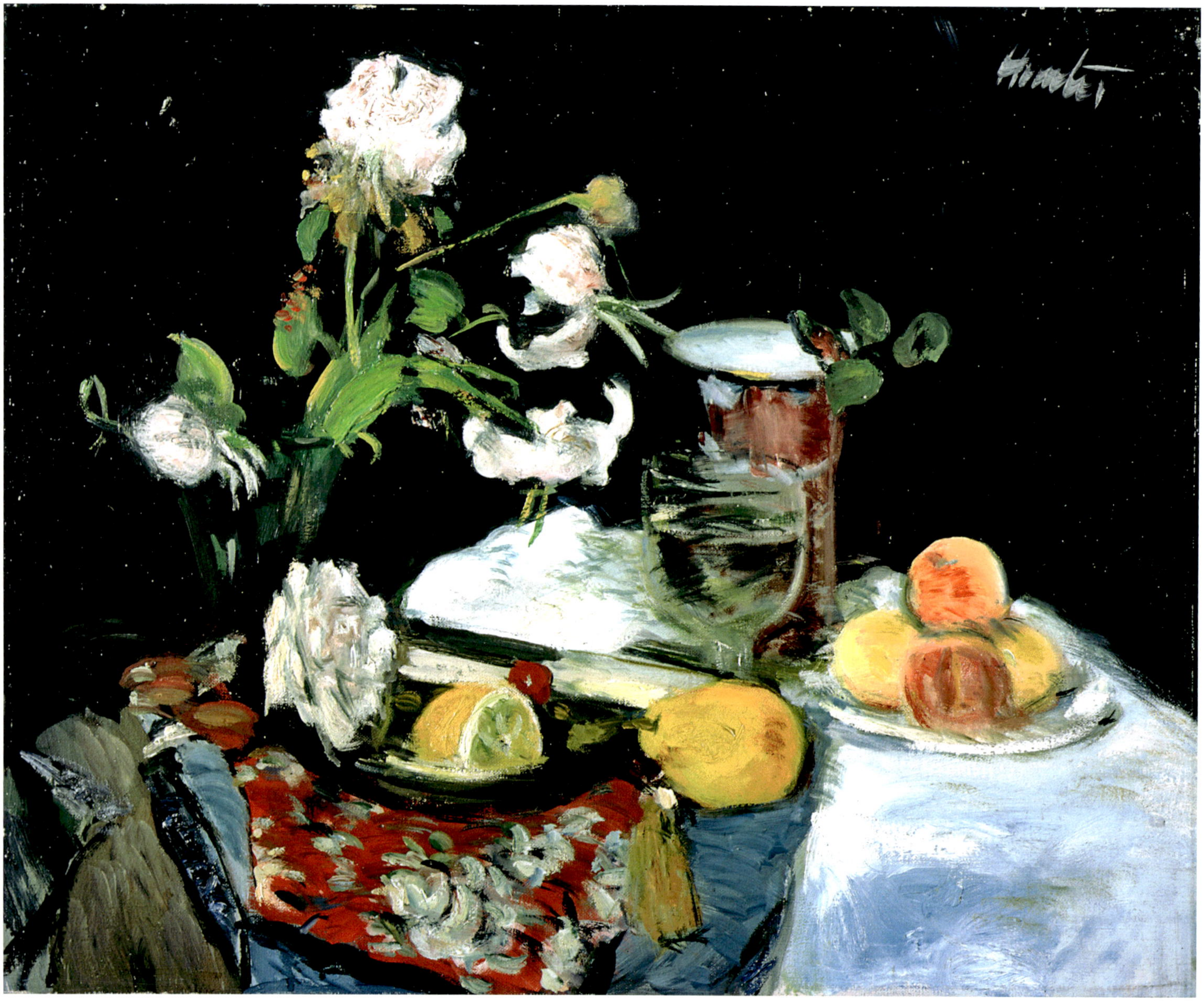

53 | Still Life
Oil on canvas, *c.*1919
Dundee Art Galleries and Museum (Dundee City Council)

Interestingly it is Cézanne's earlier rather than later work to which Hunter reacted in the first instance. Cézanne's unerring eye for the basic underlying structure in a subject is married to his superb feeling for colour as a means of registering the sensations evoked in him by the motif. Skilful use of colour binds a painting together to create harmony. Colour itself absorbs line, tone and light. Thus 'when colour is at its richest, form is in its plenitude', as Hunter jotted down in his notebook.[10] Hunter had played with these ideas. His first skirmishes are evident in his still lifes of around 1916, such as *Flowers in a Vase and Fruit* and *The Pink Tablecloth*. To an extent that is also what he was attempting in the beach scenes at Étaples in 1914. Taylor states that about this time Hunter was *'full of Cezanne'* after visiting where the painter had worked.[11]

At the beginning of 1919 Hunter's eagerness to pursue new challenges led him to experiment with still life first, which he always regarded as his forte. The paintings he had executed at Millburn Farm, *Cupboard and Kitchen Utensils* being the most obvious example, show how he was grappling with juxtaposing the simplicity of underlying structure with areas of bright colour. At the same time Hunter was unable to move away from the delight he felt in evoking Kalf or Chardin-like highlights. This same contradiction in painting style is still evident in 1919. There is also a lingering unwillingness to leave the safe haven of his Dutch-style still lifes, which proved so successful for Reid. In *Still Life* (pl.53) he experiments with blocks of colour in both the foreground and the still life itself, but seems unable to abandon the dark background and the jewel-like gleam in the cherry. Nevertheless this composition glows with vitality and colour without ever losing its overall reality.

In *The Blue Plate* (pl.55), while controlling tone more strictly, Hunter is able through the use of strong, loaded brushwork to bring alive the whole composition by stressing the sophisticated interplay of form and texture, glowing not only from specific objects such as the orange and grapes but also from areas of the blue plate and tablecloth. He has kept to his style of contrasting blocks of colour, but, with the exception of the rose, which is still Manet-esque in handling, form is created through the strong build-up of colour. Above all his experiment achieves a great harmony throughout the picture.

54 | Still Life with Apple, Fan and Roses
Oil on canvas, *c.*1919
Private collection

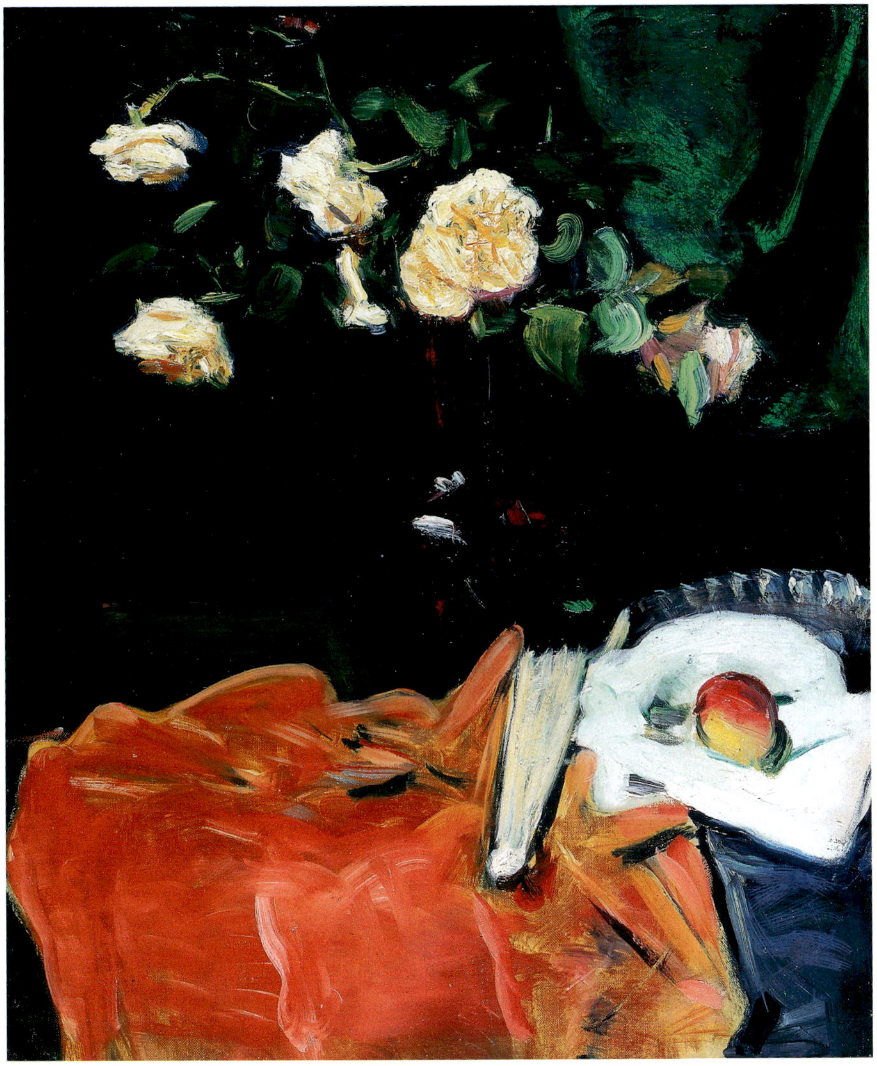

Hunter's attempts to lighten his palette and deal with colours in more sophisticated terms were beginning to be more successful too. Now he is treating areas of the canvas in a more complex and painterly manner than in his pictures of around 1916 with their straightforward blocks of colour. Furthermore there is a freshness and exuberance that have been missing hitherto. The joy in what he paints and in the quality of the paint itself is evident.

His admiration for Kalf reached its peak in 1919, when he painted a beautiful still life, *The Half-Peeled Lemon* (pl.57), based on two still lifes by Kalf in Glasgow Art Gallery.[12] From Kalf (pl.56) he borrowed the tilted blue plate, the silver platter, the unobtrusive goblet subtly glowing in the background and, of course, the peeled lemon, but it is what he has done with them that is so important. Hunter's version exhibits all the hallmarks of a deeper understanding of modern art. Note the absence of a source of light; instead Hunter uses form and colour. He takes the essence of the Kalf still lifes and transposes them into a modern idiom with over-simplification of form through bold brushstrokes and colour stripped down to bare essentials. The overall tones of blue and grey are enlivened by flashes of orange, red and yellow in the fruit, while the coiled lemon peel appears to be taut as if on a spring. Kalf offsets areas of strong colour through the introduction of brilliant, often jewel-like highlights radiating from the still life itself. Hunter adapts this technique by using crude areas of white as an alternative

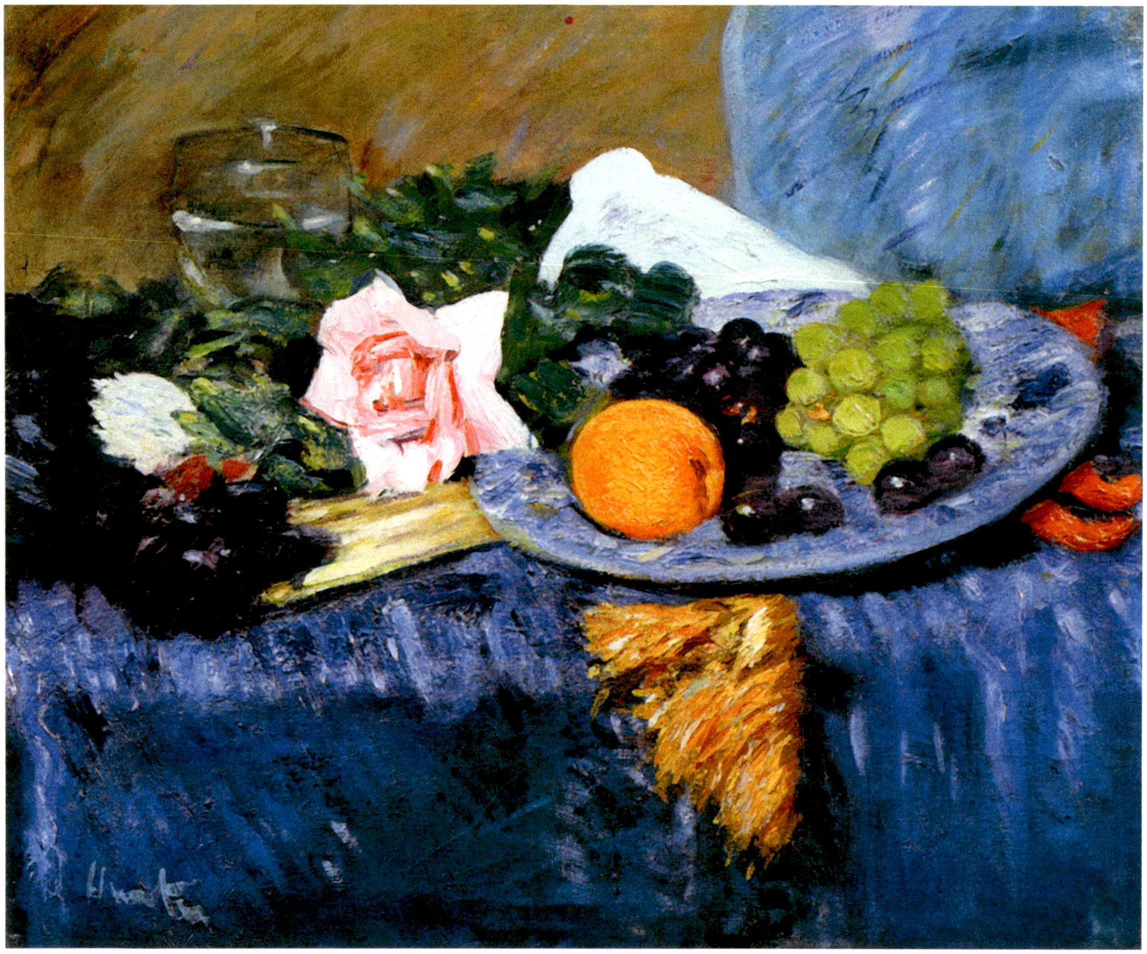

55 | The Blue Plate
Oil on board, *c.*1919
Private collection

to Kalf's jewel-like highlights, thus enlivening the composition with a distinctive vitality. Hunter's new technique of employing strong colour accents also serves to control the overall harmony of the painting.

Hunter's obvious pleasure in Kalf's work continued until 1922. After a visit to Glasgow Art Gallery, he commented to Justice: *'there are two rich and glowing still lifes by Kalf in the gallery here in the same room. The Maris, Blommers etc look executed in skim* [sic] *milk by comparison.'*[13] Those nineteenth-century Hague School artists had influenced an entire generation of Glasgow School painters, but not Hunter after his return to Scotland. His passion for vibrant colour is in total contrast to Whistler's tonal harmonies and the realism of the Barbizon painters.

In the same way that Hunter's early still life, *Chrysanthemums* is an untypical example of his

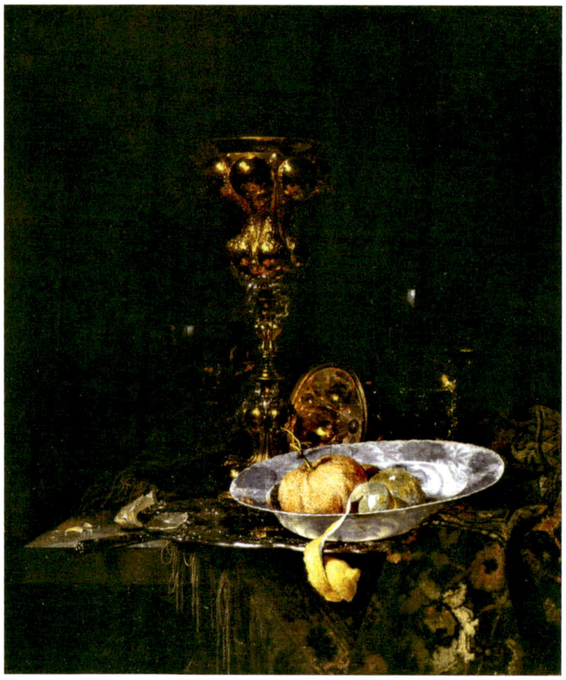

56 | Willem Kalf, *Still Life*
Oil on canvas
Glasgow Museums

57 | The Half-Peeled Lemon
Oil on canvas, dated 1919
University of Glasgow, Hunterian Art Gallery

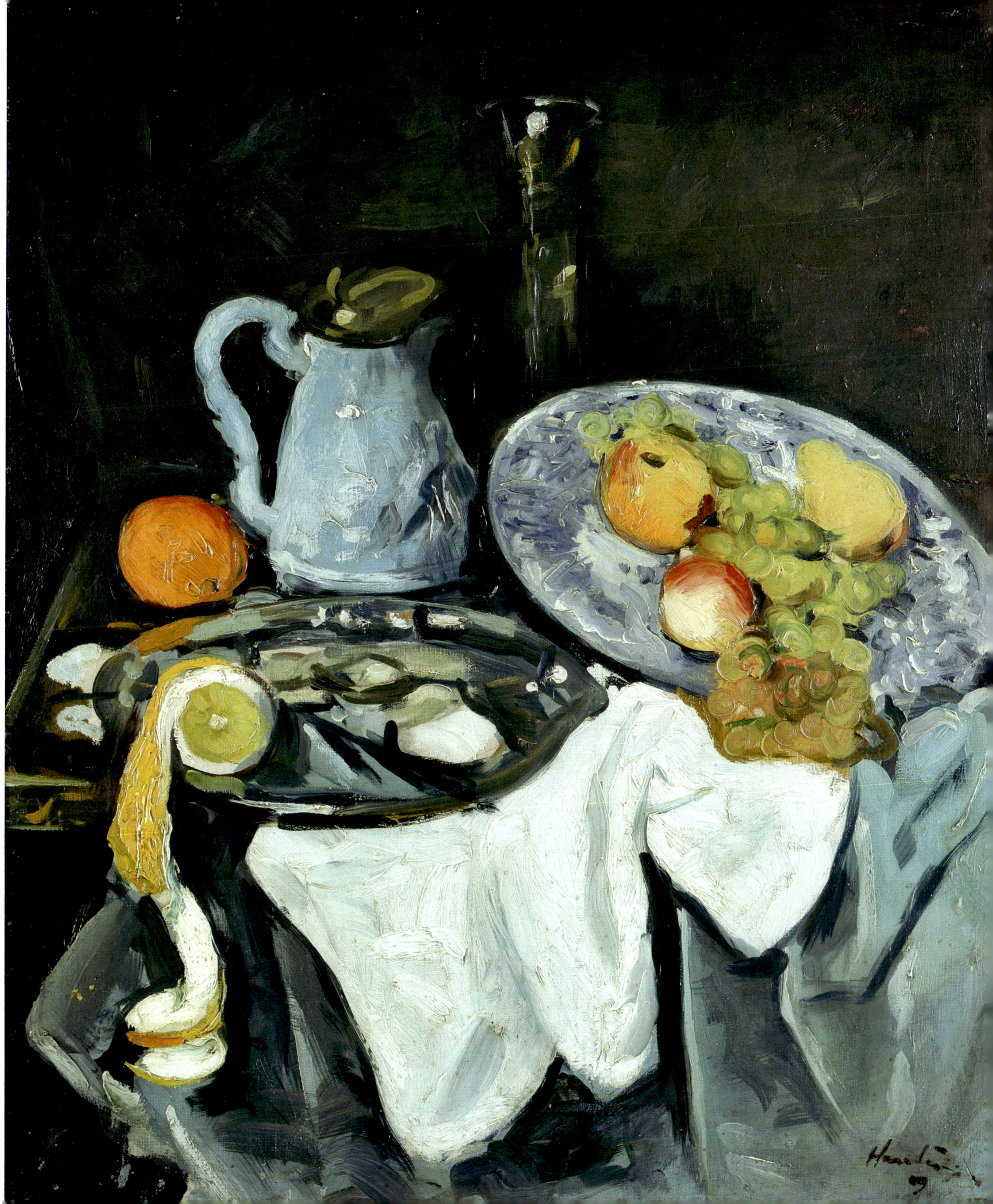

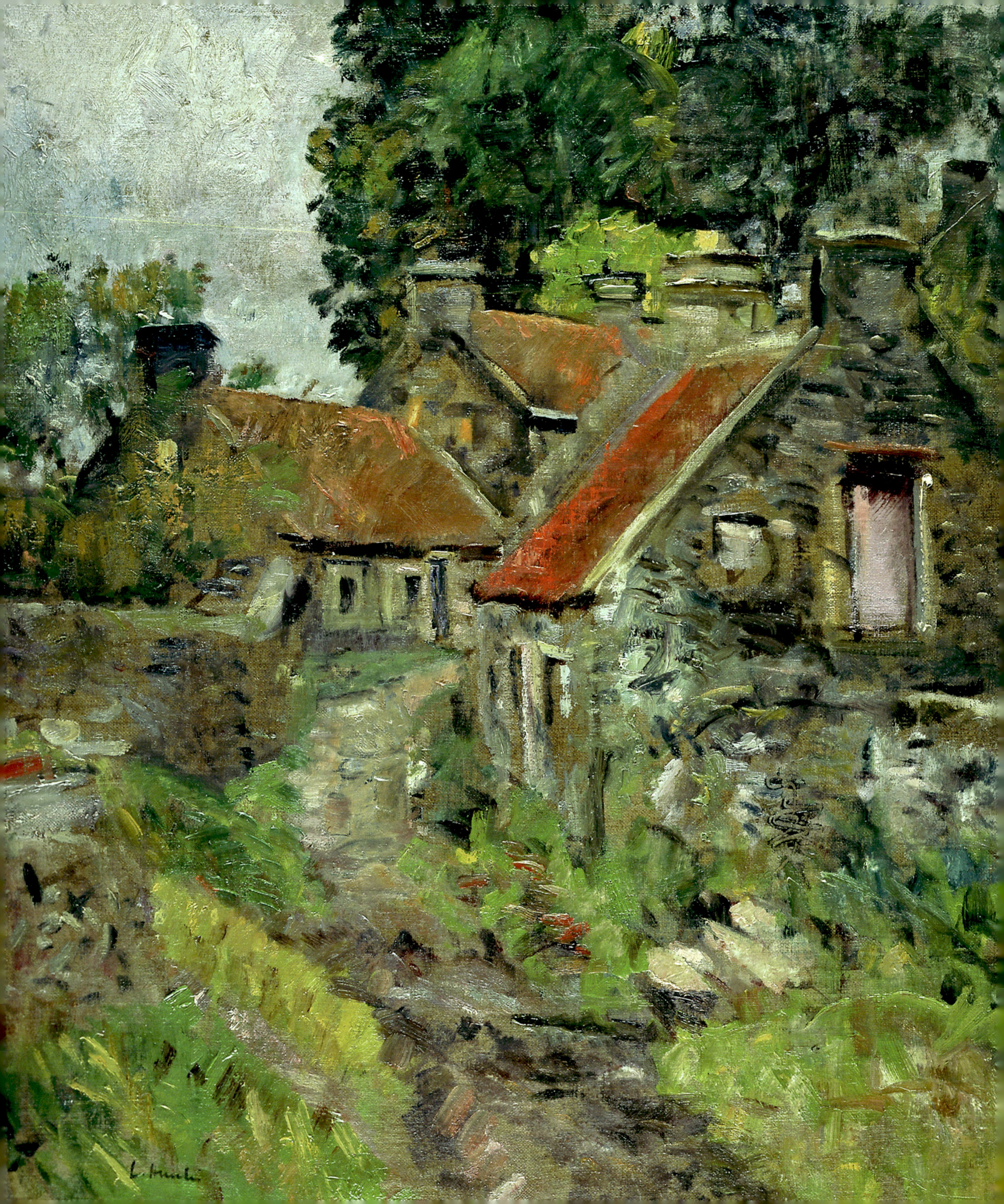

development during a given phase, so too is the serene *Dining Room Interior* of 1919 (pl.52). Here Hunter surprises us with his superb balance of form and colour, his dazzling impasto and almost impressionist feel. Perhaps it is his homage to influences he held dear, represented in the painting by William McTaggart's seascape and the blue and white oriental ginger jars, both playing prominent roles within the composition. Hunter's notebook reveals his admiration for McTaggart. The various ginger jars are used repeatedly in a series of still lifes from 1919 onwards. The interior portrayed is most likely to have been the dining room in the Broughty Ferry home of his friend, William Boyd. The sculptor, Benno Schotz, recalled Hunter painting there and apparently dropping paint all over the carpets.[14] Of Boyd's house in the 1920s Hunter himself writes: '... the harmony of the pictures, the vases, the carpet, soothed or stimulated the mind like a temple'.[15] In total contrast to Hunter's main stylistic development, this painting appears to be unique in terms of subject matter.

It was in landscape, however, that Hunter sought to find the way forward, just as it had been in 1913 and '14. Five years later he came upon an important source of inspiration through his fortuitous discovery of Fife and the possibilities inherent in its colourful landscape and rural architecture. The location probably was suggested by Justice, though it is fair to point out that Fife had long been a favourite painting ground of artists and this may have had a bearing on the choice. Whatever the reason, it opened up a whole new realm of possibilities for Hunter. Subsequently he would go to Fife in any season. It was there that he made the break to paint *en plein air.* The artistic ground he gained as a result marked an important turning point in his development in terms of modern colour, and inevitably affected his still life also.

By this time Hunter's strongly-held views about art and its future were so intense that frequently they provoked an adverse reaction – avoidance! In 1916 he had met Glasgow artists, John Quinton Pringle and his friend, James Meldrum, whose wife's portrait Hunter had painted several years earlier. When he encountered Pringle in Ceres in 1919, Hunter expressed how much he admired his originality.[16] James Meldrum's son, William, recalls Hunter had a great number of theories on art and would go to any lengths to explain them and have them understood. William and his father were in Ceres then, fully intending to avoid Hunter. However there was no escape, and Hunter invited them to tea. They went to his lodgings in the village, but there was no sign of Hunter. The landlady enlightened them: 'och, he'll be awa' walkin' wi' his dreams!'[17] It was typical of Hunter; his compulsion to draw invariably took over to the point where he forgot about other commitments.

Having gained ground by applying a measure of Cézanne's theories to his treatment of still life, Hunter felt sufficiently confident to extend the experiment to the landscape of Fife. Cézanne was the principal stimulus, but Hunter also introduced colour heightened well above reality, a technique he had identified and jotted down in his notebook concerning Van Gogh's later style.[18] In his watercolour, *Harbour in Fife* (1919, pl.59), Hunter's first instinct was to capture an overall pattern and structure in the view, which he hints at with strategically placed lines in black. However his love of bright colour takes over in a riot of strong brushstrokes, accentuating form in a manner that previously had eluded him. Equally refreshing is *Harbour Scene* (pl.60).

In *Sunrise over Fife Harbour* (pl.61) the zig-zag effect of house roofs, harbour wall, boats and the water's surface defines pattern and underlying structure. The pattern is coherently bound together by Hunter's confident, intuitive use of vivid, bright colour as he manipulates the basic elements in the view to striking effect. The constant degree of manipulation between pattern and colour that distinguishes this painting becomes increasingly evident from now on. Such was the impact of this new stylistic

58 | Ceres Mill, Fife
Oil on canvas, 1920
University of Glasgow, Hunterian Art Gallery

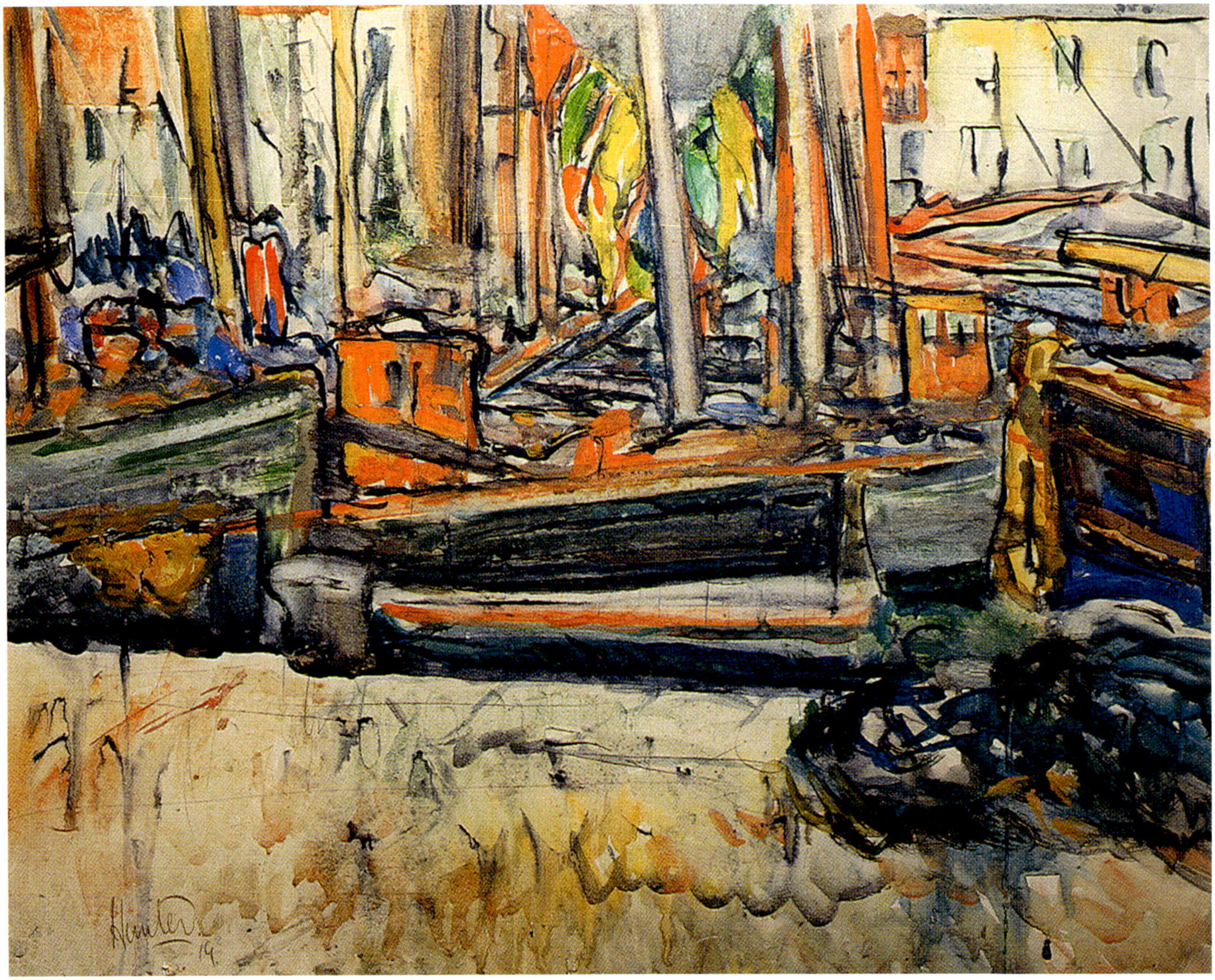

development on his friends that the picture was bought by Ion Harrison.

In December 1920, following a visit to Justice in Dundee, Hunter writes of Fife, the impact it has made on him and the pleasure he derives from beautiful things:

I have only pleasant memories of my visit to Dundee and I find the recollection stimulating still. To have cut short my survey of the exhausted aspect of nature I saw at Ceres and to talk surrounded by 'fine things' of painting of Paris and to have from you a whiff of the atmosphere of over there was a surprising recompense in the Tayside city.

To see … the more wonderful Assyrian relief – recalling Degas the modern in movement and Cezanne in volume … how lofty to live with (chez nous) perhaps too filling.[19]

From about 1920 Hunter developed a preoccupation with all things Assyrian, which is intriguing. The inference from the letter is that the Assyrian relief belonged to Justice. Hunter's comments reveal his great capacity for analysis in terms of the Modern Movement. It is difficult to identify the objects, photographs and books about which he enthuses during these years, and there does not appear to be any direct manifestation of this preoccupation in his pictures of the period. Nevertheless his passion for things Assyrian was

59 | Harbour in Fife
Pen & ink and watercolour, 1919
Private collection

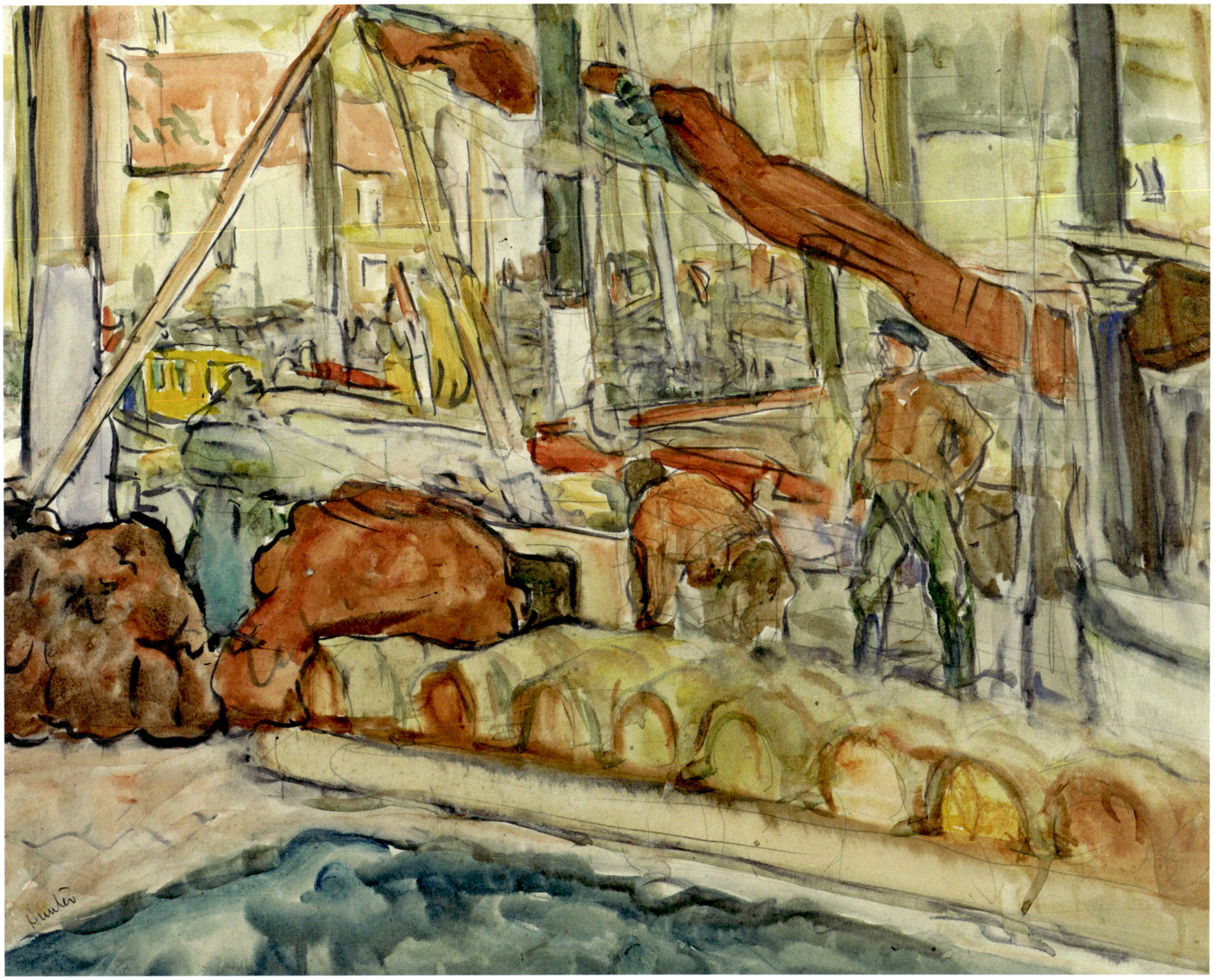

60 | Harbour Scene
Pen & ink and watercolour, 1919
Private collection

a serious source of excitement that he shared with his friends and even tried, albeit unsuccessfully, to arouse interest in Glasgow Art Club. Hunter loved to wander around the British Museum in London, where he had the opportunity to see a great variety of such ancient art. He certainly was interested in the sculpture, as he notes in a letter to Justice in the spring of 1921:

I enjoyed the sculpture in the British Museum and pictures at the National on dull and wet days and Hampton Court when the weather was promising. Indeed it was ravishing there. I made some notes and would have done more had the weather sustained. You should pay a short visit to the Italian Room opposite entrance of the National Gallery. Since my visit I have not ceased to marvel … Saw material everywhere … but feel it is not much use attempting anything unless you are settled in a place.[20]

In his December letter Hunter goes on to attempt to explain those points he identifies as fundamental to his progress as an artist:

Van Gogh, Bonnard, Vuillard follow 'the new' in a shallower channel of course but how well they sit into our modern surroundings.

It will be interesting to have Mr Turner's point of view on what I send. I have a method now of working in stages allowing each to dry that I find quite successful without fighting the material that

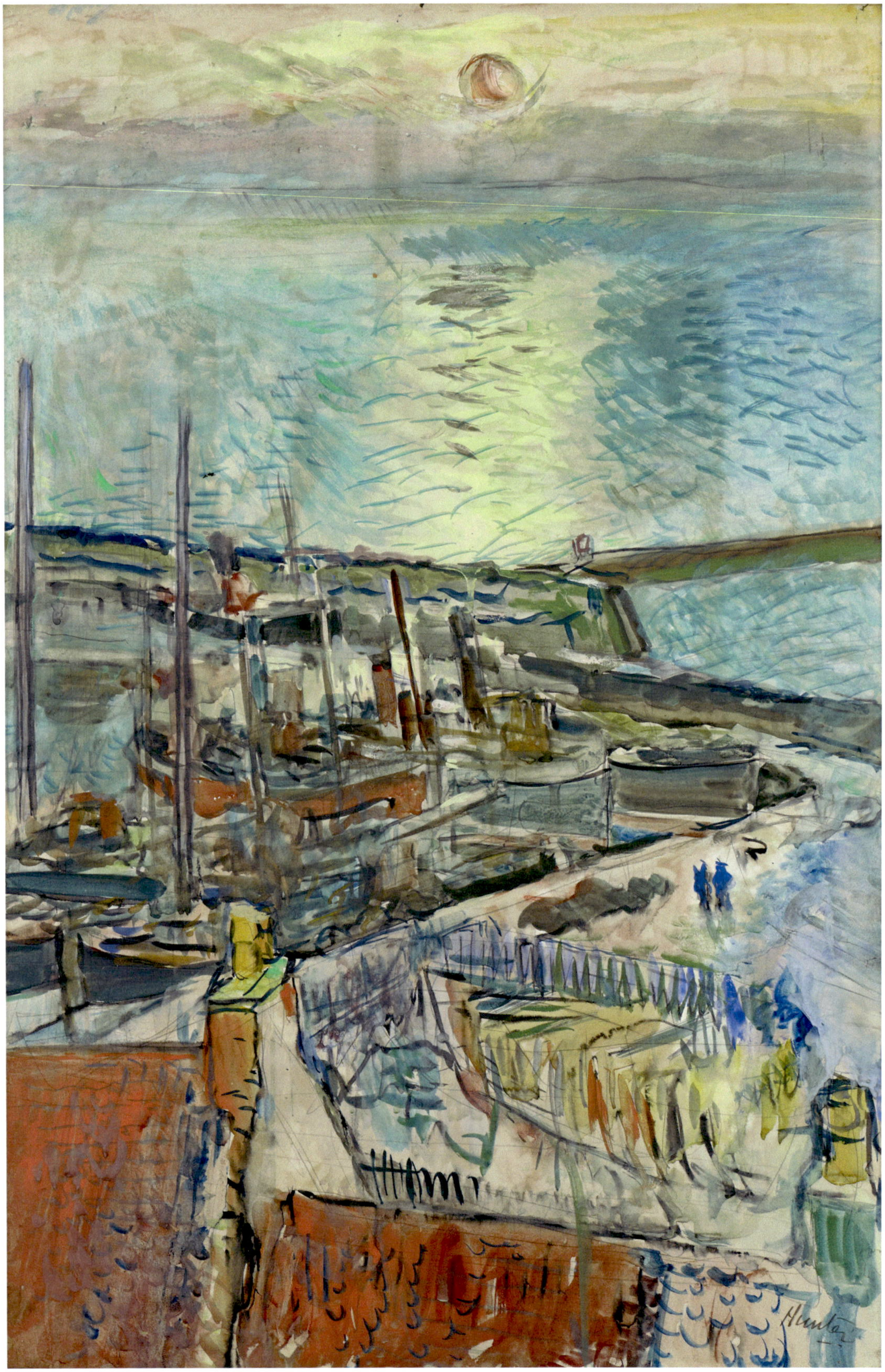

61 | Sunrise over Fife Harbour
Watercolour, 1919
Private collection

seems to bring more result with less effort. This will enable me in the coming season to shape my work better I feel. Mr Turner's desires in a picture are interesting. I too desire the statue rather than the fleeting element. It should prevail to sustain its interest. The fleeting in Impressionist work has its charm but I feel the eye wanders to more solid and sustaining things like the older men produced. There seems to me to be much post-impressionism 'a la mode' which I wish to thoroughly avoid. There is no pedantry in the old men or in Cezanne. One feels his style 'behind' nature so to speak in his pictures not in front.[21]

Hunter's admiration of Vuillard at this point is best illustrated by *The Artist's Bedroom* (pl.62). There appears to be a direct relationship between Hunter's picture and Vuillard's *Woman in Blue with Child* (Glasgow Art Gallery), which Matthew Justice owned for a short period in 1919.

The 1919 series of Fife watercolours affords an opportunity to appreciate the depth of Hunter's artistic temperament and motivation. In the offing was a show at Reid's in Glasgow and he was eager to push the boundaries of his work as far as he could. The results of his experiments in Fife were hugely successful and rapidly prompted him to apply what he had learned to his still life.

There is a strong correlation between the landscapes and still lifes that Hunter executed in 1920 for his solo exhibition in April the following year. Discussing his Fife watercolours in a letter to Justice, Hunter writes:

They are cooler in colour and I think stronger in

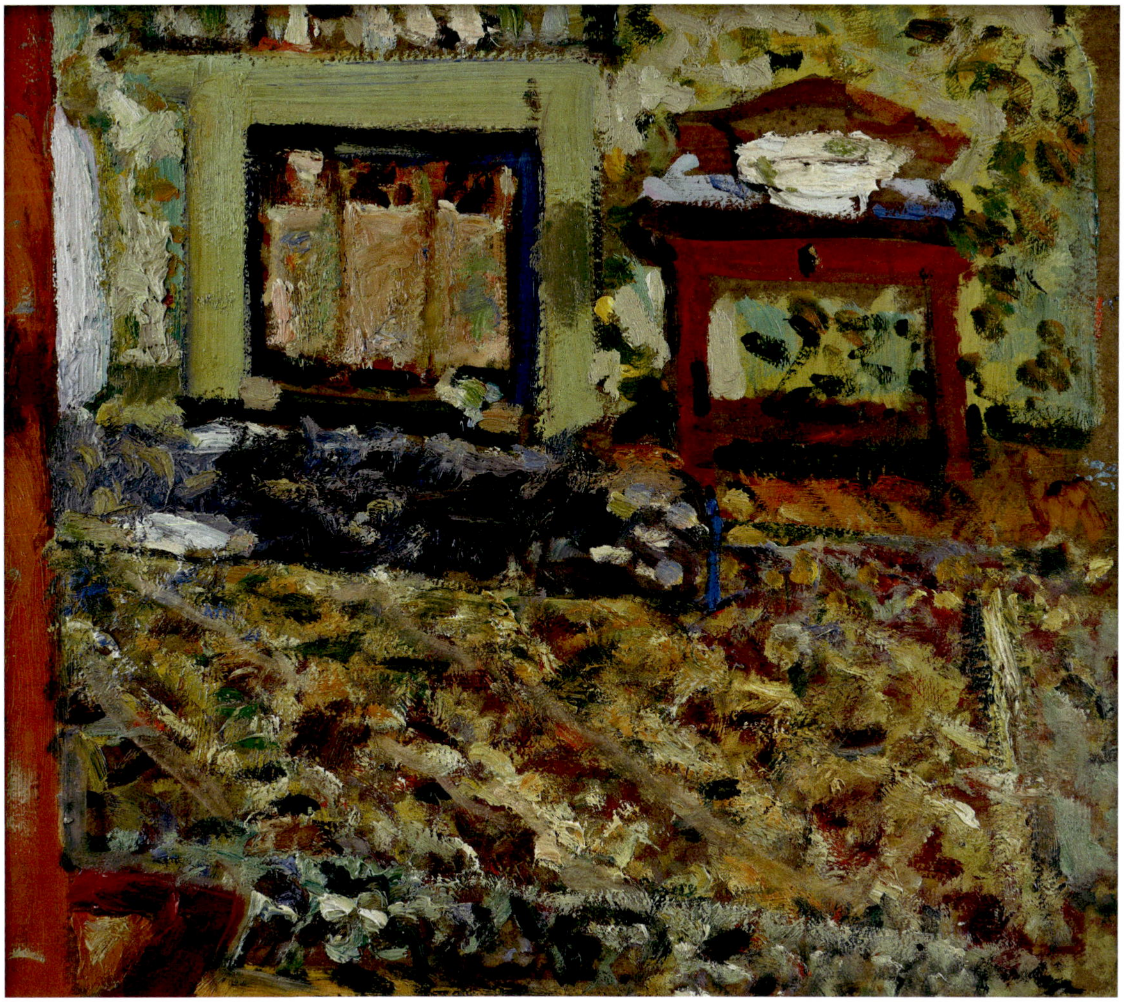

62 | The Artist's Bedroom
Oil on panel, *c.*1920
Private collection

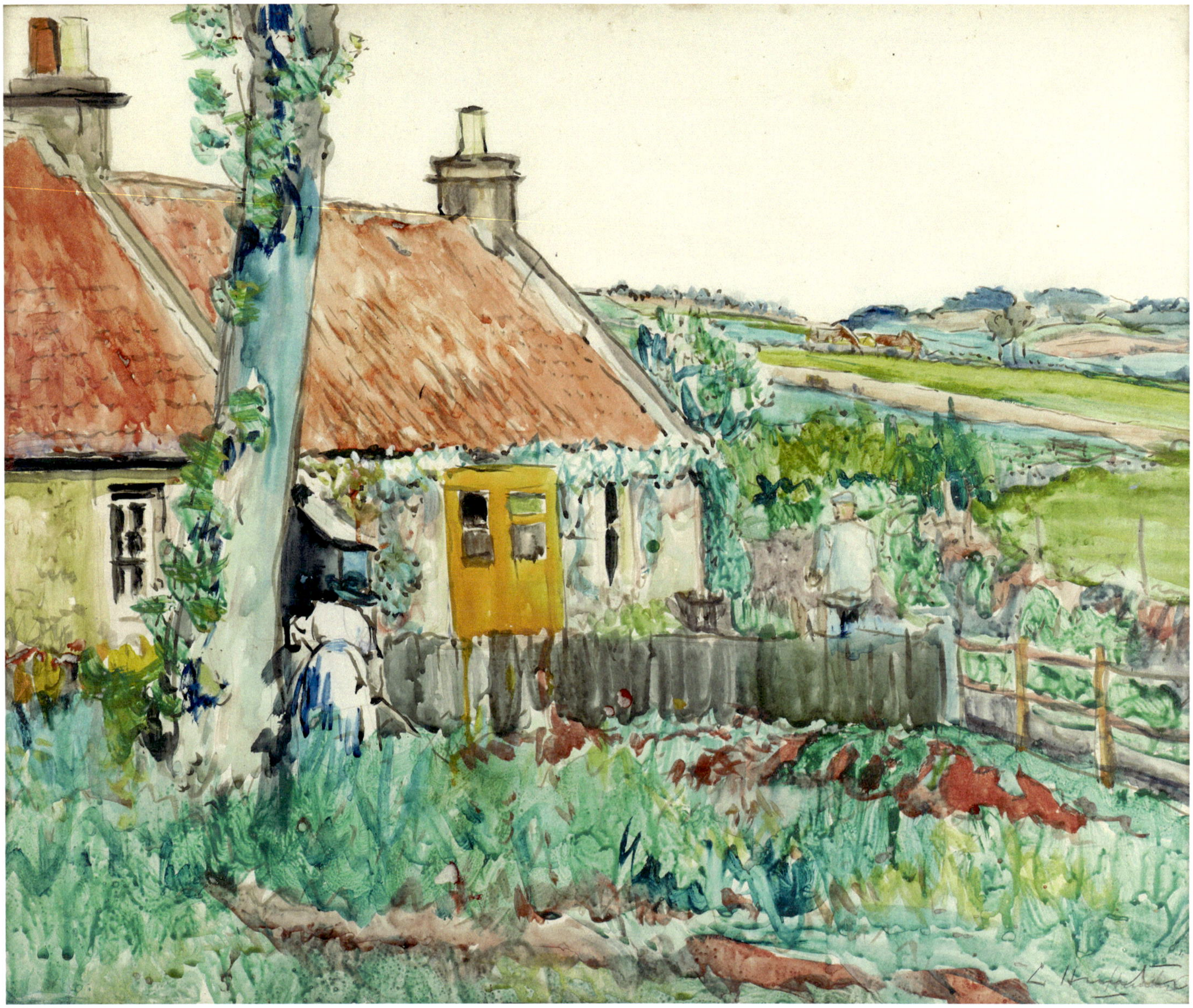

form than last years. In these studies I was concerned entirely with the animation of the landscape. The first of the season I feel I would have, had I worked on, smashed through to something, forward in strength and simplicity and backward in refinement like the few things of last year you have.[22]

In *Fife Cottage* (pl.63) the landscape is divided into simple bands of colour determined by the pattern of the fields, fence and foliage. By using the natural layout and simplifying the main colours and tones of that layout, Hunter captures the essence of the landscape itself without going into any substantial detail. The seemingly effortless simplicity belies the skill involved.

When it came to translating the Fife landscape into oils, Hunter preferred to start with small panels. The technique he employed seems more determined by the nature of the medium itself; pattern can no longer be defined using the fluidity of watercolour. In *Trees, Ceres* (private collection) the brush moves rapidly across the surface with daubs of colour that merely suggest the various textures inherent in the landscape. In *Ceres, Fife* (pl.68), which is similar in structure

63 | Fife Cottage
Pencil, watercolour and bodycolour, 1919
Private collection

64 | Figure and Cottages, Ceres
Etching, *c.*1920
Private collection

65 | Farmhouse
Monotype, *c.*1920
Scottish National Gallery of Modern Art

66 | A Village in Fife
Oil on panel, 1919
University of Glasgow, Hunterian Art Gallery

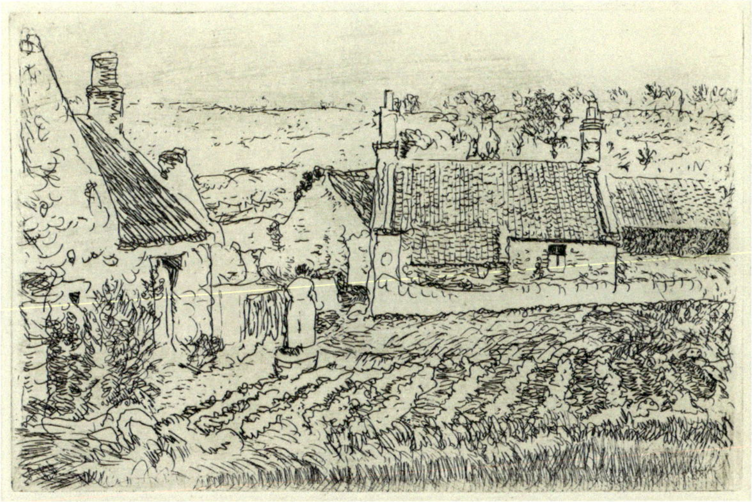

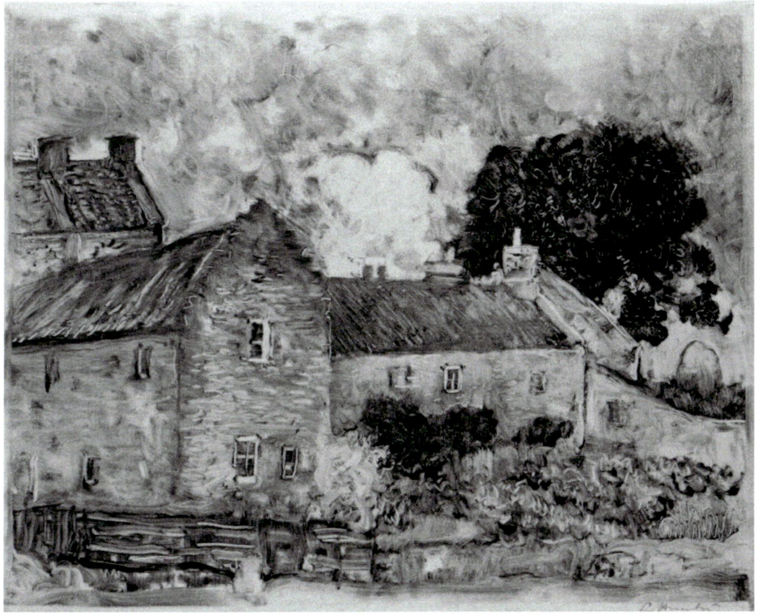

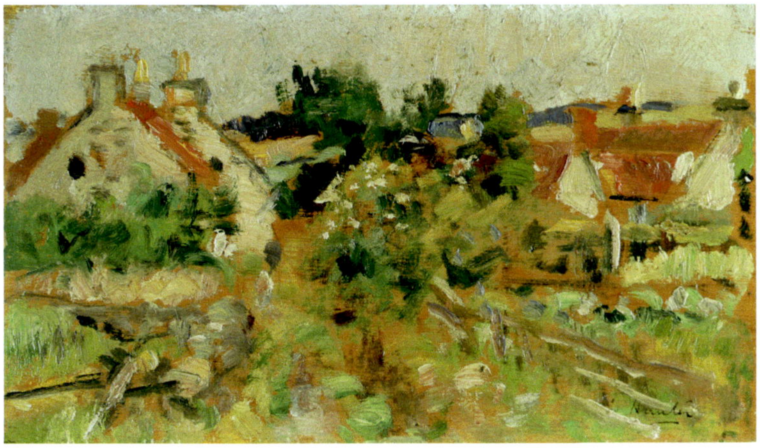

to the watercolour discussed in the previous paragraph, he reduces the landscape to bands of colour and foliage. The delightful sketch, *Distant View, Ceres* (pl.70), shows more clearly how Hunter defines his initial response to a given view in bands of colour. First he outlines the dominant elements in crayon, and then lightly fills in some of the features in oil paint. In each case he captures the essence of the landscape without losing any of its intensity. As he works up to larger, more complete canvases, he applies one or other of those techniques depending on which best suits his purpose at the time of encapsulating Nature's appeal.

All Hunter's newly-developed skills are brought into play in a fine series of paintings based on views of an old Fife mill. In *Old Mill, Fifeshire* (pl.69) Hunter binds the picture together by his instinctive sense of pattern and rapid brushstrokes of strong colour. Such is the authority of his vision, the painting wonderfully embodies Nature's timeless appeal. Equally in *Mill Dam, Fife* (pl.71) he displays a startling use of colour from right across the spectrum to build up form. In *Ceres Mill* (pl.58) Hunter's use of muted colours enlivened by a few chords of strong colour skilfully conveys both depth and freshness in this unassuming scene. Such views can never be seen as fleeting impressions. They are unmistakably deep and real. Hunter clearly demonstrates that he can repeatedly paint the same scene and through the use of subtly different techniques cleverly convey the distinctive, elusive moods of Nature.

The little town of Lower Largo provided another favoured painting ground for Hunter. This tiny stretch of the Fife shoreline – its cottages and large, square granary block (now part of the *Crusoe Hotel*) backing on to the sea, its sandy shore dotted with large outcrops of rock, its jetty and small harbour at the mouth of the Keil Burn and people enjoying the sea air – provided a constant source of challenge for Hunter. The combined impact of the sea, the physical surroundings and the people had to be contained within the picture plane.

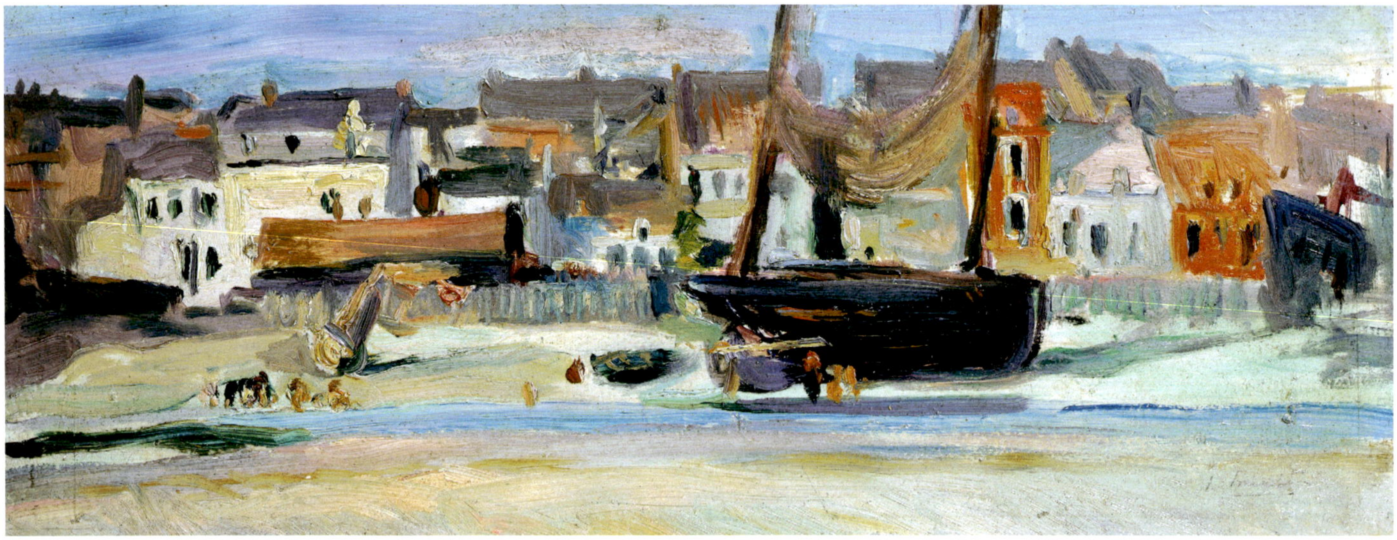

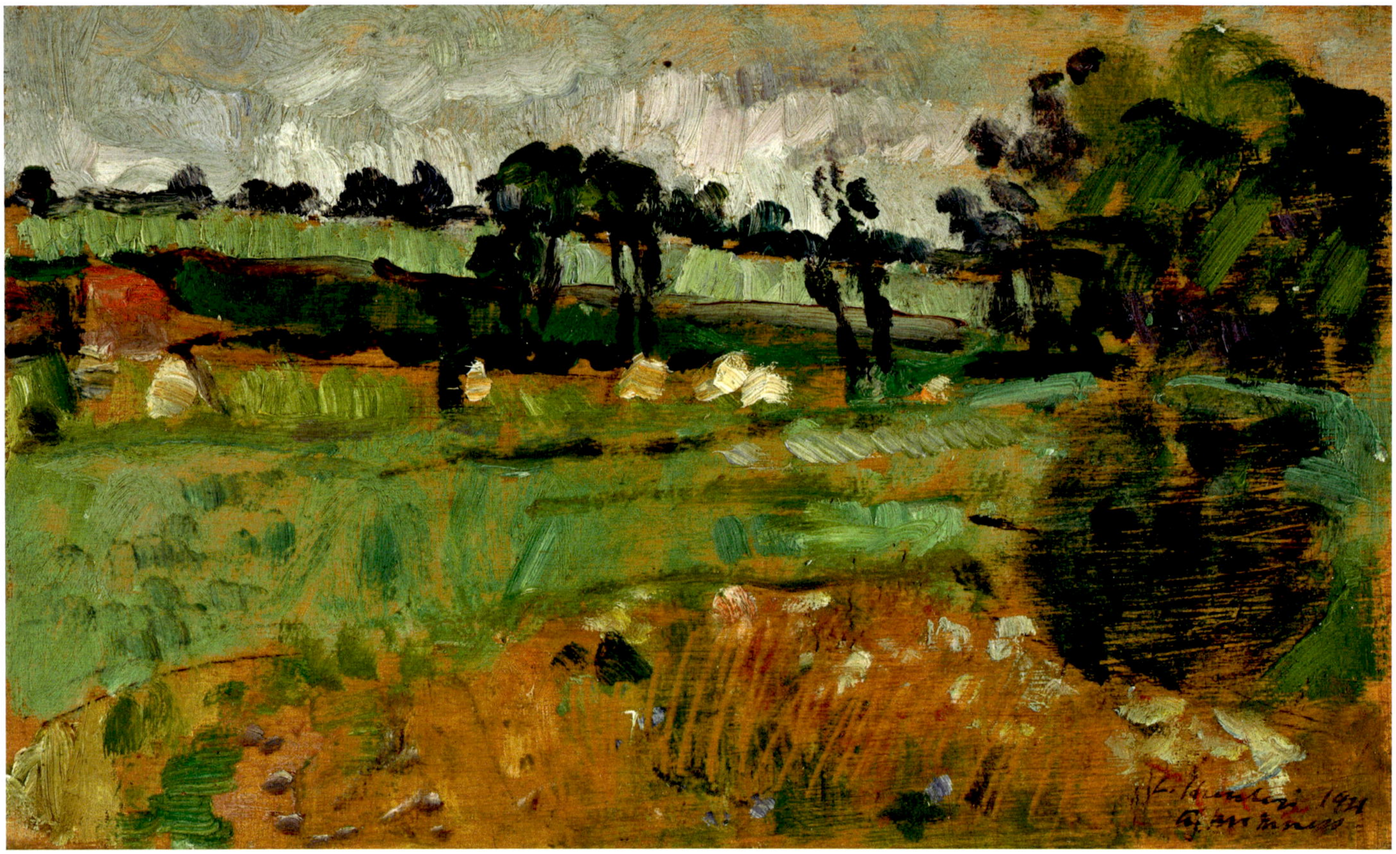

67 | Lower Largo
Oil on panel, 1919
The Fleming-Wyfold Art Foundation

68 | Ceres, Fife
Oil on panel, 1919
Glasgow Museums

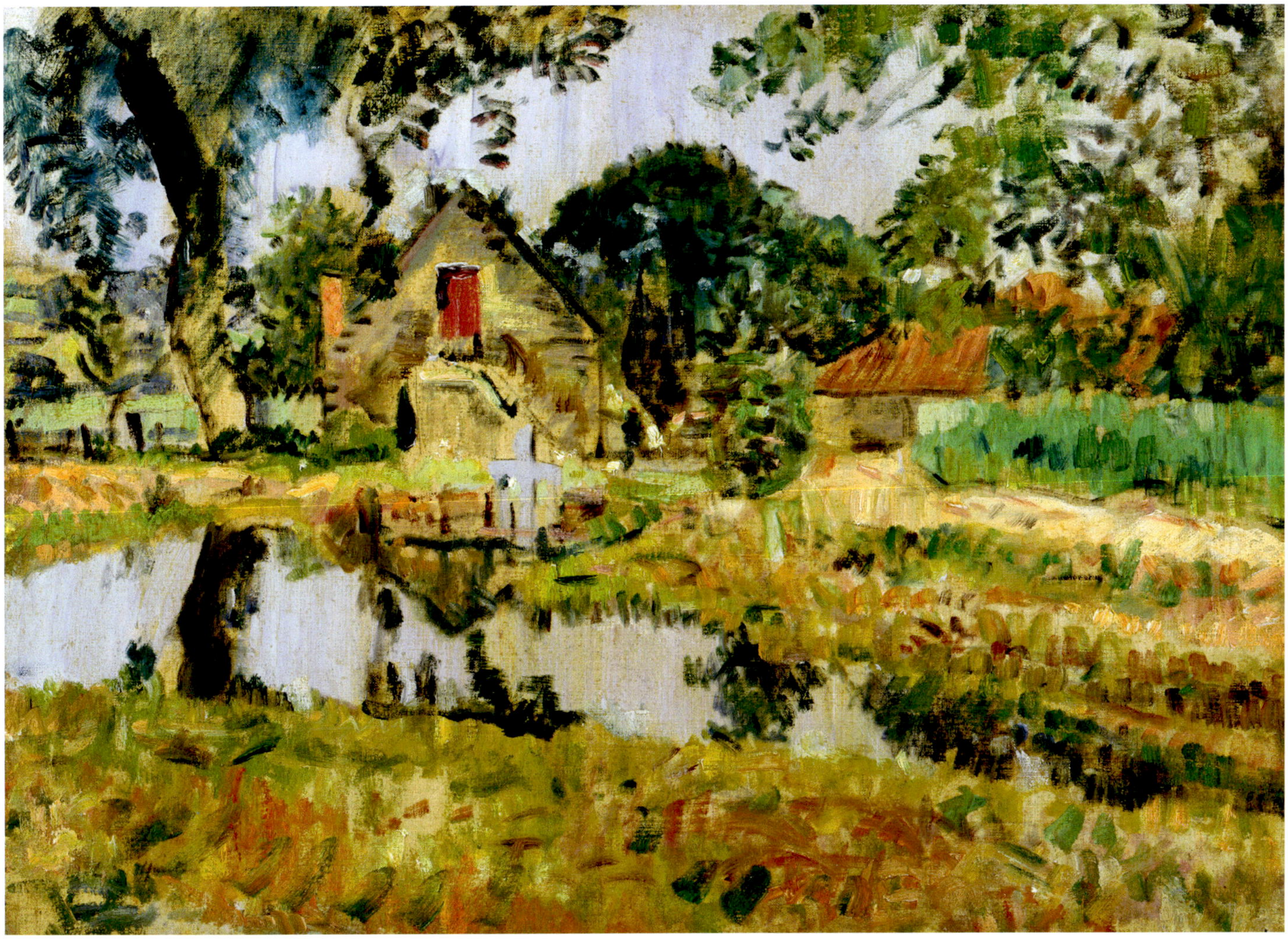

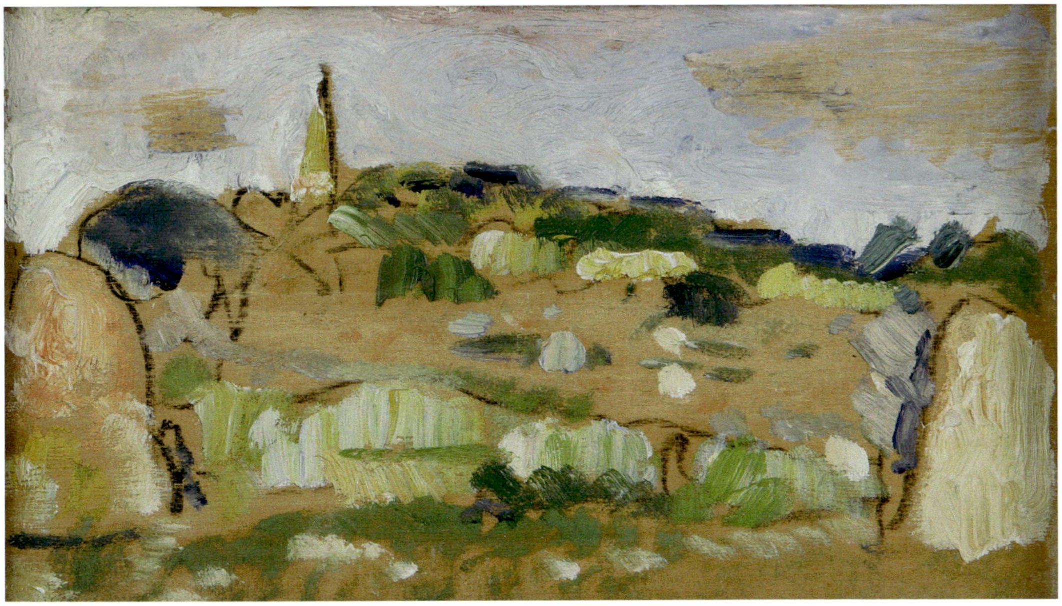

69 | Old Mill, Fifeshire
Oil on canvas, 1920
Glasgow Museums

70 | Distant View of Ceres
Oil over crayon on panel, 1919
Private collection

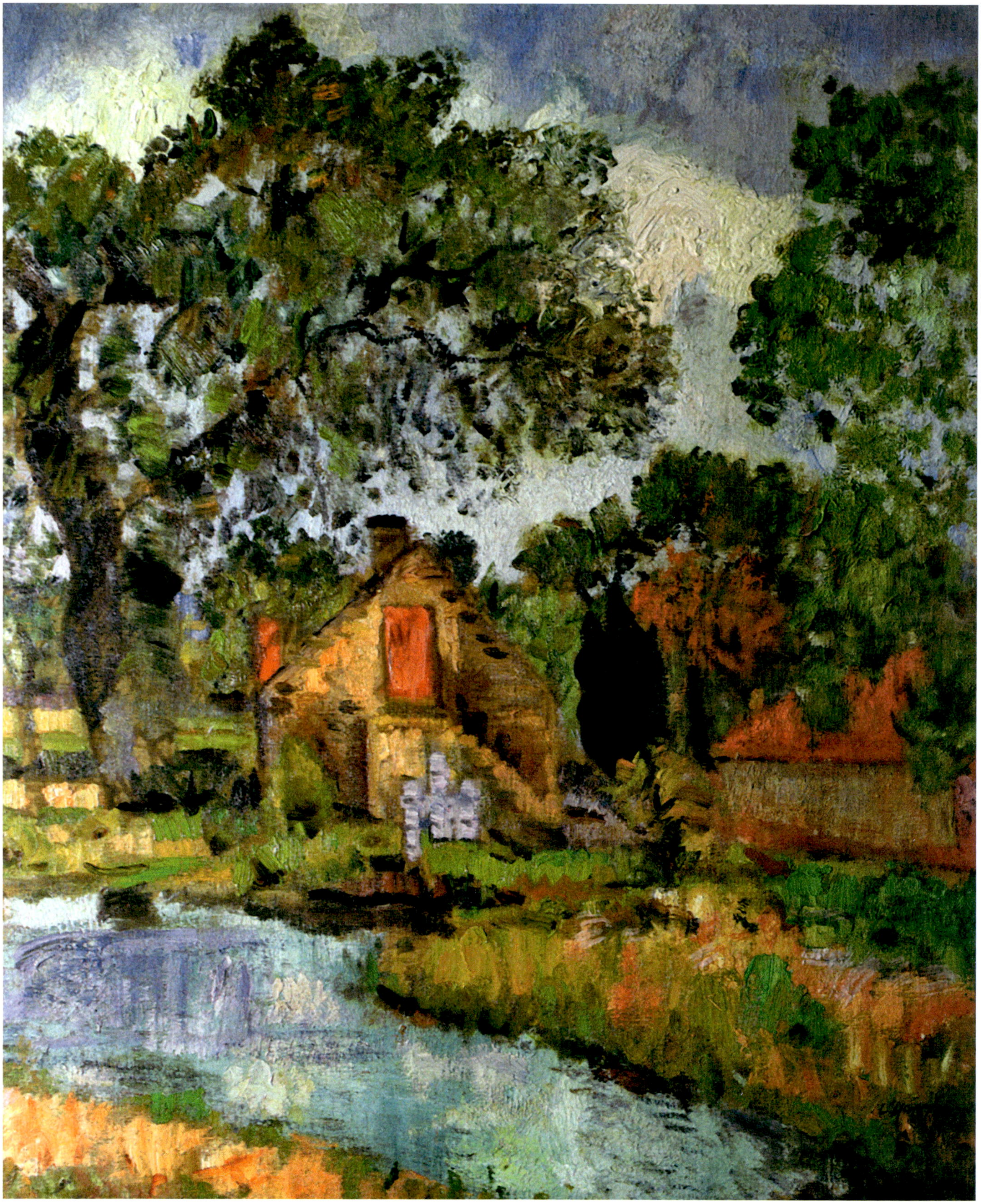

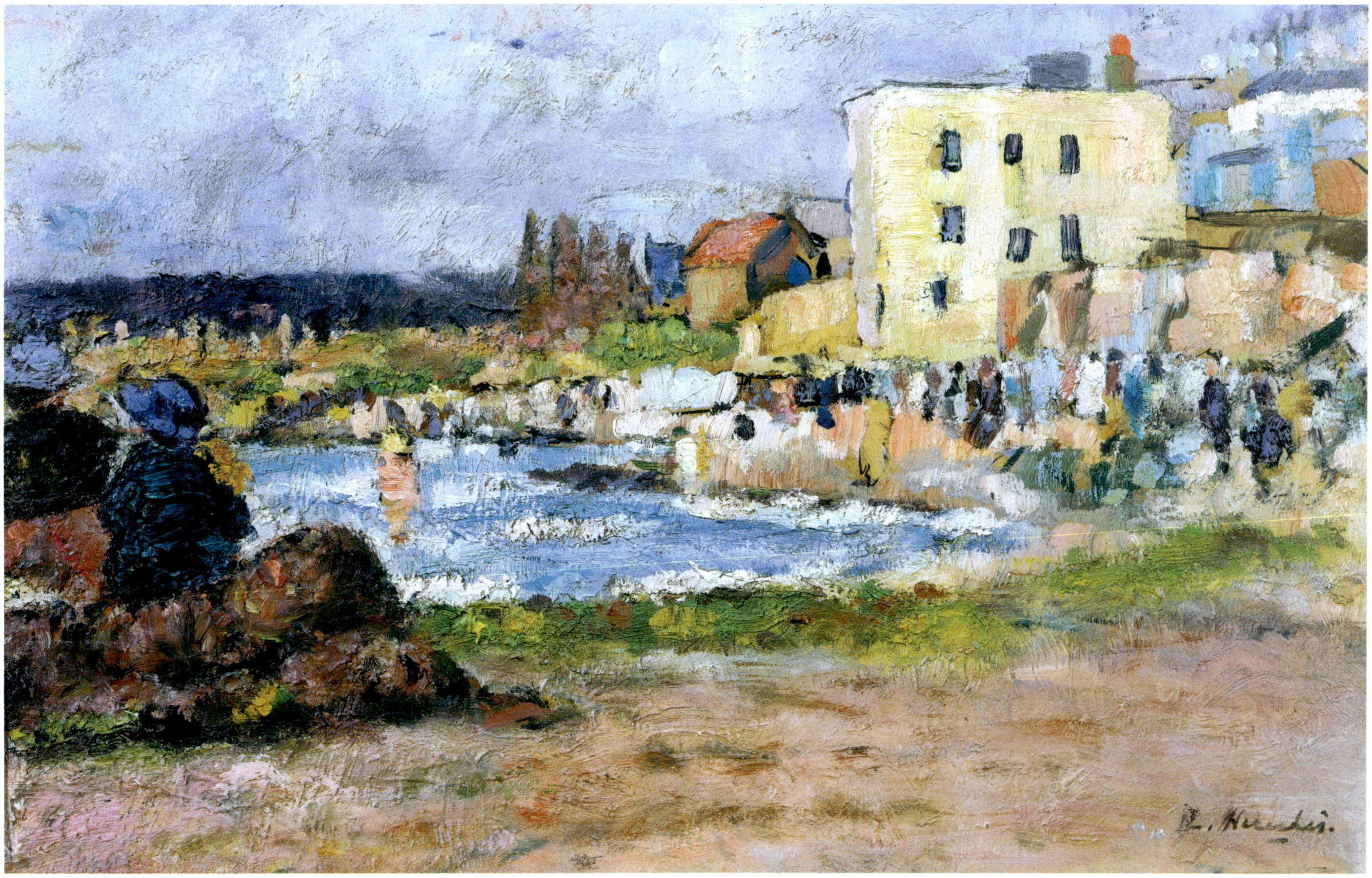

71 | Mill Dam, Fife
Oil on canvas, 1920
Private collection

72 | Summer's Day, Lower Largo
Oil on board, 1921
Private collection

Hunter had to grapple with the same problem that faced William McTaggart, namely how to convey human presence within nature without that presence being the central focus. In fact Hunter reduces human presence to the same level of form as he did with the elements of nature. He treats it as shapes and forms, as in *Summer's Day, Lower Largo* (pl.72). In various such views he evokes the sensation of bustling crowds through expert use of dabs of colour, form evolving through the texture of the paint itself. The overwhelming effect is one of activity and enjoyment. It is the textures created by the effect of strolling, relaxed crowds set against the buildings, trees and breaking sea that appeal most to the senses. Indeed the use of colour to build up form is almost secondary in importance to the effect created by texture. Such Fife views are remarkable in their strength and colour, particularly so bearing in mind the weather Hunter experienced. He constantly laments the poor summer weather of 1920. It is perhaps this factor that to a large extent prevented Hunter *'smashing through'* to better things.[23]

Constantly striving for perfection in his painting, constantly analysing the means to attain his goal, Hunter comments: 'In developing one's work one often gets one quality at the expense of another. If one loses in a change it is perhaps not so palpable to the producer as the outsider.' Of his landscapes he suggests: 'why should a landscape not be capable of silhouette like a figure? The orientals thought that way.'[24] This sense of silhouette, particularly evident in the Mill Dam series, also becomes a theme in a series of still lifes painted in 1920–21.

Still Life with Fruit and Flowers (pl.73), *Pink Rose, Fruit and Still Life* (pl.75) and *Still Life with Fruit and a Black Fan* (pl.74) illustrate Hunter's method of experimenting with different emphases. The background and foreground, if not exactly shades of white, consist of pale colours against which he silhouettes a variety of objects chosen for their shape and colour, the freshness of the flowers and fruit enhanced by the light background. Areas of thickly-applied paint create a rich, vibrant surface texture that belies the balanced order of the layout. Hunter is demonstrating his growing mastery of strong colour. Objects are grouped horizontally across the middle of the picture. Hunter deliberately highlights the contrasts in texture and colour of the fruit and roses with the smooth, dark Japanese-style vase as centrepiece, thus binding the composition together. Hunter has finally mastered Cézanne's concept of painting 'weight' in objects, which brings his art in line with that of Peploe and Fergusson, who had been grappling with that concept in pre-war Paris. It can be argued that Hunter's still life at this point is as strong as – if not surpasses – that of his fellow Colourists.

His exhibition at Alexander Reid's gallery in Glasgow opened in April 1921. The exhibition was to prove a landmark for Hunter and, more importantly, a valuable test of Scottish reaction to his current work. At the outset fate was not smiling on Hunter; he bemoans: 'What is an optimist? – a man giving a show during a coal and dock strike! … I feel I could not have struck a more unfortunate moment.'[25] He writes to Tattersall:

My show opened a few days ago as you would probably get notice. Reid himself proclaims it the best I have ever given them, but unfortunately the strike has intervened and McNeill [Reid's son] *and I are waiting for it to get settled and give the queue a chance to form. Everyone seems so pre-occupied at the present moment with the strike and we are not advertising until it is settled. Then McNeill thinks judging by the enthusiasm shown he will soon get rid of a few. Newspaper criticism too is being held over until public attention is less distracted.*[26]

Hunter was delighted that the exhibition stirred up comment in Glasgow Art Club. The club's own show was running at the same time;

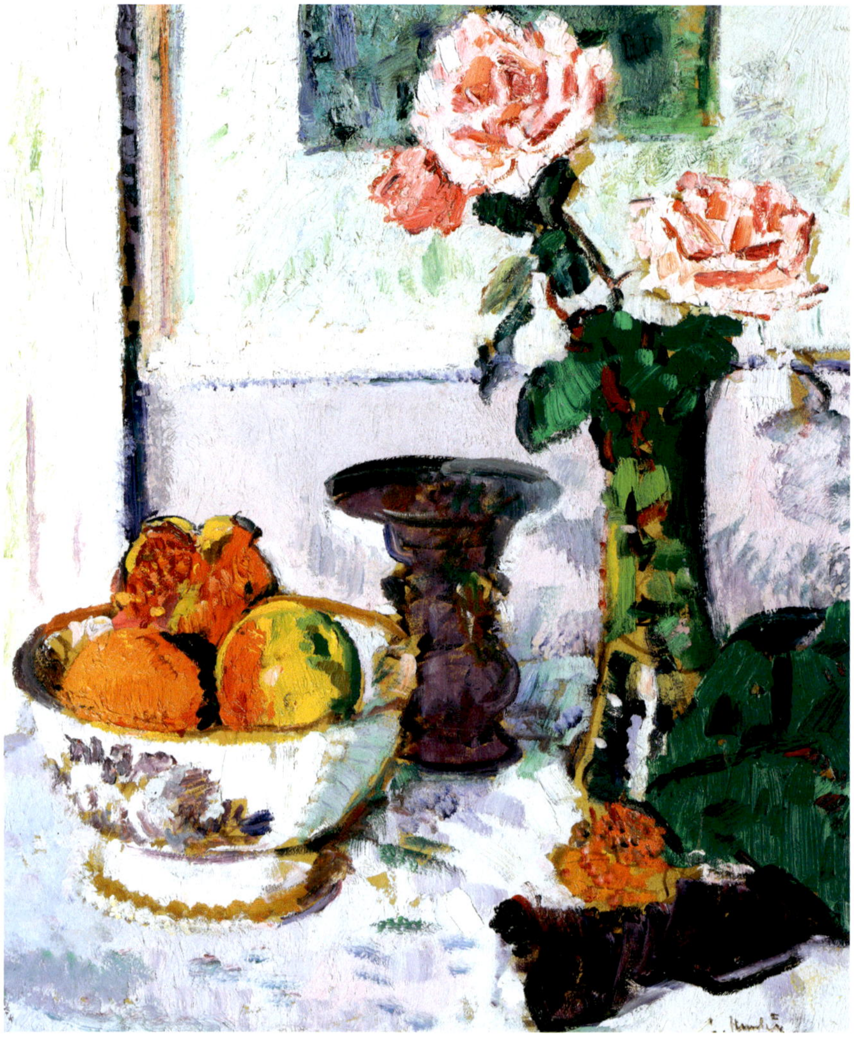

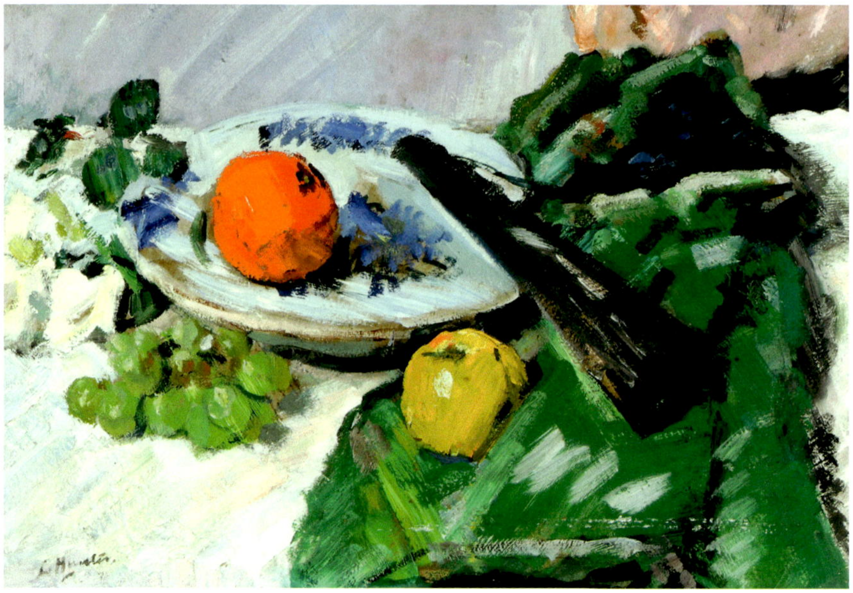

Hunter laments: 'How little there is in the present art club show, so much, and yet so little of the vital spark.'[27] An idea of how Hunter's work was received by some club members is revealed in a letter to Justice: 'Robert Macaulay Stevenson [the artist and former Glasgow Boy] has been in frequently and has been speaking a lot at the club here about "this impassioned painting" the colour of which shocked him at first.'[28] So taken with Hunter and the calibre of his work, Stevenson returned to the show with the editor of *The News*. Hunter tells Justice:

Macaulay Stevenson ... is much interested in my landscapes and has talked a lot about my work to people which will probably affect some sales lately when things are settled. He lives in France at Montreuil-sur-Mer and is anxious I should go over there and work beside him. However I think that such an expedition would be too expensive.

Despite the limited financial success of the exhibition, it boosted Hunter's self-confidence. Having turned down Stevenson's kind offer due to lack of funds, Hunter enthuses to Justice:

It is possible I may proceed to Ceres very soon, perhaps this week, to get started on the apple blossom. I have written about a room there and have been informed the blossom is just coming out. I will be glad to get out of the city for a little when everyone one meets seems to have the hump. Fife is ever a delightful thought on my mind with its beautiful valleys and villages.[29]

73 | Still Life with Fruit and Flowers
Oil on board, 1921–22
Private collection

74 | Still Life with Fruit and Black Fan
Oil on canvas, 1921
Museums Sheffield

Of course during this period Hunter's activities were not confined entirely to painting. For instance, in a postcard from Ceres dated 25 November 1920 he tells Justice that he is etching, as the colour has vanished from the landscape.[30] Hunter was an intermittent printmaker. His monotypes have been mentioned briefly in chapter three. Around 1919 he began to experiment with drypoint and etching. At that time the etching boom of 1910–29 was gathering momentum, which may have prompted Hunter to try his hand. In 1920–21 he produced nine etchings featuring cottages and landscape around Ceres.[31] They are all rather unremarkable, except for *Figure and Cottages, Ceres* (pls. 64 & 169), which is more ambitious than the rest. It is unknown how many prints he ran off from each plate; they do not appear to have been issued in customary editions, which may indicate that he executed them purely for his own pleasure. No subsequent etchings have come to light. Indeed five years or so later Hunter expressed irritation at the prevailing preference of collectors for etchings over paintings, moaning to Justice: 'Reids seem nothing but a place to show and sell etchings now a days, much to old Reid's disgust (to his credit)'.[32] At that time auction prices for etchings had reached dizzy heights. It was largely a speculative market, which shortly would be brought to an abrupt end by the Wall Street Crash of 1929.

There was also much going on in the art world at large. Justice continued to encourage debate and enliven the art scene in the east, culminating in a lecture given by Percy Moore Turner at the beginning of 1921 on the *'Modern Movement in France'*. It was hoped that the subject would stir up interest with the public and artists alike. Hunter was looking forward to attending, writing 'I sincerely hope Mr Turner's lecture will increase the 'circle' in Dundee ... It is amusing to think of Turner coming north as a sort of St. Columba of the Arts!'[33] Turner's regular exhibitions at his Independent Gallery in London's Grafton Street were a focal point for Hunter and his friends, who frequently arranged to go and see them together. Hunter went on several occasions with Justice and McInnes. In 1920 one of Turner's shows of modern French paintings and drawings impressed a correspondent of *The Burlington Magazine*, who wrote: 'Anyone with genuine enthusiasm and discrimination will take pleasure in pictures of the kind (comprising one or two broad groups) which this new gallery has brought together.'[34] Turner's extensive array of paintings included works by Matisse, Dunoyer de Segonzac, Marchand, Friesz, Luce, Rouault, Derain, Moreau, Bonnard, Frelaut, Boussingault and Vlaminck. Drawings and prints were represented by Daumier, Rodin, Puvis de Chavannes, Lautrec and Maillol amongst others.

Although Hunter was glad to view such exhibitions, he tried hard to be objective. On one occasion he wrote to Justice:

I saw the show before leaving London. Frankly I was not much impressed ... There was a little picture by Cezanne, several nude figures under a tree and very fine I thought. Also a watercolour of boats by Signac that I like. I hope it was not my apathy to the work of the show that made these and only these seem exceedingly fine. From the names I should say that the show that preceded this one must have been better ... Such art I saw of Marchand and Friesz were strong in their way and seemed the best there.[35]

Turner also provided a useful platform for contemporary artists such as Sickert and even Wyndham Lewis. Of English attempts towards modernism, Hunter comments: 'Of course there are differences in those of the "cubists" represented. The French being more interesting than the English represented.'[36]

Although Hunter was immersed in his own work, he maintained a keen interest in what other Scottish artists were doing. In December 1920 Hunter viewed an exhibition of work by 'Bunty' Cadell, arranged by McNeill Reid, Alexander Reid's son, at Warneuke's Gallery in Glasgow's Sauchiehall Street.[37] Hunter comments in a letter to Justice: '... *tres moderne*, about 40 pictures, some interesting blocks of colour.'[38] In a subsequent letter he says of the same exhibition: 'It was very bright and modern showing a bit the influence of Peploe. But Cadell has a good sense of colour. He had several interiors of his studio, rather a swagger place I believe. I have not yet seen Peploe's Iona pictures but will endeavour to do so.'[39] The general response to Cadell's style of painting provoked interesting comments, one of which Hunter relays to Justice: '... I noticed a propos of Cadell's show the Herald stated that of his bright modern work it was likely that those painters who were sneering at it today would be attempting it tomorrow and life is certainly sad enough in Glasgow in the winter without sad art.[40]

In 1921 he praises the efforts of the Dundee artist, John Maclauchlan Milne (1885–1957): 'I'm glad to hear Maclauchlan Milne had so much success as Mr Tattersall writes he had in Dundee. I hope he recruited his strength in form and colour. Apostles of that order are few enough in the Country.'[41] In December that year he writes to Justice: '... to meet Milne recently from Paris was to revive a bit of Bohemian memory. It is nice to meet men who have a genial interest in life ... oh how everywhere the stiff-necked Philistine attitude abounds.'[42]

However Hunter's closest relationship with another Scottish artist was probably with Peploe, for whom he had great respect and admiration. In January 1921 Hunter writes:

I was in Edinburgh on Varnishing Day of the SSA and spent the day with Peploe. He does not paint at all in the winter he tells me as his attempts he says in that way have only amounted to spoiling his pictures and his temper.[43]

In a later letter to Justice, Hunter writes of one of his excursions to Edinburgh in January 1922, charmingly revealing the more playful and quirky side to his personality:

When I got to Edinburgh after lunch I went to the SSA. Whew!!!!! Peploe and his wife afterwards joked me about spending sixpence in that fashion or throwing it away rather. I went into the National Gallery for a little when at the door as one enters I find some wonderful primitives that regale one's spirit. I found Peploe waiting in, rather impatiently, owing to my detour in the above places.

I produced the Cigars des Magiques, I revealed the price in Bohemian fashion, we regretted we could not cash them and then proceeded to light up. I had been thinking all the way in the 'Name of Les Assyrians' and now how their art could be put in to paint ... but I opened up with Peploe first on the new era. The post war and the great future with an art to typify Les Seneplusis-Assyrien plus colour [sic]. *A world brightened by science and a higher ideal growing out of peace. Peploe to my astonishment rose to the occasion on every point. II est tres fort Monsieur Peploe! Mrs Peploe chipped in occasionally and the two kids were open-eyed. The creative idea in this world! And then we discussed the marvellous contours of the Assyrians*

75 | Pink Rose, Fruit and Still Life
Oil on board, 1921
Paisley Museum and Art Galleries

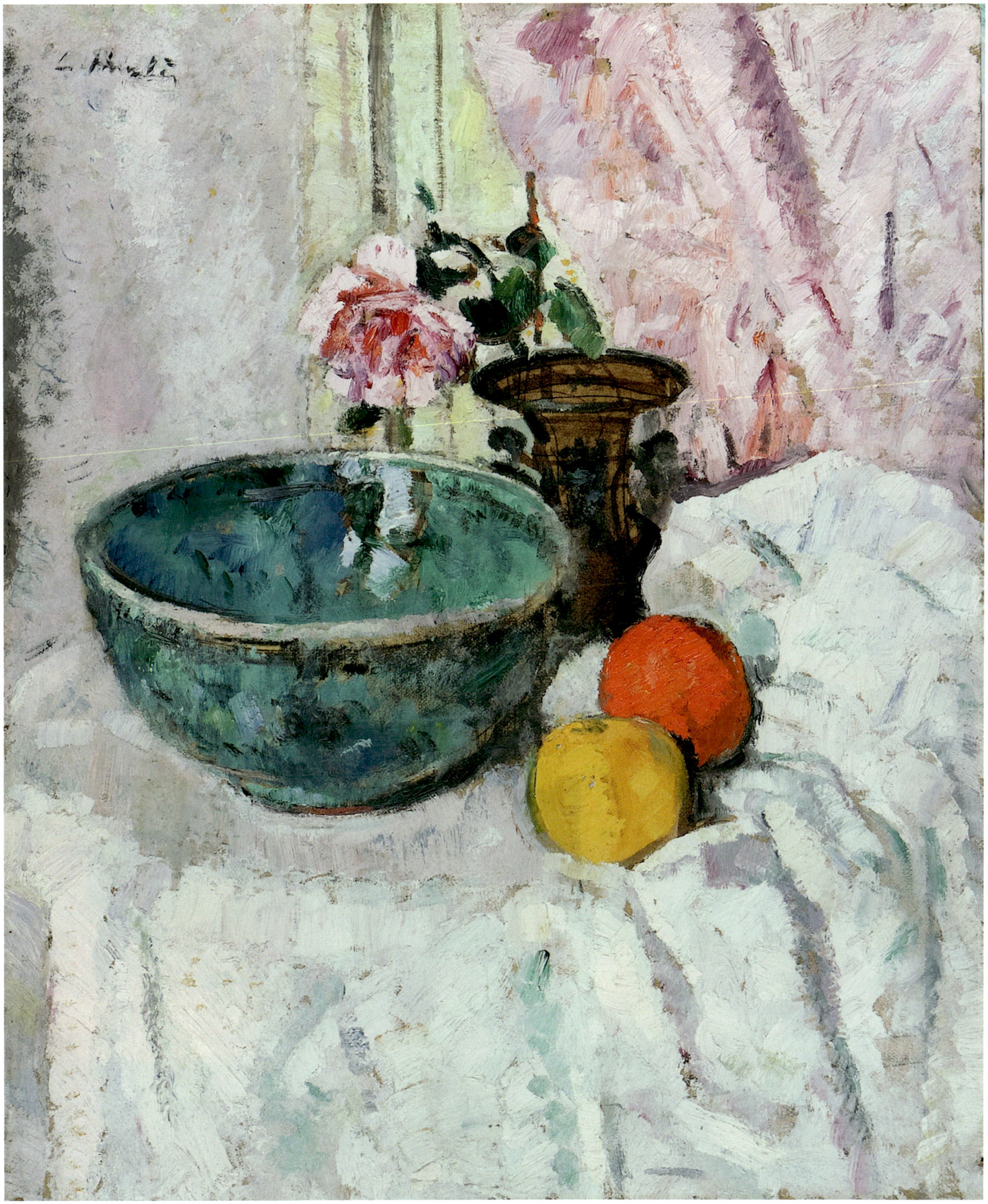

and how to express them in paint. Time fled. I left him buzzing over the problem as I had been in the train. I had to make my usual 'dash' to catch the 6-45 express with my usual fractional surplus of time.[44]

By the latter half of 1921 Hunter's painting was going from strength to strength. In common with a number of French and Scottish painters a certain oriental feel appears in some of his compositions, especially in still life. In a series of still lifes – see for example, *Still Life with Japanese Print* (pl.76) – he makes use of a thin, black-framed Japanese print against a white wall as a backdrop to the still life of fruit, flowers and objects. The paint is applied in flowing, textural sweeps, almost in a manner akin to Peploe's early work of *c.*1905. Hunter is silhouetting the foreground against the background to an extent, but he also reduces the still life shapes to bold statements of plain colour, producing a coherent and striking ensemble. The areas of strong colour, most notably found in the fruit, are very close in style to Cézanne's still lifes with fruit and flowers of circa 1886, attesting to the command Hunter now had in applying Cézanne's techniques as a core upon which he could build.

Silhouetting form against a light background again and displaying an almost oriental sense of decoration is evident too in *The Showcase* (pl.77). The vases, jars and bowl are arranged by shape – long, short or squat – on the various levels of the sideboard. Then to enliven a potentially static display, Hunter adorns the largest vase with a magnificent display of foliage and picks out accents of bright colour in the other vases. The piece of furniture is still in the possession of Hunter's family.

Hunter rarely dated his pictures, but *Still Life with Fruit and Fan* (1921, pl.78) is an exception. All Hunter's experimentation based on Cézanne's theory of colour and pure form comes to fruition in this painting. In his study of Cézanne's concepts and technique, Hunter had jotted in his notebook 'as for colour the more the colours harmonise, the more the design will take place itself'. By 1921 Hunter's highly developed instinct for pattern, form and colour enabled him in

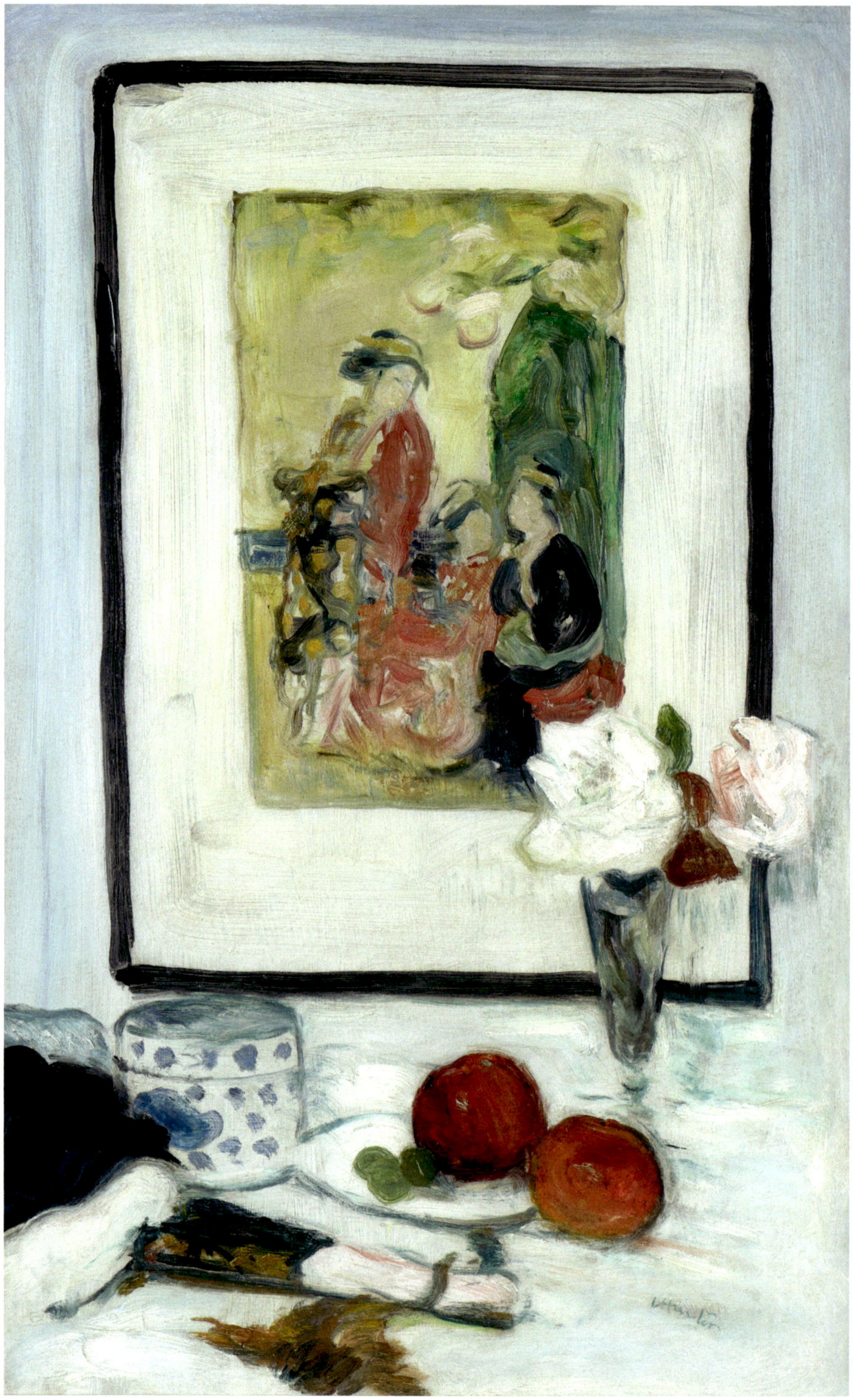

76 | Still Life with Japanese Print
Oil on panel, 1921–22
Private collection

77 | The Showcase
Oil on board, 1921–22
Scottish Gallery

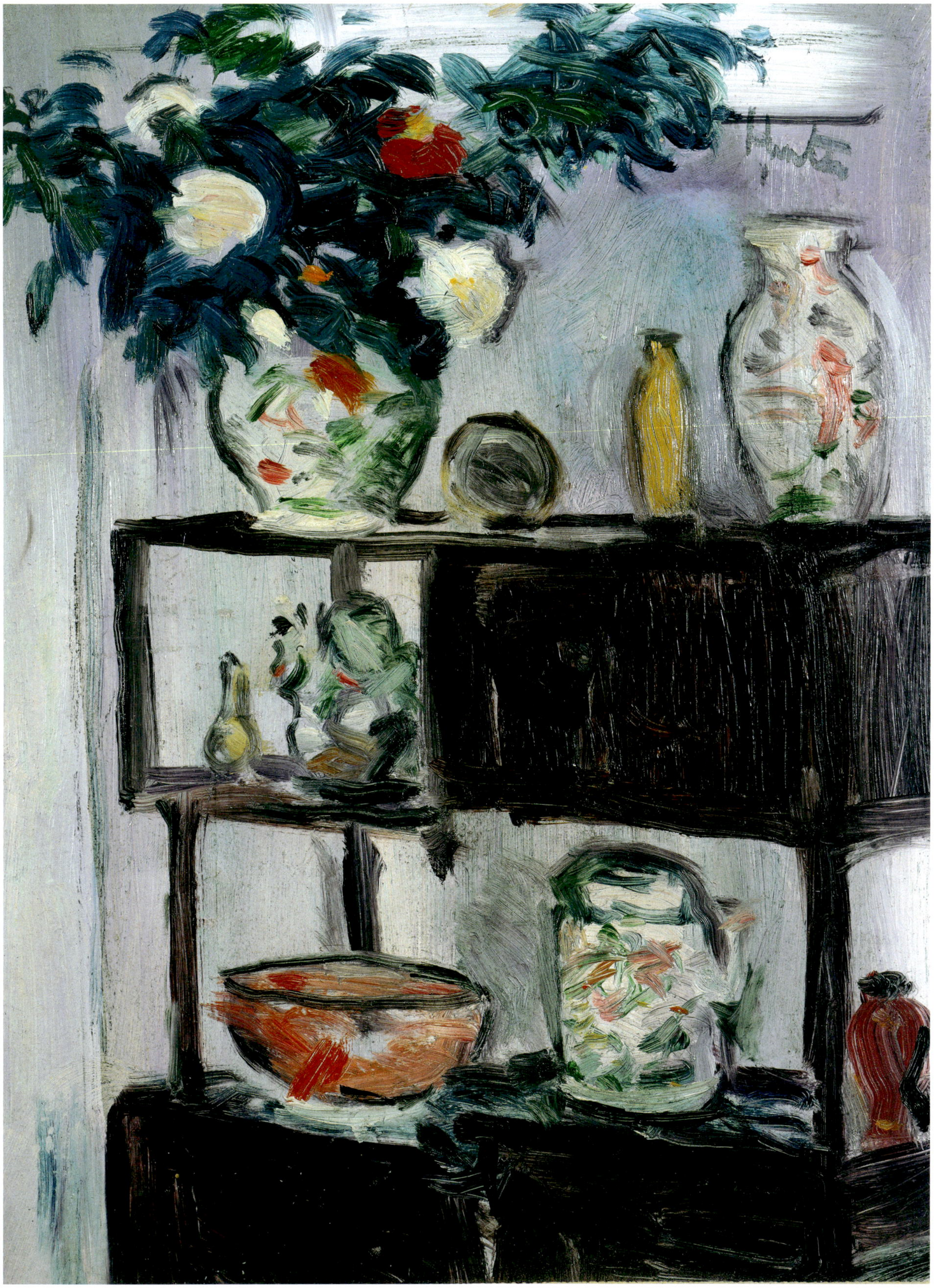

this instance to create a superb, harmonious and colourful still life from a variety of fruit, platters, glass and fan, which, were it not for his hard-won skill, could so easily have been a clumsy, cluttered array of miscellaneous objects. More to the point, the painting is in an advanced modern style rarely found in Scottish, or indeed British art of this date.

In November 1921 Hunter showed around thirty pictures, mainly Fife landscapes and still lifes, in Dundee with James Foggie of Thomas Murray & Son, fine art dealers and frame makers in the Nethergate. McNeill Reid, Hunter's dealer, had agreed to the exhibition on condition that Hunter paid him a commission of 10% on all sales.[45] The correspondent of the *Dundee Advertiser* was very supportive of the show, writing:

It is as a colourist that Mr Hunter is distinctive, and all his works show his exceptional talents in this direction. The artist has gone back to some of the old French masters, notably Cezanne, for his essentials – those schools which presented in paint the richness and vigour of a subject in its appeal for response from

78 | Still Life with Fruit and Fan
Oil on board, dated 1921
Private collection

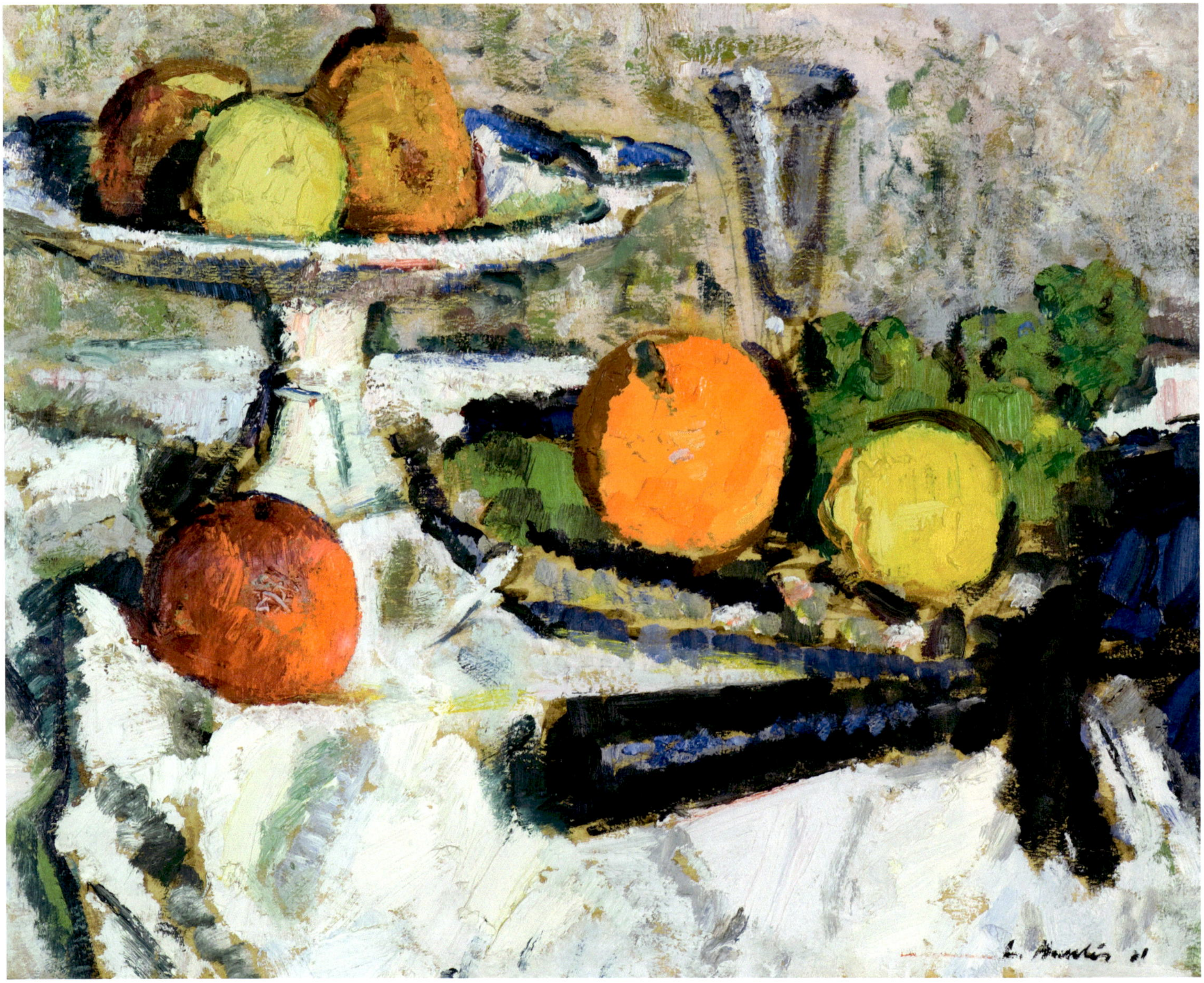

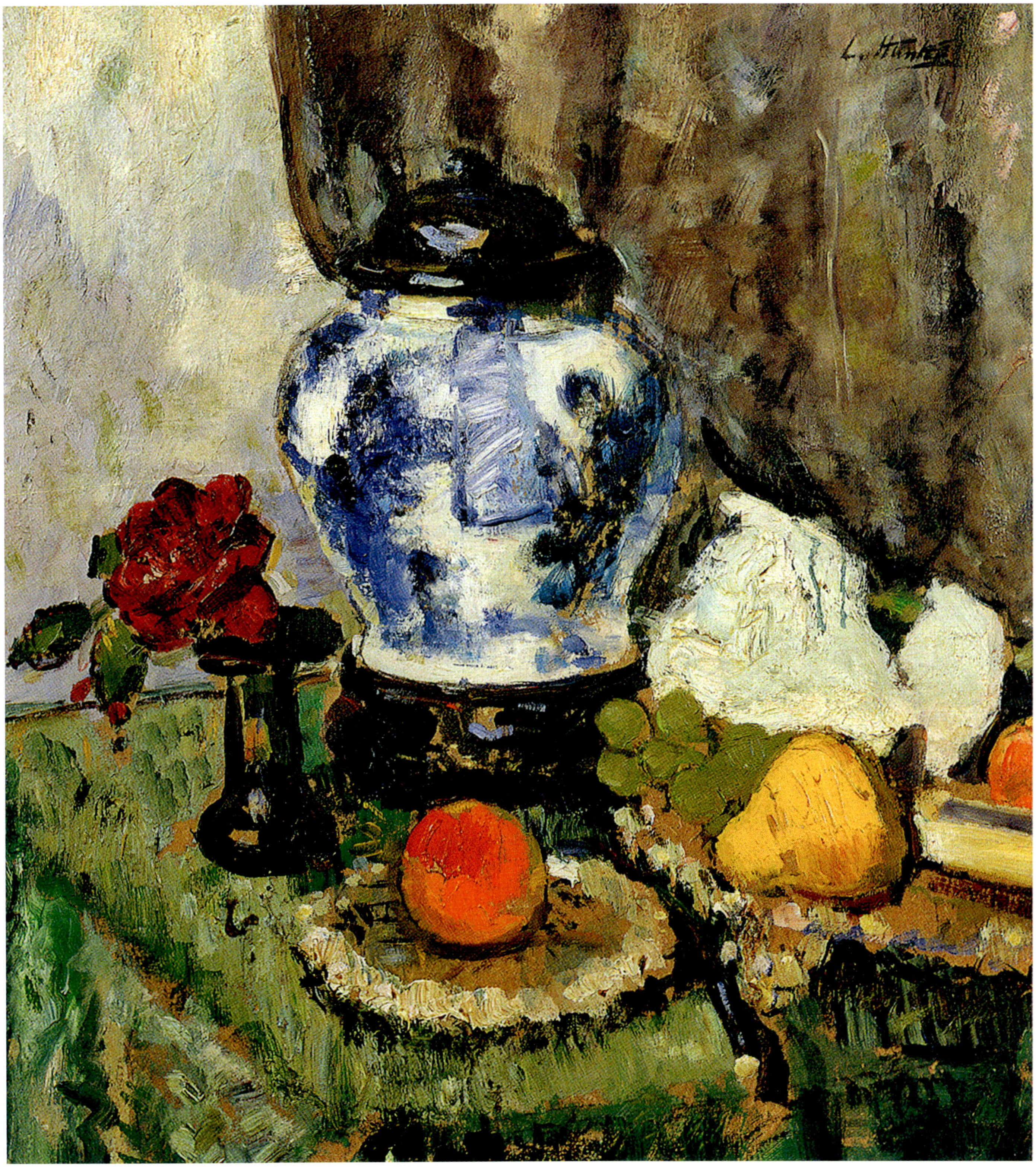

79 | Still Life with Blue and White Jar
Oil on canvas, 1921
Private collection

the senses ... The sincere lover of art will find in the exhibition much to interest and stimulate responsiveness in a phase of artistic development.[46]

Hunter had a good following in Dundee and the exhibition was reasonably successful, netting him £187.10/-.[47]

By 1922 Reid believed that Hunter's recent work outclassed his previous work. Hunter, however, was growing weary of the style he had developed and, following the critical success of his exhibition the previous year, felt that once again it was time to push forward. As if to underline a change in direction, early in 1922 he embarked on a series of still lifes based upon *Chrysanthemums* (1913; see pl.22), totally reworking the motif in his current style. However not all of the paintings are successful. He experimented with altering the main emphases within the composition. In turn he would concentrate on form or employ his silhouette theme. In the wonderful *Still Life with Chrysanthemums in a Chinese Vase* (pl.80), Hunter concentrates on texture, sensitively bringing out the beauty of the blooms. The dark background enhances the quiet mood of the painting and accentuates the glowing colour of the flowers and fruit. The picture captures the essence and polish of the original 1913 still life, but is on a totally different level. This still life series was possibly the last he painted for the next two years.

Hunter's eagerness to push forward proved to be his undoing. His head filled with ideas, he worked long and arduous hours. His physical and mental health began to suffer. Hunter's attempts to lift himself out of his depression, listlessness and increasing homesickness for his beloved California resulted in a decision to go to Europe.[48] By the beginning of March 1922 he was in Paris, his first visit since the beginning of the war. He writes to Justice:

... I have been making up for seven years absence, and am now 'full up' and anxious to get away South to work. I called on Epstein and saw the Matisse show. They seem to have sold very well.

I found the Louvre interesting as ever. The Camondo [Musée Nissim de Camondo], *of course, less so – the Cézanne still lifes Yes! Impressionist art seems so fleeting. To pass on to the wonderful Poussins – what a fillip to the spirit! This afternoon I visited B.* [Galerie Bernheim-Jeune] *and saw the Dufresnes. He is certainly a colourist ... I'll be glad when I am settled down to work and hope there will be no psychological disturbances. After dinner tonight I am going round to the 'Rotonde' where the crowd is, and imitations of recent 'Masters' on the walls. It is very amusing and not to be taken any more seriously than the pictures. I see the sickness in the art of today here in Paris. How sober the old men seem in comparison!!*[49]

Matisse had a thoroughly eclectic attitude towards art from foreign cultures. He freely

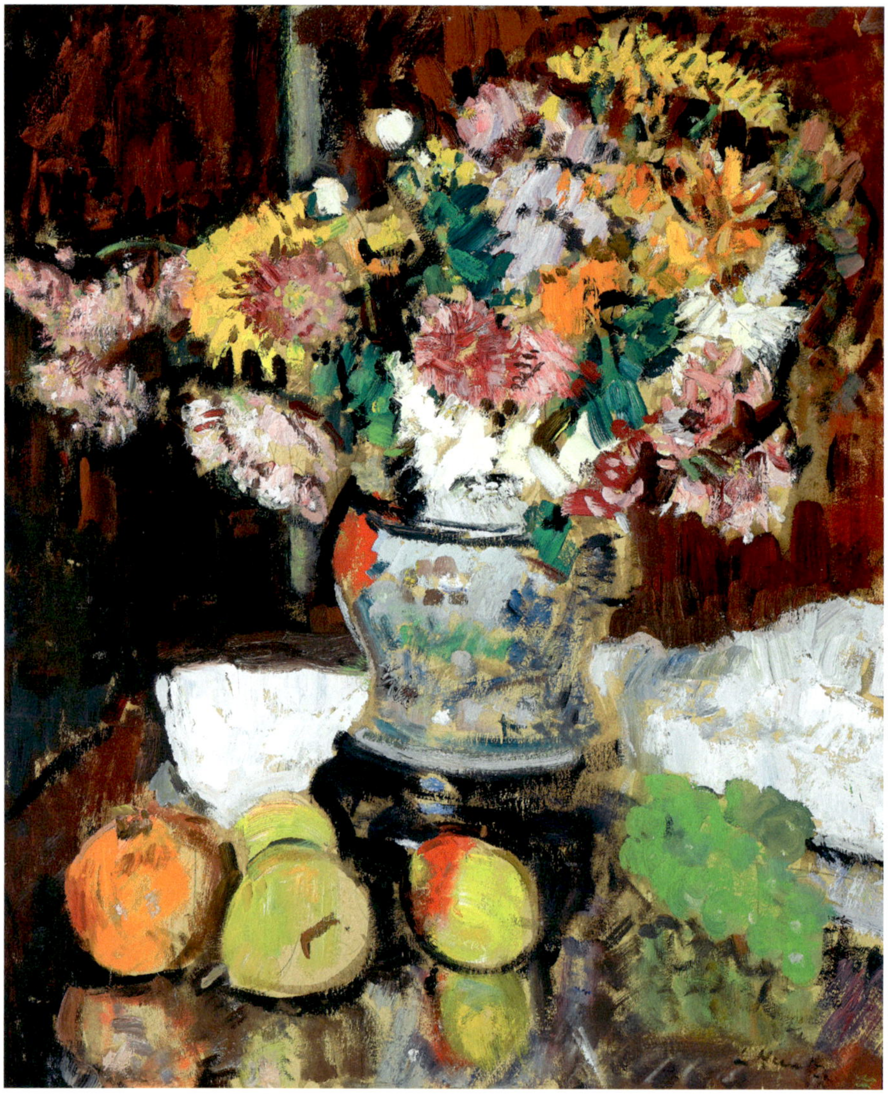

80 | Still Life with Chrysanthemums in a Chinese Vase
Oil on board, 1922
Private collection

81 | Interior of a French Church
Watercolour, *c.*1922
Private collection

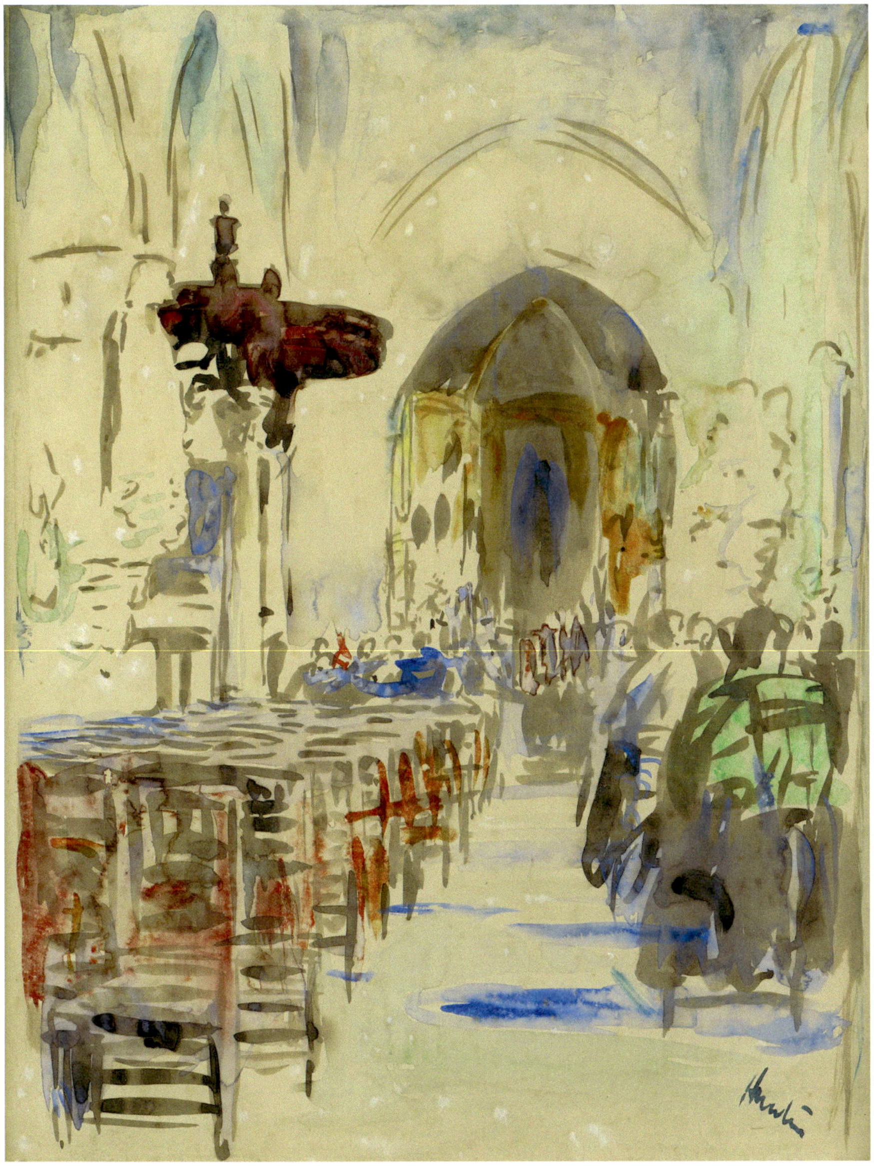

adapted techniques and motifs from Chinese, Japanese, Persian and North African art. Hunter always admired and responded to the decorative aspects of Oriental art. This was especially true of all things Chinese, an interest dating back to his early days in San Francisco. Hunter's still lifes frequently featured Oriental porcelain, such as the oft-used blue-white ginger jars and the Chinese ceramic jade bowl, which feature noticeably in his work of 1920–21. It is fair to say that over the years Hunter's interest in Oriental art ran parallel with that of Matisse. The impact of seeing Matisse's latest paintings set Hunter thinking. The means to move forward artistically was beginning to take shape in his mind. What he needed was time to formulate his ideas and to experiment, but that was impossible while he was travelling.

By the middle of April 1922 he was in Rome, and then moved on to Venice. Consequently he found himself unable to complete any pictures, executing only sketches. He wrote later: 'I know Reid pere liked my Venetian watercolours very much. They were, I thought, only rough notes, done in the fashion of my early work, done spontaneously and the only training I ever had.'[50] Honeyman relates that initially Hunter was attracted to Venice for its colour;[51] a typical example of his work, *A Canal in Venice* (pl.83), demonstrates clearly that his interest is in the patterns created by the facades and roofs of the buildings. Although no figures are present, the strong accents of colour in the trees and canal posts significantly animate this delightful scene.

Hunter did not confine his efforts to watercolour alone, but made a stunning series of small oil sketches of Venetian canal views. The spontaneity of the work is expertly captured in *Sails, Venice* (pl.85) and *Grand Canal, Venice* (pl.84) through strong, bright colour and lively brush-work. In some of his views of Venice Hunter reduces the forms to a minimum, preferring to accentuate them by leaving areas of panel bare, allowing charged brushstrokes to convey the thrill of the scene.

The Italian journey gave Hunter the opportunity to enjoy a different climate and landscape; he told Justice it 'fulfilled that vague nostalgia for California'.[52] But the visit to Paris left him feeling unsettled, as if his art was merely at the beginning of its development. Seeing Matisse's current work made Hunter more determined than ever to achieve a further breakthrough. The artistic advances Hunter had made between 1919 and 1922 came mainly through the combination of a deeper understanding of Cézanne's principles on colour and form and Hunter's increasing ability to put them into practice. He had moved on from simple colour blocks arranged across the canvas surface, creating form by skilfully manipulating pattern and colour. Now Hunter was convinced that the way forward could be found only through the 'modern' use of colour. With the enthusiastic encouragement he received from his Dundee and Glasgow friends, he could largely ignore the general disinterest of the Scottish art establishment. It certainly was not for lack of trying on the part of Hunter and his friends that the message had fallen on stony ground. If in certain quarters he was regarded with distaste and thought of as eccentric, then so be it. His time would come.

Hunter's talent lay in his extraordinary sensitivity to the moods of nature. The Fife landscape had brought out the best in him, allowing him to exploit its natural beauty in all seasons. The delights and rigours of the 1922 Italian visit had come to an end, leaving him anxious to return to Scotland and the Fife landscape, where he longed to experiment and develop his style further. The strength of Hunter's emotional attachment to Fife is touchingly revealed in a letter to Justice:

The 'valley' was very fine at night. When the sun was down one felt the elegiac spirit of Corot in the willows and that of quality men Poussin and Claude in the classical sweep of the hills. I was the sole spectator often in the twilight fragments that haunt – nature seen to unfold her rarest aspect – while Ceres slept.[53]

The remainder of the year was divided between painting in Fife and in his Glasgow studio at 104 West George Street, where he concentrated mainly on working up his landscapes. According to Honeyman, much of what he did dissatisfied him and he struggled to produce any important pictures to send over to Reid for sale. Apart from occasional visits to Dundee, Hunter

82 | St Mark's Square, Venice
Ink and wash, 1922
Private collection

83 | A Canal in Venice
Pen & ink and watercolour, 1922
Glasgow Museums

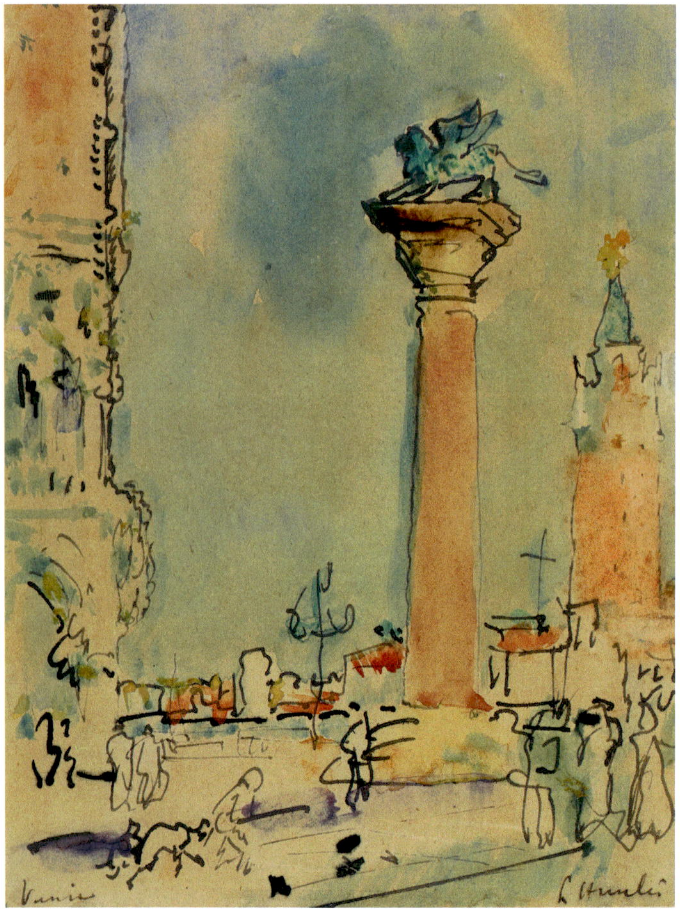

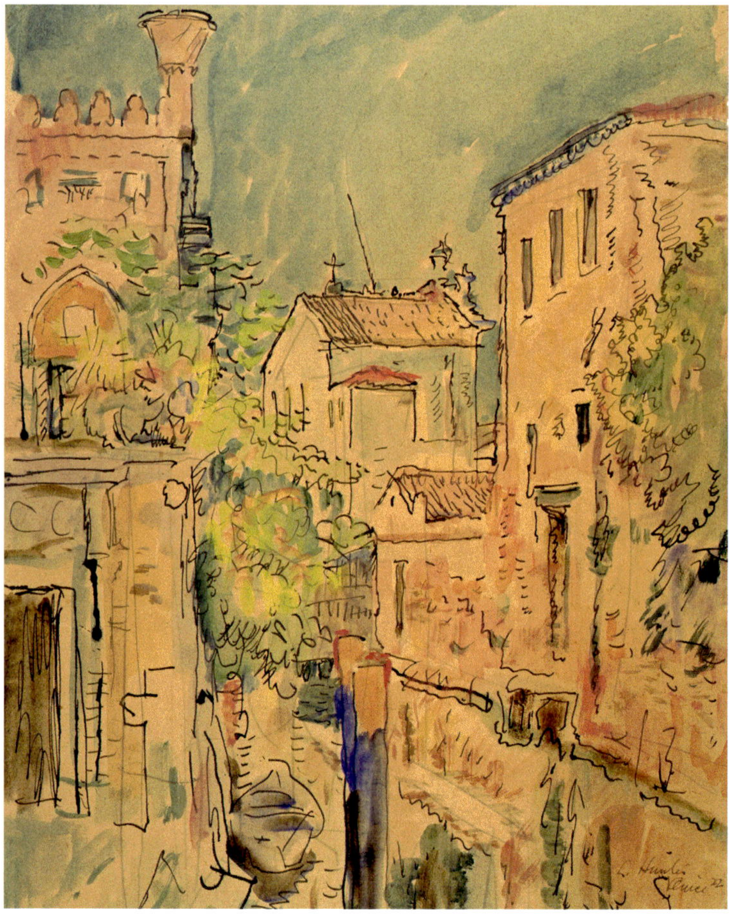

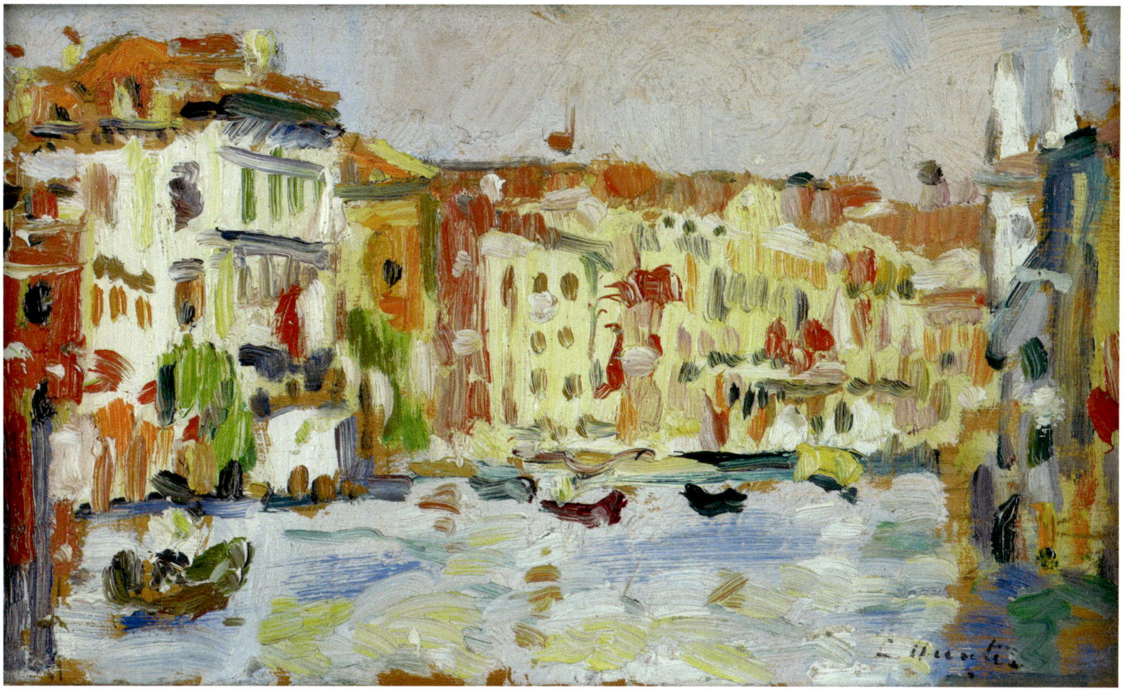

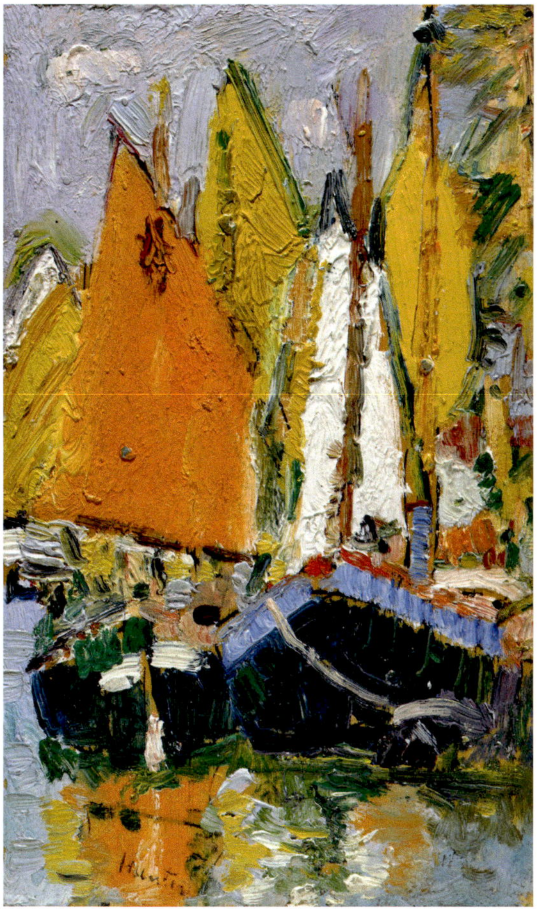

'cut himself adrift from social recreations, and seemed continually to be deeply occupied with problems which defied solution'.[54]

On the bright side, McNeill Reid had arranged Hunter's first showing in London for early 1923. It was to be a group exhibition of the work of Peploe, Cadell and Hunter at the Leicester Galleries. Hunter realised that he did not have the luxury of time to experiment. He had to produce a sufficient volume of work for the exhibition, which would tax his physical and mental resources to the full.

84 | Grand Canal, Venice
Oil on panel, 1922
Private collection

85 | Sails, Venice
Oil on panel, 1922
Glasgow Museums

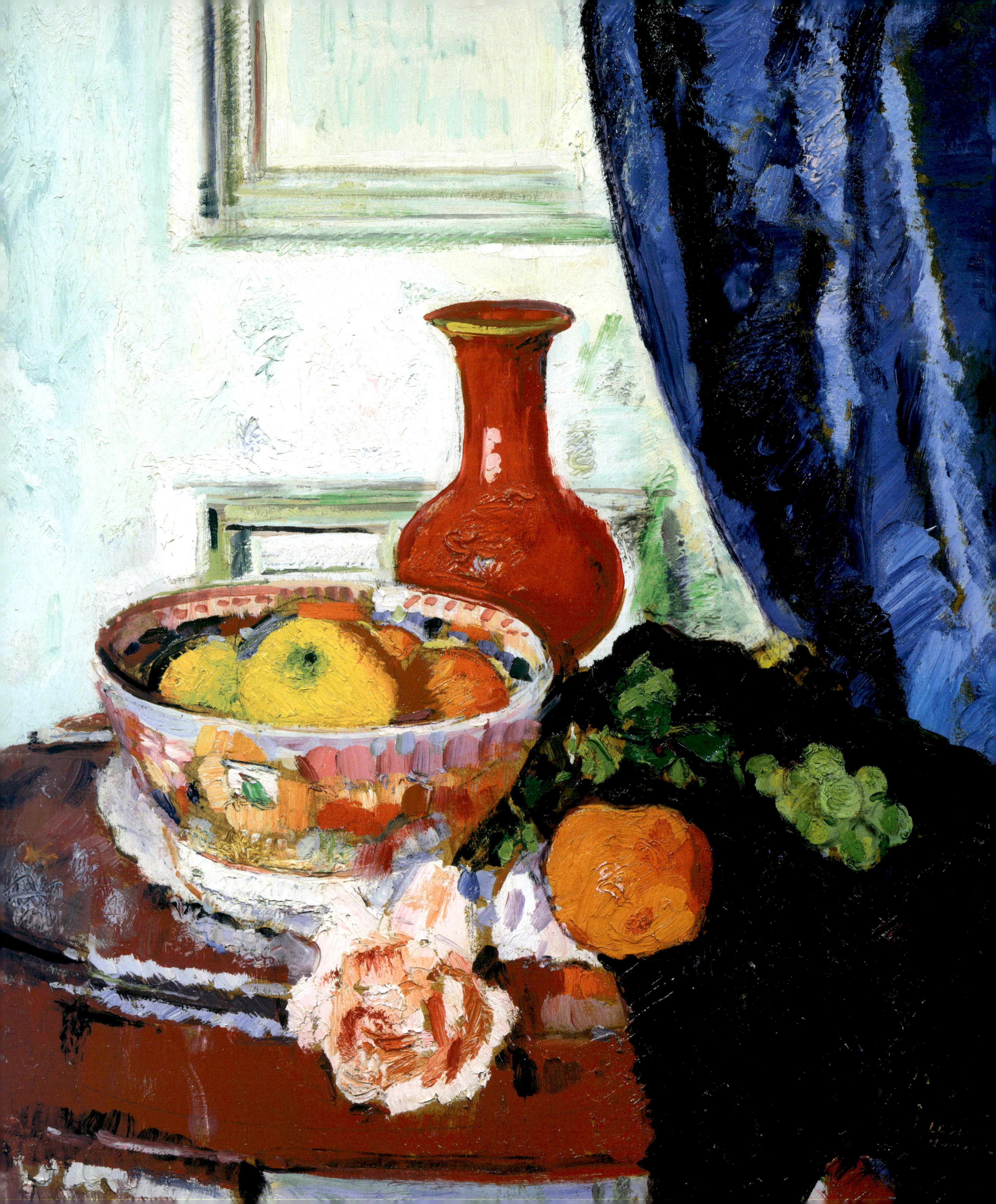

6 Struggle and Triumph

THE FIRST JOINT EXHIBITION by three of the four painters known today as *The Scottish Colourists* opened at the Leicester Galleries in London at the beginning of January 1923. However it would be another quarter of a century before that group name was used to describe all four artists together – Peploe, Fergusson, Hunter and Cadell – when only Fergusson was still alive. Of course the four never regarded themselves as a group. They were individuals, following separate careers and developing at different rates. It seems likely that Hunter did not meet any of the others until after the First World War, though, as mentioned in a previous chapter, he may have come across Fergusson in pre-war Paris, and he tried unsuccessfully to see Peploe when they both happened to be in the French capital just before the outbreak of war. The four artists never worked as a group, although occasionally they painted in pairs – for example, Peploe and Fergusson in Brittany in 1904 and Cadell and Peploe on Iona from 1920.

They had somewhat contrasting personalities: Peploe was shy and retiring; Cadell was an extrovert; Fergusson was very precise in his dress, his studio very clean and ordered; Hunter was the true Bohemian, the very antithesis of Fergusson. The Colourists had many similarities, however. All came from comfortable middle-class backgrounds. All were drawn to Paris, spending various periods in that city. All were attracted by the intense light of the south of France, returning there a number of times to paint. Above all, they were influenced in their work by the French Impressionists and Post-Impressionists – particularly Manet and Cézanne – and, with the exception of Cadell, by Matisse. It is fair to say that they all had a greater experience and understanding of what was happening in French painting in the first two decades or so of the twentieth century than did the vast majority of their counterparts in Scotland and England.

The exhibition at the Leicester Galleries was organized by McNeill Reid. The gallery was gaining an enviable reputation for its outstanding exhibitions of modern art. Reid felt that a show there would bring contemporary Scottish art before a much wider and, hopefully, appreciative audience, as well as raising the profile of the three artists back home in Scotland. None of the three had shown a body of work in London before. Hunter welcomed the initial approach from Reid, writing to him:

Thanks very much for your note of the 9th inst. à propos a proposed show in London with Peploe and Cadell. I am thinking over the matter favourably and will talk over matter and particulars in two or three days when I return.[1]

Hunter exhibited nineteen paintings, Peploe twenty-six and Cadell thirty.[2] Peploe received the most praise from the critics, and was described by *The Times* as 'the most learned' of the three. Cadell was criticized by *The Morning Post* for 'superficial cleverness'.[3] Hunter's pictures received a somewhat ambiguous reaction from *The Times*, the bewildered critic describing what he saw without perhaps having a full understanding of the work:

86 | The Red Vase
Oil on board, 1923–24
Private collection

Mr Hunter loves paint and the flatness of paint. He loads it on lusciously; yet his painting is not luscious in its effect. His still lifes are strong and simple in design and gorgeous in colour. Only his firm taste and his mastery of colour saved him from being blatant; but, missing that, he makes the heart glad, like wine.[4]

The *Glasgow Herald* was more responsive to Hunter's work:

While the art of Mr Cadell has much in common with that of Mr Peploe, Mr Leslie Hunter's pictures aim at something different from clarified emphasis on design and colour. Alike in his studies of the environs of Florence and in those of fruit and flowers he works with a fully loaded brush, and with a desire, it would seem, to empower his themes. Contours are all along the line broken up, and delicately rich colours used, though not always consistently or conclusively.[5]

The *Daily Mail's* critic best summed up the general consensus when he wrote that Hunter 'revels in beautiful colour. In structure he is not as firm.'[6]

It is uncertain whether or not the exhibition was a financial success for Hunter. Reid's Glasgow sales journal for 1920–1925 records the sale of two oils: *Still Life* for £55 and *Environs of Florence* for £30 (plus three works by Peploe and five by Cadell). If total sales were indeed only two, Hunter made little if anything from the exhibition, because Reid charged him £10.15/ – and £12.15/6 for insurance, packing and freight of his pictures to and from London respectively.[7]

Only a few weeks after the show at the Leicester Galleries closed, Alexander Reid held an exhibition in Glasgow of watercolours Hunter had executed in Italy the previous year. Hunter had enjoyed working in Italy, telling Justice in a somewhat rambling letter written early in 1923:

I was disappointed in Ceres this time [presumably autumn 1922]. *I found it did not suit my palette as Italy did* [spring 1922]. *Italy, too, fulfilled that vague nostalgia for California, that a trip out there might have cured. Florence is the hard difficult stuff. Venice is more superficial, water and buildings and shipping – studies of which the earthquake interrupted in San Francisco.*

Had I departed in November [1921], *I would have liked to have spent a few months in Paris drawing the figure. What I'll probably do* [in spring 1923] *will be to go over the ground I went last year, and make sure of a number of completed pictures. I would love to devote myself to line and form for a while. The instinct for the former is even rarer than that for colour …* [8]

The watercolour show was described by the *Glasgow Herald* as 'a small but striking collection of watercolour drawings of scenes in Venice and Florence'. The newspaper's critic continued:

The drawings, which for the most part show streets, canals, and buildings in Venice, are decoratively treated and brilliant in accomplishment, gladdening the eye, even if they do not always evoke intensity of emotion. Vivid colour is the keynote of most of the drawings, with a marked predominance of the warmer tones, and yet the colour is applied with due regard for the purity of the medium and always with exhilarating effect. Perhaps the most attractive drawings in the collection are those of Venetian canal scenes, in which there is much virility of vital colour and a sense of the brightness of light … The views of Florence are rendered in somewhat cooler tones, and are pleasing and satisfying. In all the drawings there is a commendable striving after harmonious unity, which is in a large measure achieved.[9]

Thus it was no surprise that six were sold almost immediately, including two to Leonard Gow, senior partner of Gow, Harrison, and two to William McInnes, also a partner in Gow, Harrison.[10]

Now Hunter was making plans to return to Italy. Reid had arranged another solo exhibition in Glasgow for December 1923, giving Hunter under eight months to put together a body of work worthy of him. A letter from Hunter to Justice reveals that his recent work was not giving him the pleasure painting normally did. Hunter writes:

Resilience is the great thing in painting. I feel I have been at the mercy of my temperament for two or three years, and too much inclined to take 'knockdowns' for 'knockouts'. A little success a few years ago gave me a great deal of enthusiasm, a little success again will do the same with wider facilities; meanwhile I hate this 'hugging' of colour. I feel it will be said yet that my sense of line (that supplement of form that the ancients all used) is greater than my sense of colour, and yet I've hardly used it.

... Meanwhile I am off to Italy. What I mean to get there this year is some determined studies and some finished pictures. I want a base, and mistrust being carried away too much with my feelings, for never in a landscape have I been 'si bien émotionné', yet this I take confidence from too.

Italian landscape appears to me the least local. I mean, the green there is the eternal Spring for all the world, and by the streams and the cascades in the early morning one could feel the spirit of Virgil. Noonday in the olive orchards or the unforgettable sky of the evening I left! My early studies seemed to help me there – a lovelier California embalmed in a thousand years of art.[11]

Hunter's expectations for his second trip to Italy were high. After a brief visit to Paris, accompanied by his Dundee friend, Tattersall, he arrived in Italy. On parting in Paris his friend had been worried about Hunter's health. However Hunter wrote a long letter to him from Italy, revealing his astonishing ability to revitalise his view of the world with an optimism that confounded the true state of his physical well-being. The letter, which is worth quoting in full, not only reveals Hunter's intense feeling for his surroundings, but his interest and genuine delight in all that is going on around him:

Dear Mr. T.,

This is Sunday night, and I am all out of writing paper. My friend has gone to Rome for ten days, so I am working here alone. I should have answered your letter sooner, but what with surveying the wonders of the galleries and the wonders of the landscape hereabouts, I am usually tired enough to go early to bed.

It is difficult in the small compass of a letter to write of a new country one is travelling in and living in. I am beginning to get used to things and like it here on the whole very much.

Florence is in itself a wonderful city – the city itself with all its places of interest would take weeks to see and one could spend months in the galleries, where there are some truly marvellous things, especially by the great Italians, Florentines and Venetians. One has to come to Italy to see how great they are. Then there are the great frescoes in the churches. I can assure you their greatness simply stuns one. Settignano is about three and a half miles from Florence, so I have been glad to have intervals of nature gazing after regarding these marvels of the mind. It reminds me very much of California here and I feel at home somehow among the olive trees and the orchards more so perhaps even than my friend who was from the north, but who otherwise speaking Italian has made himself quite at home with the people.

Last Sunday for instance we were at a village fete. It was a lovely day. A nut and wine festival on the slope of a hill overlooking a great historical valley. My friend knew a farmer who regaled us with some good wine. The Tuscan architecture is so very beautiful and the farms too are striking. This one was of the fourteenth century.

Everywhere one is reminded of the great paintings of Poussin and Claude. It is all so far removed from what is modern, northern and commercial. The difficulty in so much is to get settled down to work, but I have been busy with drawings and have started a few things. It is very interesting to be here with my friend with whom I have so many old associations. Today another sculptor from San Francisco was over here with his wife. We visited the villa of Stein [Leo Stein, brother of Gertrude Stein]*, who had a famous collection of Matisse in Paris years ago. He was one of the first to buy Cézanne. He has a collection of very fine earlier drawings by Picasso. They are truly beautiful, finer much than Segonzac, but the collection of drawings by Matisse are N.D.G. – that's my final opinion of them. It seems with him Rubens now is the dernier cri and Renoir his follower the man of the present and future. I see Stein often. There are a number of Swedish painters here. I have met one or two of them but have not seen their work and believe they are all quite modern.*

We had very fine weather the first week but this last has been full of storm and rain. There have been wonderful skies but now showers have been too frequent to get on with what I had started. There has been a drought for months so the farmers welcome the rain but I hope it will not spoil the blossoms that are out in the hillsides peeping through the sombre olive trees.

Berenson [Berenson] *the great critic has a villa near here.*

I find my friend besides having the most amiable personal qualities has the broadest appreciation possible on art and nature alike so that it is a pleasure to go to see anything with him. He paints not badly and has made immense strides in his sculpture though is modesty itself.

We hope to proceed to Venice about the second week of April. There I hope to get some 'water' pictures for here we rest on a hill and this landscape is therefore dry.

I was mighty glad McInnes did not get the Cézanne. When I saw it in daylight I had not much enthusiasm. The Daumiers were very fine. McInnes would be better with a good Renoir than a second rate Cézanne. Renoir's youngest son comes of age soon, Stein tells me, and there will likely be a great sale of his pictures.

I doubt if I will go to Provence this season … if I do not go to Venice I may see more in Paris on my return. I may discover ground of my own here and think it best only to make plans as I go along.

I hope things are beginning to revive a bit in the north. Mr Justice in his last letter seemed to think that they were. It seems difficult to think of business here. I saw two women and one man dragging a plough, one man holding it but mostly it is sleek white oxen that shove up and down the furrows leisurely and they all fit in their landscape.

Well I hope this finds you and Mr Justice in good health and spirits. With kind regards to you all.
I remain yours sincerely, Leslie Hunter

P.S. It's cold enough for a coal fire here today.[12]

The friend to whom Hunter refers is the sculptor, Ralph Stackpole. The two knew each other in California and subsequently had gone round Paris and the north of France together in 1907 or '08. It highlights the interesting point that Hunter frequently preferred the company of Americans when he was abroad. The reason for this is probably that Americans in general had a far more relaxed attitude to life and Hunter had always been more comfortable with this than the relative formality of the British abroad.

According to Honeyman, the Italian visit lasted about five weeks and produced little of value in the way of pictures.[13] Hunter's run-down physical state eventually conspired with his self-imposed pressure to 'make sure of a number of completed pictures', driving him to a nervous breakdown, which forced him to return to Glasgow and the loving care of his sister. With hindsight the causes of the breakdown become clear. In a letter to Justice written from the refuge of his sister's home, Hunter states:

I should have taken a rest before leaving this country and made the mistake of thinking I could find rest and change in Paris before passing to Italy. I have probably been taking too much out of myself.

My friends, it seems, have thought I was too preoccupied with my work and too little with life in its other phases, with athletics and women and children, and human beings in the usual run of things. These things, however, holding in my own mind's eye such a normal and healthy position, I felt like pushing on with all my energy to a more definite point in my work and then returning as rapidly as possible to these other necessities and advantages. I felt strong enough and sane and healthy enough to go on through the last six months. I have, indeed, felt at times fatigued.

But one can't, can't fight long against a consensus of opinion and when it was backed by medical opinion of a high order I collapsed and came back here to recuperate.

I saw the Independents in Paris and was not at all impressed. The new school does not paint from nature, and there were things in consequence fearfully and wonderfully made.[14]

Back in Scotland Hunter had regained his strength by identifying the causes of his breakdown and soon, as his letter indicates, he was back making plans and discussing modern art. His comments on contemporary French art are interesting, for they define more clearly Hunter's philosophy when it comes to his art. He firmly

87 | Anemones
Oil on board, 1925–26
Aberdeen Art Gallery and Museums Collections

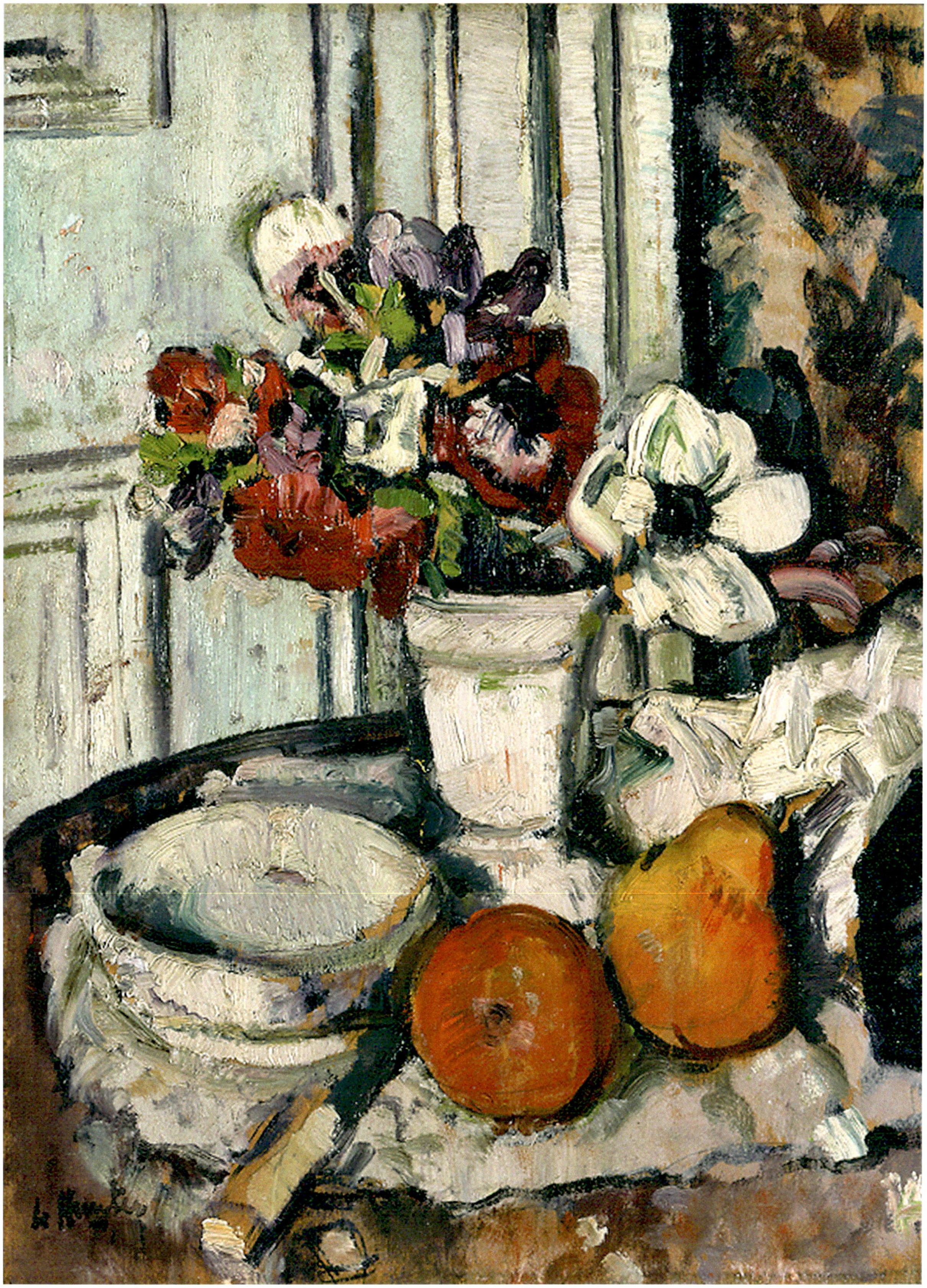

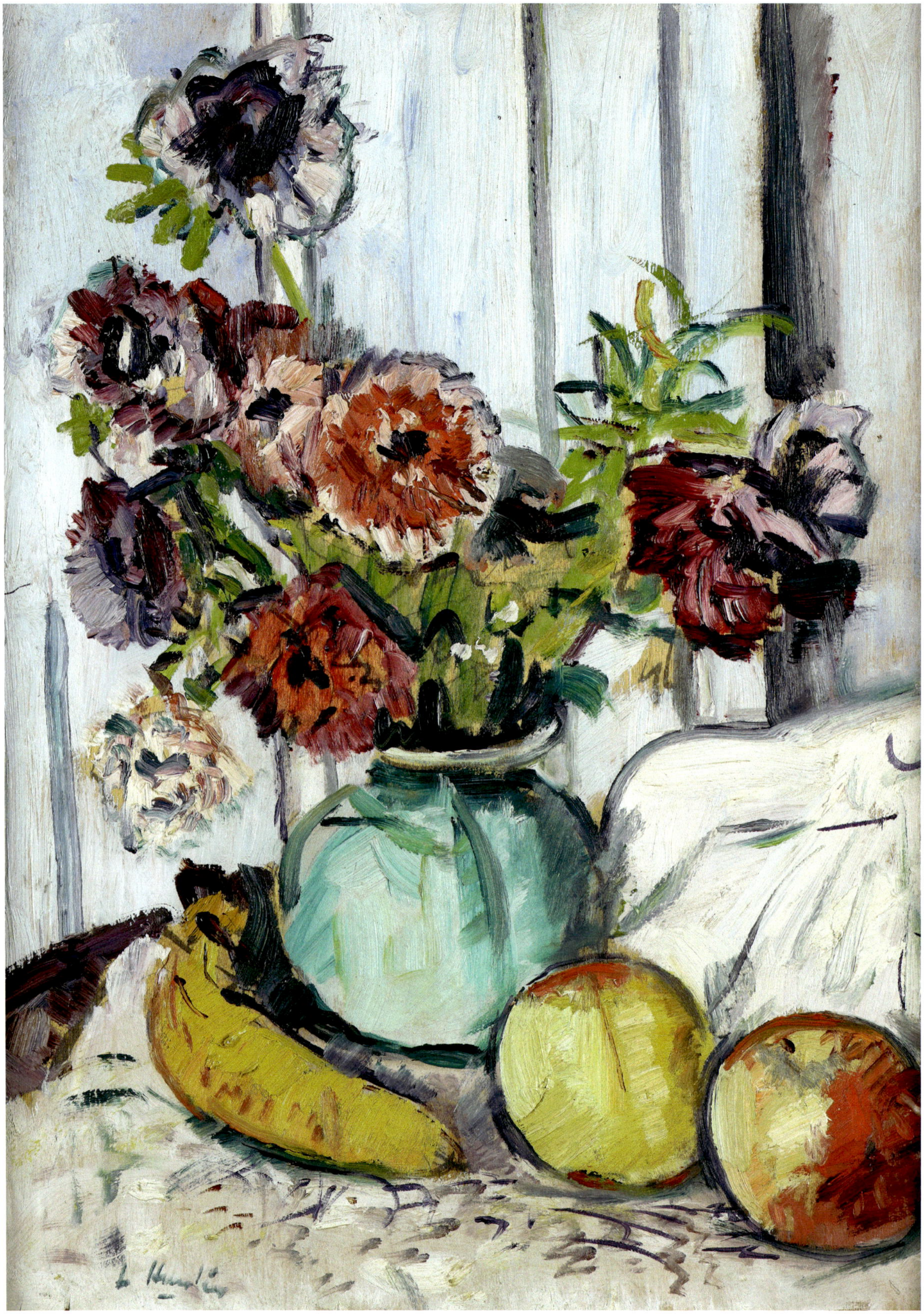

believed that Nature should be at the very heart of modern art; he never wavered from this standpoint. What he had seen in Paris were the extremes to which certain painters were willing to go in their art.

Following the exciting and almost abstract work of the Fauves with distortions, flat patterns and violent colour, and the Cubists with complex breakdown of volumes and spatial inter-relations, post-war French painting in general was returning – perhaps retreating – to a more realistic basis. For artists such as André Derain, Georges Braque, Marie Laurencin, Dunoyer de Segonzac and André L'Hote, such a tendency did not lead necessarily to the surrender of Fauve or Cubist techniques. It was more a case of returning to Cézanne's insistence of Nature as the base from which creative art springs. Fauve or Cubist forms could be relied on as a style, but in terms of inspiration and content only the direct study of Nature could provide that. Of course the opposite side of the coin was provided by artists such as Fernand Léger and Robert Delaunay. Their interest in mechanical and industrial constructions and geometry produced an art glorifying the energy of the material world, and in Leger's case turning them into monumental emblems. One can understand Hunter feeling that by not painting directly from Nature the pictures were 'in consequence fearfully and wonderfully made'.

88 | Anemones in a Green Vase, Banana and Two Apples
Oil on panel, 1925–26
Private collection

Given the general development of French art between the wars, it is perhaps more obvious why Hunter found the work of Matisse to be so exceptional. Matisse was very much his own man, constantly building upon what he had learned from Cézanne. However it was the way in which Matisse rendered colour that struck a note in Hunter's heart. The warm and intense emotional stimulation engendered by the series of still lifes and figures by a window executed by Matisse in the 1920s appealed strongly to Hunter.

One of the highlights of the artistic year in Glasgow in 1923 was the outstanding exhibition of French paintings organised by Alexander Reid in conjunction with the London art dealers, Thomas Agnew & Sons. There were twenty works in all: five by Manet, four by Renoir, three by both Cézanne and Degas, two by Sisley and one each by Courbet, Couture and Monet. Amazingly Reid managed to persuade the civic authorities to show them at Kelvingrove Art Gallery, a triumph for him considering it was a selling exhibition. By then Hunter was back on form, commenting on the exhibition:

Impressionist work for the most part now somewhat fails to satisfy. I liked the Renoir woman. The Manet still life did not seem to me so infinitely finer than some of the things I used to do. The show certainly makes the other 'modern' things in the gallery look like muck and tripe.[15]

Hunter spent the summer and autumn of that year chiefly in Fife, where he concentrated on landscape. His principal concern was to have sufficient paintings ready for his solo show at Reid's Glasgow gallery in December. There was renewed pressure on him to produce pictures in quantity. Hunter continued to work hard, but he was not prepared to compromise on quality. His trusted 'advisory board of selectors', consisting principally of Justice, Tattersall and McInnes, became invaluable as he battled on.

The exhibition was a resounding success. Hunter showed about forty paintings – still lifes, landscapes, seascapes and harbour scenes – though it seems unlikely that they were all new work; several may have come from Reid's existing stock. Many of the paintings were sold before the exhibition opened officially.[16] In financial terms the exhibition must have pleased both Reid and Hunter. Twenty-three oils, two watercolours and four drawings were sold in little over a month, the top price of £50 being paid by Hunter's friend, William McInnes, for *A Cornfield in Fife*.[17]

The *Glasgow Herald* told its readers that the show 'should not be missed … nothing so important by him has been seen for several years'. The newspaper's critic continued:

The old idea that a picture should be 'restful' and charged with repose does not appeal to Mr. Hunter and he never falls into a groove in his vigorous presentation of the beautiful in Nature. On the contrary his works act as stimulants, stirring one into thought.

... It is undoubtedly as a colourist that Mr. Hunter has attained a distinctive and recognised position among the younger generation of artists ... He paints with an opulent palette and is ever reaching after a fuller and more prismatic range of colour harmonies. This tendency is seen in an admirably rendered still life, showing a dish of fruit set in front of a richly designed Persian curtain and there is perhaps nothing more vital, more beautiful or more harmonious in the gallery than this painting. In this and some other works the artist – while his style is his own – appears to have gone back to the Old Masters for essentials and especially to Tintoretto, who was considered by Ruskin as the world's greatest artist.

... Mr. Hunter's drawings also display in a marked degree the qualities of vitality and strength combined with the vigorous presentation of essential details.[18]

The critic's comment about Tintoretto and Ruskin is at first sight somewhat curious. At that time Hunter was interested in John Ruskin, the art critic and so-called arbiter of late Victorian taste, as he told Justice in a letter:

I'm reading Ruskin! Lately I've been letting myself become much absorbed in Turgenev and Flaubert. Their marvellous insight into modern psychology stuns me, but alas, their morbidity depresses. The picture art is simpler, gives more and demands less than literature. One does not have to recall the beginning or 'wait' for the end. But these long nights one must pass somehow and I read. So I'm risking Ruskin![19]

Although the sixteenth-century Venetian painter was noted for his colour, one can see little connection between Tintoretto and Hunter's still life. Possibly the *Herald's* critic picked up on Hunter's views on Ruskin and felt it would lend some weight to Hunter's standing by drawing, somewhat erroneously, a comparison.

The year 1923 was one of mixed fortunes for Hunter. His breakdown while in Italy was serious and highlighted a fragile physical and mental state, brought about in part by his bohemian lifestyle and his disregard for anything but his painting. His health would remain a great worry for his friends right up to his death in 1931. On a positive note, he had exhibited in London for the first time, alongside Peploe and Cadell. His exhibition of watercolours in Glasgow had met with an enthusiastic reception. The high spot of the year, however, was the very successful exhibition at Reid's gallery in Glasgow. Hunter must have felt that at last he was being taken seriously.

By this time Hunter had re-focused his attention on still life, executing a series of paintings featuring a darker background than usual and incorporating a richly designed Persian curtain. The use of the Persian curtain as a principal element in his still life, along with the introduction of a panelled door, was to fascinate Hunter for several years to come. This can be viewed as the beginning of Hunter's response to Matisse's decorative interiors and still lifes of the early 1920s.

89 | Still Life with Roses and Fruit
Oil on board, 1924–25
Private collection

Hunter had reached a point whereby colour, form and harmony were instinctively assured, allowing him to experiment with a variety of features as integral parts of a stronger design. Of course not all this change can be attributed to Matisse. Indeed the root of this transformation lies more fully in Hunter's extensive knowledge of Cézanne's *oeuvre*. The late still life paintings of Cézanne frequently include a floral-patterned curtain that drops behind a table, acting as a distinctive colour field with which other distinctly-coloured areas of the composition can interact. One of the most stunning examples of this is Cézanne's *Chrysanthemums* [Barnes Collection, Pennsylvania].

When works such as *The Red Vase* (pl.86) are compared with Hunter's still lifes of 1921 and '22, a marked difference in approach can be detected. The combined effect of the form and grouping of the central still life elements has a wonderful sculptural quality, while the colours almost vibrate with energy. This new emphasis is borne out by his stated intention in early 1923 to devote himself to line and form.

Other late-1923 still lifes also demonstrate a response to Matisse's decorative interiors and

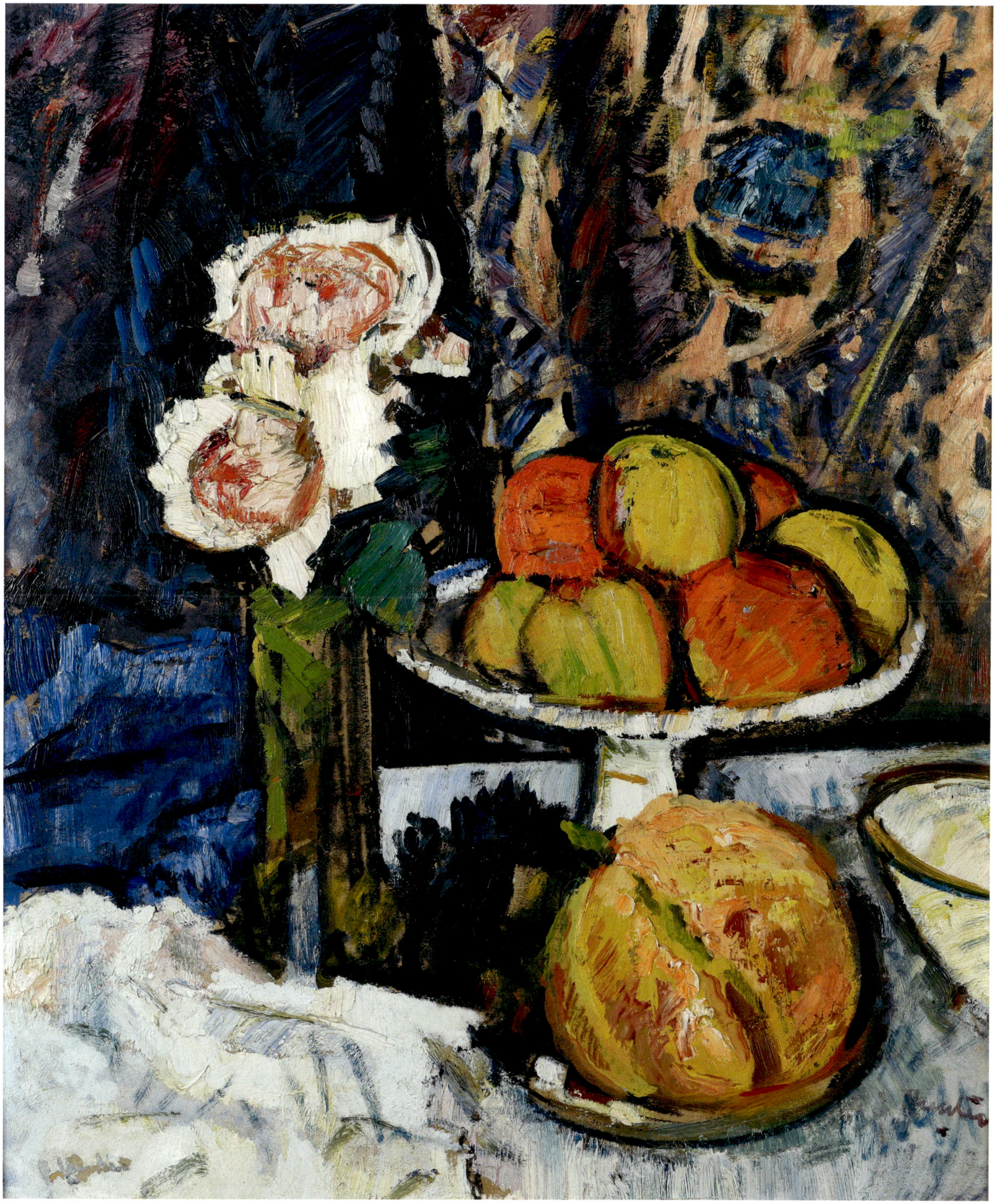

still lifes of the early 1920s. In *Still Life with Blue Glazed China Vase* (pl.90) Hunter has expertly combined colour, form and design to achieve a stunning overall harmony and vitality. He has injected solid notes of strong colour in the fruit, book and cloth and juxtaposed a richly-textured table covering and Persian curtain to striking effect. What is apparent now in his still life is his treatment of the whole picture surface as a coherent, balanced entity in itself, coupled with exquisite individual passages of paint.

In the same manner Hunter's search for line and form finds wonderful and harmonious expression in his Fife landscapes. He captures the essence of late summer scenes in well-balanced, coherent compositions that command attention. The exciting immediacy of his emotional response to Nature is found in *Cornfield, Drumeldrie* (pl.91). The contrast between the radiant, sunny, ripened corn and the timeless backdrop of a red-roofed cottage nestling amid mature trees at the foot of a hill excites the senses. Justice gives a rare insight into Hunter's *modus operandi* when describing one of his visits to Hunter at Largo in October 1923:

Along with Roland I went over to Largo today, and on calling at the house Hunter was staying at I found he was out painting. Fortunately he had left this plan of the route and I got him in about half-an-hour's time [at Drumeldrie]. *The farmer was clearing the cornfield of the stooks and he* [Hunter] *was anxious to get his picture completed before the stooks were removed. It is a fine picture, full of fine form and the true spirit of Scottish landscape.*[20]

Although the visit was pre-arranged, Hunter felt unable to wait for Justice, so he left him a map of where he would be painting. Hunter's urge to complete the picture before the stooks were removed, suggests that such was the appeal of the scene before him it was of great importance to capture the essence of the moment, rather than rely on memory.

The control Hunter had gained through his sense of line enabled him to create a feeling of timelessness. In *Ceres, Fife* (pl.92) his sense of line competes with a generally flatter perspective, indicating how his tentative response to Matisse reveals itself in subtle ways. The *Glasgow Herald's* critic admirably summed up the Fife landscapes in Reid's December show, writing: '[they] are delightfully rendered with the fullest resource of the palette, express the generous bounty of nature and the effect of all pervading sunlight'.[21]

Hunter should have been well pleased with the positive response, reflected both in critical acclaim and financial terms. During the first half of 1924, however, he was still preoccupied with the interminable battle between his sense of colour to create form and colour as an organizing principle in design. Looming

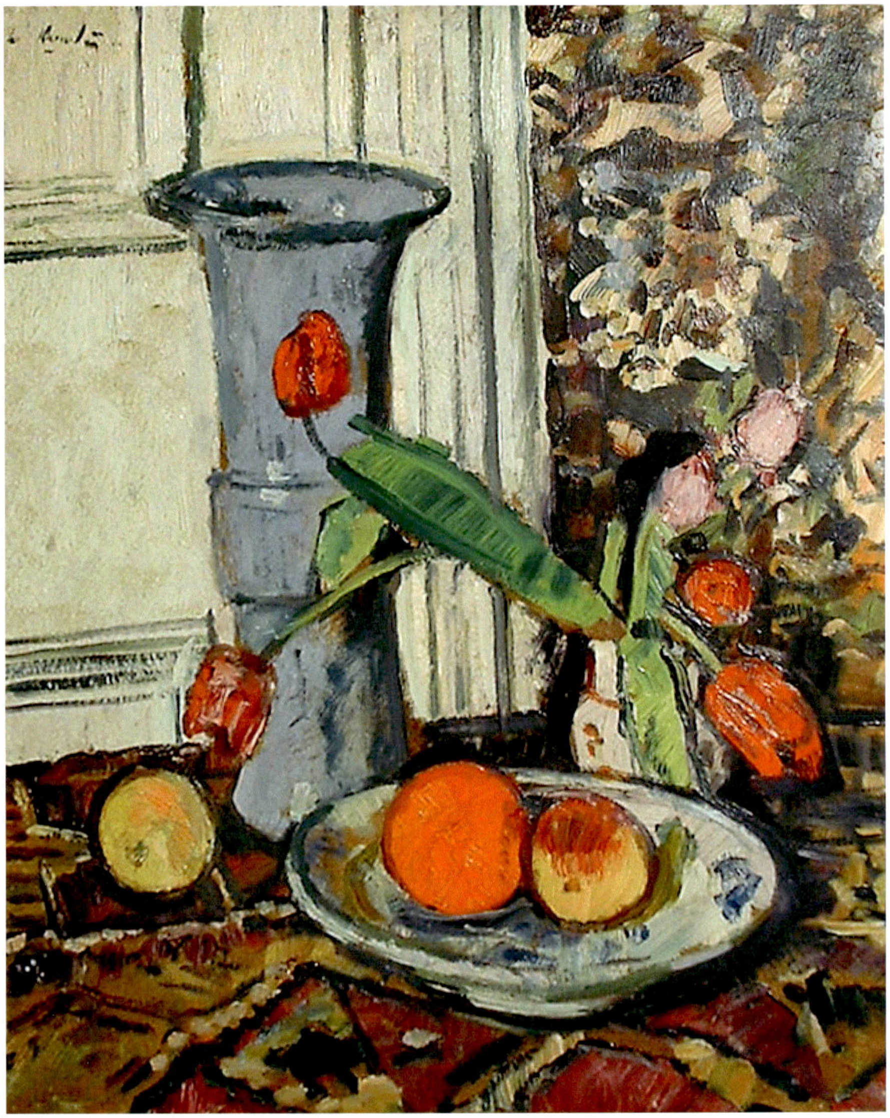

90 | Still Life with Blue Glazed China Vase
Oil on board, 1923
The University of Edinburgh Fine Art Collection

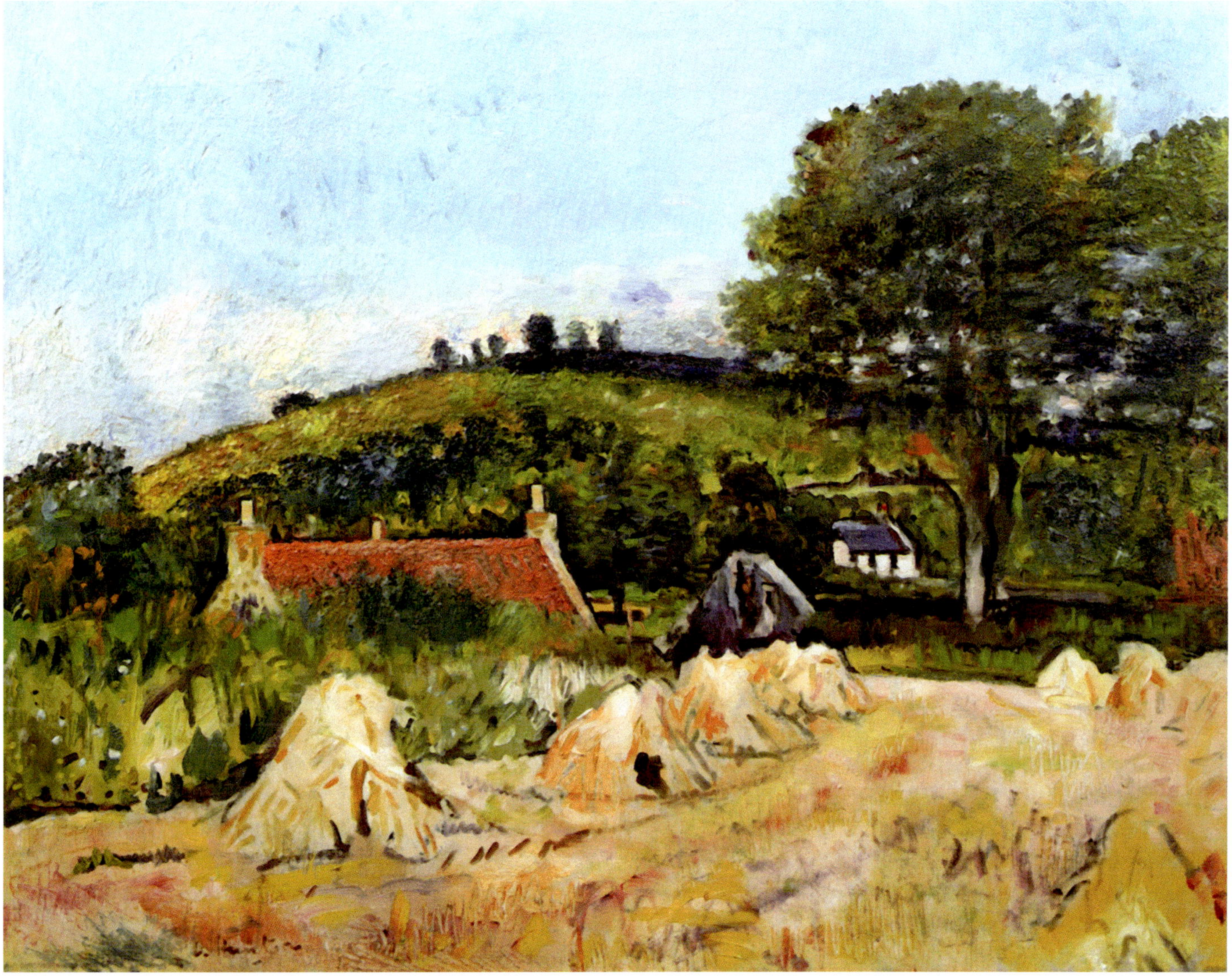

91 | Cornfield, Drumeldrie
Oil on canvas, 1923–24
Private collection

on the horizon were commitments to a solo exhibition in March with the Edinburgh art dealer, Aitken Dott, and in June an important group exhibition organised by McNeill Reid at the Galerie Brabazanges in Paris of work by Peploe, Fergusson, Hunter and Cadell, the four colourist painters selected to represent the modern movement in Scotland. It seems likely that the Paris exhibition was organised in conjunction with the Parisian art dealer, Etienne Bignou, who later played a crucial role in the international development of Reid & Lefevre in London. In a letter to Justice, Hunter remarks 'Bignou told McNeill he thought Matisse the only man in Paris the equal of Peploe and myself.[22] Egotistical though that may seem, it is indicative of how highly thought-of Peploe and Hunter were in certain circles at the time.

Hunter continued working hard to produce sufficient work for both Edinburgh and Paris. In total contrast to Peploe and Cadell, who never worked over the dull winter months, Hunter's compulsion to paint meant that he was incapable of putting down his brush even for a short period of time. He was well aware of being one of the few artists who did paint over the winter; the short, dank days, and the consequent lack of light, sorely taxed his patience. With

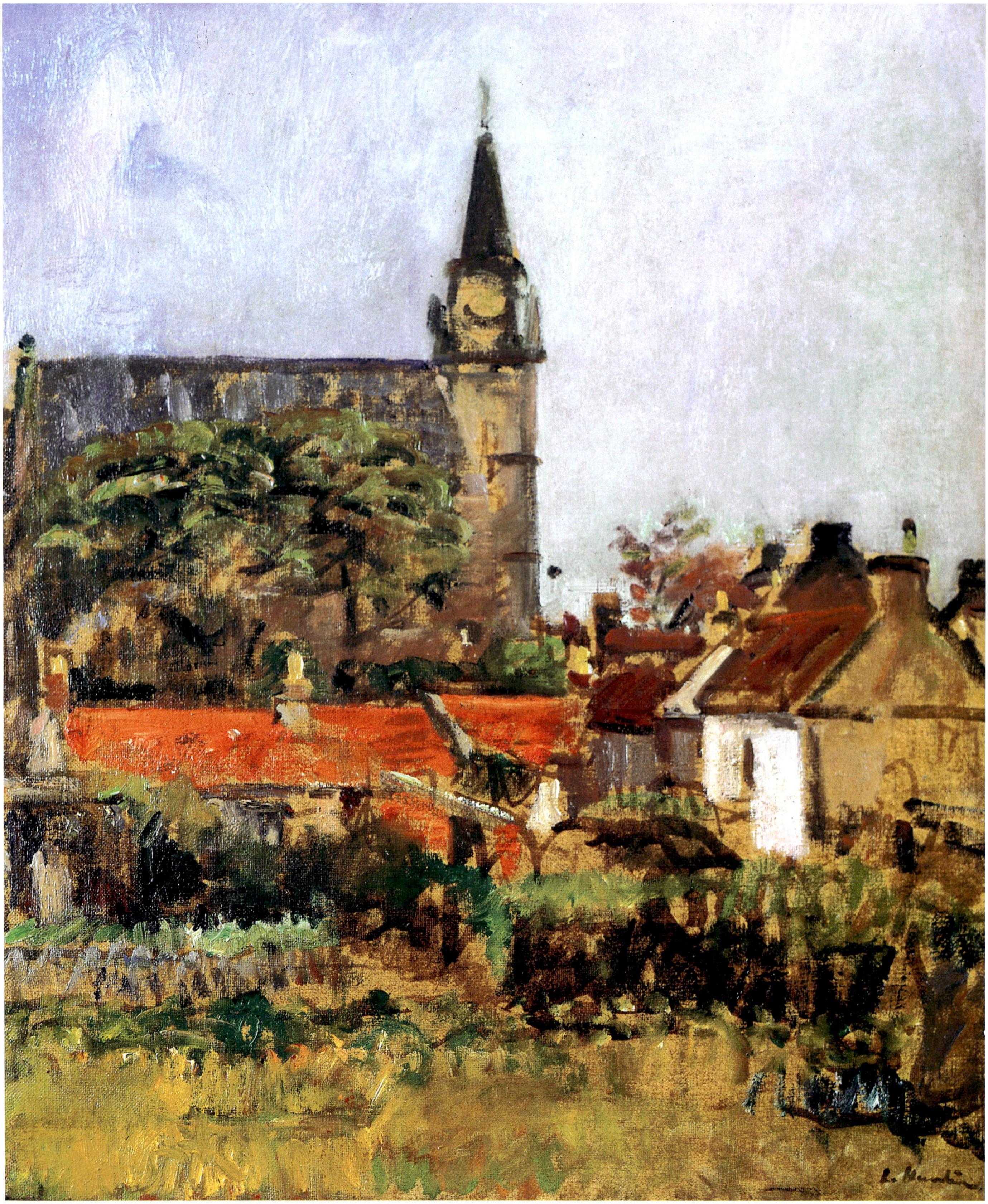

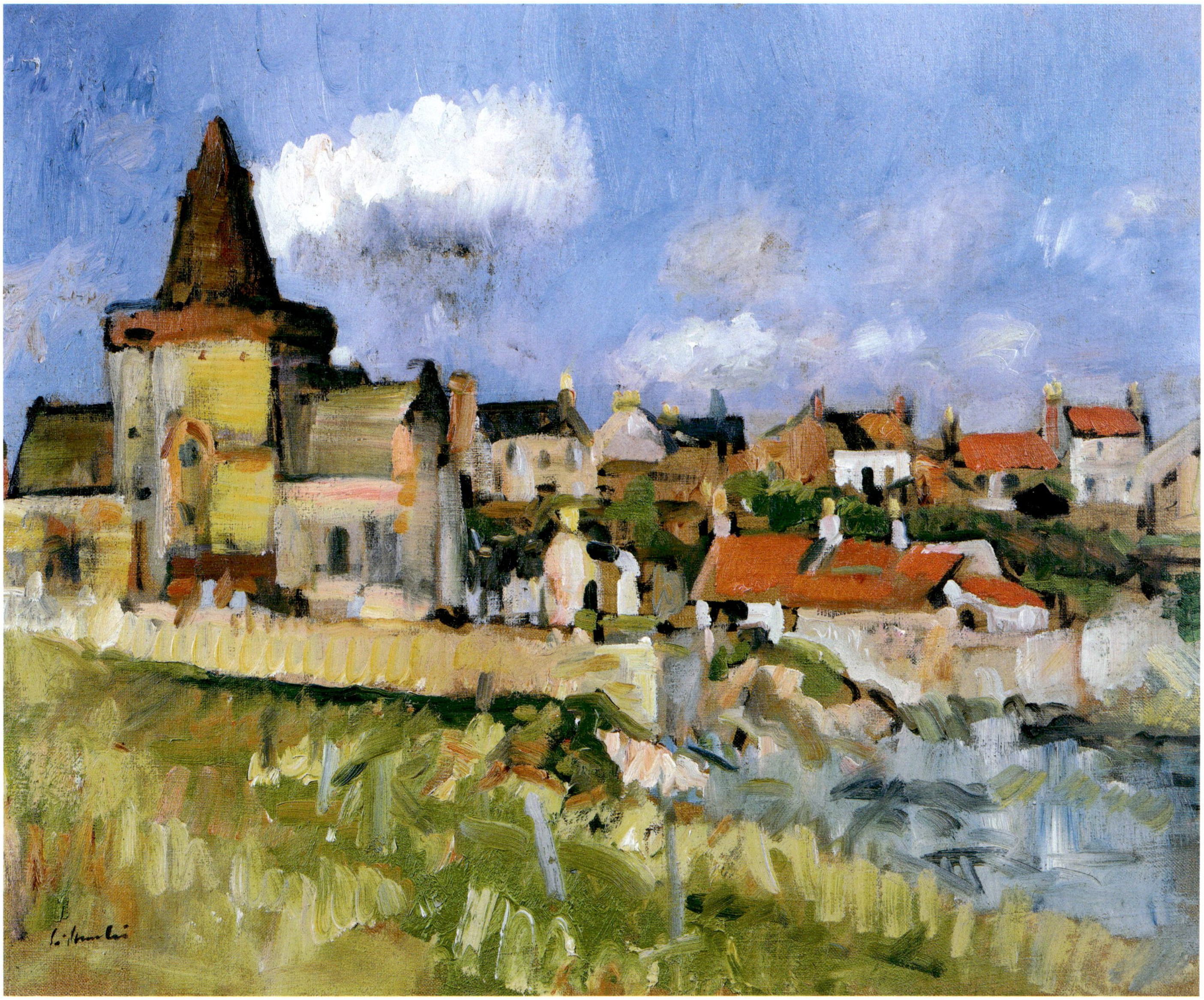

92 | Ceres, Fife
Oil on canvas, 1923–24
The Fleming-Wyfold Art Foundation

93 | St Monance, Fife
Oil on canvas, 1923–24
Private collection

the Edinburgh show beckoning, Hunter also was travelling through to Edinburgh more frequently. His strong admiration for Peploe's work and artistic integrity meant that whenever he could he made a point of visiting Peploe's exhibitions, most of which were held in the capital. Through Peploe, Hunter's contact with Fergusson increased. Writing to Justice about Peploe's show at Aitken Dott in late 1923, Hunter comments:

The Peploe show looked very fine after the insipid stuff at the academy. His old comrade Fergusson is here. His show is commencing at Dott's. He is eager that the three of us should give, as a Scottish group, shows in London and possibly Paris and New York. Fergusson is a most likeable chap, determined yet sympathetic, and was a confrere in the group of Derain, Friesz and Segonzac …

Hunter went on to commend his friends in Dundee for their appreciation of modern art:

After France, Scotland for appreciation of painting, but indeed to talk modern art one has to go from Glasgow to Dundee which seems to become what Florence was to Rome. Did I tell you I saw some fine things by Dufresne [Charles Dufresne, 1896–1938], *a man you don't hear much about? He is perhaps the greatest colourist living if not the greatest artist, in my opinion.*[23]

On international art matters, he comments on McNeill Reid's praise of Picasso's new work, showing the influence of the French nineteenth-century master, Ingres: 'After so much slop it would be well, it seems, if everyone would hark back to the probity of drowsing that the Masters believed in. A landscape by Ruysdael or a still life by Kalf are beautiful to look at from the point of drawing, aside from anything else.'[24]

Hunter's first solo exhibition in Edinburgh duly took place in March 1924 at Aitken Dott's gallery in Castle Street. Although it did not generate the same level of sales as his show with Reid in Glasgow the previous December, according to Honeyman it established his reputation more firmly.[25] The growing enthusiasm for the work of Peploe, Cadell and Fergusson also helped appreciably to boost Hunter's reputation and introduce him to a wider following. After the Edinburgh show Reid and Aitken Dott decided to join forces as far as Hunter's work was concerned. A tripartite contract was signed in April 1924, which was to run for a period of three years. In return for first call on his work, Reid and Aitken Dott guaranteed Hunter an income 'of not less than £600' in *each* of the three years. Any sales made by Hunter himself, either at public exhibitions or privately, would entail him paying a stated commission to the joint account of Reid and Aitken Dott, but pictures sold by Hunter in America were exempt from this commission.[26] It seems a generous contract as far as Hunter was concerned; now he would not have to worry unduly about his financial state. Just as important, however, it was a crucial vote of confidence in his work at a difficult time for him.

Over the winter months the pressure and hard work as a consequence of the impending Edinburgh and Paris shows were beginning to tell on Hunter. His views on what he considered 'real' art were being met with a decidedly narrow-minded attitude among his fellow members of Glasgow Art Club. Hunter had been a member of the club since 1917; over the years he despaired over their lack of interest in modern art. On 11 April he writes to Justice:

Between the apathy of the public and the hostility of the 'artists' real art seems to have but a poor chance in the country. It is truly disheartening at times. Mr. President of the Art Club last night became furious that I defend anything that came after Fantin or Boudin and this is as far as they get advanced! … Thus the Art Club represents 'taste' in Glasgow. I feel I am in it but not of it.[27]

This lack of curiosity or a recognition that there was so much to be learned from early twentieth-century French art thoroughly frustrated Hunter. It was something that he found increasingly hard to ignore. To Hunter's mind the club's rejection of modern French art ultimately extended to a rejection of him as an artist, and this was eating away at his mental well-being. Hunter did not hold the Royal Glasgow Institute in any great esteem either. Commenting on his submission for its 1923 annual exhibition, Hunter bemoans: 'That old bridge picture accepted by Institute, other two refused as too extreme. Ha! Ha!'[28]

Fortunately Hunter was a little wiser after the trials and tribulations of 1923 that led to his mental breakdown that year. After completing the pictures required for Paris, he sensibly decided on taking a proper holiday. His cousin, Arthur Leyden, lived in New York and – no doubt emboldened by his new-found sense of financial security – it seemed to Hunter a trip to New York would more than cheer him up. Some of his old friends from California had moved there, and there was Tom Hunt, his artist friend from pre-war Paris days, whom he would want to see again. It is also very likely that his brother, William, and his family, who had emigrated to Los Angeles in September 1920, were in New York at the same time.[29] Hunter was hoping to 'see some good Cézannes and Renoirs' there too.[30] The plan was to go to New York, and upon his return he would go on to Paris for the opening of the exhibition there. With the help of McInnes, McNair and Hunter's framer,

Gibson, he had already decided on what work to exhibit. With characteristic kindness McInnes intended accompanying Hunter to Paris.

On 26 April Hunter boarded *SS Cameronia* at Glasgow bound for New York.[31] Typically he drew sketches of the passengers to while away the time. The American holiday was a success, engendering a renewed sense of purpose. The only record of the visit is a postcard to Justice: 'The Metropolitan Museum here is quite an important collection, but the Cézannes are easily the best of the more modern stuff. I am tired seeing things and people, though it has been a change to rest, and am anxious now to get back to Fife and get some work done. Met Augustus John here.'[32] Hunter's stay in New York was a short one. He travelled back on the *Cameronia*, docking in Glasgow on 15 June. Three days earlier his brother and family had arrived in Glasgow from New York on board *SS Orduna* for a family visit to Scotland lasting some ten weeks.[33]

The Paris exhibition, *Les Peintres de l' Écosse Moderne*, at the Galerie Barbazanges was generally well-received. Due to the many years Fergusson had lived and worked in France, it was natural that he was the best-known of the four and commanded most of the attention. Peploe fared well in sales and had the added honour of one of his paintings being purchased for the Luxembourg. Hunter exhibited seventeen pictures and for the first time received some attention from the French critics. A little later that exposure led to a favourable review in the French art magazine, *Revue du Vrai et du Beau*. Commenting on a still life by Hunter shown at that year's annual exhibition of the Royal Scottish Academy in Edinburgh, the magazine's critic wrote:

One of the outstanding exhibits in the RSA is the still life painting by the British artist, Leslie Hunter ... Like all modernists who have followed Cézanne, Hunter has profited by the great lesson given by the illustrious Provencal and has applied the instruction to his own proper development, for he is not, in any sense, an imitator of the Master.[34]

Around this time Hunter purchased some very attractive little paintings by Félix Ziem (1821–1911), Van der Velde [probably Willem van de Velde the Younger 1633–1707, a marine painter] and Adolphe Monticelli (1824–1886). Honeyman points out that these pictures bore no relation to the work Hunter was doing and were not even in the style that had given their creators a degree of popularity. Hunter had chosen them because he liked them and 'probably because it felt good to be in the position to make such purchases'.[35] Notwithstanding Honeyman's observations, Hunter commented in a letter to Justice: 'I have an old master that is so full of depth, recession and volume which Cézanne preached – a landscape', signifying one aspect of why he was attracted to one of his purchases (presumably the van de Velde).[36]

An important outcome of all this activity in the first half of 1924 was that Hunter felt refreshed and eager to continue developing his growing sense of colour and design. In terms of style 1924 marks a turning point. As previously mentioned, Hunter had long held a desire to explore his sense of line. Perhaps it was with this in mind that for a time he chose to change his painting ground from Fife to Loch Lomond. Honeyman relates that Hunter considered it a happy interlude, though his friends and critics were not so certain.[37] Yet five years later one of the 1924 series of paintings featuring houseboats on Loch Lomond was purchased by the French government. Whatever the truth of the matter, Hunter had achieved a different emphasis in his efforts and was able to transfer this to his subsequent still lifes and Fife landscapes.

There were two concentrations of houseboats to be found on Loch Lomond. One was centred on the River Leven at Balloch at the south end of the loch. The other was at a secluded, sheltered little bay, just south of the village of Luss on the western shore. The houseboats were fashionable at the time, in general used as weekend retreats by city-dwellers. They were colourfully painted and had a unique and peaceful charm. Hunter was particularly taken with the lively contrast between the colourful houseboats, the lush green foliage and the ever-changing subtle reflections they create on the surface of the water. Their rectangular shapes set against the density of the encompassing green foliage provided the challenge for which Hunter was searching.

In a departure from his usual style, Hunter has flattened the paint and perspective in *Houseboats, Loch Lomond* (pl.95), providing a clever contrast between a powerful line, colour and tone and, by setting out the basis of the composition with strong dark lines, introduced a livelier contrast of colours. The reflection of the yellow houseboat is quite solidly defined, yet with the flatness of paint he achieves a strong, coherent view without sacrificing its tranquil setting. This period at Loch Lomond marks a watershed for Hunter. The flattening of paint and perspective reflects only one aspect of his response to the work of Matisse, demonstrating his burgeoning development in strong pictorial design. Later that summer he returned to Fife determined to paint his familiar territory in the light of his new style.

Hunter's favourite painting spot at Drumeldrie, a hamlet close to Lower Largo, did not escape the new treatment. A series of drawings, of which *Drumeldrie* (pl.96) is a strong example, clearly demonstrate his new thinking. First he isolates the main shapes he wishes to emphasise, organising them into three distinctive planes. Each element enlivens it, in some cases by almost furious cross-hatching. In a series of oil paintings, some of the same view of

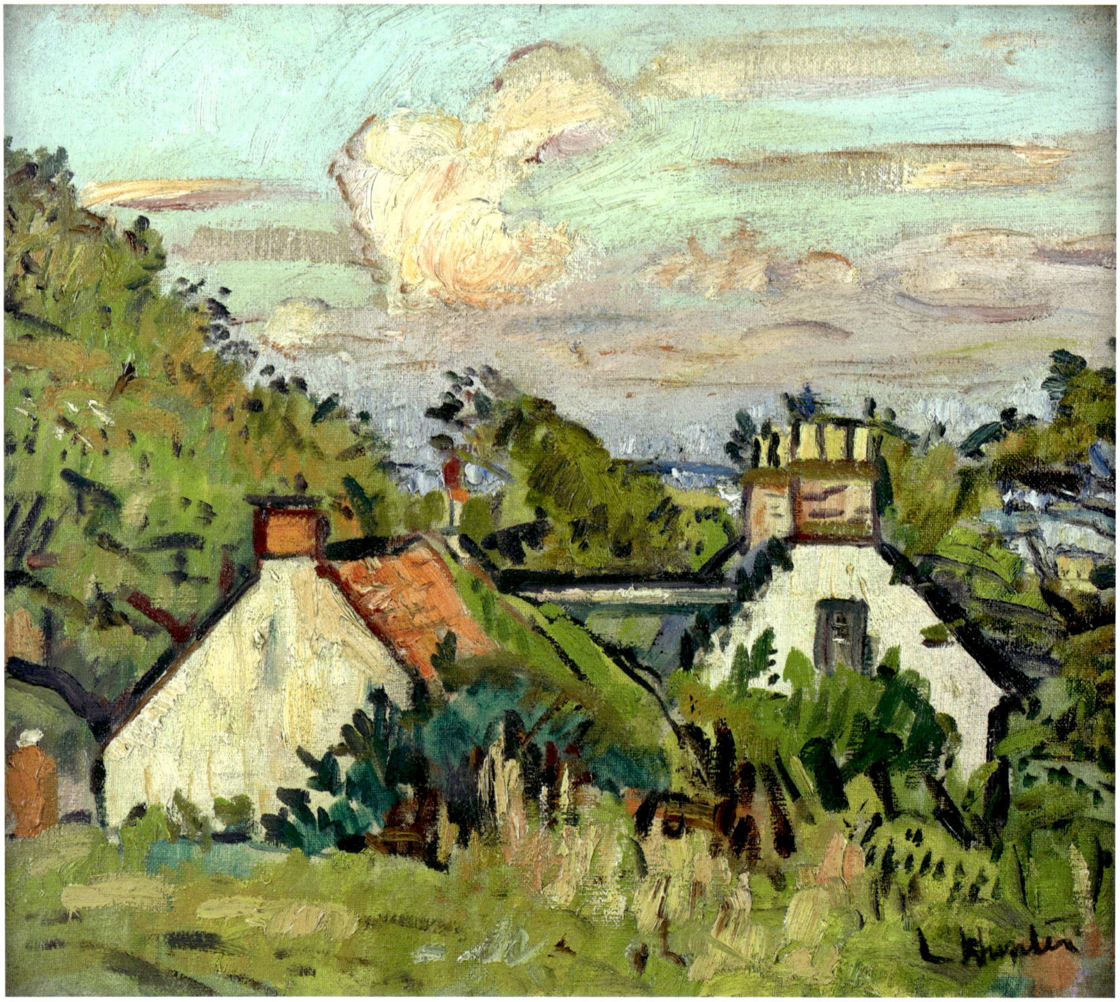

94 | Cottages and Landscape, Fife
Oil on canvas, 1923–24
Private collection

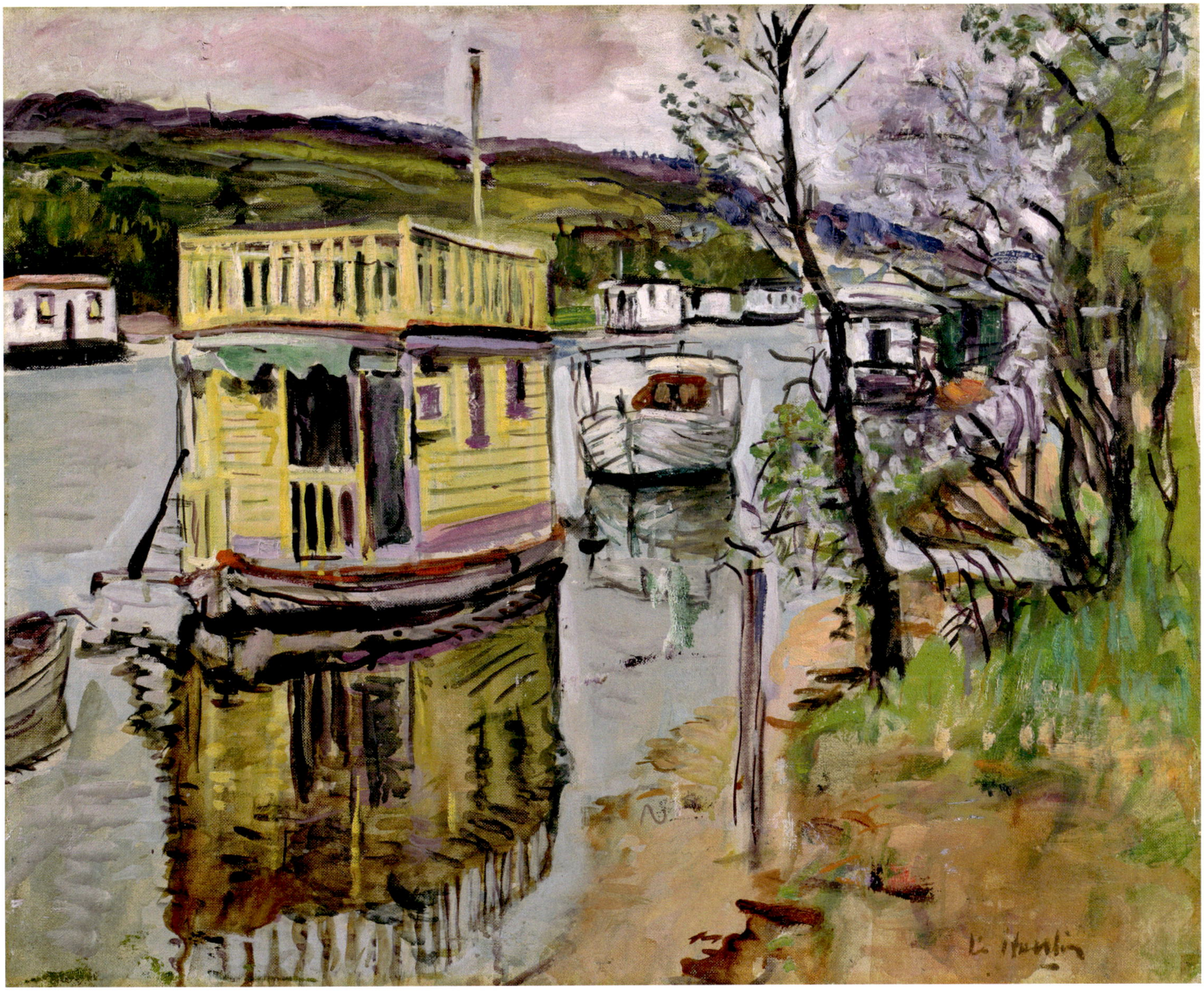

95 | Houseboats, Loch Lomond
Oil on canvas, 1924
Glasgow Museums

Drumeldrie, Hunter picks out with strong lines and areas of colour the shapes that form the main components of the design.

Employing much the same technique, Hunter achieves a stunningly fresh evocation of the *Mill Dam, Fife* (pl.98) with a surprisingly flat perspective. The pattern of the roofs of the farm building is offset by the treatment of the soft foliage and its corresponding reflection in the pond in the foreground. Rather than the result being principally one of striking colour, as it was in his Fife paintings of 1920–22, this particular picture epitomises the overall difference in his approach. No one element dominates; each comes together to form a stunning whole.

After several years of dissatisfaction, 1925 was to be a triumphant year for Hunter in terms of his painting, even if it was not so in his personal life. He had found the breakthrough for which he had been searching. It must have been a great relief to him, and he spent the remainder of the year building on his new-found experience. With the confidence he had gained in late 1924 Hunter was more than ready for the proposed group exhibition at the Leicester Galleries in London in January 1925. On this second occasion the show included Fergusson as well as Peploe and Cadell. The English artist, Walter Sickert, wrote the preface to the catalogue, although one feels he missed the mark on Hunter when he wrote: 'He uses the refractory, and how much and how shamefully abused, tubes to inspired ends on normal and traditional lines'.[38] Considering Sickert's artistic development is more in keeping with Whistler's tonal values and with Degas, Hunter's affinity with Cézanne and Matisse hardly can be described as along 'normal and traditional lines'. Perhaps such unhelpful comments deflected attention away from Hunter towards the equally strong and colourful offerings of Peploe and Fergusson. Honeyman sums up the critics' reaction:

The exhibition served to establish more firmly the London reputations of Peploe and Fergusson. The press notices featured these two, and although some were very appreciative of Hunter's ten pictures, they did not submit them to any real criticism.[39]

This must have been disheartening for Hunter and his supporters, but the reality was that his work was still too advanced for most tastes. Determinedly Hunter worked on in his Glasgow studio with the crucial encouragement and assistance of his Glasgow and Dundee friends. Once again, however, he was beginning to feel mentally and physically weary. The dull winter weather was not helping. In a letter to Justice in April he laments the problems he is suffering:

... The few lines in my last note about bloodsuckers did not apply to Dundee of course, of which I have only happy memories, but of Glasgow here when I have unfortunately been friendly out of pity for one or two neurotic 'temperaments' and a 'has-been' painter [as yet unidentified]*, who made my studio a rendezvous of depression and I out of pity put up with it foolishly – for there are those who by their nature if you tell them to take a flower in the garden proceed to pull up the rose-trees!! Strange, today E.A. Taylor, Peploe's friend, who is giving a show here, told me the same party in an experience made him feel life was not worth living. I got rid of them at the time*

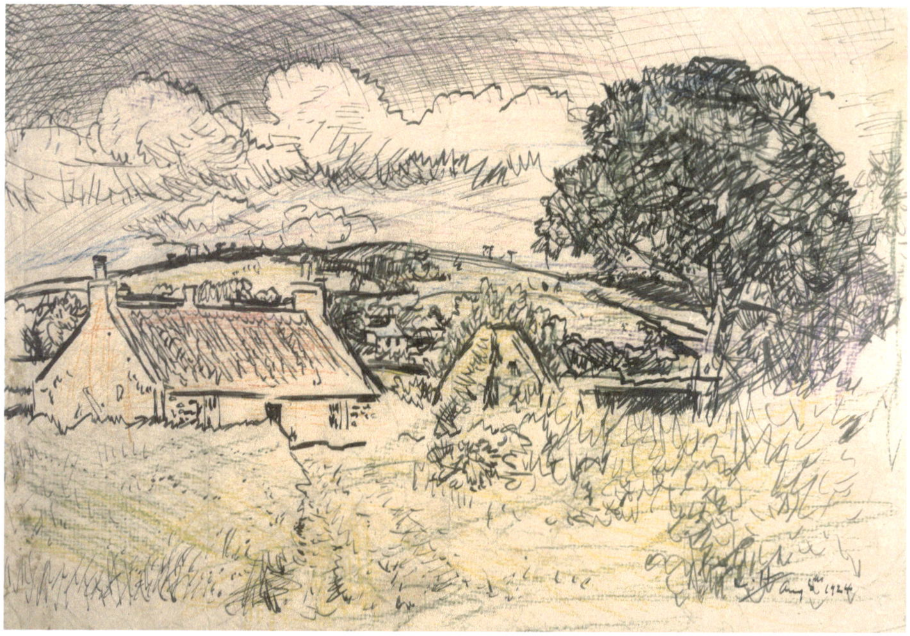

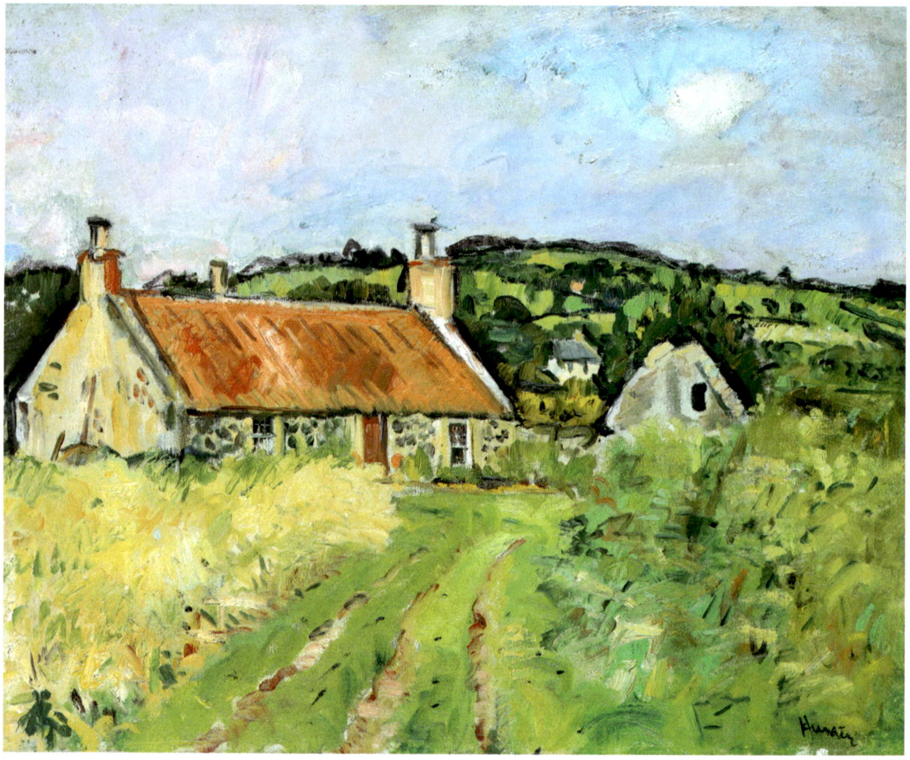

96 | Drumeldrie
Pen & ink and coloured crayons, 1924
University of Glasgow, Hunterian Art Gallery

97 | Drumeldrie
Oil on canvas, 1924
Private collection

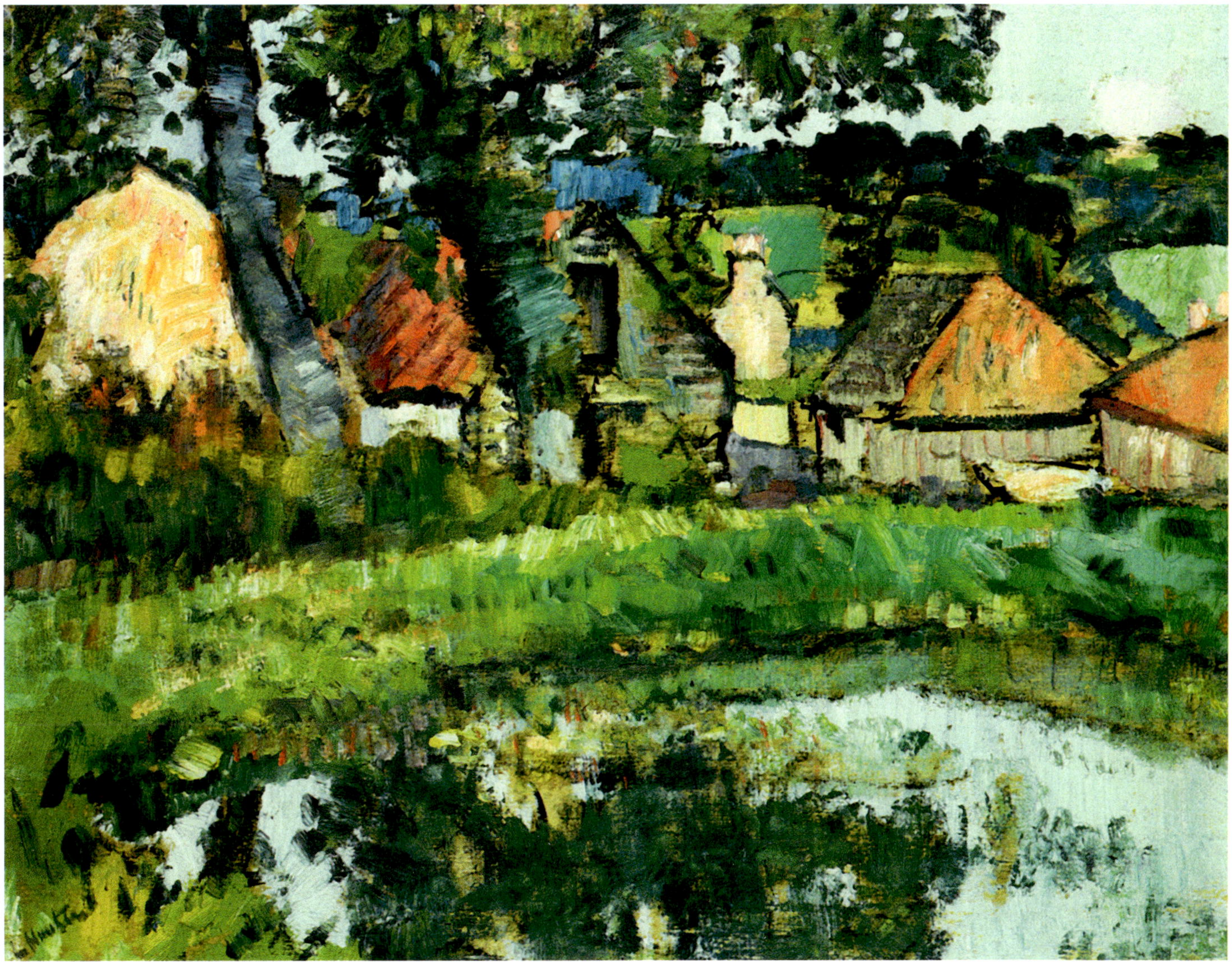

98 | Mill Dam, Fife
Oil on canvas, 1924
Private collection

of my nerve attack some time ago, but the aftermath of these temperamental complexes is sometimes as bad as the actuality.[40]

Three weeks later Hunter tells Justice: 'I will be glad of a little rest and change before starting the season's work. How I worked in that damned studio I don't know. Another six months I think would have done me in.' The only hope lay in his plans for the summer: '… I will do some good things this summer … line will be a passion for a few years … There is a marvellous charm in the Fife coast especially in the long twilight evenings.'[41]

Aware that Hunter was in desperate need of a change, his friend, McInnes, suggested Hunter accompany him to Paris at the end of May. This was just the tonic he needed to motivate him. In Paris they viewed an exhibition of Matisse's current work. Hunter and McInnes were stunned by what they saw. Such was the impact of the exhibition that McInnes, fervently encouraged by Hunter, decided that he should acquire a Matisse. McInnes's financial state can best be described as comfortable; emphatically he was not the wealthy industrialist that in recent years he has been made out to be. The cost of buying a Matisse was well outside the limits McInnes would normally spend on works of art, particularly a work by a contemporary artist. After much soul-searching and a family

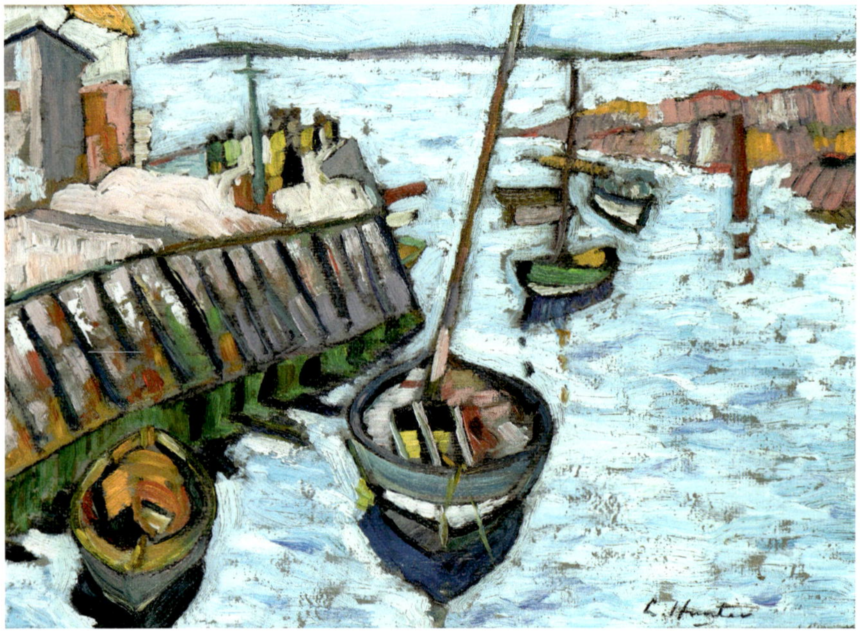

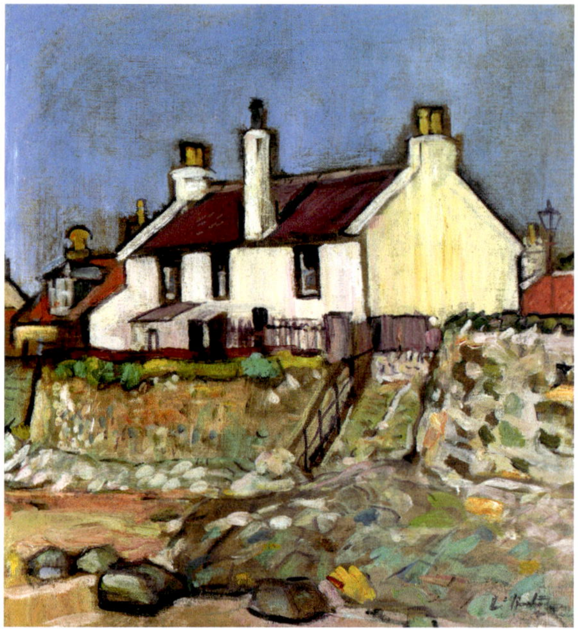

99 | Largo Harbour
Oil on board, 1925
Private collection

100 | Robinson Crusoe's House, Largo
Oil on canvas, 1925
Private collection

debate, he bought the wonderful still life *La Nappe Rose* ('The Pink Tablecloth', see pl.139), which is now in Glasgow's Kelvingrove Art Gallery. Over the years McInnes carefully put together a collection of modestly-priced works by Monet, Renoir, Degas, Seurat, Vuillard, Cézanne, Picasso and Braque. However no acquisition required the courage and conviction it took to buy the Matisse.[42] Yet McInnes never regretted buying the picture and over the years obtained much pleasure from it. Even during his lifetime it was loaned to several exhibitions, including one in Paris in 1931. On that occasion Hunter comments in a letter to Justice: 'McInnes' brother writes from Paris that McInnes' still life is the best in the Matisse show. I urged him to buy two others at the time but he baulked!'[43] How typical of Hunter. McInnes is taking a major and very expensive step in buying a Matisse, and Hunter, filled with enthusiasm and impervious to the cost, berates his friend for not buying three!

Hunter returned from the French trip refreshed and ready to immerse himself in the summer's painting. He had moved into a new studio in the same building in West George Street, which gave him a renewed zest for painting. Writing to Justice, he can barely hide his enthusiasm:

Just a line to say I have just got moved into a new studio – a large one on the same floor and which I have 'had up' in a nice arrangement of French grey to blue. Entering into it is like a new lease of life.[44]

The French trip and the new studio created precisely the right atmosphere to motivate Hunter. His first solo exhibition for two years was only five months away. Eager to showcase his recent progress, Hunter was determined to have plenty of work available for the exhibition.

The exhibition at Reid's gallery in Glasgow in December 1925 was both a critical and financial success, proving beyond doubt that Hunter's decision two years previously to explore a new approach in his painting was fully justified. Over the last two years or so the conflict between his accomplished sense of colour as form and his increasing desire to exploit colour for design had been a painful, but necessary episode for him. Now he was able to put all that behind him. Hunter had produced some of the most stunning landscapes and still lifes he had ever painted. The critic of the *Glasgow Herald* reacted to them with genuine delight:

Like all progressive artists, Hunter's art has advanced

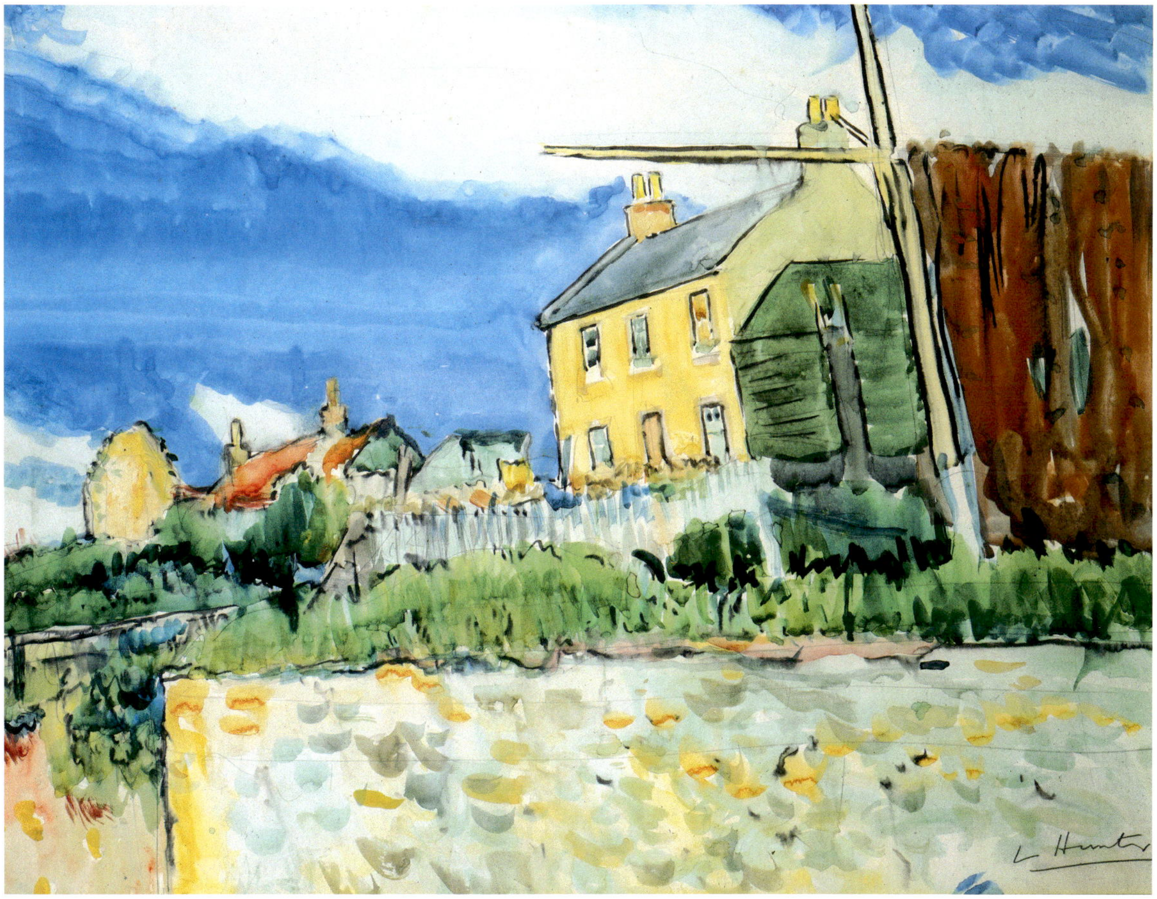

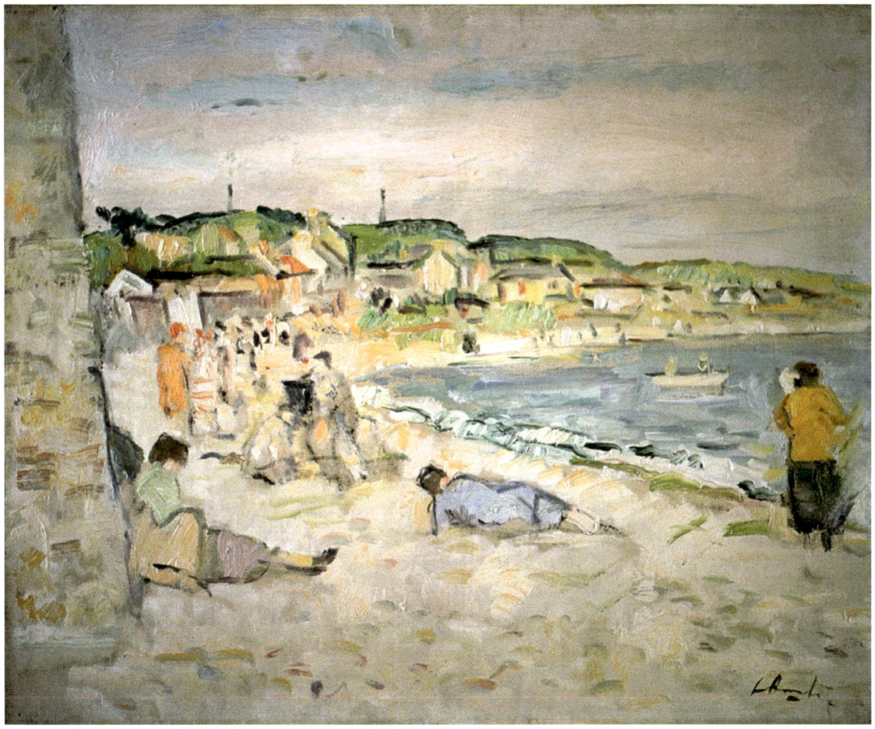

101 | Drying the Nets
Pen & ink and watercolour, 1925
Private collection

102 | Largo Beach
Oil on canvas, 1925
University of Glasgow, Hunterian Art Gallery

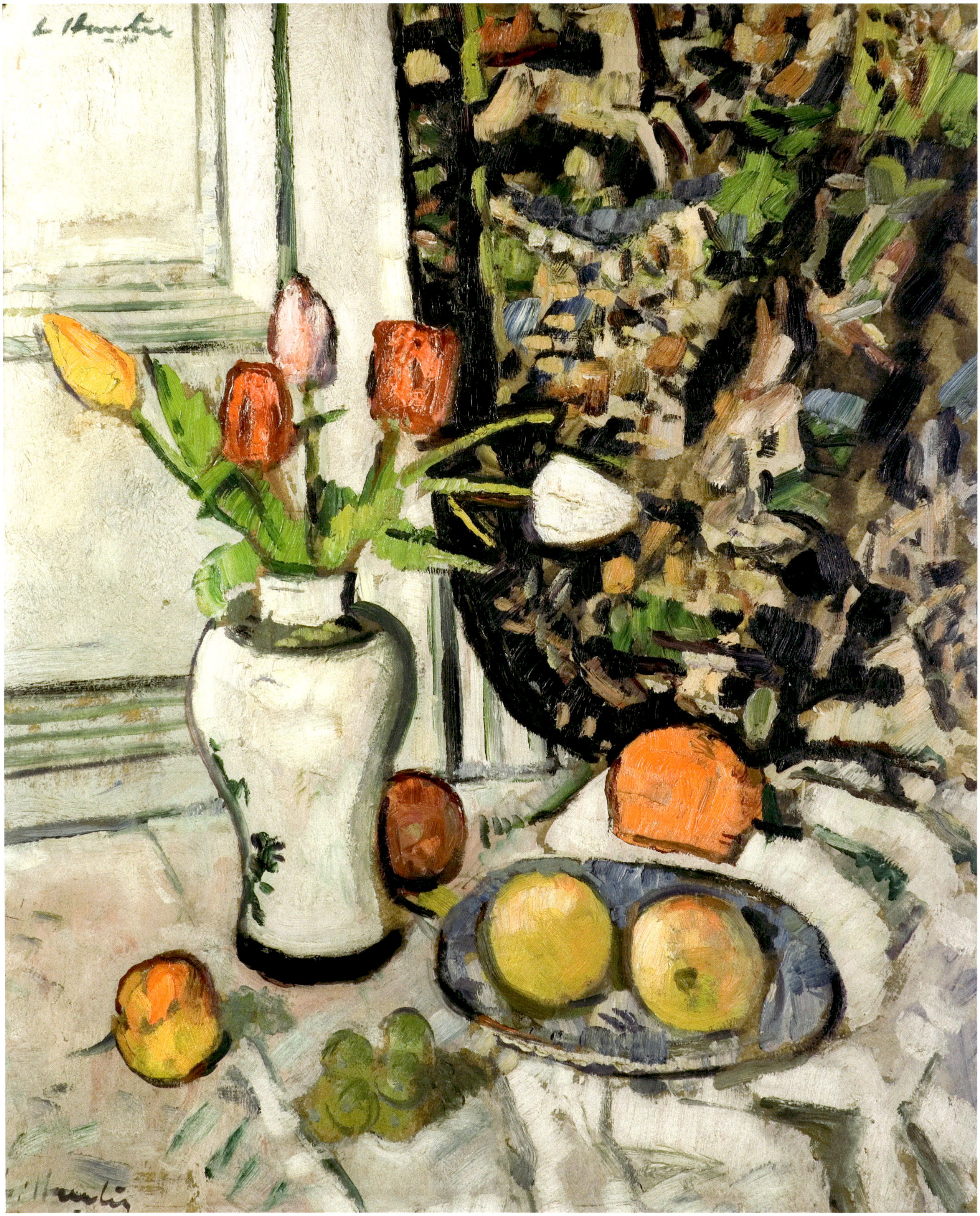

103 | Still Life with Tulips
Oil on panel, 1925
The Potteries Museum & Art Gallery, Stoke-on-Trent

104 | Peonies in a Chinese Vase
Oil on board, 1925
The Fleming-Wyfold Art Foundation

stage by stage until he has now evolved a style of his own, which in its compelling power and decoration and realistic elements is well in advance of anything he has hitherto achieved ... The big planes which he introduces into his landscapes give unusual solidity and breadth to his compositions and if his colour schemes are sometimes daring they are always harmonious ... presenting the essence of his subject with directness and vigour that is yet elastic, sprightly and joyous ... also characterised by a fine rhythmic sense of design, a subject to which the artist has devoted a great deal of attention in his most recent work.[45]

Hunter's new-found confidence is epitomized in the pictures in the exhibition. The big design is at once apparent without competing with the other elements that go to make up the whole.

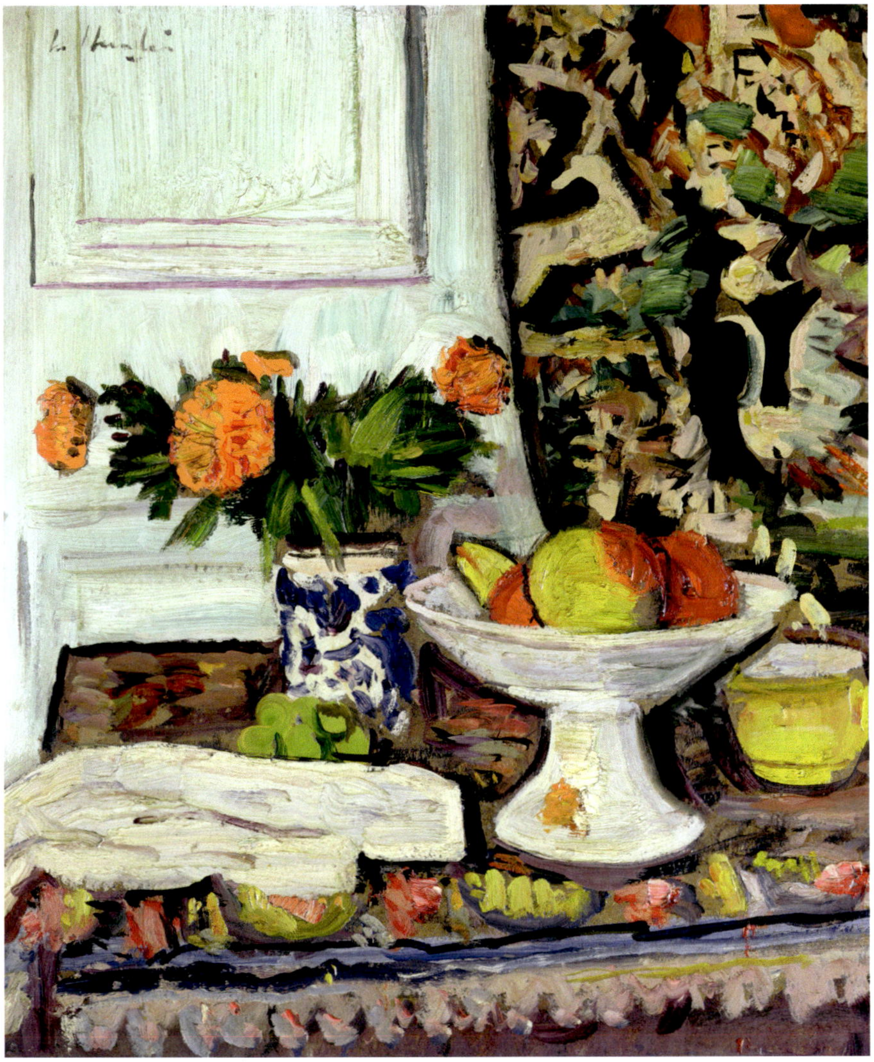

For instance in *Largo Harbour* (pl.99) Hunter has chosen to emphasise vivid colour as opposed to strong design, successfully evoking the idyllic and restful sensation of a hot summer's day by the sea. *Drying the Nets* (pl.101) is still within a flattened perspective, whereas the bold appeal of *Robinson Crusoe's House, Largo* (pl.100) is achieved by Hunter's highly-developed sense of colour, confidently controlling the design.

In this exhibition Hunter showed for the first time a considerable number of figure subjects. Commenting on them, the *Herald's* critic declares that the 'feeling of life and the joy of living are strongly brought out, while at the same time the pictures have distinctly decorative qualities'.[46] *At the Window* (untraced) is in the same vein as Matisse's series of female figures at a window from the 1920s, but Hunter has achieved a clearly different effect. In general Matisse completely flattens perspective, relying on intuitive application of bright colour both to bring out the intrinsic design and to communicate the scene's immediate warmth and intimacy. Hunter, on the other hand, is unable to abandon form to such an extreme degree.

The lessons Hunter learned in landscape in 1924 and subsequently are brilliantly applied to still life. The *Herald* describes them as 'strong and striking in design and gorgeous in their colour harmonies. His favourite theme in this connection is a vase of flowers or a dish of fruit set against a richly patterned curtain.'[47] An excellent example of Hunter's new verve is found in *Still Life with Tulips* (pl.103). What might have been a cluttered still life becomes instead one of strong line and striking intensity. Colour, form, tone, texture are all brilliantly handled and harmoniously assembled. In *Peonies in a Chinese Vase*[48] (pl.104) Hunter's mastery of colour and texture reveals a new sensuous quality. While perspective is flattened, it is not to the severe extent of Matisse's oversimplification. His liberated sense of pattern comes together, striking colour chords that vibrate across the surface. Hunter's inspired brushwork ensures the richness of colour glows with energy. Clive Bell, the noted English art critic, was greatly impressed when he viewed the painting in an exhibition at Reid and Lefevre's London gallery in the 1930s of work by contemporary British artists – some well-known, some less so – and commented 'That is the finest picture in this exhibition and I do not know who painted it'.[49]

An interesting feature about all these paintings is that, although Hunter flattens perspective, unlike Matisse he is unable to completely abandon it. It is more a case of Cézanne's views on form being confidently integrated with Matisse's sense of design, leading to a vision entirely of Hunter's own creation and one which, while uniquely Scottish, is also quite distinct from his fellow Colourists, Peploe, Fergusson and Cadell. Hunter manipulates the impact of the individual strong shapes he wishes to pick out with vigorous brushwork, while at the same time controlling the flat perspective planes with striking colour. The *Herald's* critic was sufficiently impressed to insist that Hunter's exhibition 'should not be missed!'[50]

Glasgow's Kelvingrove Art Gallery also was impressed and purchased three drawings for its permanent collection: *The Pierrots, Largo*, *Fife Landscape* and *Largo Harbour*. The gallery already had the superb *Old Mill, Fifeshire* (see pl.69) and a still life by Hunter, both gifted in 1921 by William McInnes. *The Pierrots* is one of a series of drawings Hunter did of the open-air theatre near Largo jetty. Since his days in San Francisco he had maintained an interest in the theatre, as much as anything for its colourful spectacle. The Pierrots at Lower Largo staged a popular form of vaudeville entertainment for summer visitors; often Hunter depicts scenes of the audience milling around, capturing on paper the casual seaside atmosphere (pl.105).

At last Hunter had overcome his difficulties of the last few years to emerge triumphant, though it had taken its toll in terms of his mental well-being. The pressure to produce work for exhibitions, combined with the fact that when painting Hunter would be totally absorbed in the work, frequently led him to forget to eat or sleep for unnaturally long periods at a time. It was not uncommon for his sister, Jeanie McFarlane, to go along to the studio and insist he come back with her to rest and recuperate. However his family and friends could only do so much.

His sense of having achieved success in Scotland was tempered by the depressingly conservative attitude of his fellow artists. He had no one with whom he could discuss art, except for his loyal band of friends, which had widened and now included Fergusson's friend, the writer John Ressich. Honeyman describes how some of Hunter's Art Club acquaintances 'had reached the conclusion that his views on art were a trifle fantastic and that he himself was 'a bit queer'. His artist neighbours in the West George Street studio would report frequent noisy altercations going on in the Hunter studio, and on investigation they would find that Hunter was alone.' The vehement argument was with himself, no doubt concerning the merits or demerits of a painting or paintings. According to Honeyman, who was a doctor of medicine before becoming an art dealer, it was the 'only objective symptom of the neurosis which afflicted Hunter for the remainder of his life'.[51] Perhaps 'neurosis' may be too strong a word to apply to Hunter's

105 | The Pierrots, Largo
Pen & ink and coloured crayons, 1923
Glasgow Museums

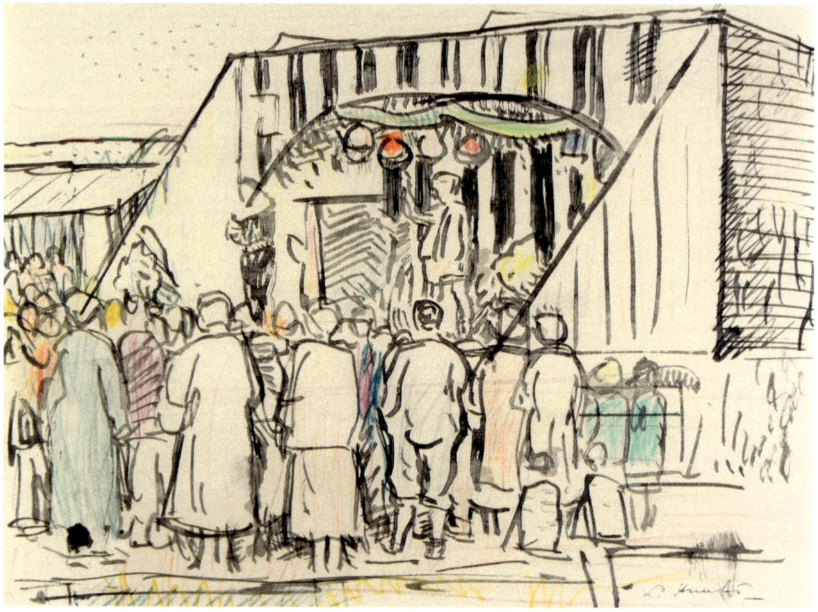

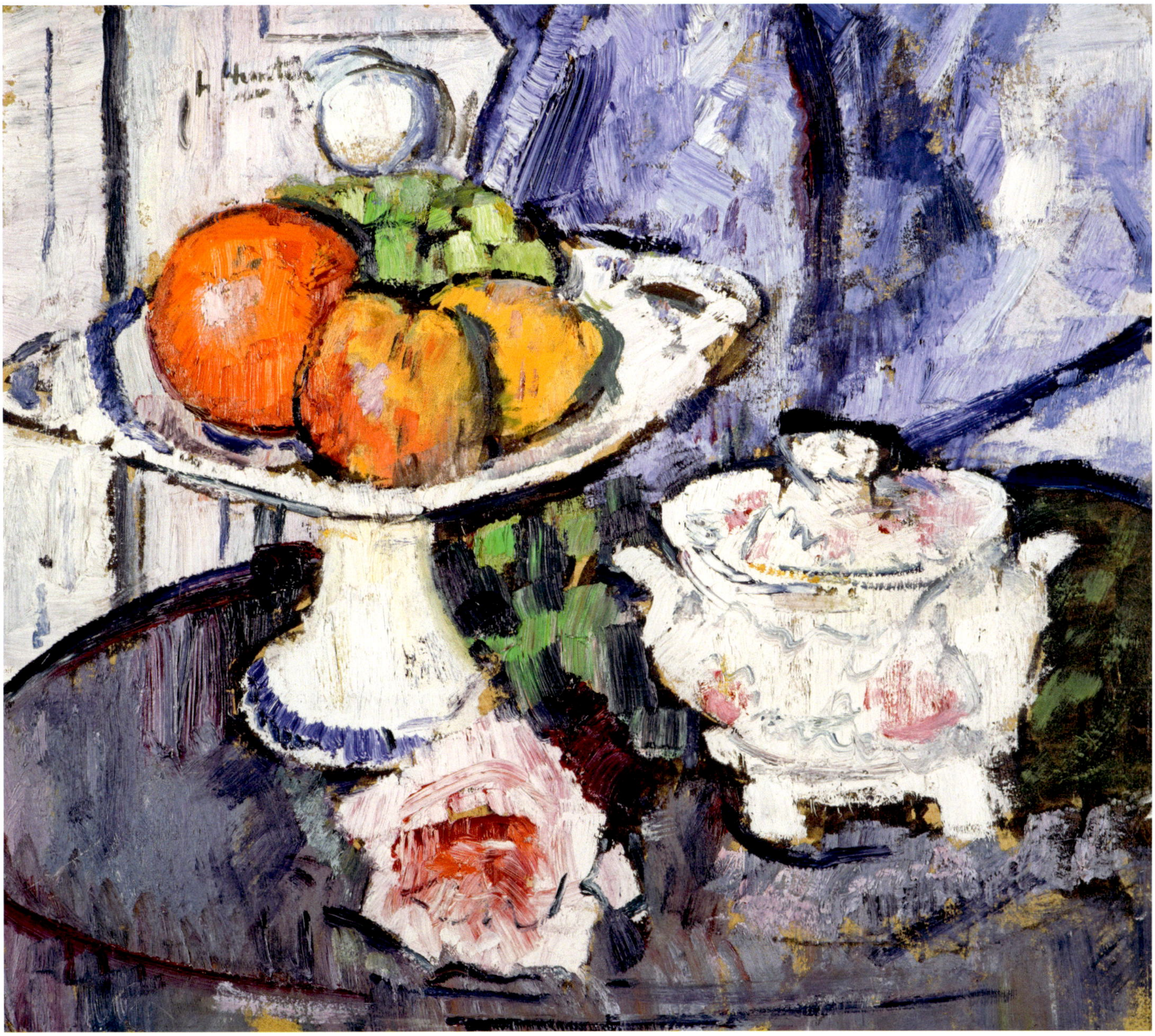

106 | Still Life
Oil on board, 1925
Scottish National Gallery of Modern Art

mental state. He does not seem to fall within any particular category of known mental illness. While it is obvious he was not normal in the usual sense of the word, his mental anguish appears to have stemmed from extreme overwork, tackling difficult abstract concepts and their physical application, and a form of paranoia resulting from a lack of understanding by others in what he was trying to achieve.

Having painted some of the finest pictures of his career, by 1926 Hunter felt drained and in need of a major change. The variable Scottish weather seriously affected Hunter's ability to paint and the long, dark winter months seemed to drag on interminably. His constant need to move forward made him realise that he had to find somewhere new to work. However he was undecided where to try next, telling Justice: 'I will go back to Fife again and this season I think wind it up definitely … I may go to Lanarkshire, Clydeside for the Spring blossom. Indeed this year I hope to go over the scenes of

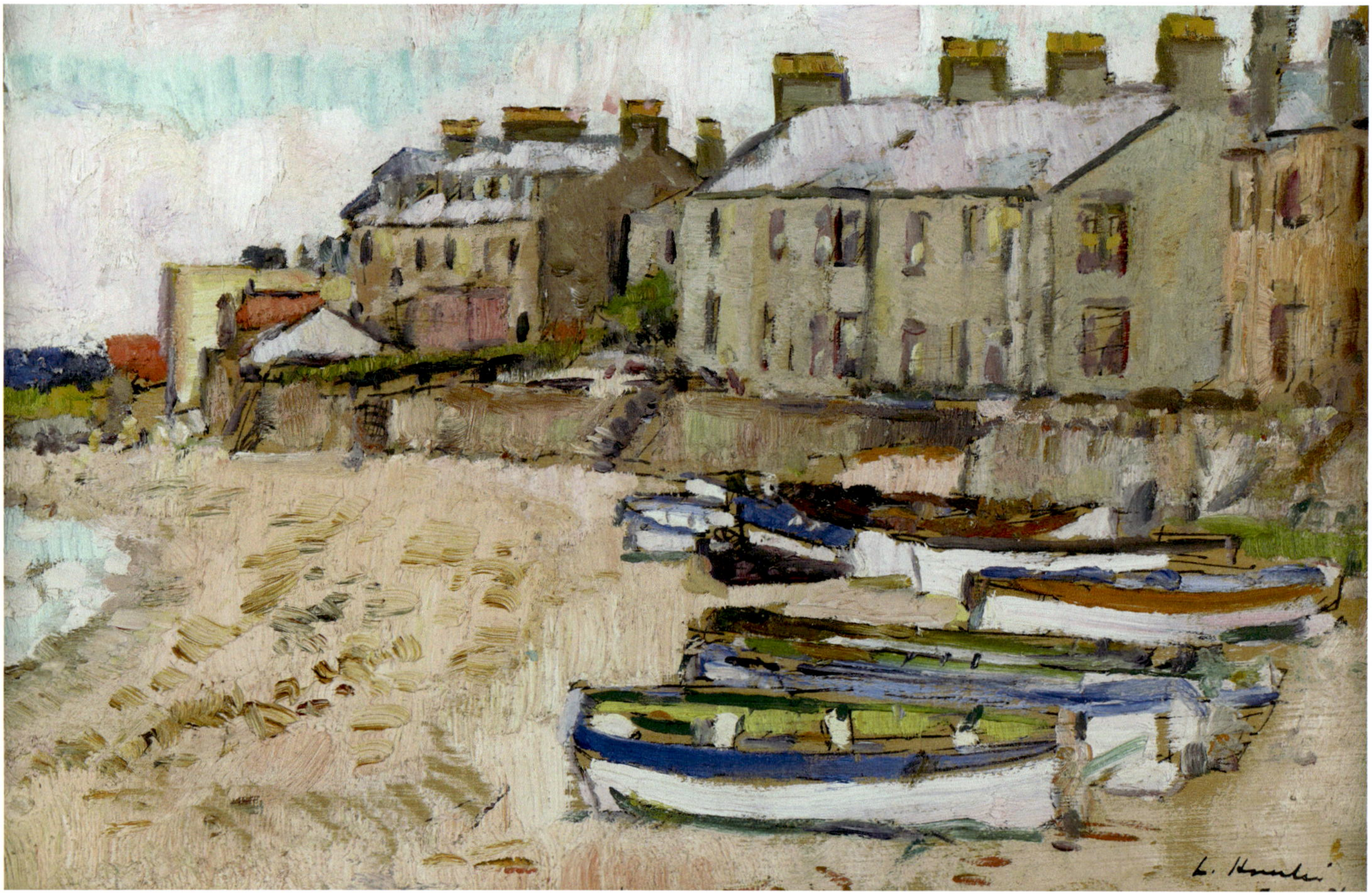

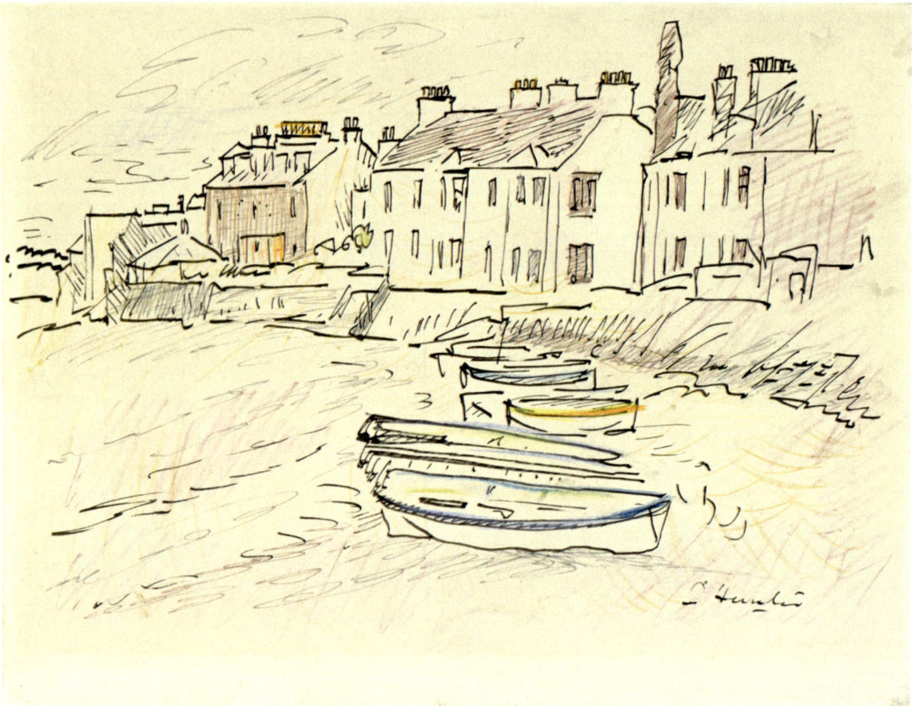

107 | Boats, Lower Largo
Oil on board, dated 1926
Private collection

108 | Boats and Houses, Lower Largo
Pen & ink and coloured crayons, 1926
Scottish National Gallery of Modern Art

my exploits this last five years. I hope to go to Paris next winter and work like a demon on the figure then go to Italy in the Spring.'[52] His friends urged that it would be sensible to have a proper holiday. He was undecided on that point too, writing to Justice:

Just a line to say that I saw Mr McInnes yesterday. He expects to go to London this week and see the show of Charles Dufresne and some other shows. Do you intend going this week? I've been thinking as I have to go to London anyway I might take a run over to Paris with you for a week instead of going to Ilfracombe as I had intended.[53]

Evidently his friend, Tattersall, won the day and Hunter accompanied him to Ilfracombe for two weeks that April. 'Mr T. and I had some delightful walks and drives, the country being very charming' was all he had to say of the break.[54]

After his holiday Hunter felt sufficiently refreshed to try Fife again. *Boats, Lower Largo* (pl.107) clearly shows his compelling interest in pattern and colour. However for his friends it was an anxious time, because Hunter believed he *had* to have a significant change of location in order to continue moving forward in his art. In a letter tinged with regret he writes to Justice of his last days at Ceres:

I took a walk around the morning before I left to say my adieu to the old mill. I looked over a wall hélas there were new vistas in the valley. Nature is never still![55]

He was not losing what he had gained, but neither could he stand still. His thoughts regarding new territory turned increasingly to Italy:

Of course, I cannot plan anything yet although Florence and Venice opened up such a vista for my work that I feel I could start out and walk if only to see them again.[56]

Ultimately it was Peploe's opinion that carried the most weight. Hunter had been discussing with him for some time the delights and challenges of painting in Italy and of how it had opened up possibilities for him. In turn Peploe confessed that he was tiring of Iona and told Hunter that Cassis in the south of France now was one of his favourite sketching grounds. He considered the setting ideal for both serious work and for relaxation.[57] This was precisely what Hunter needed to hear. The additional attraction of artists of the stature of Matisse and Segonzac being based in the south of France probably was the deciding factor.

Having gained so much ground in his painting over those difficult years, Hunter felt the pull of foreign lands too strong to resist. Encouraged both by Peploe and Fergusson, Hunter once again turned his attention to France and, in particular, to Provence.

109 | Still Life with a Bowl of Fruit and Vase of Pink Flowers
Oil on board, 1925–26
Private collection

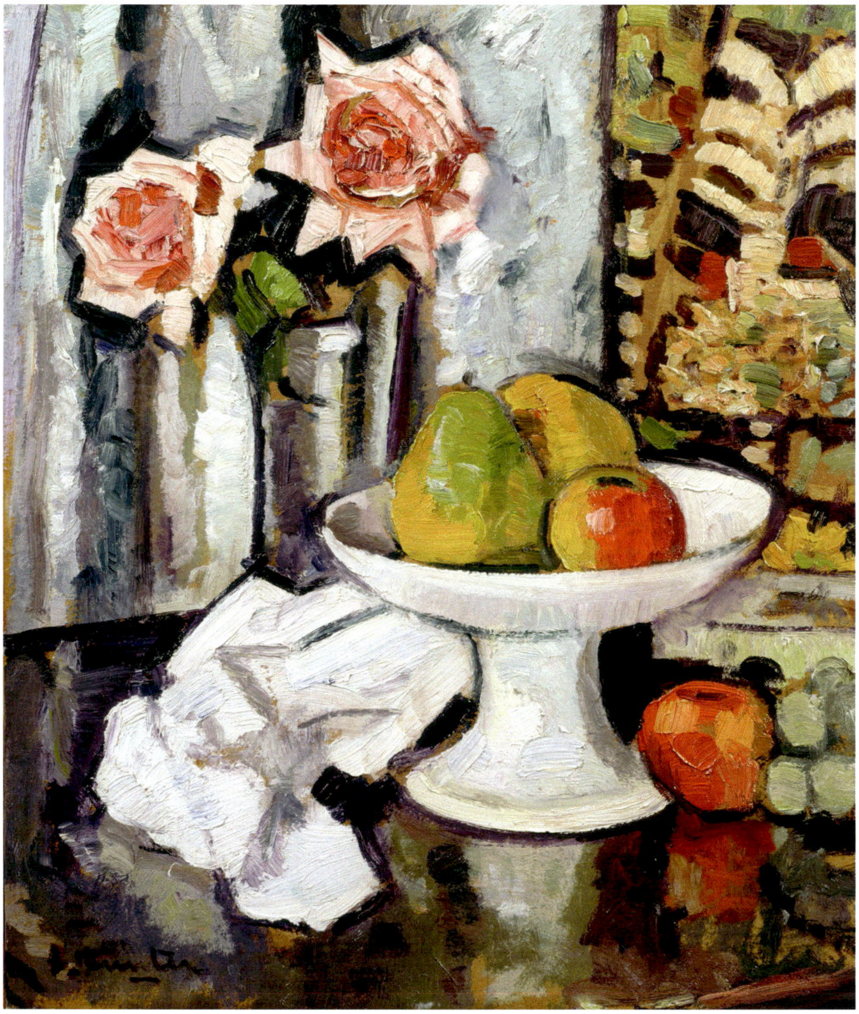

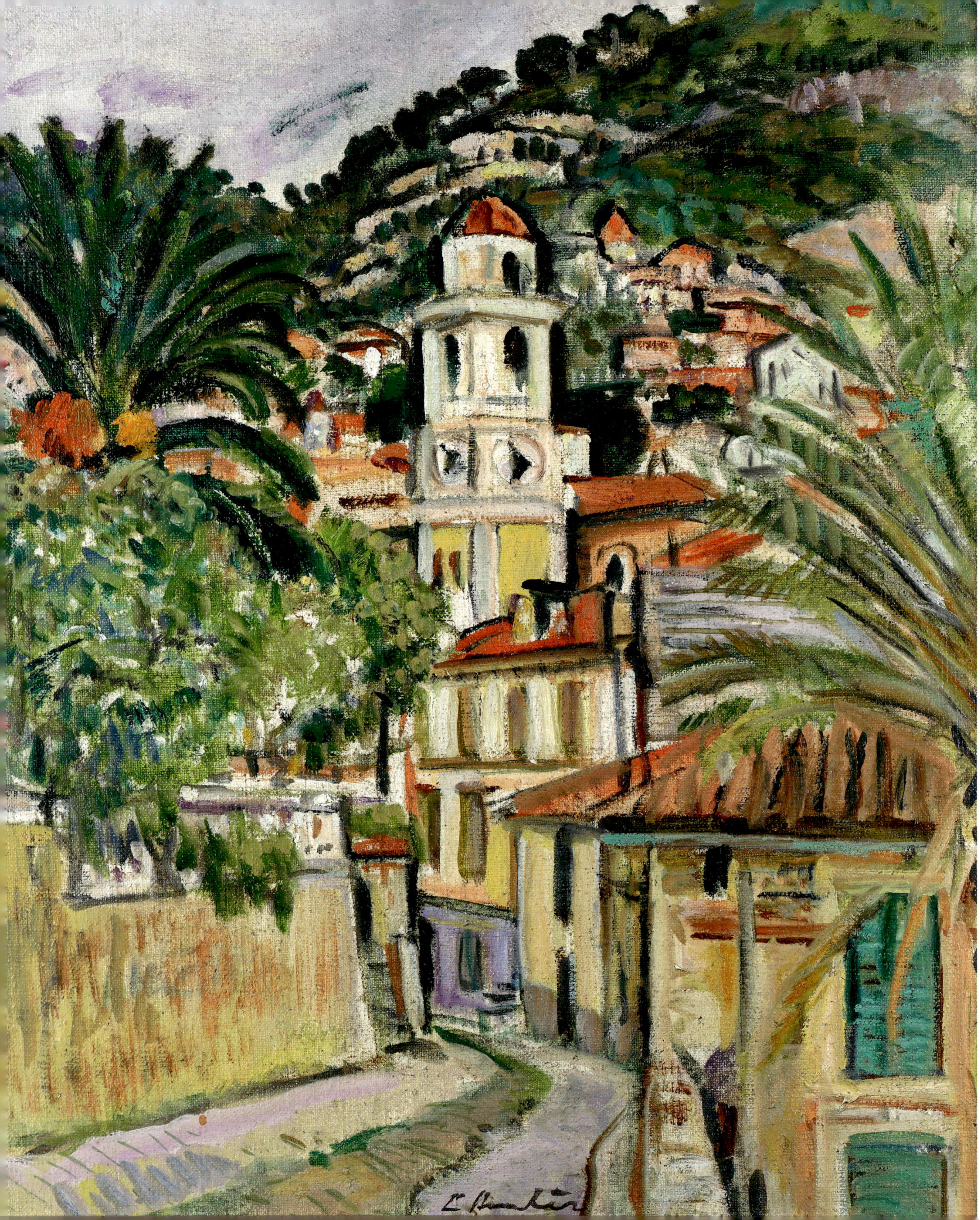

7 A Breath of Fresh Air

Writing to Justice, Hunter could not conceal his enthusiasm and sheer delight at being in Provence:

I like this country very much and am sorry I did not come here six years ago in place of going to Fife. I feel six months here was worth six years there. I have been in St. Paul a week and have just got into a new little studio attached to this hotel where I can paint still life as well as landscape. Still life that is different from in Glasgow. Fruit is just coming on and flowers are abundant. This is a painter's country.[1]

For Hunter it was a breath of fresh air. The change of location brought about a radical shift in his painting. He did not abandon what he had gained from his analysis of the work of Cézanne and Matisse; rather it was the dramatic landscape, bright sunshine and outdoor life engendering in him a renewed sense of purpose and direction. His remark about Fife should be seen in its proper context, for Hunter loved Fife. However painting in Scotland had become a struggle in his somewhat agitated state of mind. Now France opened up so many more opportunities for moving forward. The three years he would spend in Provence were very productive. He was among like-minded artists, unlike in Glasgow, but on the other hand a great distance separated him from his sister and close friends in Scotland. They would not be able to care for him as they had done up till then. Painting was Hunter's *raison d'etre* and in his passionate and single-minded pursuit of it he would again neglect his health.

It is uncertain when Hunter arrived in Provence, but it seems likely that it was in the early spring of 1927. It was not long before he settled on the idea of making St Paul de Vence his base. St Paul is a beautiful medieval hill village about five miles inland from the Mediterranean coast between Nice and Cannes. In Hunter's day St Paul had an impressive view across scented, flower-cultivated valleys to the sea. There he found an irresistible, yet inexpensive auberge, *La Colombe d'Or*, run by Paul Roux and his wife. Hunter writes: 'The proprietor is very friendly to artists. He has had some fine studios built and for 40 francs a day one can have an elegant place with hot and cold water, bed and excellent board.'[2] Food on a regular basis was exactly what Hunter needed.

St Paul was sufficiently far from the cosmopolitan coast not to attract too many of the wealthy tourists, and so it provided an ideal environment and a pleasant existence for struggling artists. Indeed Paul Roux, himself a keen amateur artist, often accepted paintings in lieu of cash from his tenants, some of whom subsequently became the most important and influential painters of the twentieth century. Today *La Colombe d'Or* is renowned as a first-class hotel and restaurant, where guests can enjoy Roux's collection of paintings by Picasso, Braque, Matisse, Miró and of course Hunter, sculpture by the hugely-influential American, Alexander Calder, and an unusual variety of creations such as a ceramic mosaic by Fernand Léger on the terrace and a Braque mural by the swimming pool. On one occasion Hunter designed the cover of *La Colombe d'Or's* Christmas menu.[3]

110 | Villefranche
Oil on canvas, 1928
Private collection

A large community of artists was spread loosely along the Côte d'Azur. From 1917 Matisse was based in Nice and André Dunoyer de Segonzac was at the centre of artistic activities in St Tropez, surrounded by artists such as Derain and Friesz. Hunter kept in contact with Fergusson and Peploe, who were based at Antibes and Cassis respectively and, of course, knew Segonzac from their early days in Paris. In September 1927 Hunter writes of one of several memorable occasions: 'I met Lefevre [retiring partner of Alex Reid & Lefevre in London] at St Tropez and had dinner with him, Segonzac and others at St Maxime – a very delightful evening in which I got very friendly with the French painters'.[4] All that Hunter observed on the Côte d'Azur would have strengthened his resolve to follow his instincts.

Hunter was immediately drawn to the Provencal landscape. As in the past, he used landscape to develop and explore his response to the fresh, exciting aspects of Nature, eventually transferring what he learnt to his still life and figure painting. His three years in Provence produced works of wonderful colour and vitality. Indeed the immediate simplicity of his vision belies the compelling strength of his highly-developed sense of line and colour. Being so far from Britain – and, in particular, his dealer – he felt free to indulge his passion to record the landscape, experimenting with ways to capture its enthralling potency and luminescence. Wholeheartedly embracing the Provencal landscape, Hunter writes of his method: 'Peploe thought my plan of making innumerable drawings to learn the country an excellent one.'[5] By September 1927 he reports in a letter to McNeill Reid: 'I know the coast now between Monte Carlo and Cassis and have made about 100 drawings in colour.'[6] Those drawings demonstrate his immediate rapport with the landscape.

Hunter continued to strengthen and develop his technique. In *Street in Villefranche* (pl.112) he picks out the basic design with strong black ink lines, while his economical but inspired use of coloured crayons captures a scene of

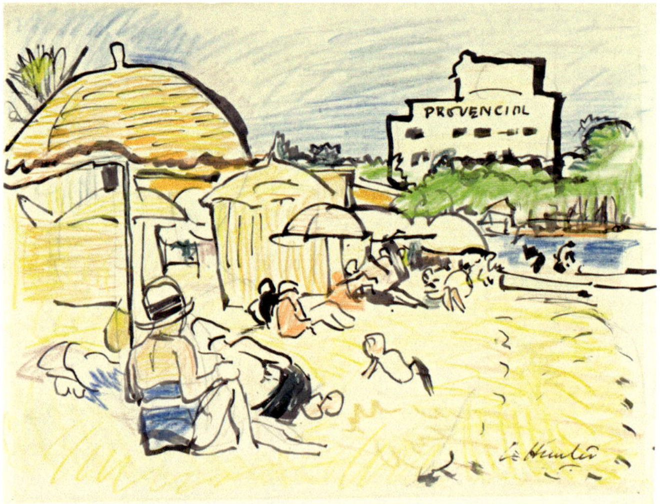

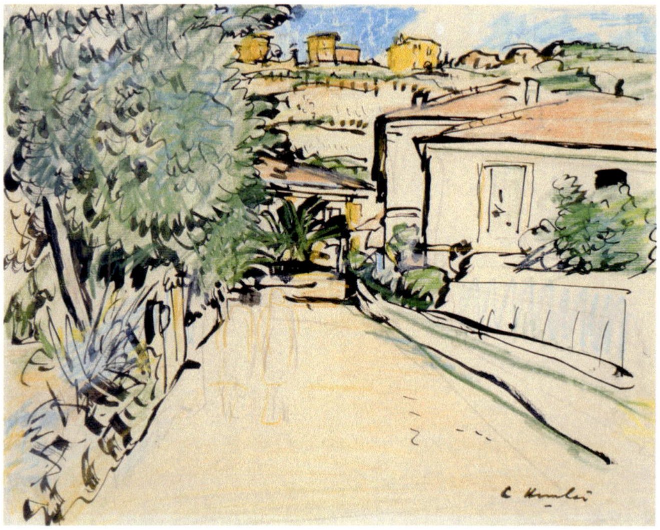

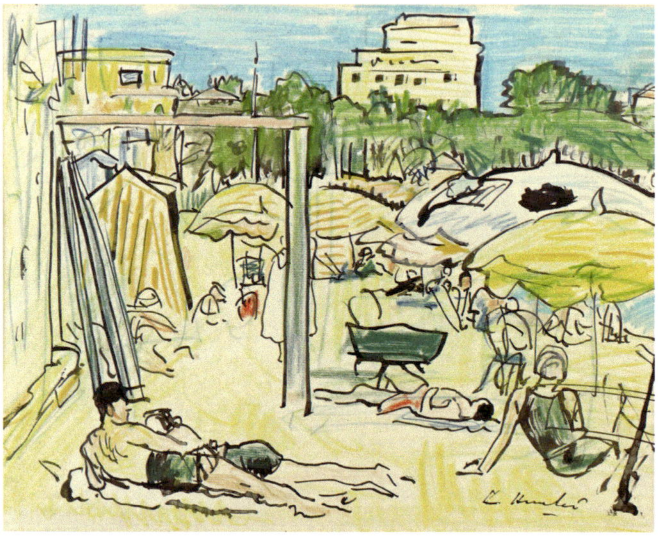

shimmering light and lingering sensuality. As in Fife, Hunter found his subject in the people relaxing by the seashore. At once he was attracted to the challenge of capturing that simple relationship between man and his enjoyment of Nature. There are many such views of which *Plage, Juan-les-Pins* (pl.113) is a particularly strong example. Again Hunter flattens the perspective, delineating the basic design in thick, black ink lines and relying on colour to evoke the sensual delight of Nature. This is achieved with a skilful yet understated simplicity new to his work.

Hunter's fascination for views through a window, as in *The Café, Cassis* (pl.115), affirms his continuing regard for Matisse's latest work. However, whereas Matisse made his passion for strong decorative design the main thrust, Hunter has achieved a stimulating counter-view by marrying the strong design of the architecture with the simple, fresh appeal of the marine view outside. He employs much the same technique in *The Balcony* (private collection), in which the qualities of the architectural design are well emphasised, while the colours in the buildings with the hill rising behind the rooftops subtly bind Nature to the man-made view below. When he was in Paris with McInnes in 1925, Hunter had seen examples of Matisse's current theme of women in exotic interiors by a window. However Hunter's window motif is really a continuation of his experiments in Largo that same year. The Provencal setting merely opened up new avenues for manipulating different aspects of form, tone, colour and texture.

Café, Vence (pl.116) is Hunter at his most perceptive. With striking simplicity, he has captured both the setting and ambience of the local square in Vence, a market town close by St Paul de Vence. The thick, black ink marks do not intrude

111 | Juan-les-Pins
Ink and coloured crayons, 1927
Scottish National Gallery of Modern Art

112 | Street in Villefranche
Pen & ink and coloured crayons, 1927
The Fleming-Wyfold Art Foundation

113 | Plage, Juan-les-Pins
Pen & ink and coloured crayons, 1927
Private collection

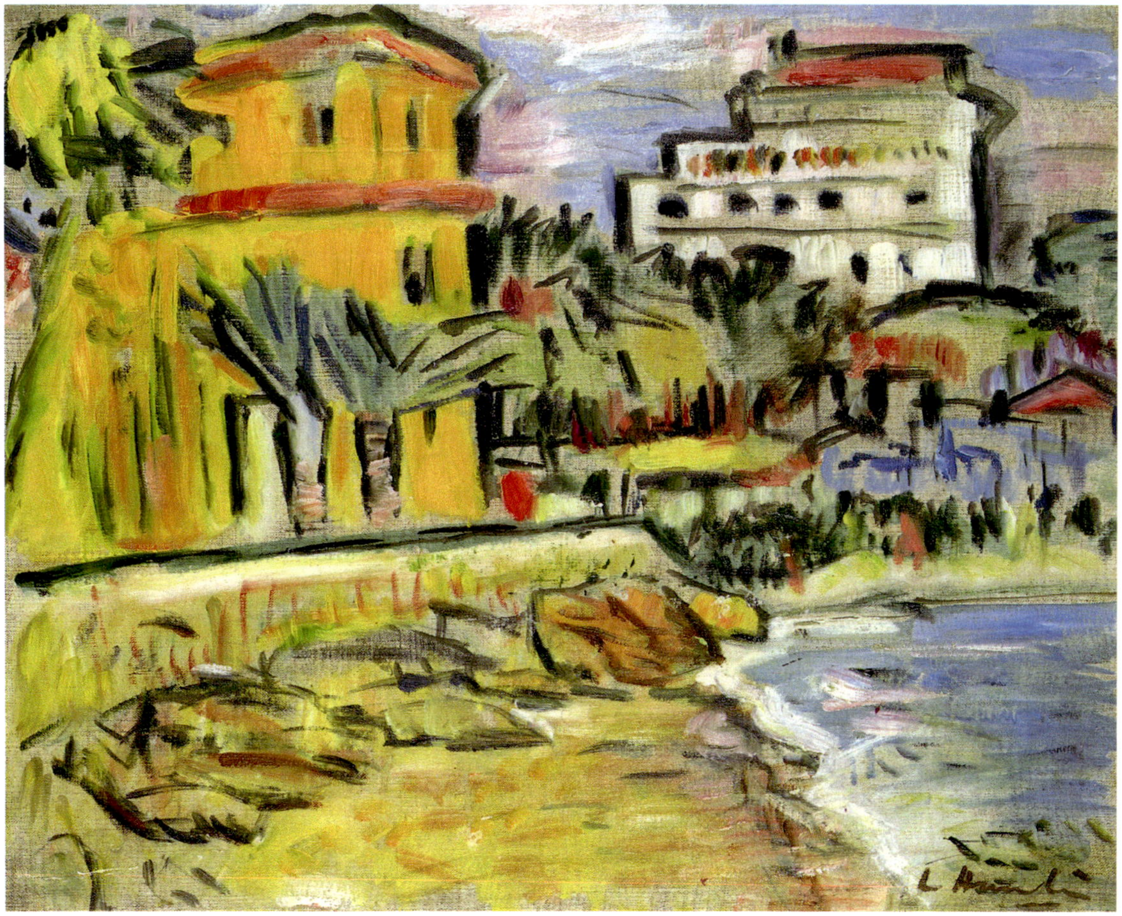

114 | Juan-les-Pins
Oil on canvas, 1928
Private collection

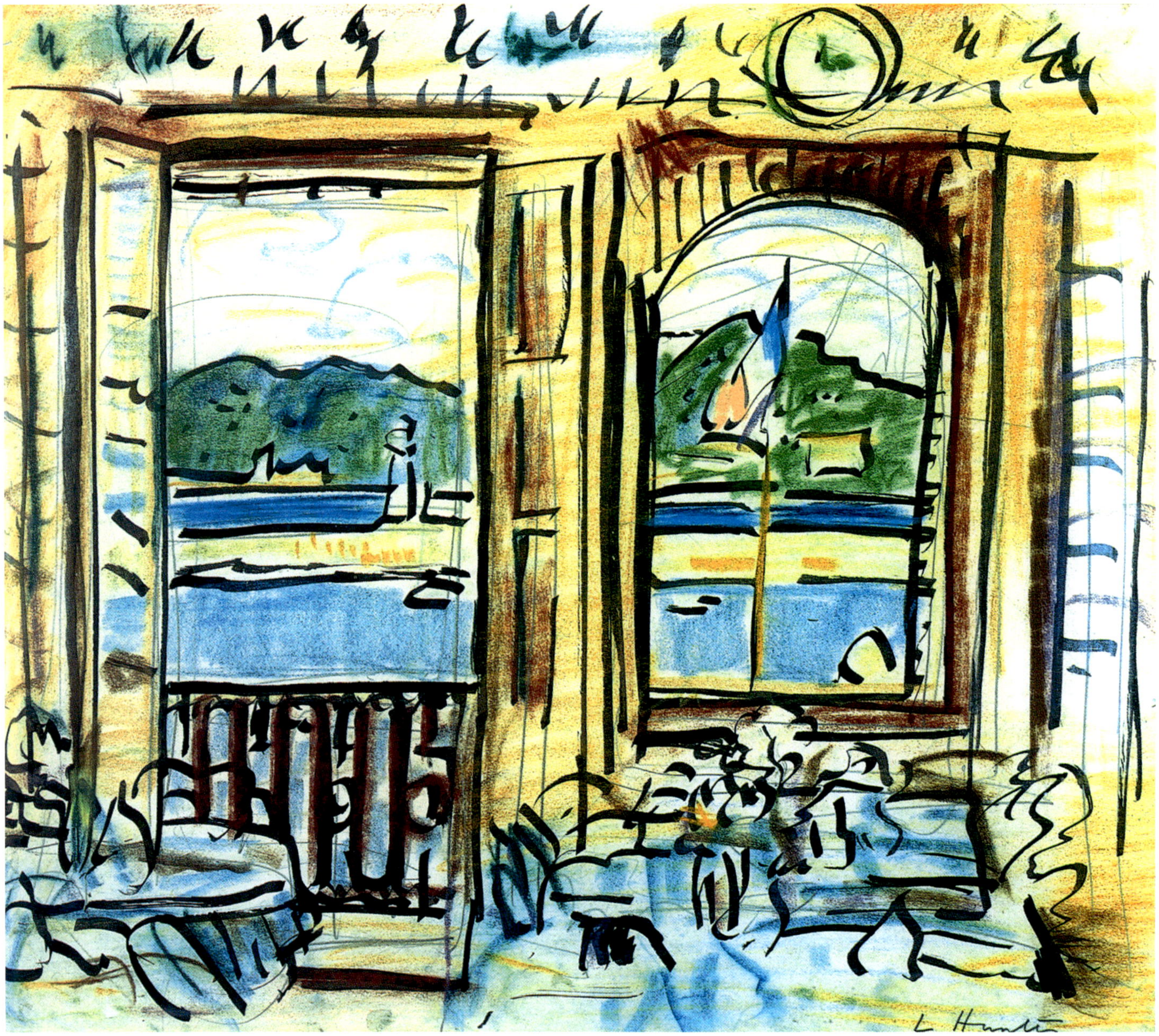

and the warm colour of the buildings and sun umbrella contrast with the blue and green of the sky and foliage, brilliantly conveying the very essence of a typical Provencal town.

Reid's reaction to Hunter's drawings was one of cautious optimism, however, telling Hunter in a letter in August, 1927:

I duly received the parcel of drawings. These in themselves are, of course, very slight, but the subjects are extremely interesting, and if you can carry through finished pictures they should prove good sellers for our forthcoming Exhibitions. We hope to give you a Show in London, Glasgow and Edinburgh during the coming winter.

See that you get all your pictures finished before you leave the South and don't make the mistake again of trying to get the Mediterranean atmosphere in a Glasgow studio … I will pass on your kind regards to all your friends as requested, and look forward to hearing from you that you have been producing masterpieces.[7]

Hunter's reply indicates a feeling that Reid has

115 | The Café, Cassis
Ink and pastel on paper, 1927
Private collection

not considered the drawings properly:

They may seem slight but if you try one or two in white mounts, as I have done here, with white paper behind them, as the paper is thin, you will, I think, find them more solid and substantial, especially at a little distance.

Of course, my paintings are the main thing. I may stay down here another month or two, and thereby take your advice to finish everything before returning.[8]

Hunter heeded Reid's advice in part, staying on at St Paul de Vence until almost the end of the year. However the reason for his extended stay is more mundane; he was genuinely happy in this simple, almost bohemian environment, and he had his eye on greater things. Hunter's letter confirms his faith in his work, and this new-found confidence had given rise to ambitious ideas of showing in New York. He writes to Justice:

I'm hoping to go over to New York in the late autumn [1928]. Fergusson's two shows in America were very successful and they have asked him to come over and my friend Ressich [John Ressich] is hoping to place a novel in the movies – so we will make a two.[9]

A little later he tells his cousin, Arthur Leyden, who lived in New York, of his intentions:

... There is just a slight chance I might run over your way and try to arrange a show. Peploe has one on in February at the Kraushaar Gallery ... My friend Ressich mentions to go over to try to get his novel filmed in which case I might go too but will let you know.[10]

The reason for the hesitation in the second letter was the result of one of Hunter's more outlandish escapades. In the two months or so between writing the two letters, Hunter embarked on an incredible piece of sheer folly. In such cases it was invariably his naivety and trusting nature that were to blame.

During several of his frequent visits to Nice, he had made the acquaintance of a Spanish Duke and a Count. Naturally Hunter took the Spaniards at face value. They praised his work and, when they heard he was planning to go to New York, they introduced the idea of his going to Palm Beach in Florida as their guest. Excited by such a prospect, he readily agreed to travel with his new-found friends. It was late December 1927 and, having raised the necessary funds for his New York trip, Hunter was on the point of leaving on the first leg of the journey, stopping first in Britain. Though unknown to Hunter at the time, it turned out the two Spaniards had out-stayed their welcome and their credit. By duping Hunter, they could see a way of extricating themselves from the south of France and moving on to Paris in a manner

116 | Café, Vence
Brush with ink and coloured crayons, 1927
Private collection

117 | Café Scene
Pen & ink and coloured crayons, 1927
Private collection

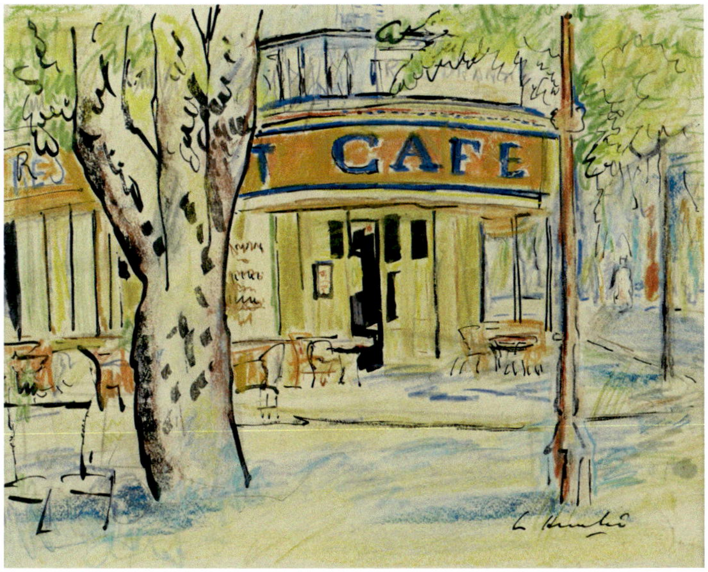

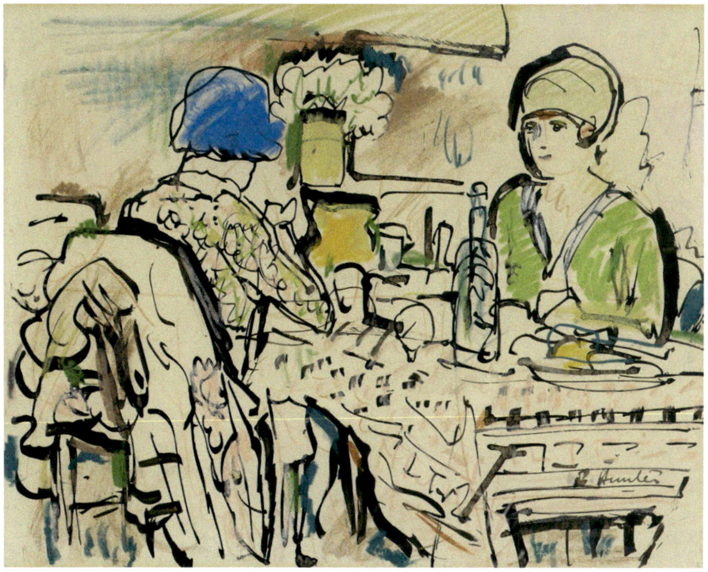

to which they had become accustomed, and someone else would pay the bills.

Perhaps their outrageous idea of travelling in a leisurely manner across France in a taxi was Hunter's innocent perception of what he imagined the rich would do. The project was swiftly agreed and, as their guest, Hunter need not even think of paying any share of the expenses. All the same, if he paid the bills *en route* and kept a note of the amounts, he would be repaid in full when they reached Fontainebleau, where they assured him they had direct access to their bank account. Unbelievably it was only after eight days of travel and a short stay at Fontainebleau that the taxi driver's proprietor cabled for the fare to be settled in the staggering sum of 11,000 francs; the hotel bill stood at 5,000 francs. Already the unfortunate Hunter had spent practically all the money that he had laid aside to take him to New York, but, not surprisingly, he had not received the promised refund. However worse was to come. The Spaniards' trail of debts in the south had come to light and swiftly all three travellers were apprehended by the police.

The last time Hunter had been arrested, he had fled out of the front door of the *gendarmerie*. On this occasion, however, it was not so easy. Eventually the French police were able to satisfy themselves that Hunter was not involved in the fraud, but was a victim. Instructing the police to contact Étienne Bignou, the Parisian art dealer who worked closely with Reid & Lefevre, Hunter was assured of his credentials being verified. Bignou agreed to collect him, but, having met Hunter on several earlier occasions, he was apprehensive about his quirky behaviour, which he found somewhat disturbing. The police had failed to explain why Hunter was in jail. So taking into account the possibility that Hunter's eccentricities might have got worse, Bignou gave firm instructions to his chauffeur to seat Hunter in the front of the car, where he could be watched. In addition Bignou provided his chauffeur with a revolver in case of any 'funny business.'[11] In such a manner Hunter was extricated from his predicament. The end result of this sorry tale meant Hunter was left without funds for New York. Later on, his adventure became a favourite and much-embellished anecdote, although at the time Hunter mentioned it only to Leyden:

While travelling in France in company with a Spanish Duke and Count we were arrested – the two having overlooked the payment of certain bills. I was let go. I spent several weeks with them and found them very charming.[12]

With the exception of the art business, about which he was passionate *and* well-informed, Hunter really could not imagine anything bad in people.

The season's work completed, Hunter's desire to stay on in Provence was very strong. He wrote to Justice:

I'm in love with this country and wish you all could come down here. Nice is charming – like Paris before the war. This country is like California only cooler and is commencing to be known as a summer resort. I am sorry I did not discover it sooner. It must be the best part of Europe with sunshine every day, fruit, flowers, fine colours and everything the heart could desire.

One meets numerous Americans here and to me it is a pleasant change from the Glasgow life and the awful Glasgow weather.

... We dine out here on a charming terrasse under orange trees with a fine view and the Alps beyond.[13]

Originally Hunter had been expected back in Glasgow in the autumn of 1927, but of course his return had been delayed. He found that however hard he worked, he could not translate his drawings into oils. Honeyman suggests that at the time Hunter was only really happy when he was drawing, and to 'transfer these notes was like trying to complete something already complete in itself'.[14] It would take a fresh summer season before he could pick up his brush again with any confidence. By the end of that year Hunter certainly needed to sort out matters with his dealer. His failure so far to produce oils meant that the proposed winter exhibitions would have to be postponed. In order to accommodate a compromise, Hunter agreed to commit himself to a London show the following May.

Over the space of a few years there had been a significant change in the setup and personnel of La Société des Beaux-Arts, Hunter's dealer. In 1925 Alexander Reid had retired, leaving the gallery in the hands of his son, McNeill, when the firm was renamed Alex Reid & Son. Conscious of the fact that he would need assistance to run the gallery, McNeill took on Duncan Macdonald, a talented young man then working for Aitken Dott, the Edinburgh dealer.[15] Times were changing and Glasgow's industrial and commercial predominance was showing signs of decline. Reid Senior had often discussed with his son the possibility of opening a branch in London, as it appeared business was shifting in that direction. Over the years he had built up a good working relationship with Ernest Lefevre of the Lefevre Gallery in London. Lefevre too was on the point of retiring, so it was to their mutual advantage to merge their respective galleries. This they did in April 1926, when the firm became Alex Reid & Lefevre. The French dealer, Étienne Bignou, also became a director,[16] further strengthening the company's position in the international art market. Macdonald moved to London to work alongside Lefevre until the latter retired, when Macdonald took charge of the London gallery. Thereafter Macdonald's career blossomed into one of international renown, a career that to this day Scotland has steadfastly failed to recognise. Until Macdonald's death in 1948, his successful partnership with McNeill Reid was marked by the sheer virtuosity, energy and imagination with which both men enlightened and assaulted the art world's imagination with modern exhibitions in their galleries in London, Glasgow and, after 1935, in New York. Macdonald, a stylish man with a keen eye for quality, was also an astute businessman. His commitment to modern art was absolute. In the face of ignorance and stubborn attitudes, he never lost his enthusiasm. Amusingly he tells of a weekend in the country with clients, when he was introduced to an elderly and much respected judge: 'We had the most terrific arguments on modern painting and literature. These old chaps think everything must and ought to be as in the days of Victoria the Good. Annoying to speak with if they don't have elastic minds!'[17]

Hunter now had to deal with two directors at Alex Reid & Lefevre, and Macdonald would prove to be less mild-mannered than McNeill Reid. Indirectly the changes had a significant bearing on Hunter's future. Since his exhibition in Glasgow in December 1925, Hunter had not produced nearly the amount of finished work that Reid and Aitken Dott had expected when his contract with them was drawn up in 1924. Indeed the contract had had to be renegotiated in 1926, McNeill writing to George Proudfoot at Aitken Dott:

I have just had a talk with Leslie Hunter regarding our arrangement for guarantee and he is agreeable to make some alternative agreement on whatever lines we mutually arrange. He does not propose to let us off with the total sum, but he is willing to spread it over a longer period and suggests either that we should give him £450 for 4 years, or that we should slightly increase the total and make it £400 for 5 years.
I thought he might have been prepared to wash part of it out altogether, seeing that he has not drawn anything like the sum we originally guaranteed [£600]. *He is a businessman and having got something he does not propose to give it up.*[18]

Although Hunter gave the impression of being a painter totally wrapped up in his art to the exclusion of almost everything else, McNeill's letter proves that he was not as detached from reality as might have been thought. At times he must have been a sore trial for his dealer in more ways than one. Over the previous two years Reid & Lefevre had had to pay most of Hunter's outstanding bills without seeing much of a return in the way of completed paintings.

With a London show fixed for May 1928 – just four months away – and the need to raise funds all over again for his projected New York trip, Hunter was very anxious to return to the south of France and begin painting in earnest.

In a generous act of faith given the circumstances – and probably to test reaction – Reid held a small exhibition in Glasgow of Hunter's recent drawings of the south of France. The new direction that he had taken was not well received. Honeyman records that some of Hunter's following 'professed a regret that he should have fallen so heavily under the influence of Segonzac, Matisse and the other "degenerate" Frenchmen'. Honeyman goes on to comment:

There was, if any, the merest trace of such influence, but, presumably, because of Hunter's delight in having met these artists, this was an explanation for the great change in the character of his work. Many of the oil paintings which he made from the drawings at this period did unquestionably pay homage to Matisse, but the rapid, spontaneous sketches which he did in ink, pastel and watercolour between 1926 and 1930 are among the most personal of all his output. Nevertheless, the confidence of his friends and especially of his dealers was a little bit shaken.[19]

Of course the public's reaction to the drawings was the very reason why Hunter had fled to France in the first place. Fortunately, by the time the exhibition opened Hunter was again resident in the south of France, thus escaping any ill effects that this kind of reaction could have triggered.

However Hunter had more pressing problems to contend with. In order to build up to painting in oils, he began once again by concentrating on his drawings. Removed from day-to-day contact with his dealers and friends, time slipped by, and though the drawings multiplied, the oil paintings he fully intended to finish did not materialise. As time ran out, it was inevitable events would overtake him.

Hunter would never wilfully hurt people or let them down. However a preoccupation with his art was totally ruling his life now. The short term casualty was his unwitting betrayal of Reid & Lefevre's trust, but the longer term damage was to his state of mind. With the deadline for the London show fast approaching and Hunter still having next to nothing to send over to London by way of oils, he received a plea from Reid: 'Macdonald is on tenterhooks over your forthcoming exhibition as he has no news of your pictures. Their non-arrival would be very disastrous for us all.'[20] At the eleventh hour Hunter attempted to salvage the situation as best he could:

I got your letter shortly after I had sent over 40 pastel drawings to Macdonald with Peploe's boys who were leaving that day. April here turned out as bad a month as the one that preceded it and I found it a very hopeless struggle trying to finish the canvases I had started the preceding month.

I found working against time and in the conditions of mistral and rain, that many of the best things were spoiled and many unfinished. I saw Mrs Macdonald [Duncan Macdonald's wife] *here and she seemed to think the show should be postponed. I sent on the drawings hoping they might be a substitute if necessary. They are very much better than what appeared in Glasgow and were only possible during the short days and bad weather when oil painting was difficult and almost impossible, as Peploe found.*

After receiving your letter I waited to hear from Macdonald but failed to hear anything tho' I wired what to do.

It seemed a pity to give an imperfect show done under adverse circumstances and subject to criticism when by delay if possible when the real season that is now coming on, is making painting really possible. I am, now that the days are longer, getting very effectively on with things while thinking of your letter about bringing what I had. I kept waiting to hear from Macdonald and felt in a dilemma what with.

Perhaps you can explain how things are going. You may be sure I am concerned and interested having heard nothing.[21]

Peploe's son, Denis, remembers vividly the day he delivered the parcel of drawings to Duncan Macdonald. There was Macdonald eagerly awaiting a large consignment of oil paintings, when the boys had but a small parcel of drawings. The shock wave was palpable! The exhibition had been advertised and it would have to be cancelled, which would be an extreme embarrassment all round.

When matters had calmed down a little,

Hunter wrote again to Reid, though on this occasion he found it a struggle to justify his position:

I had a letter from Macdonald re the show in London. I'm vexed at the amount of upset and annoyance my defection in the matter of his show has caused him. I had hoped to be able to find enough canvases to make a reasonable showing but April seemed even worse from the weather standpoint than March. It resulted in many unfinished pictures that I had hoped by April to finish in time. But the last two weeks were chiefly Mistral and rain.

... I found the days here as in the North very short which made painting difficult ... I had no idea how much preparation had been made about the show in London thinking only how things were arranged in Glasgow – advertising had started with the show. I feel I must make up for the delay and upset. Sincere regrets for the unavoidable postponement of the London show.[22]

Hunter had been totally unrealistic in his expectation that he could produce the necessary work at a time when sensibly other artists all but ceased painting. He had managed in the past to produce work over the winter and early spring, but then he was in the strong position of having good friends with their measured encouragement close by, helping him to focus on priorities. He had no such safety net in France. However, as Macdonald pointed out to Hunter, the problem was not that he had failed to produce finished pictures, remarking 'that is a thing that might happen to any artist', but that he had not let him know in time to make other arrangements.[23]

Hunter's relief that the exhibition had been cancelled allowed him to concentrate on the coming season. Now pleased with the way his work was developing, he writes to Reid:

The forty drawings I sent were in pastel than in paints. Truly very much stronger in design and colour than what were exposed at Glasgow and would make a reasonable show. However much the show has been postponed, I will be able to give a very representative one in oils. The summer after all is the only place one can work here as elsewhere and I am hoping to get figures as well as landscapes and marines which I will have ready by the autumn.

The good weather is just starting as I write, soon fruit will be arriving so that I can get a lot of still life done.

I have a friend here who is Matisse's most intimate friend in Nice. He expects to bring Matisse up to see me.

Hunter finishes up with the inevitable request for funds:

Material for painting I find expensive if you could let me have £30 or £35 to pay my bill and order some canvases to colour.[24]

Hunter was as good as his word. By the autumn he had produced the landscapes, marines, figures and still lifes that he had promised.

Hunter's work in the south of France had developed along what his friends and dealers considered to be a more extreme line, one for which they were unprepared. His new environment, experience of Matisse's creativity, and lively contact with numerous artists based in Provence provoked in Hunter a renewed passion for experimentation. The dramatic forms of the Provencal landscape, wonderful colour

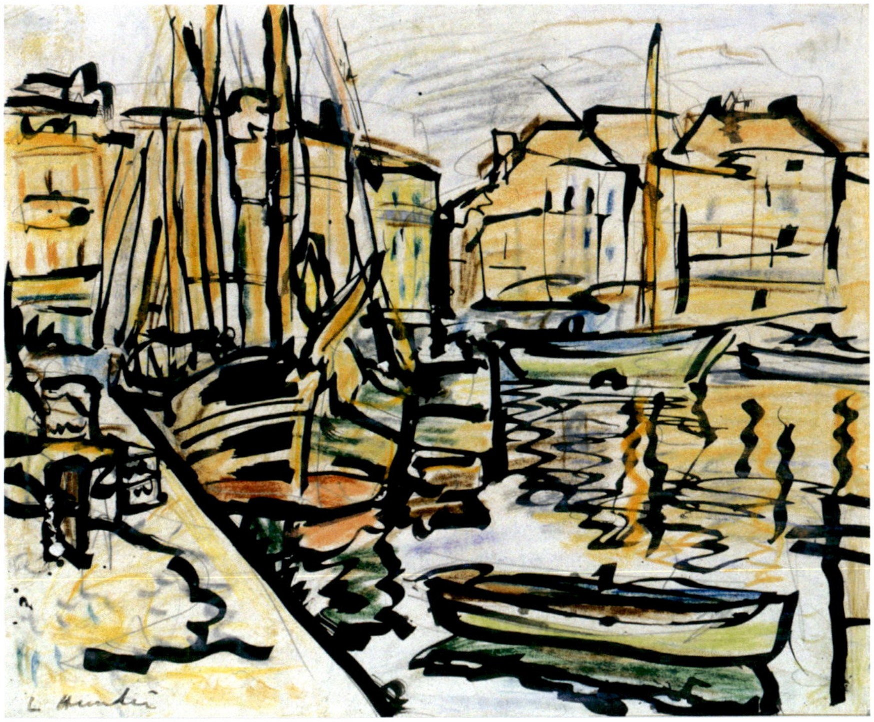

118 | The Harbour, St Tropez
Brush with ink and coloured crayons, 1927
Aberdeen Art Gallery and Museums Collections

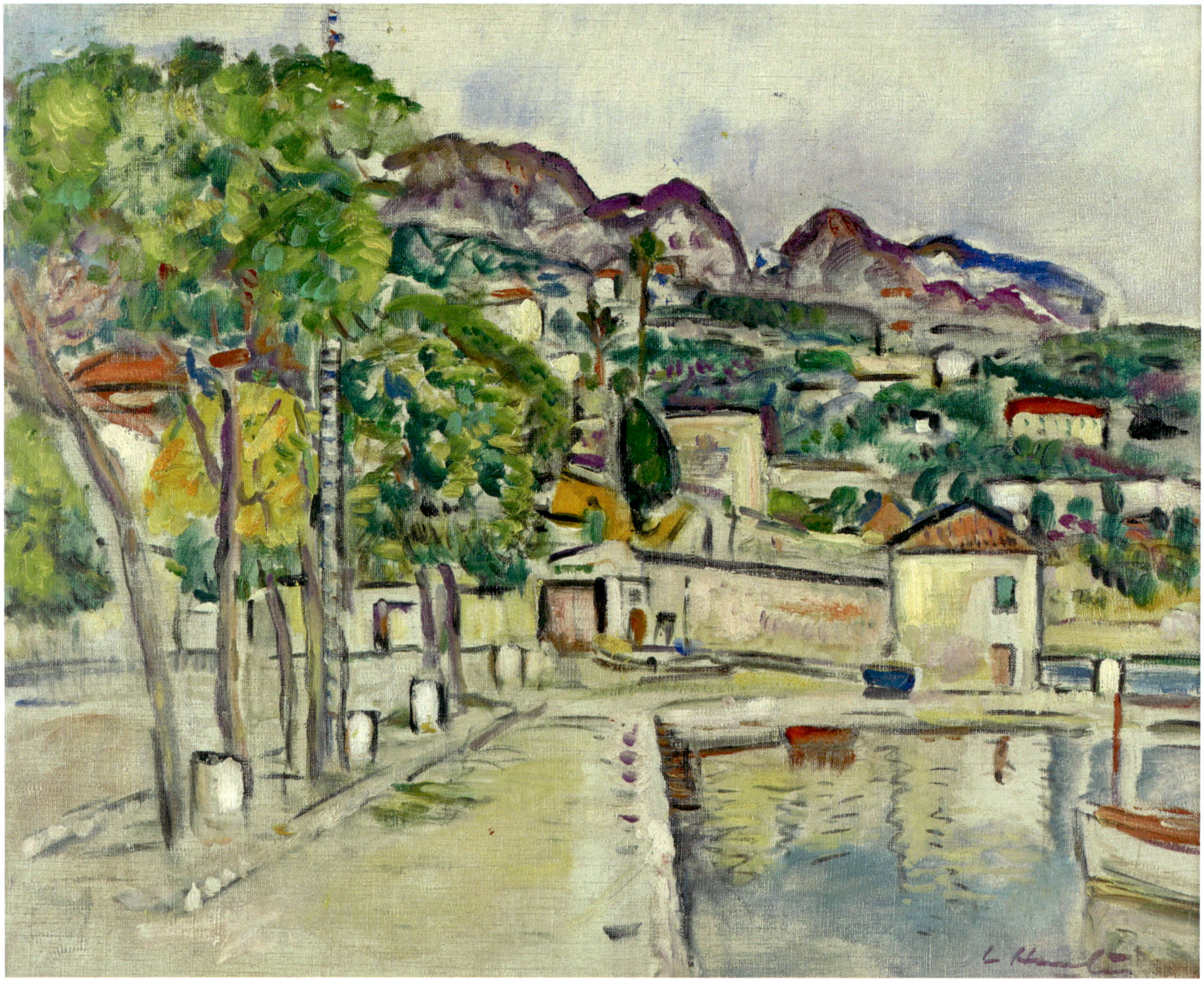

119 | The Harbour at Villefranche
Oil on canvas, 1928
Private collection

and strong, bright light also forced Hunter to reconsider his technique. He tells Reid: 'I am working in a thin fashion and see my way to get the luminous nature of the country here'.[25]

Painting in a thin fashion was a new and interesting concept for Hunter. Again there may be a connection with Matisse. The still life by Matisse that had been purchased by McInnes is painted almost transparently in places and overall the paint is thin, yet there is no loss of intensity in the colour. Contrary to what might be expected, painting in a thin fashion did not mean that Hunter would have to sacrifice colour strength. His 1928 paintings of both still life and landscape clearly demonstrate that there is no moderation in his use of bright colour.

For his oils Hunter still prepared the way with drawings, but now they were distinctively stronger in design than those of 1927. In *Harbour, St Tropez* (pl.118) the unmistakably bold black ink lines reverberate with energy, while the contrasting areas of warm and cool colour merge together to inspired effect. Such strong lines define both volume and design, but it is the colour that dazzles. In using thick dark lines to define design, then applying strong areas

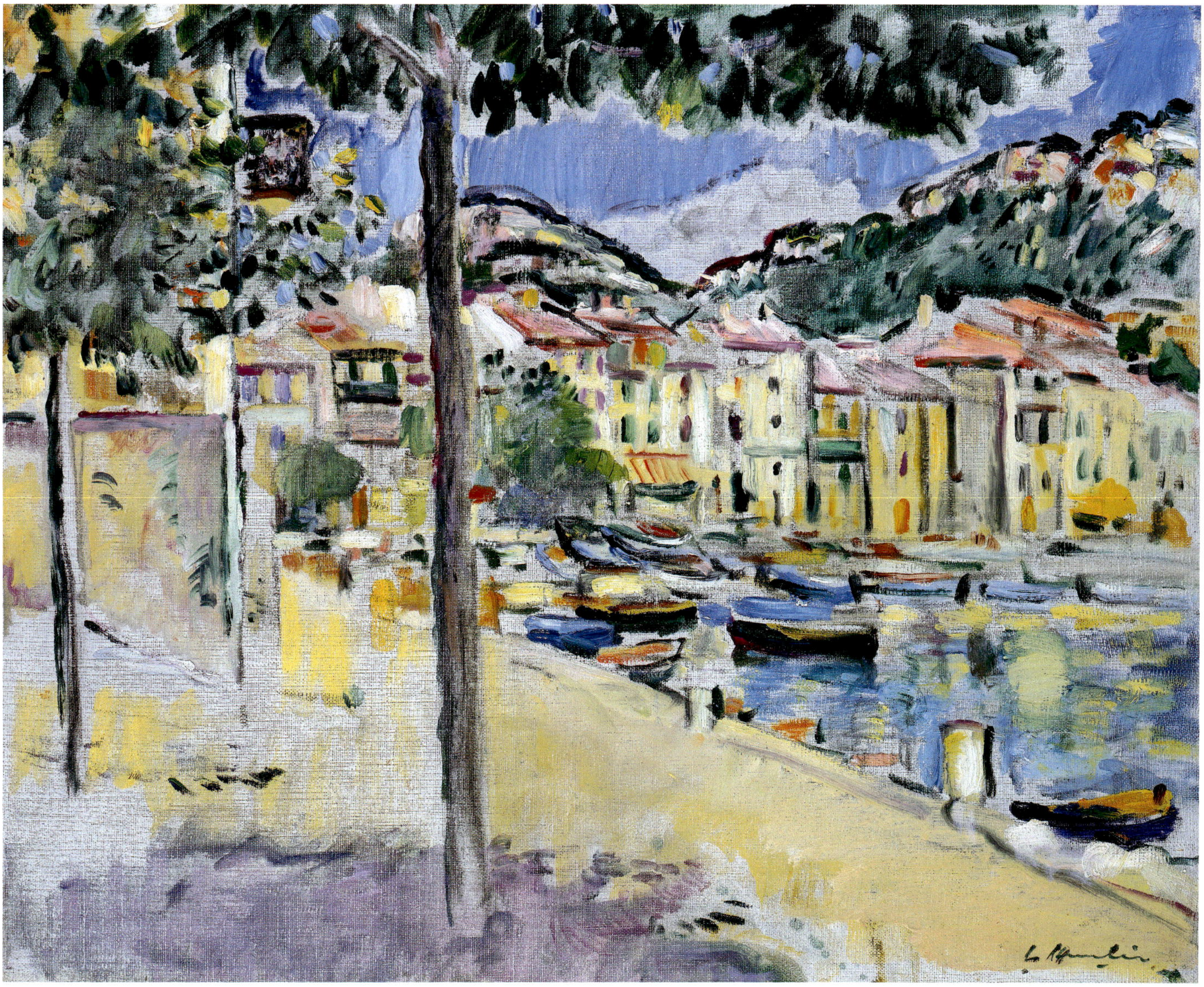

120 | Mediterranean Harbour (Villefranche)
Oil on canvas, 1928
Private collection

of colour within a flattened perspective plane, Hunter is returning to what he had originally started to experiment with in his 1924 series of Loch Lomond houseboats. The difference now is found in his more confident, sophisticated sense of design. Hunter had come a long way from his innovative Fife pictures of 1919–20.

There is another factor to be considered, namely Hunter's knowledge of the French artist, Othon Friesz (1879–1949), and his sunlit harbour scenes painted at Toulon in 1927. Friesz also used strong dark lines to define pattern and movement, albeit to different ends, but there is a similarity in approach between the two artists in their bold delineation and singular application of paint. Friesz, a good friend of French artist, Segonzac, had also known Fergusson in pre-war Paris. Along with Matisse, Friesz had been among the original group of Fauve artists in 1905. There were many points of contact; Hunter's encounter and subsequent acquaintance with Segonzac the previous year and, of course, his close contact with Fergusson at Antibes would point to the strong possibility of Hunter and Friesz having met at some stage. Based at St Tropez, Segonzac's villa was well known as a popular meeting place for artists. Hunter had long admired the work of both Friesz and Segonzac, having seen it regularly at Percy Moore Turner's London gallery. In fact Turner and Segonzac were very good friends, as was Turner with Segonzac's biographer, Paul Jamot. With such strong connections to Segonzac and Friesz there is every reason to suppose that Hunter's radical new style attained the same standard as the work of this important and creative group of French artists. At the same time it should be stressed that the roots of Hunter's current style firmly lie in his own long and highly individual artistic development.

Another of Hunter's favourite painting grounds was Juan-les-Pins. There he found the beach alive with activity (see pls. 111 & 113), wealthy tourists strolling along the promenade and the kind of architecture that naturally appealed to his sense of design. In *Juan-les-Pins* (pl.114) it can be seen how compatible his new technique is with the landscape. Hunter adeptly contrasts the monumental shapes of the two buildings with the pattern of the palm trees, shrubbery, shoreline and sea. All these elements fuse together, producing a wonderful depiction of the warmth and languor of the Mediterranean. Interestingly this effect is not achieved by applying strong colour in thick broad sweeps as in his Scottish views. In almost contradictory terms he limits his choice of strong colours to a few – mainly yellow, green and blue – and applies them thinly, deliberately leaving almost bare areas of canvas.

Hunter's radical new style shifts the emphasis from form to design. To an extent he is fulfilling aims he laid out for himself in 1923, namely to develop his sense of line.[26] Yet, intelligently building upon his experience of Matisse's design-based approach, Hunter's own artistic consciousness still holds on to a need for volume, albeit much reduced. This streak of independence resoundingly confirms Hunter's artistic integrity. From here his work moves into a maturity rich in colour and expression.

His compositions invariably have a point of reference that forms the key to his treatment of volume. Frequently it is found in the strong outline of a building. The white building on the right hand side of *Juan-les-Pins* is the *Hotel Provencal*. In its heyday it was the epitome of the smart, luxurious hotel. In his series of paintings of Juan-les-Pins, Hunter consistently highlights the hotel's irregular outline, using its prominent mass in the same way he did with the granary building at Lower Largo in his coastal scenes of 1924–26; it forms the initial focal point. Applying the same technique in other south of France views, Hunter achieves superb results. In *Harbour at Villefranche* (pl.119) the combination of harbour building and front acts as the main focal point to lead into the view that fills the eye with sensations of timeless purple-hued mountains, a clutter of red roofs, yellow buildings and rich foliage and the dazzling shimmer of the reflections on the surface of the water.

When Hunter wished to introduce a wider range of colours, he obtained a subtly different effect. By drastically toning down the use of strong black lines, the tree in *Mediterranean*

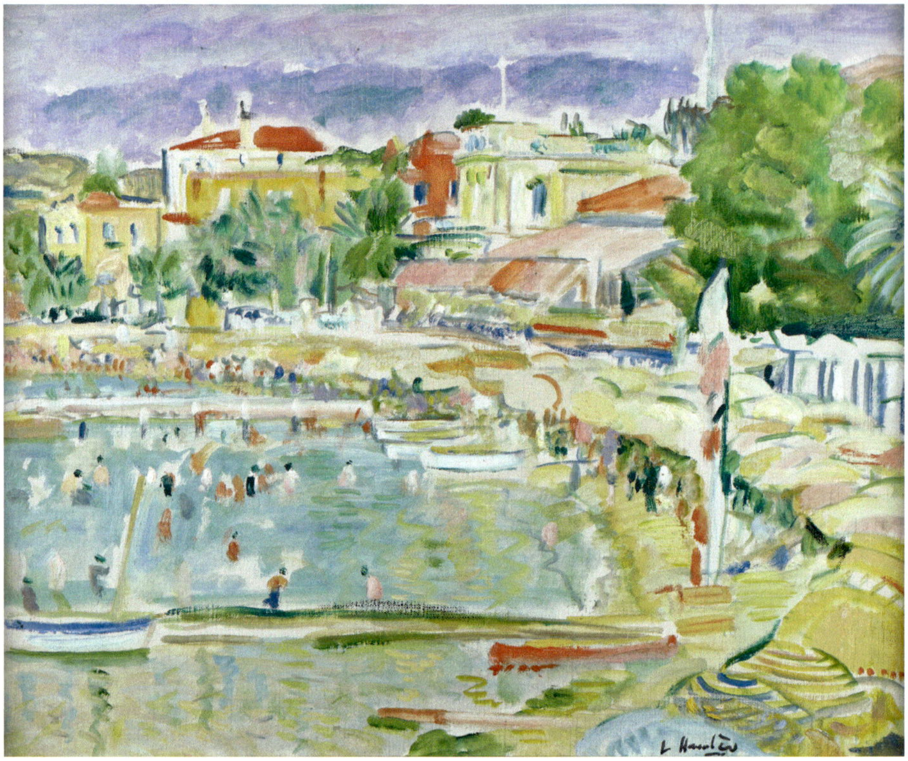

121 | The Bay, Juan-les-Pins
Oil on canvas, 1928
Private collection

122 | Summer Spray
Watercolour, 1928
Private collection

Harbour (pl.120) provides the focal point. The contrast of the conglomeration of roofs and windows and the collection of small boats, their dappled reflections punctuating the water's sparkling surface, evoke the same sensual feel, but in this case through a more complex application of colour and tone. Equally, in *The Bay, Juan-les-Pins* (pl.121) the animation and sparkle is brought about by the jumble of roofs, umbrellas and trees juxtaposed with the numerous bathers in the water. However this intricate application of colour should not imply the pigment was applied thickly. On the contrary it aptly illustrates Hunter's desire to paint in a thin fashion. Despite his radical change in style, these paintings brilliantly retain the harmony and vitality that had long been Hunter's hallmark.

The Côte d'Azur, famed for its cultivation of flowers for the perfume industry, provided a wonderful location for sustaining Hunter's love of still life. With an abundant choice of brightly coloured, fresh blooms for the greater part of the year, Hunter was now more than ready to transfer his newly-developed style from landscape to still life. As always, drawings furnished Hunter with a base from which he

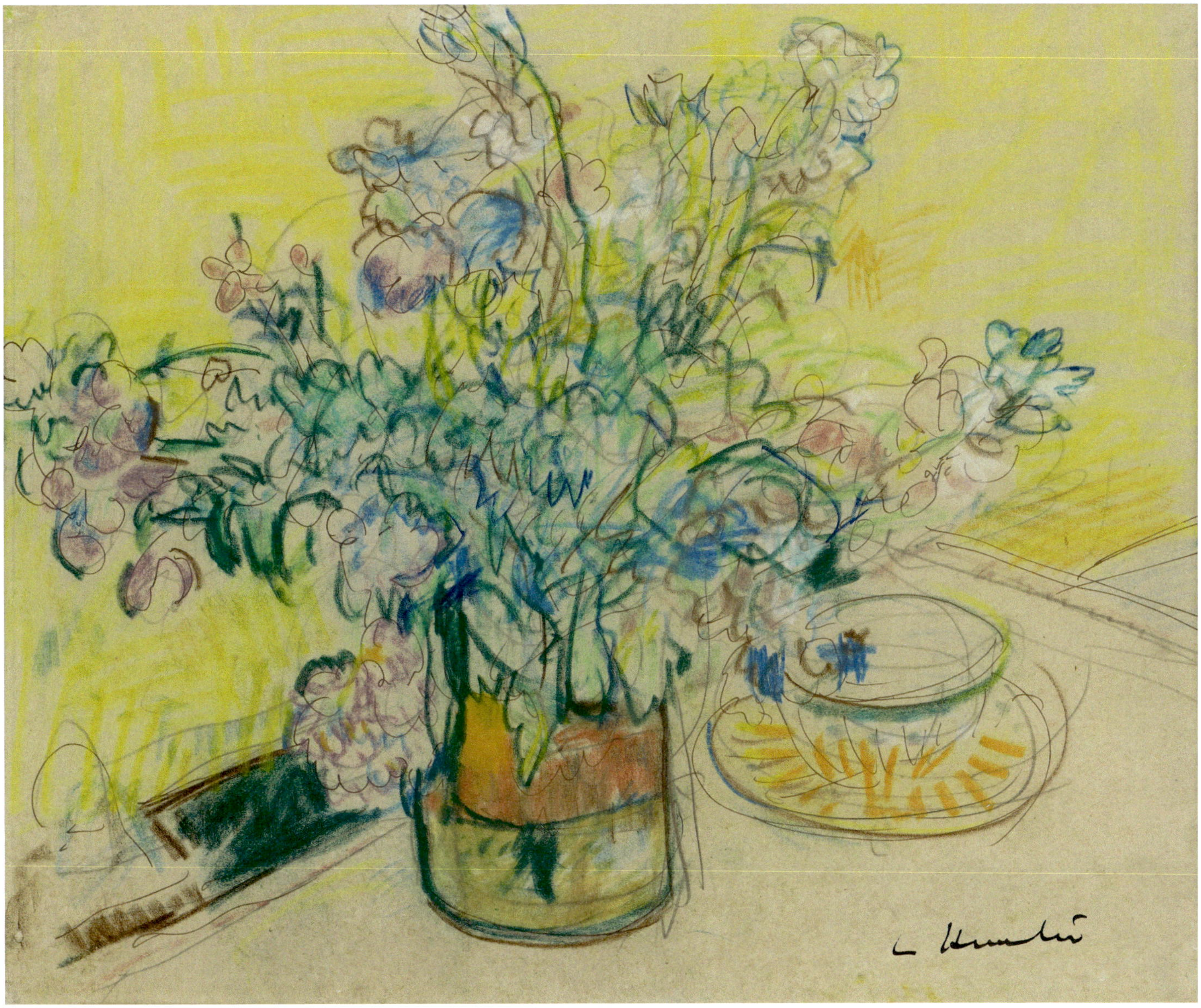

could form his ideas. In *Summer Spray* (pl.122) Hunter is at his most vibrant; the unruly tangle of blooms and foliage burst outwards from the simple vase. The composition is balanced by the angular shape of the surface on which the vase stands and the symmetry of the solitary yellow teacup and saucer.

Still lifes painted in oils reflect the two basic approaches he applied in his landscape. There is the strongly patterned style with its attendant thick black lines, and at the opposite end of the scale the thinly painted, almost liquid application of rich colour and tone. The latter style is vividly demonstrated in *Still Life with Flowers in a Yellow Vase* (pl.123). The flowers dance across the surface of the canvas, merging with the delicate indeterminate background in an almost virtuoso performance of flat perspective. Tension, created through the contrast between the soft petals and the bold fruit, further serves to heighten the sense of vitality. The fruit is given a distinct sense of volume through bold colour, offset against a transparent table top. Only a few strategically placed dark lines remain to hint at any further substance or form.

In complete contrast, Hunter attacks the picture surface in *Still Life with Flowers in a Jug* (pl.124), its strong black lines predominant. In 1925 Hunter relied on his skilled use of bright colour to prevail as the sole creator of form, whereas three years later he allows the strong accents of colour to act in partnership with the black lines to create above all a dynamic pattern. Neither Peploe nor Cadell took such risks in still life; they adopted a much more formal approach. Nor was Hunter's lust for pattern confined exclusively to painting flowers and fruit. His widening array of props extended to baskets, books, vegetables and even implements such as scissors, as in *Still Life with Bible and Scissors* (pl.126). Many of these pictures were sent to London for his first solo exhibition in the capital in October 1928.

Working hard over the summer, Hunter's confidence in his work increased. It was bolstered further by being among like-minded painters and residing in a country more inclined

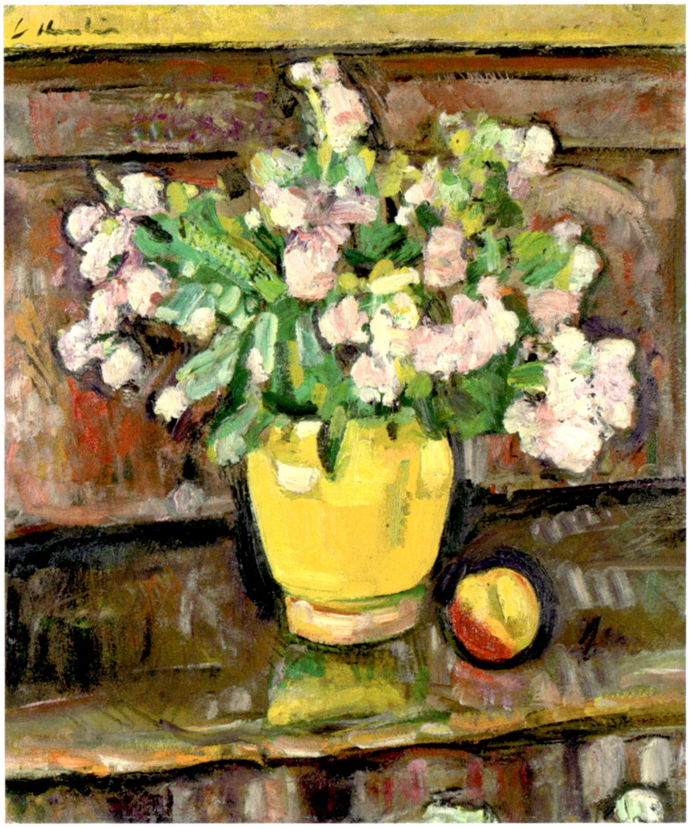

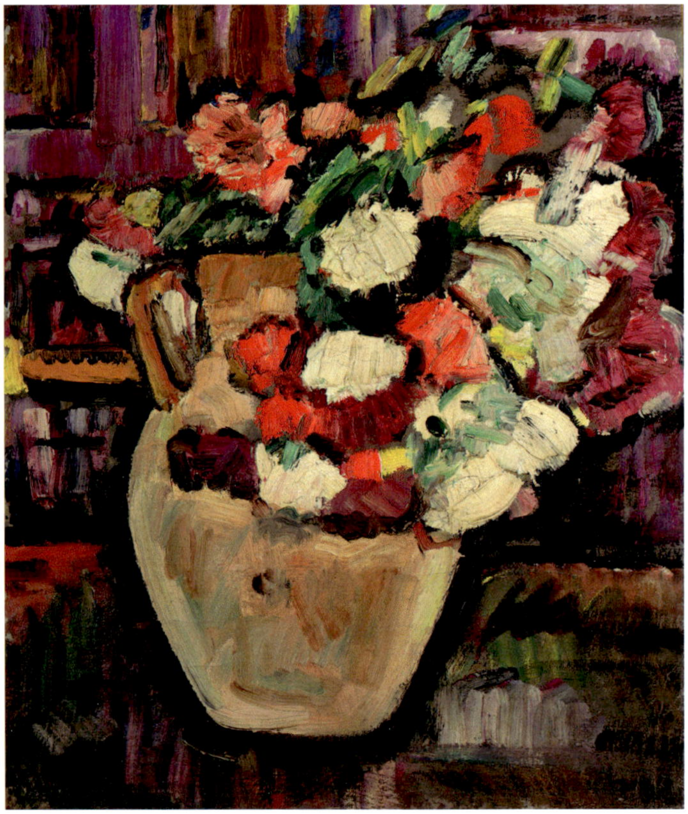

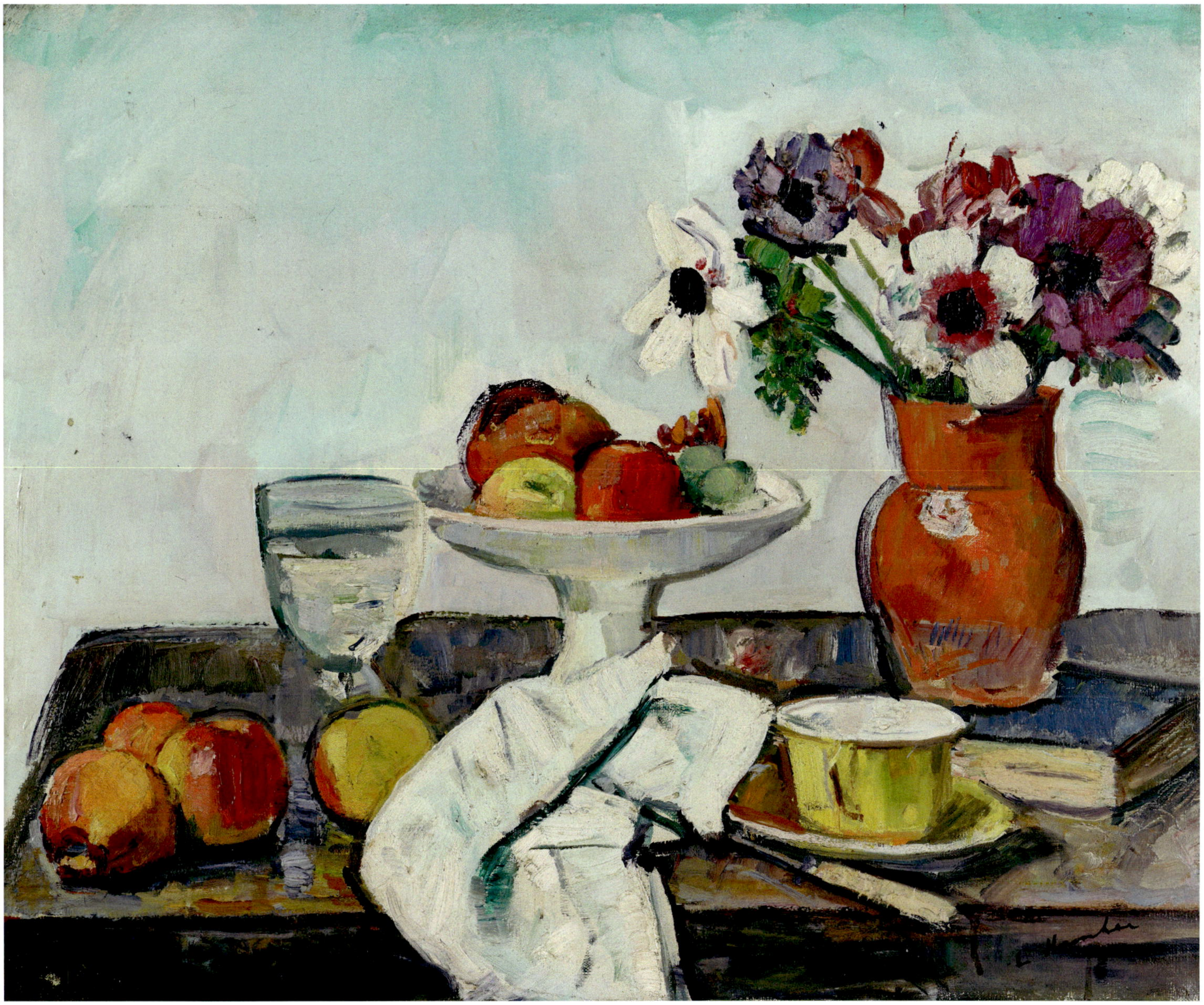

123 | Still Life with Flowers in a Yellow Vase
Oil on board, 1928
Private collection

124 | Still Life with Flowers in a Jug
Oil on canvas, 1928
Private collection

125 | Anemones in a Red Vase, Yellow Teacup and Apples
Oil on canvas, 1927–28
Private collection

to embrace artists and modern movements. In contrast London was not so disposed to such advanced trends. With the adverse reaction to Hunter's February show imprinted on Reid's memory, he was understandably nervous when Hunter wrote to him that the season's work was impressive and that his friends thought highly of it. Reid's immediate response followed swiftly: *Remember, in your painting do not be led astray by all the nice things your friends say about your work, for it does not cost them anything. Sit down in the worst temper you can get and pull them to pieces or get Peploe to be absolutely candid, and you should then be able to find out their merits and defects.*[27]

Understandably Reid was apprehensive about the reaction to Hunter's new style. In the event his fears were justified; very few sales materialised. The reaction of the critics did not help. Honeyman summed it up well when he wrote that they were 'patronising, and if they showed any appreciation they were careful to qualify it with a reservation'.[28]

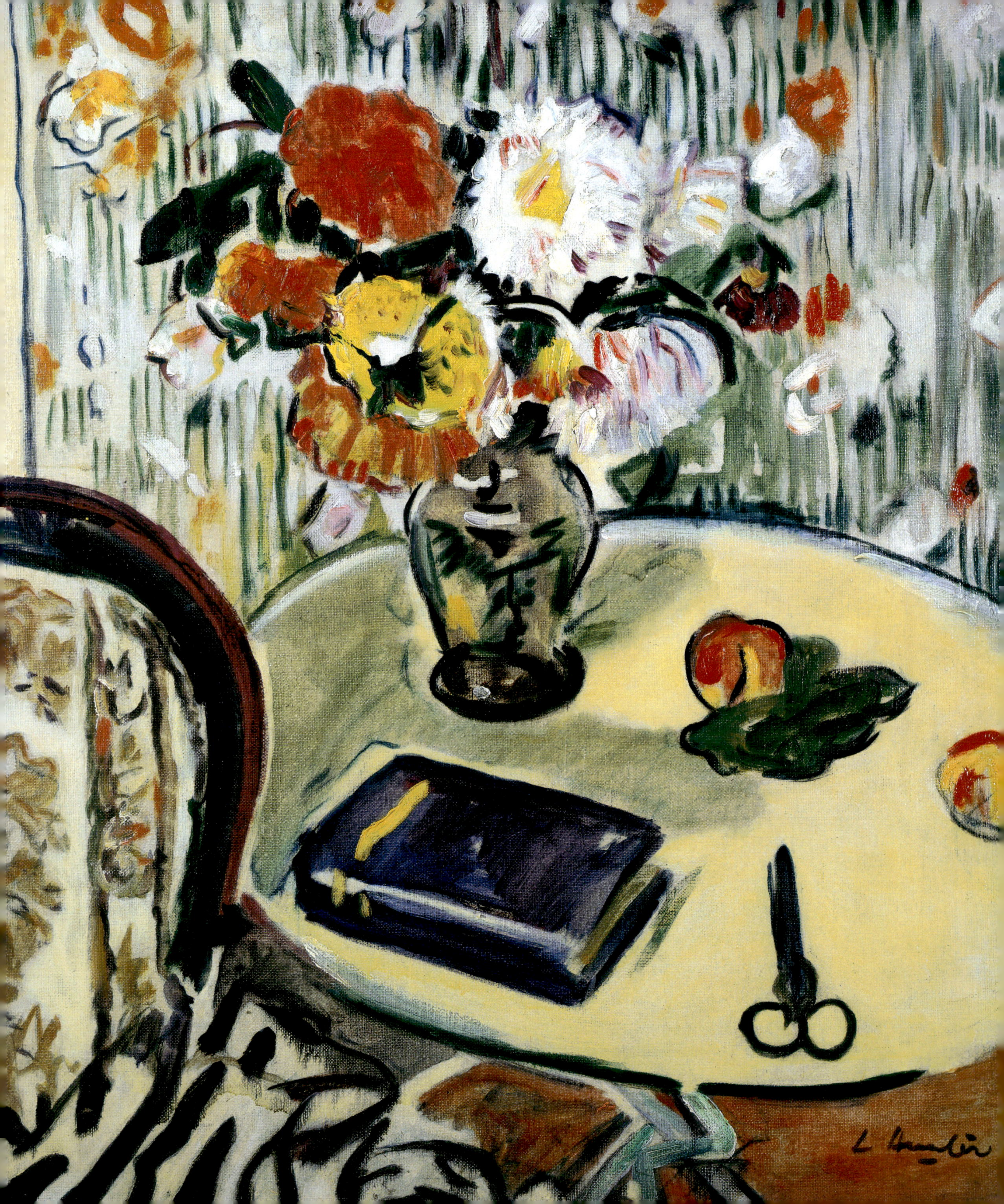

126 | Still Life with Bible and Scissors
Oil on canvas, 1928
Private collection

The Times considered that Hunter's still life 'gives the best entertainment':

His designs are firm, well balanced, energetic in movement, and lively in colour ... The chief disadvantage of such painting is that it says all that it has to say at a glance, unless the design is made very complicated, and Mr Hunter's pictures must be looked at as intended, frankly for wall decoration. That he does not shirk the problems of recession, which are hardly present in still life subjects, is shown in such landscapes as 'Street in Cassis' and 'Bathing Hour, Juan-les-Pins', which attain sufficient depth by colour relations alone. So far as it goes this is a stimulating form of art, but it excites rather than satisfies.[29]

Commenting on Hunter's change of style, *The Morning Post* offers:

... He now depends mainly upon sumptuous colour-patterns and the blinding light of the South as motives for his principal essays in painting. Sacrifice of the third dimension and structural firmness is not always atoned for, especially in the still life pieces, but some of these are most attractive ... His skill, however, finds fullest expression in pictures such as the 'Bathing Hour, Juan-les-Pins' (45), 'Port of Villefranche' (33), 'Rue de Poillu' (18), and 'Street in Antibes' (48).

In these the glamour of the Riviera region is suggested with uncommon power.

Still, his brilliant methods occasionally lack the reticence which betokens thought and gives permanent significance to art.[30]

The Observer sourly states:

Mr. Leslie Hunter ... belongs to the group of Scottish painters headed by Mr. Peploe and Mr. Fergusson whose whole work constitutes, as it were, a protest against the cold Calvinism and the dourness that tinge the life and outlook of their land. From the bleakness of the moors and the featureless, grey grimness of Scottish buildings in town and country, he, like his fellow workers, seeks refuge in a riotously-gay palette; but whereas Mr. Peploe draws his colour from the store of his fertile imagination, Mr. Hunter found it necessary or advisable to go South, where a kindlier sun does the preparatory work for him by painting the world in a lively, high key.

The critic cannot have viewed Hunter's exhibitions in Glasgow in 1923 and 1925. Then Hunter and his Fife landscapes full of colour and light had more than proved that Scotland itself could inspire paintings in 'a lively, high key'. Also it could be argued that in this case it was not so much a 'fertile imagination' that was needed, but the vision and skill that allowed the paint to transcend the initial task of representation to a higher plane of emotional response, qualities that Hunter had proved he possessed. The newspaper's critic continues:

In one notable respect Mr. Hunter's recent work marks a departure from his earlier manner. He seems to have lost interest in the search for volume and to be more exclusively attracted by pattern and arabesque as though he had transferred his admiration from Cézanne to Matisse.

This implies a more liquid sketchy use of the pigment – a calligraphic manner which agrees better with his predilection for emphasised contours than did his more solid and plastic use of the medium, and which makes for greater unity. Mr Hunter is sufficiently varied in his general treatment and in the degrees of colour intensity that he manages to hold the spectator's interest even through his repetition of very similar themes ...

Unlike many painters of the entrancing neighbourhood of Marseilles and the Esterels, Mr. Hunter has not merely produced a few more additions of 'Views', but has absorbed no small amount of the seductive charm of that happy land. Often enough, he contents himself with sparsely-used colour and lines sketchily indicated with a brush. They are all that is needed, for his line has meaning. The drawings deal with landscape and other forms simply expressed in black outline, heightened by loose colour, generally yellow and red, on thin tissue paper. The treatment is again quite in keeping with what the artist means to convey.[31]

However *Art Weekly* was much more responsive and encouraging:

Mr. Hunter is one of those artists who has both deserved and received fortune's smiles. Along with three artists he held an exhibition in the West End three years ago; now he is holding a one-man show, and the brilliant quality of his work more than justifies this independence. His work has come on apace, and in design and colour his pictures show a maturity that was lacking in his earlier efforts. In the best of his pictures at this exhibition he suggests with great skill the wonderful sunlight and glitter of Riviera scenery. The finest of these are 'Port of Villefranche' and 'Street in Antibes'. In these and many others of his pictures there is power, atmosphere and wonderful colour. This is a show to be seen.[32]

Hunter's reaction to this decidedly mixed response was philosophical. He genuinely felt a strength and satisfaction in the way his painting was developing. He knew that much of the criticism had more to do with the somewhat archaic attitudes of the British art world than a personal attack on him. Frustrating though it was, he was a victim of people's misplaced distrust of the new.

During the 1920s Impressionist and Post-Impressionist paintings were rare in the London salerooms, confirming a narrow and unadventurous approach to art in Britain. On the other side of the Atlantic, however, buyers showed much greater enthusiasm.[33] In America there were a substantial number of collectors appreciative of modern art, and willing to spend money on it. Perhaps Hunter's desire to show in New York was not as optimistic as it might at first appear. Letters to his cousin in New York confirm that Hunter knew of the enthusiasm in America for Matisse and the School of Paris.[34] Other factors, such as Reid & Lefevre's intention to expand into the American market and the measured success of Fergusson and Peploe in New York, held out further hope for Hunter. Any disappointment he felt in London was offset by the challenge of breaking new ground.

On 19 November 1928, very shortly after his exhibition closed in London, Hunter sailed for New York, travelling first class aboard *SS Transylvania*, accompanied by Hunter relatives who were travelling home to America.[35] It must have been his intention to stay for several months, because he asked Honeyman to arrange renting out his Glasgow studio. Obviously Hunter was enthusiastic about his prospects in New York, but Honeyman, who by then had given up medicine for a career as an art dealer with Reid & Lefevre in Glasgow, was all too aware of the pitfalls, writing to him:

I was pleased to know that your pictures were favourably impressing the New York Dealers, but without wishing to discourage you, the test of sales will be the real one. Dudensing might be quite a good man to show your work. He did exceptionally well with Lurcat, and although in his case there is the speculative interest of Modern French Pictures, he has evidently a clientele who would take advanced work.[36]

In addition to having the questionable benefit of showing the unsold London pictures, Hunter had kept aside paintings specifically for America. He planned to show a total of thirty-two works, enlisting the help of his cousin, Arthur Leyden, to arrange storage. Thus the paintings were in New York by the time Hunter arrived.

Leyden and his French wife, Marcelle (pl.127), had moved to the United States shortly after the war, when he was appointed as sole agent for Staines Linoleum. Linoleum was a new product in America and had a wealth of applications.

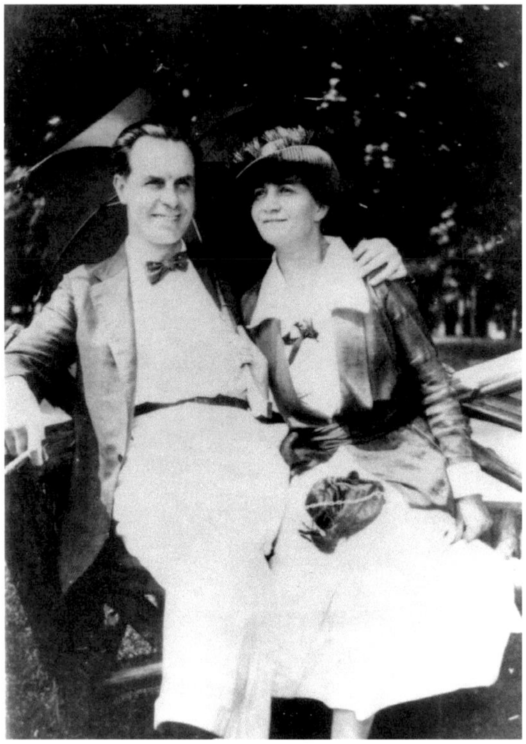

127 | Arthur Leyden, Hunter's cousin, and his French wife, Marcelle

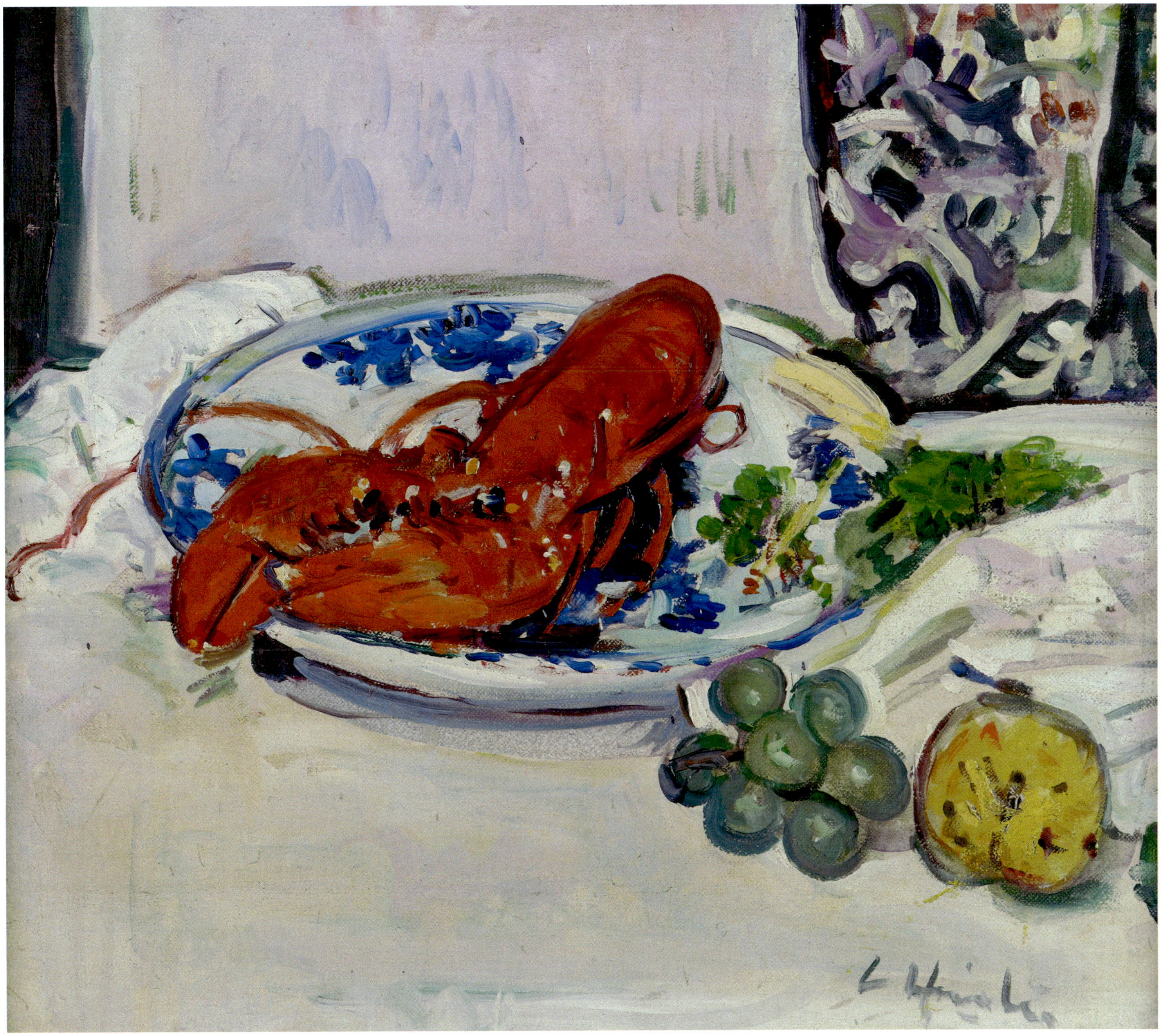

128 | Still Life with Lobster on Blue Plate
Oil on canvas, 1928
Private collection

It proved very successful, and over the years Leyden had made many good contacts in New York and elsewhere. Leyden never lost his interest in art; he was particularly friendly with Hunter's artist friend, Tom Hunt. Without these contacts it would have proved very difficult indeed for Hunter to achieve what he did, as he was organising this exhibition on his own. Reid & Lefevre had no part in the arrangements and no financial interest in the outcome. On arrival in New York Hunter set about generating interest in his work, eventually succeeding in arranging a show at Ferargil Galleries, which took place between 24 April and 11 May 1929.

Towards the end of 1928 Hunter's work was taking on a much fuller and more assertive expression. His New York show represents a watershed on two levels, first, confirmation

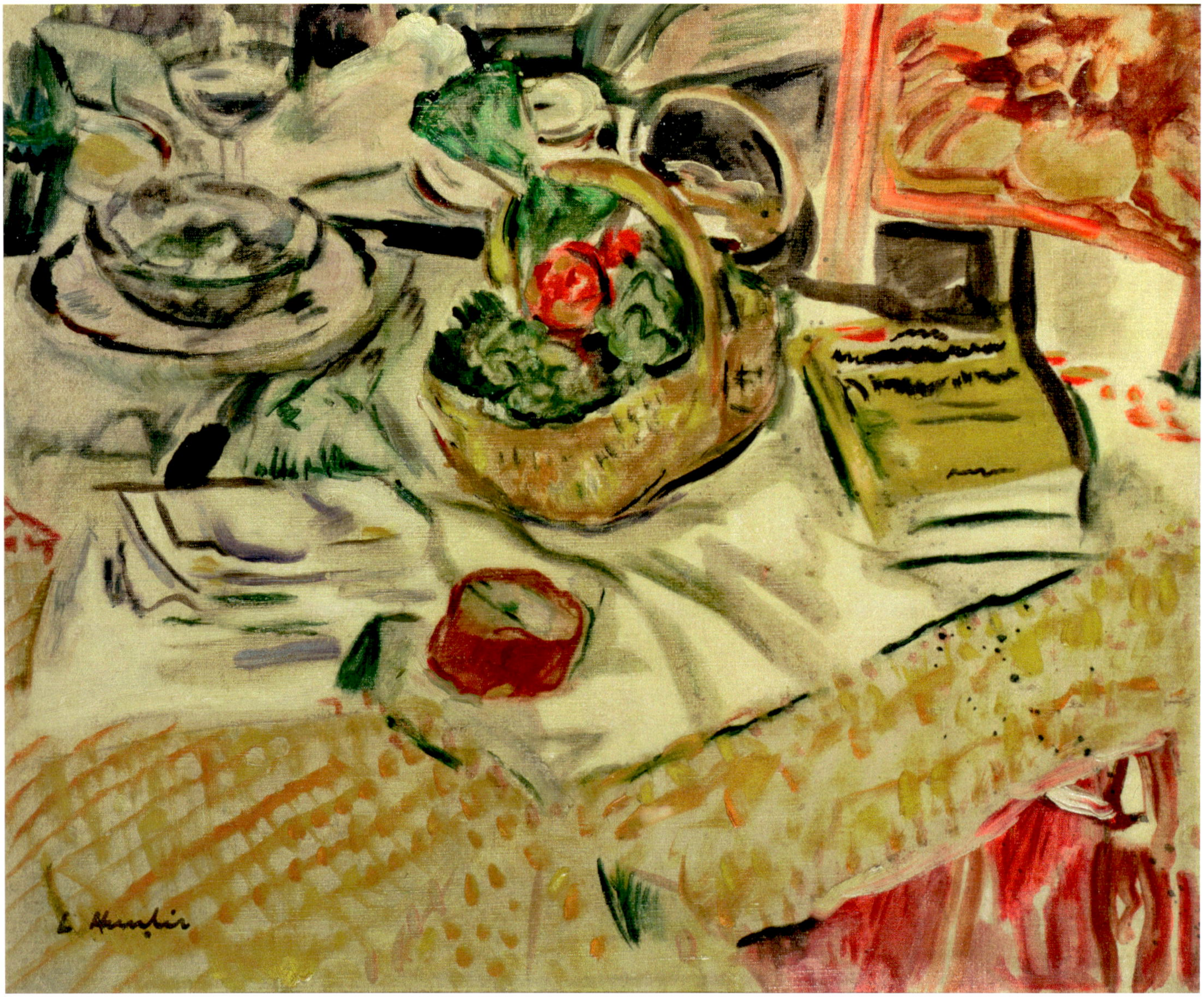

129 | Still Life with Basket of Vegetables
Oil on canvas, 1928
Private collection

of his assured, mature style, and second, the positive response his latest work generated in a new audience. The exhibition offers an excellent opportunity to appreciate the real advances in his art and status at this point in his life. In still life he continued to allow pattern to dominate over form, such as in *Still Life with Lobster on Blue Plate* (pl.128), exploiting its luminescent quality by using the pigment thinly. This is demonstrated well in *Still Life with a Basket of Vegetables* (pl.129). If the illustration of a bold, almost graphic still life [untraced] on the catalogue cover is anything to go by, Hunter's move towards a much stronger phase in his art is confirmed beyond doubt. Nowhere is this more evident than in Hunter's landscape. In *Après le Bain* (pl.132) Hunter continues his exploration of achieving a luminescent quality. On the other hand, looking to strengthen the impact implicit in his reaction to landscape, he applies brief but emphatic lines of black, and then with lively brushwork allied to colour accents and understated tone he unites the individual elements to create a powerful, enduring image, such as *St Paul de Vence* (pl.130).

Hunter was forever toying with minor

changes in approach. In *Provencal Landscape* (pl.131) he reduces the emphasis on refined tone to striking effect by substituting bold individual areas of colour. Although there is an underlying pattern, it is the direct impact of strong colour that instantly captivates, brilliantly conveying Nature's timeless appeal. One continues to detect in such views a satisfying and wholesome depth that is very much Hunter's hallmark. In comparison to his Fife paintings, the principal difference is his shift in technique from the importance of form to that of pattern.

The American press were favourably impressed with the show, although it has to be said that a witty and lively introduction by award-winning journalist, Will Irwin, Hunter's friend from his San Francisco days, greatly helped to establish the quality of Hunter's impressive background. That introduction is worth reproducing in full, because it is an example of the lasting impact Hunter made on his American friends:

Leslie Hunter, as I review the good old days, seems to me all-pervasive. I knew him first in San Francisco, and we lived the care-free Bohemian life and were unaware of it. I moved to New York; and he came down Broadway as accustomed as a piece of the scenery. Paris – and there was Hunter sketching on a street corner. London – and Hunter hailed me from the next table of a Chelsea restaurant. Glasgow – and Hunter, finding my name at a hotel in an obscure newspaper paragraph, called me up on the telephone. I have no doubt that if ever I visit Damascus, I shall find him there ahead of me. And always the same Hunter; Scotch from his accent to his walk, quietly friendly, quaintly witty.

I had laughed with him many times over these recurrent meetings of ours before I realized how much the boy I knew and starved with in San Francisco was coming to mean in modern art. When in the first decade of this century painting shook off the Victorian shackles, he found himself. Reid, the famous Glasgow dealer, a leader in the modernist movement, 'brought him out'. Reid it was who introduced Degas, Manet and Renoir to Great Britain; tradition says that he was one of the few men whom the crusty Degas would admit to his studio. He sold most of Whistler's paintings. And Reid's verdict that Hunter is 'a more powerful colorist than Matisse and equally refined' carries authenticity.

Hunter belongs to that school which Paris calls 'Les Ecossais Moderne'. This group has of late given exhibitions at the Leicester Galleries in London and the select Brabazanges Gallery in Paris; in both instances the force and purity of their color attracted sensational attention. Fergusson and Peploe of this modern Scotch group have already exhibited in New York; but although Hunter grew up in California this is his first appearance in an American gallery. He lives and paints, now, on the Cote d'Azur; and that richly colored country is the inspiration for most of these landscapes.[37]

The critic of the *New York Herald* declared:

... his expression is unmistakably French, being more particularly allied with the Matisse tradition ... his landscapes are direct and vividly presented, with a vivacity of pattern akin to the effects produced by the Frenchman.[38]

The *New York Times* commented:

Mr Hunter's strongest point is his colour, which is gay and attractive, attaining a luscious brilliancy in some of his handsome decorative still lifes. He is one of those artists in whose style spontaneity plays a large part.[39]

The *Brooklyn Daily Times* focused on the impact of Hunter's attitude to painting:

... like many and many an American artist, Mr Hunter went to school with the French.

However by his own admission he trusts to a personal and healthy reaction to nature. His paintings attest to this with no explanations on the part of Mr Hunter necessary. They are stimulating, vital and present the same purity and force of color that the artist himself suggests. There is nothing half-hearted or theoretically lugubrious about his work. It sets forth the 'healthy and personal reaction' with a casualness that almost conceals its art. It repudiates formalism and yet it is aesthetically sound and real. And above all it is individual and personal. There is none of that visiting alien sort of politeness and reserve about his presentation of the Cote D'Azur.

... It is all there, in substantial reality, whether

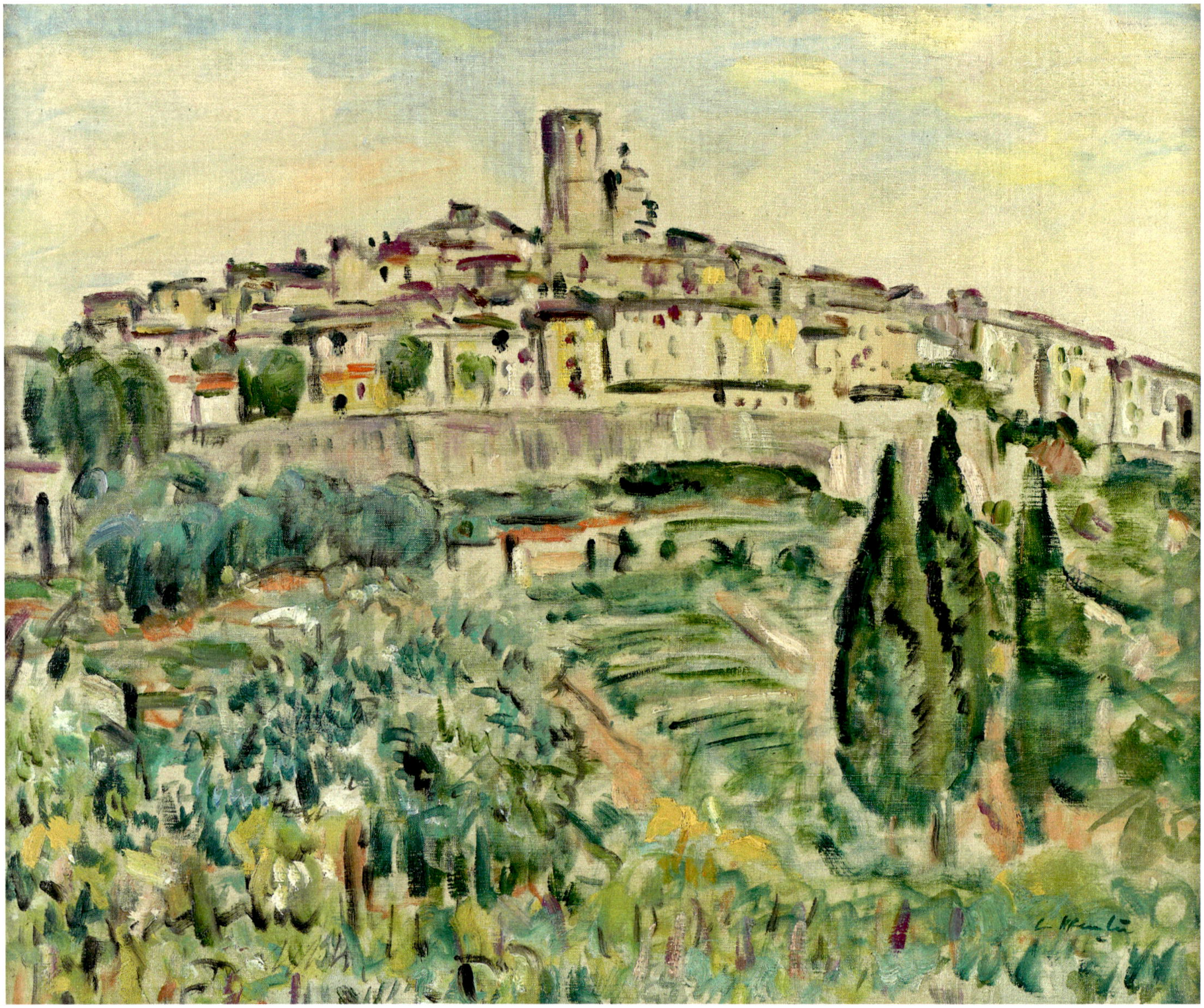

130 | St Paul de Vence
Oil on canvas, 1928
Private collection

it be a still life or a rugged hill – by the force of his colour alone.[40]

Hunter was heartened by these and other press reviews, though sales were more difficult to achieve. However his prospects were improving at last. Honeyman records that 'there is some evidence of one or two dealers willing to admit that Leslie Hunter was worth cultivating'.[41] He had left a still life with Knoedlers, the renowned New York fine art dealers, at their request, and later received a letter from them stating: 'We are very agreeably impressed with your still life and the writer hopes it will not be long in stock'. Honeyman records that the asking price was $1,500 [£300].[42]

On 9 June Hunter arrived back in Glasgow, having crossed the Atlantic on board *TSS Caledonia* on a first class ticket.[43] Perhaps sales had not been too bad after all! By the beginning of July he had returned to the south of France feeling refreshed, confident and eager to start the coming season's work, as a letter to Leyden reveals:

I got here about a week ago and am getting settled down to work. I travelled along the coast stopping at Cassis and St. Tropez which has become a very gay place at night.

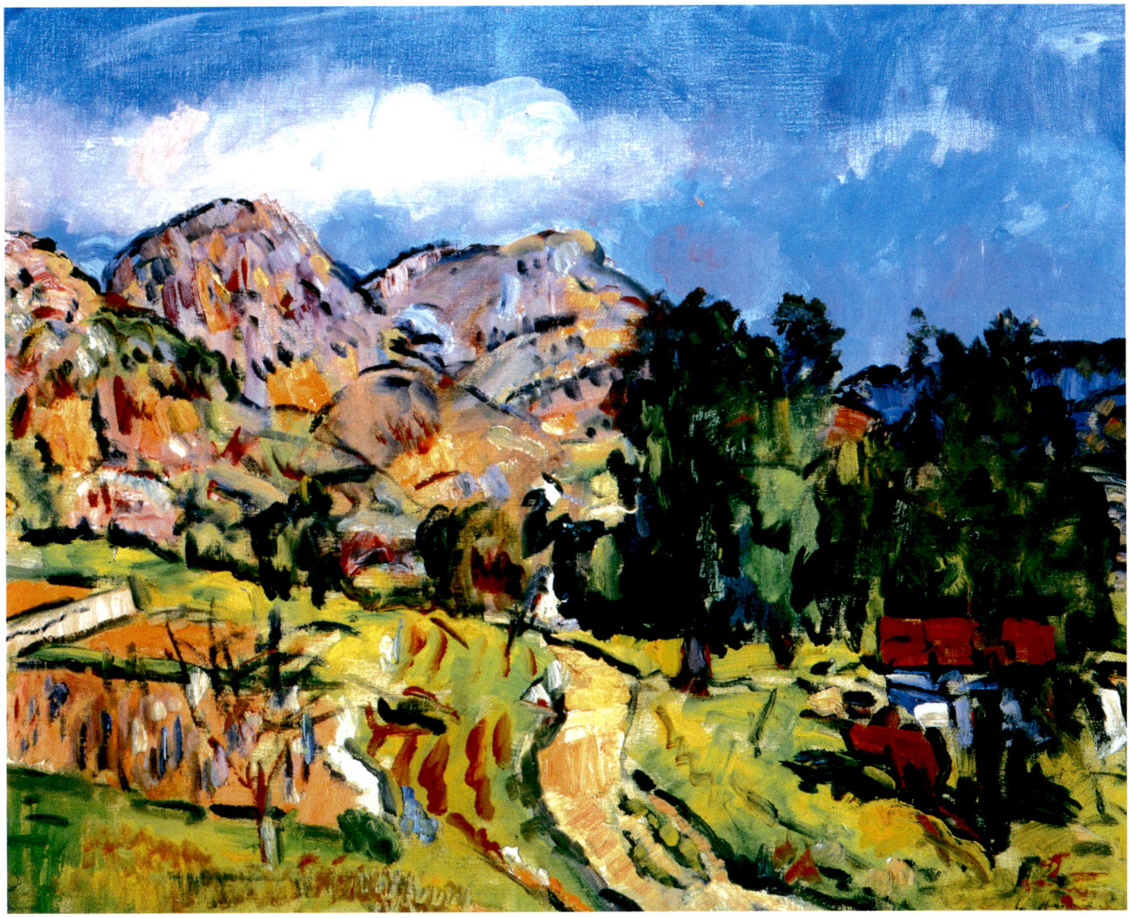

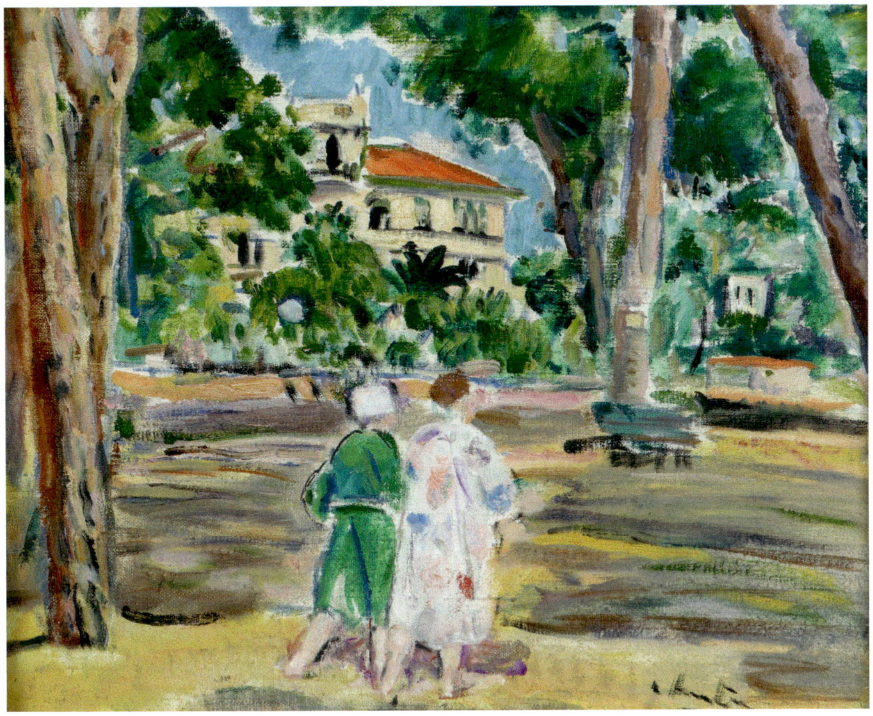

131 | Provencal Landscape
Oil on canvas, 1928
Private collection

132 | Après le Bain (The Bathers, Juan-les-Pins)
Oil on canvas, 1928
Private collection

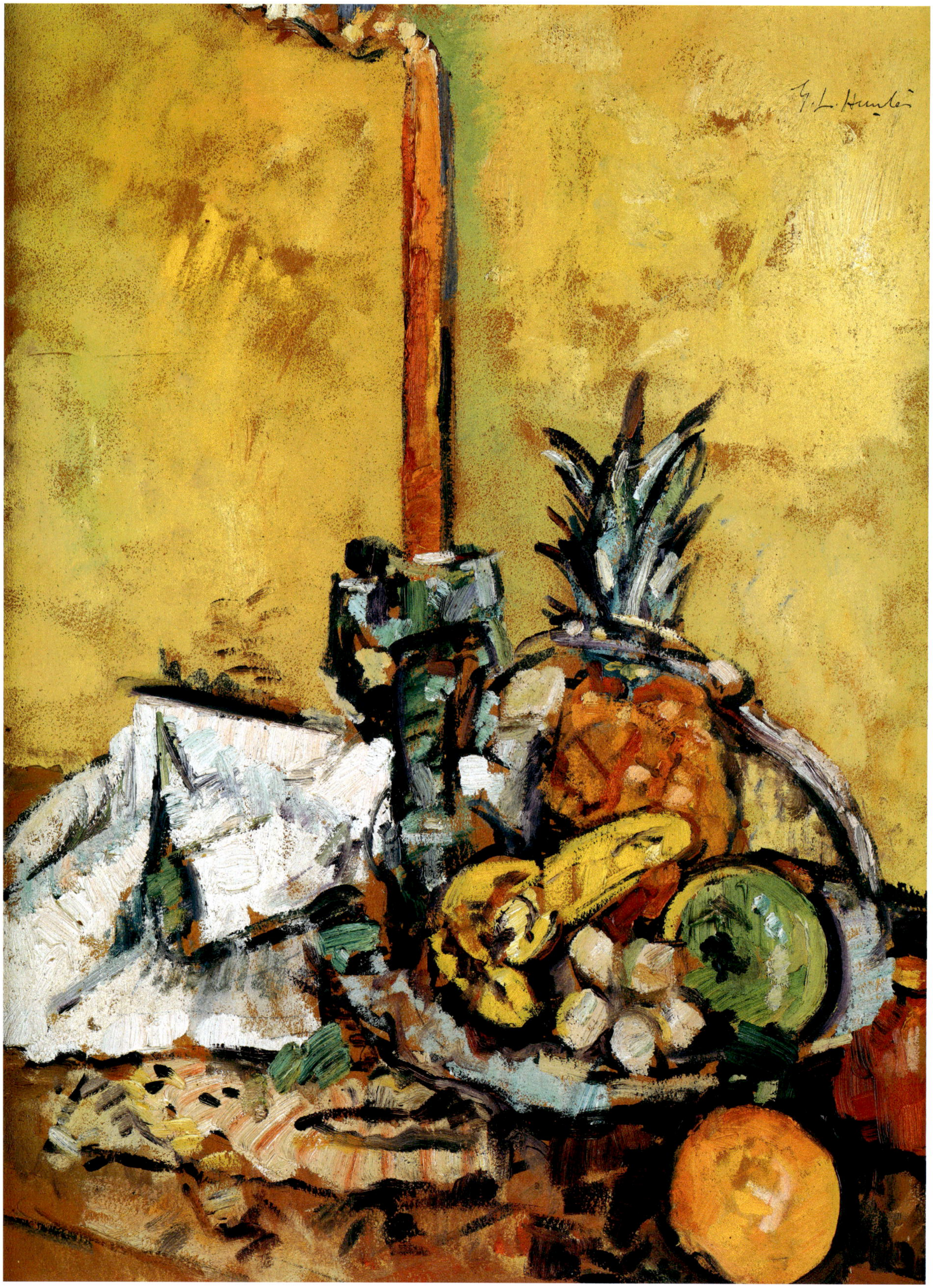

... Bignou of Paris showed the reproduction to Bernheim Jeune and there seems a proposal of my giving a show in Paris next Spring. As he only shows very high class stuff this show if it comes off will help my American prestige. This is an ideal country I live in and I wish I could simply loaf around and enjoy the sunshine and the cooking as most of the people around me but to loaf (and be loved) one has to work. I'm starting out with still life.

... Two American painters who visited the Luxembourg with me agreed there was nothing to touch it [presumably the still life with Knoedlers] *among the Modern French pictures there. Matisse alone came near it in colour but his is much weaker in every other respect. The French are all advertised from Paris far beyond their value.*

Fergusson and his lady friend have taken a studio flat in Paris on the strength of his New York show. They were here the other night at a studio dance.

I enjoyed my trip to New York and I am looking forward to crossing again if I get a good batch of stuff. Thanks for all the trouble you went to on my behalf when I was there.

I am feeling in very good health and spirits and am beginning to get some amusement out of life again.[44]

133 | Still Life with Candlestick
Oil on board, 1928
Private collection

Hunter's uncharacteristically immodest statement relating to his still life with Knoedlers appears somewhat extravagant. Honeyman suggests that it might have been fuelled by either Bignou's encouragement or the excessive praise of American friends.[45] It is equally likely, however, to have been a manifestation of the passion Hunter felt about his most recent work. Much as he admired Matisse and the École de Paris, he also had great faith in his own abilities, which in his mind were quite distinct from those of Matisse *et al*. Hunter felt that he too could compete with the best on an international stage. It was a source of great frustration to him that the enlightened American collector appeared to desire the work of French painters above all, when he believed his work to be every bit as strong and relevant – and at a much lower price.

However his letter to Leyden confirms that life was getting very much better for him. The New York adventure certainly had stimulated interest in his work. Bignou was working hard to promote his art to Bernheim Jeune, one of the foremost dealers in Paris, and Knoedlers in New York were showing a healthy interest too. In the south of France Hunter settled back into his Bohemian environment once more. But there was another reason for his present contentment – Hunter was in love.

On one occasion Hunter produced a photograph of a beautiful woman, confessing to Honeyman: 'If it had been possible for that woman to have married me, everything would have turned out so differently.' Later Honeyman was able to identify the woman as Helene Vanel, who in partnership with Lois Hutton owned and performed in a little theatre in St Paul devoted to dancing, mime and masque. Unfortunately Hunter's love was not returned, and that in part may have led to a rapid deterioration in his health. Another factor was the pressure he put himself under in his drive to paint a sufficient body of work for Paris and New York.

Among his circle there was one very special friend to whom he could turn in his despair. Described as a 'very energetic and alert young lady', Joan Smith lived in St Paul, where she ran an attractive little curiosity shop. It also functioned as the meeting place for St Paul's English-speaking residents. According to Honeyman, Hunter owed a great deal to Joan Smith; she 'mothered' him, finding him 'utterly incapable of making a fight for things material and completely over-matched in the hard battle of life'.[46]

During that summer of 1929 Hunter threw himself into his work, pushing towards a new mastery of thick paint with interesting results. While staying with Leyden in New York, Hunter had painted two still lifes that clearly illustrate the direction in which he was going. *Still Life with Candlestick* (pl.133) retains the dark lines, which act as a device to define the overall design, but by fleshing out the array of fruit and objects with rich colour and decisive brushwork, the overwhelming impression is one of sensuous texture in which all the individual elements blend together well. Taken a stage further in *The Blue Teacup* (not illustrated), he reintroduces his concept of creating monumentality within a flat perspective. With an application of impasto, he builds up the powerful individual masses of the various objects and allows the pattern to intrude to the point of levelling the entire sense of volume, creating a still life of considerable impact, rich in colour and bold in design.

Hunter's continual ability to subtly alter the final effect through a minor adjustment in emphasis is well demonstrated in *The Black Hat* (pl.134). By placing a highly polished black vase in a half-concealed position, he is able to introduce the head of a girl in a black hat without allowing her presence to intrude. It is the vitality of the flowers (now lacking the soft definition of the petals) and the bold prominence of the solitary orange that are striking. Hunter achieves all of this by means of loaded brushstrokes that heighten contrasting textures, binding together the whole design.

As the summer season advanced and the volume of affluent tourists increased, Hunter turned to the coast at Antibes, where he found some willing sitters for his figure studies. Exclusively painting women, he embarked on a series of pictures that are remarkable for their natural sensitivity and understatement. *The White Hat* (pl.135), one of the most stunning, reveals yet another facet to Hunter's approach. Originally the painting was of an elegant lady wearing a Chanel suit and white hat and posed against a white background. The white on white affects an air of sophistication, while her warm complexion glows with sensuality. When the painting was being cleaned recently, the restorer discovered that the white background was a layer of gesso applied over a different background. The decision was taken to remove the gesso, revealing a luscious, exotic background. The resultant picture acquired a depth and fullness of a totally different quality to that which it had previously (pl.136). Gone was the feeling of quiet sophistication, to be replaced by a compelling air of mystery. Presumably Hunter was not satisfied with the first version (perhaps it was too personal) and sought to achieve a different impact by drastically altering the background.

Totally immersed in his work, Hunter painted all summer, increasingly neglecting to eat or sleep. It was only a matter of time before his physical and mental health broke down. By September 1929 it became clear that Hunter was

134 | The Black Hat
Oil on board, 1928
Private collection

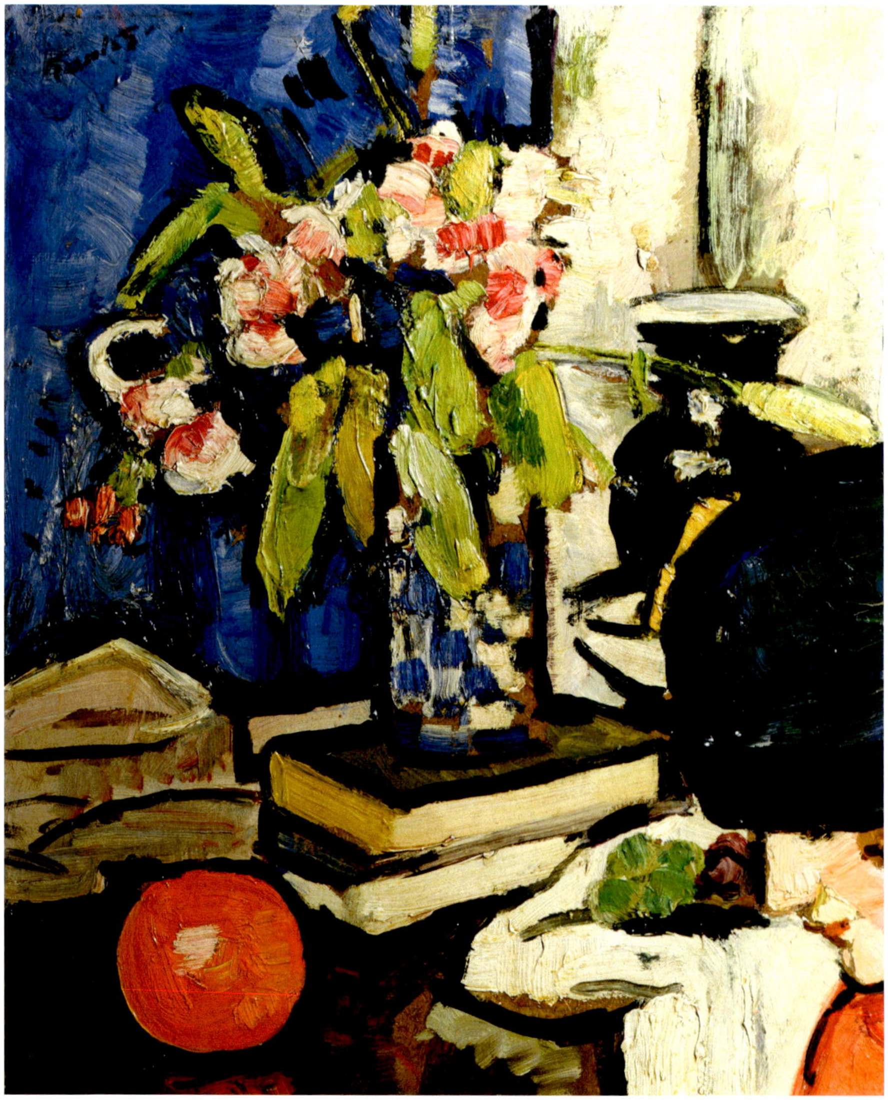

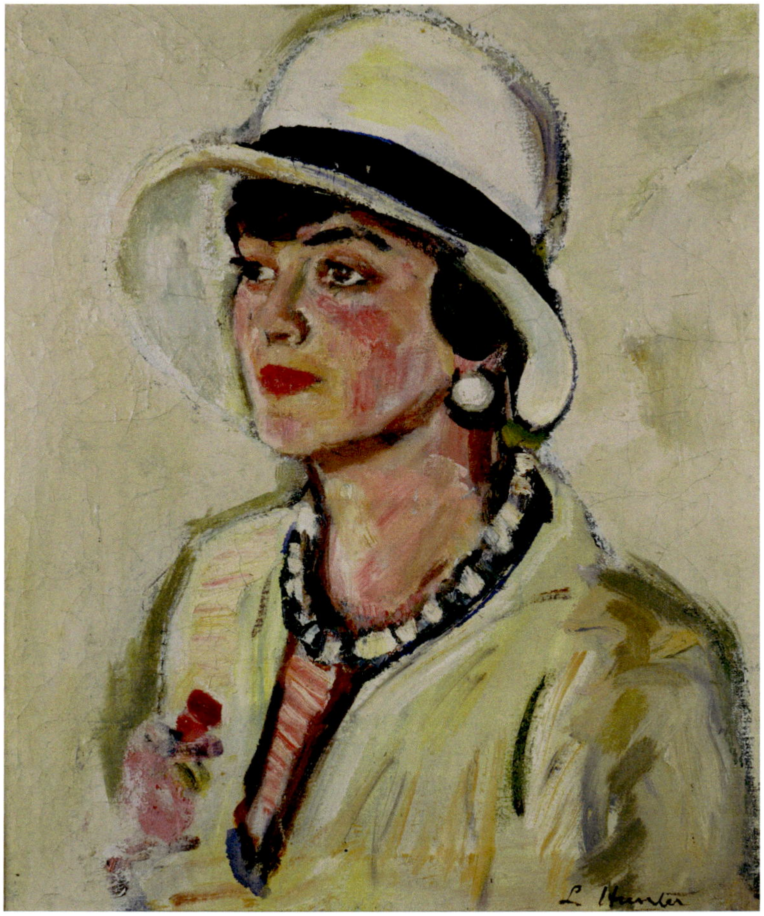

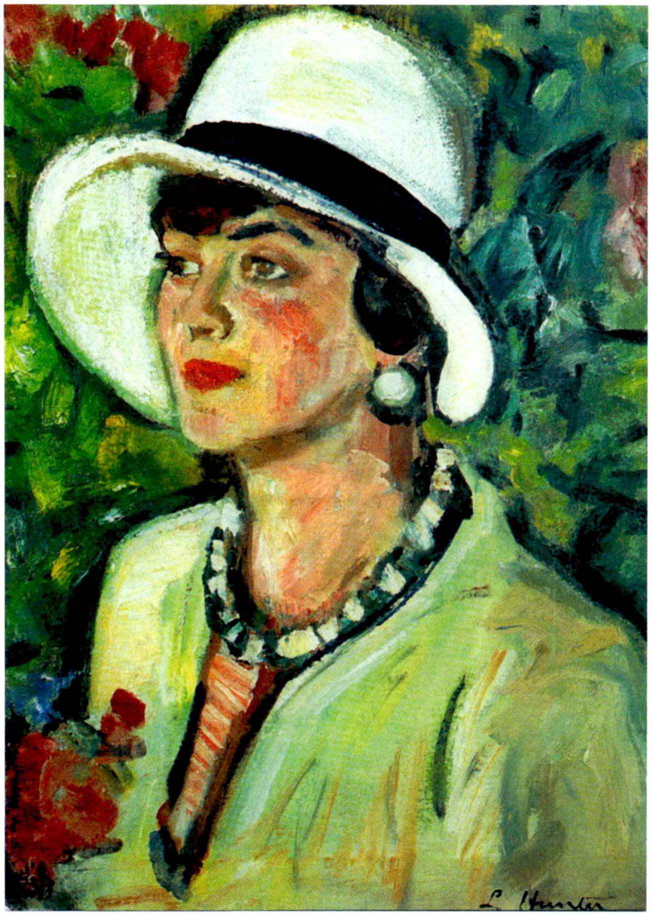

135 | The White Hat
Oil on canvas, 1929
Private collection

136 | The White Hat
(after cleaning)
During cleaning, the background was found to be a layer of gesso applied over a different background. The decision was taken to remove the gesso, revealing the original exotic background.

heading for a breakdown. On holiday in the Mediterranean, McInnes met up with him and they had dinner together in Toulon. McInnes was shocked by what he saw. Hunter was 'miserably thin and unhappy', distracted and unable even to sustain a conversation.[47] Though he was greatly troubled by what he saw, there was little that McInnes could do in the short space of time he had with Hunter.

Not long after McInnes met with him, disaster struck. Hunter mistakenly swallowed some turpentine mixture he had stored in an empty wine bottle in his studio. How Hunter could have mistaken turpentine for wine is puzzling, as turpentine has such a distinctive smell. However he was very untidy and disorganized and it is probable that the studio was reeking of turpentine anyway. Be that as it may, it was typical of Hunter that it was not until the onset of unpleasant symptoms that he took any action, going straight to his friend, Joan Smith. Horrified, she took him immediately to a clinic in Nice. Her prompt action probably saved his life. Jeanie, his sister in Glasgow, was sent for. So ill was Hunter, that it would be several weeks before he was sufficiently well to return with her to Glasgow. Hunter's three idyllic and productive years in the south of France had come to an abrupt end in dramatic fashion.

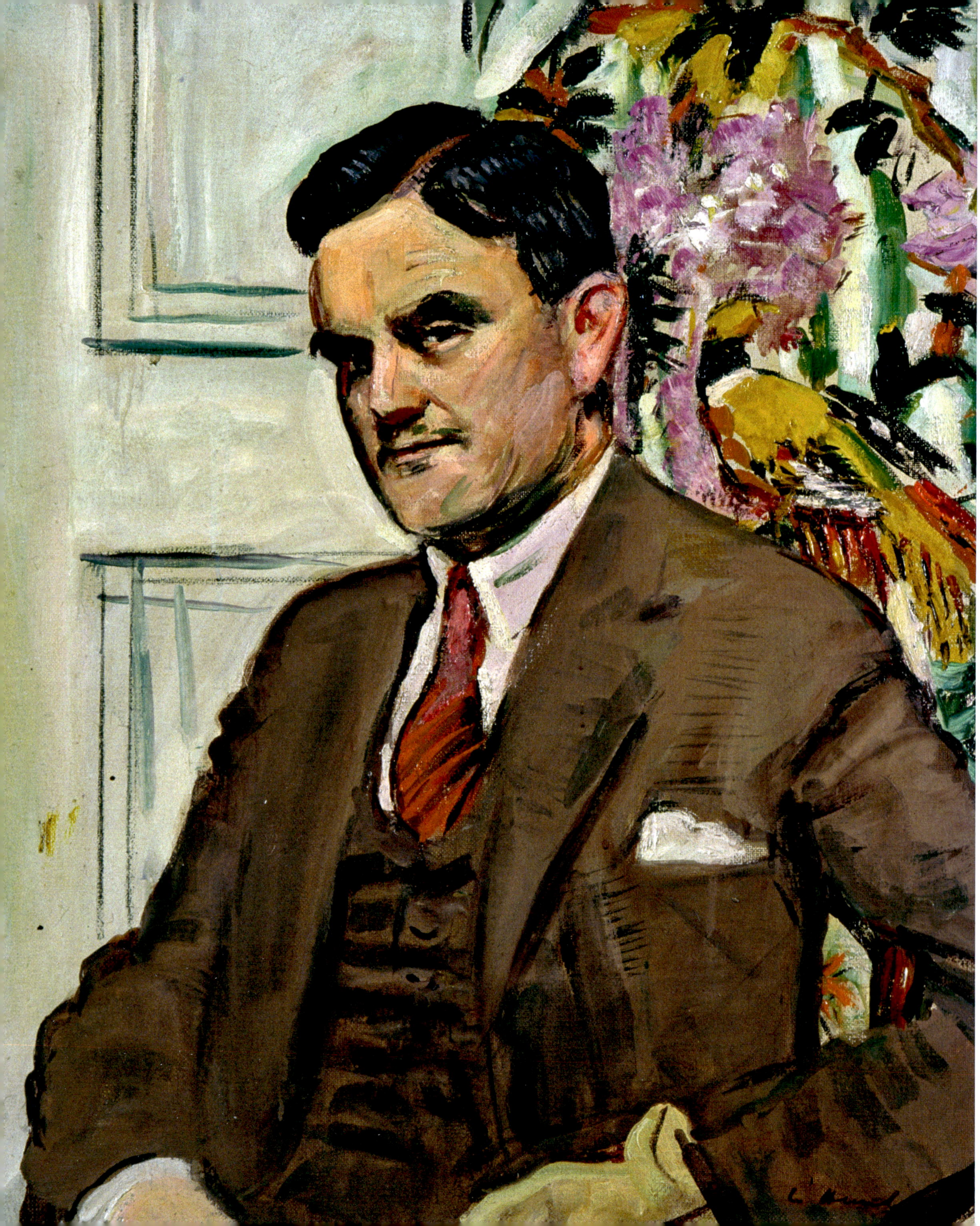

8 Triumph and Tragedy

Hunter returned to Glasgow and the tender care of his sister, Jeanie, in October 1929. He was in poor shape, both physically and mentally. Overwork and misfortune had forced him to leave behind his bohemian lifestyle. In the south of France he left the inspiriting company of like-minded artists, fine weather and brilliant light, striking landscape and an abundance of exotic flowers. As well as the lack of light at this time of year and the 'dreich'[1] Glasgow weather, he had to contend once again with the backward-looking attitude of his fellow members of Glasgow Art Club, and a new feeling among a few of his supporters that his most recent work had been disappointing at best. On a broader front his return coincided with the Wall Street Crash in America, when the speculative bubble fuelled largely by borrowed money had burst, sending the New York Stock Exchange plunging some forty per cent within a couple of weeks and causing fortunes to be lost virtually overnight. The stock market crash brought about the Great Depression that lasted for much of the 1930s. In the art market it killed the speculative boom in etchings and made selling pictures a more difficult and often lengthy task.

All this might have proved too much for Hunter had it not been for the devotion of his sister, who nursed him back to health, and the companionship of his trusted friends in Glasgow and Dundee: McInnes, McNair, Harrison, Justice, Tattersall and Ressich. They were adept at handling him in a lively but compassionate manner, as is demonstrated by the following anecdote that illustrates one of a series of simple gestures that gradually put Hunter back on his feet:

On one occasion Hunter appeared at Gow Harrison's offices to see McNair who exclaimed 'Look here Hunter, that's a hell of a hat you're wearing!' and promptly took him out to lunch, buying another hat on the way.[2]

Although Duncan Macdonald had serious misgivings, which to a lesser extent were shared by McNeill Reid, Reid & Lefevre continued to support Hunter. This was despite the fact that he had not delivered the expected number of paintings and thus was still in debt to the firm in respect of expenses he had incurred in the south of France. While Hunter was away in France, Tom Honeyman (pl.137) had given up a career as a doctor in the East End of Glasgow to join Reid & Lefevre. Honeyman and Duncan Macdonald had been firm friends for twenty years or so and it was Macdonald who persuaded him to become an art dealer.[3] Honeyman had developed a passion for art. He was a man of undoubted integrity, and this, combined with a remarkable talent for communicating all that there was to enjoy in modern painting, made him an ideal partner. At Reid & Lefevre, and later as Director of Glasgow Art Gallery, Honeyman was to make a significant and lasting contribution to the arts in Scotland.

By December Hunter had regained his physical health. Mentally, however, he was still not fully recovered. He felt he was back where he had been three years ago, before his move to the south of France. His sentiments for

137 | Dr Tom J. Honeyman
Oil on canvas, 1930
Glasgow Museums

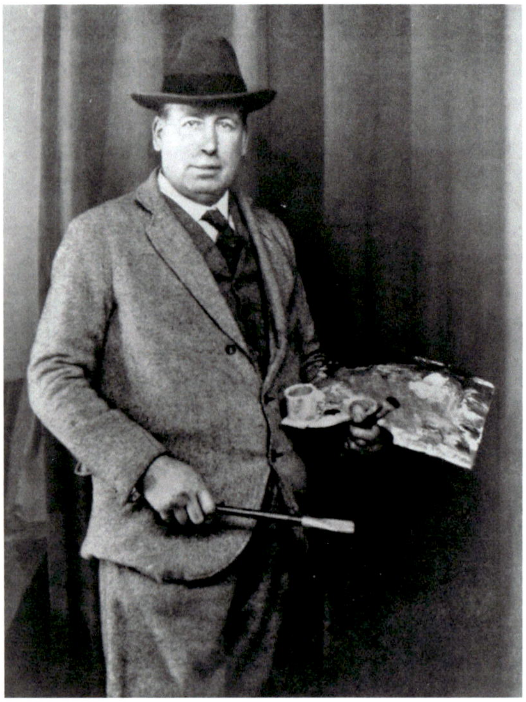

138 | Leslie Hunter, aged about 50
National Library of Scotland

Glasgow and the majority of the artist-members of Glasgow Art Club had not changed in the meantime. His last exhibition in the city, when he showed his 'modern' drawings, had not been a critical success, and the following he had built up had dwindled somewhat. However much he believed in his new style, he found it difficult to pick up his brush again with any conviction. It was an uphill struggle to shake off the feeling of despondency. However with the help and encouragement of his friends, and of Honeyman, who was to become a good friend, Hunter's depression gradually lifted and he began to regain his old form.

When McNeill Reid moved south in 1929 to join Macdonald in London, Honeyman took charge of the Glasgow gallery.[4] Not surprisingly, he was concerned about Hunter's level of indebtedness to the firm, writing to him:

We must come to some arrangement about this financial business … as it is not much fun paying out money all the time and not getting any in. I will try a show later in the year with some of the pictures you had in London and see if I can raise the wind.[5]

There must have been times when Honeyman doubted whether Hunter could repeat the success of his 1925 show. However in March 1930 he put on the promised exhibition of Hunter's work held in stock by Reid & Lefevre, which included pre-south of France pictures. As well as being an attempt to reduce Hunter's debt, it was intended to encourage Hunter and to announce his return to the firm's clientele. Over the next two years Reid & Lefevre would mount a further three exhibitions of his work, two of which were solo shows in the Glasgow gallery and one, *Les Peintres Écossais* at the Galeries Georges Petit in Paris in 1931, a group show by the four Colourists – Peploe, Fergusson, Hunter and Cadell – along with George Telfer Bear and Ronald Ossory Dunlop.

Among collectors there were a few who considered that Hunter was finished and several more of the opinion that although his earlier work would stand the test of time, his new modern style did not merit serious consideration. Hunter himself had no such qualms. On seeing one of his paintings of chrysanthemums executed in 1916, he smilingly remarked: 'I've gone a long way since I did that.'[6] Indeed he had. To a suggestion in a letter that he should return to his earlier style of painting he replied: 'I cannot go back. It is impossible for an artist

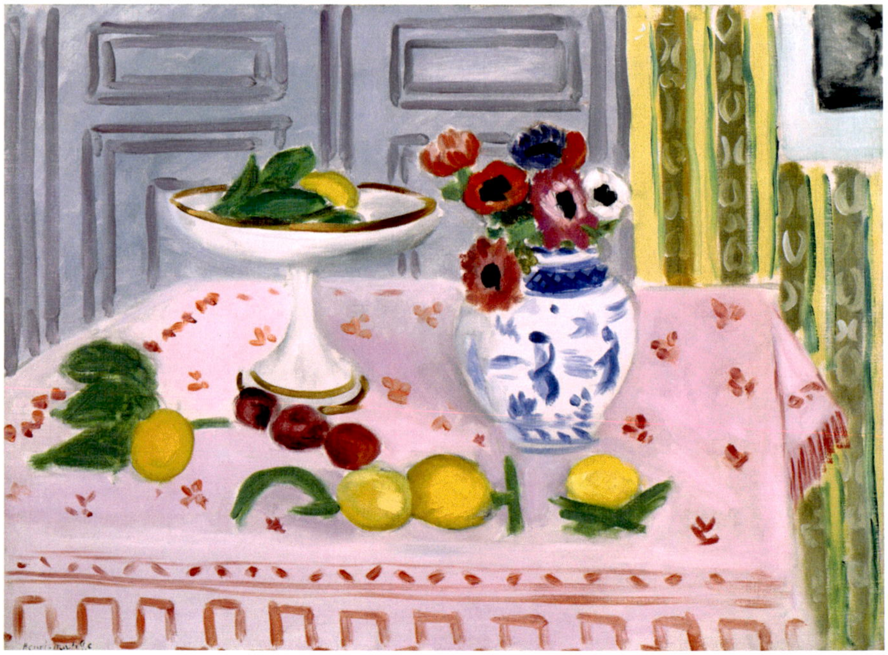

139 | Henri Matisse, *La Nappe Rose*
Oil on canvas
Glasgow Museums
© Succession H. Matisse / DACS 2012

to retrace his steps. He must go forward.'[7] The few who kept the faith were McInnes, McNair, Harrison, Matthew Dickie and, in Glasgow Art Club, Robert Macaulay Stevenson, Stuart Park and Telfer Bear. Although the exhibition did not bring Hunter or Reid & Lefevre much immediate financial relief, it did remind Hunter of how far he had come and provided the impetus for him to pick up his brush again.

Hunter spent 1930 in and around Glasgow, gradually picking up the strands of his life again. He moved into a very small studio at 65 West Regent Street, where other artists, such as David Gauld, also had studios. His habit of making noisy outbursts resurfaced, arguing in his studio with an imaginary opponent, and were stoically tolerated by his fellow artists, eventually being accepted as a normal part of his character that could neither be changed nor eradicated. Such noisy outbursts had been evident in 1923 and in 1928–29 in the south of France. As his confidence returned, so his passion for painting brought on his customary pattern of neglecting to eat and sleep. When grappling with a problem, the hours became blurred and coalesced into an indefinite lacuna, a situation that sometimes lasted several days. His sister and his friends did their best to see that he ate and slept as regularly as possible, but they could only do so much.

Hunter began by painting still life, going on to produce pictures unsurpassed by his earlier works. Unquestionably the strength and depth of those still lifes make lasting statements. Honeyman confirms that many of the paintings pay homage to McInnes's still life, *La Nappe Rose* by Matisse (see pl.139). According to Honeyman,

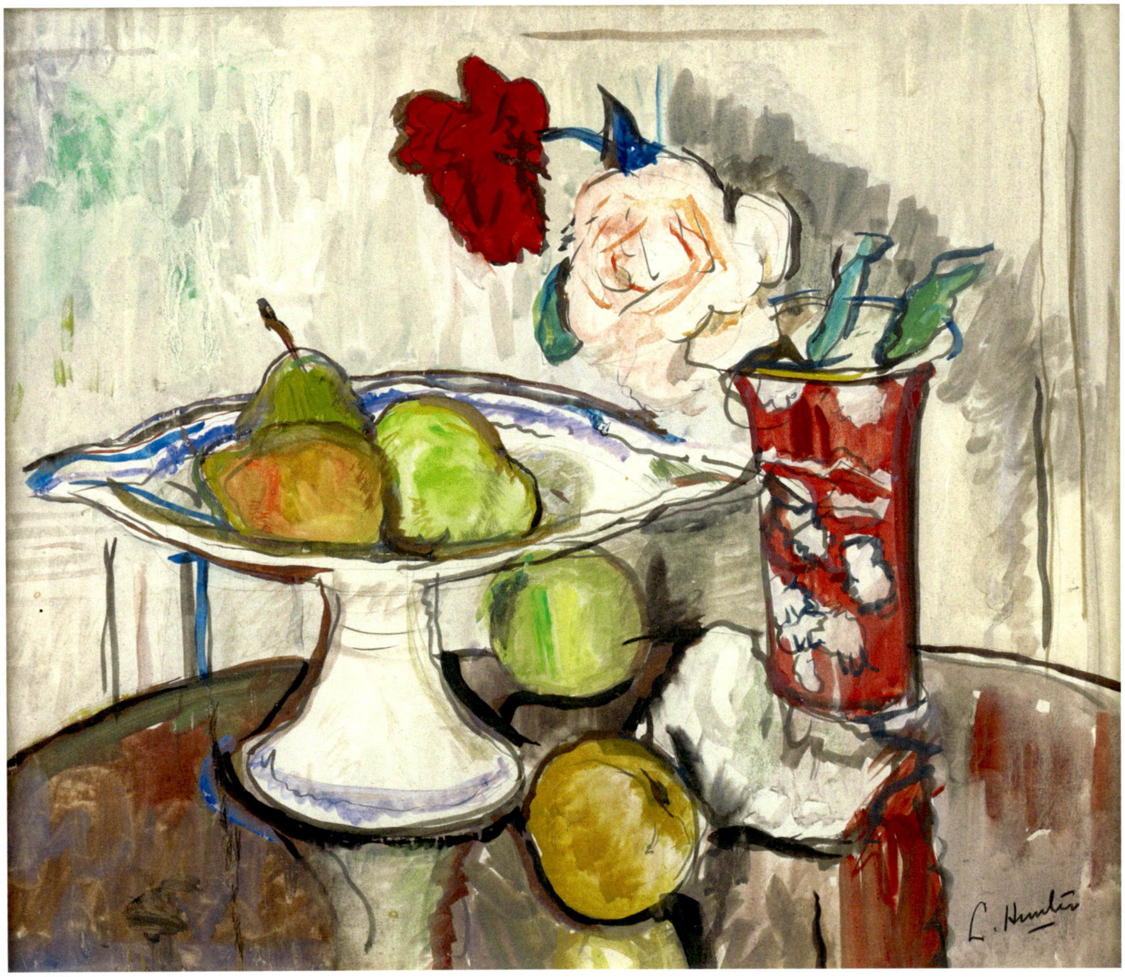

140 | Fruit and Roses in a Red Vase
Watercolour, 1930
Private collection

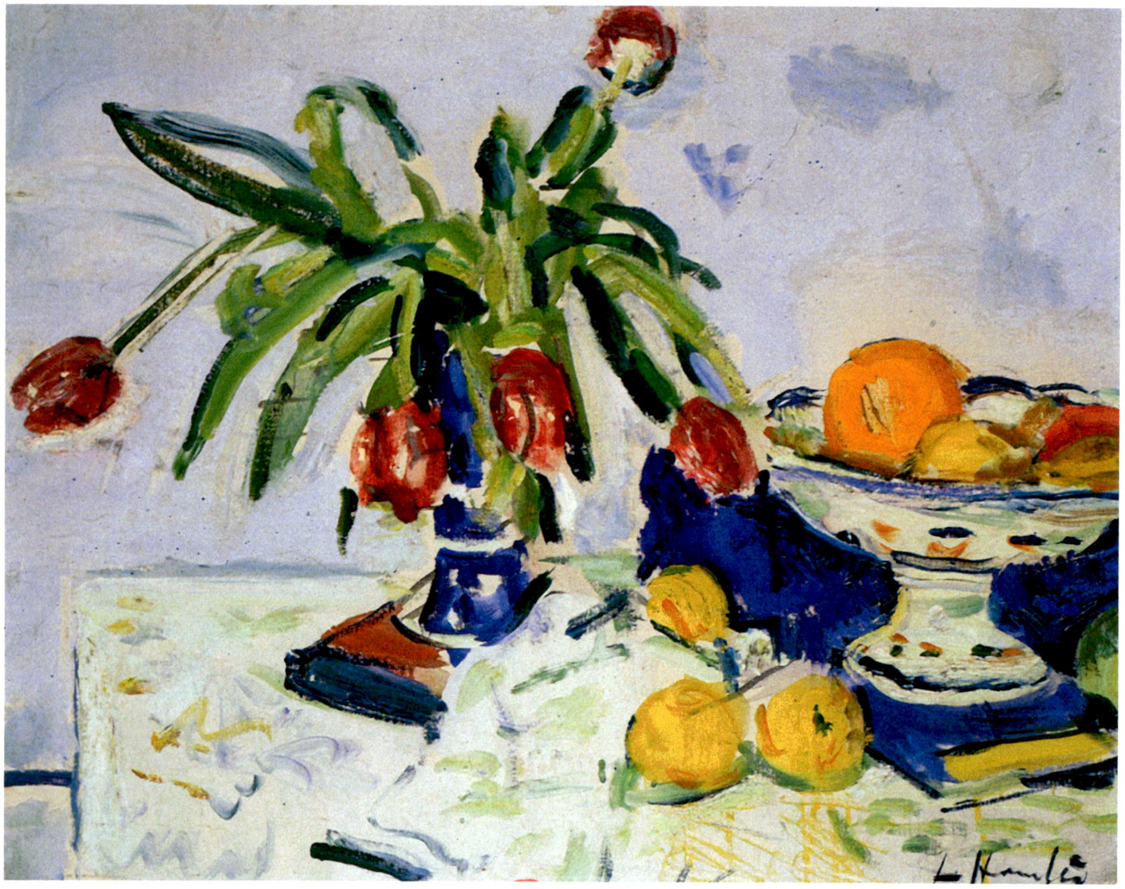

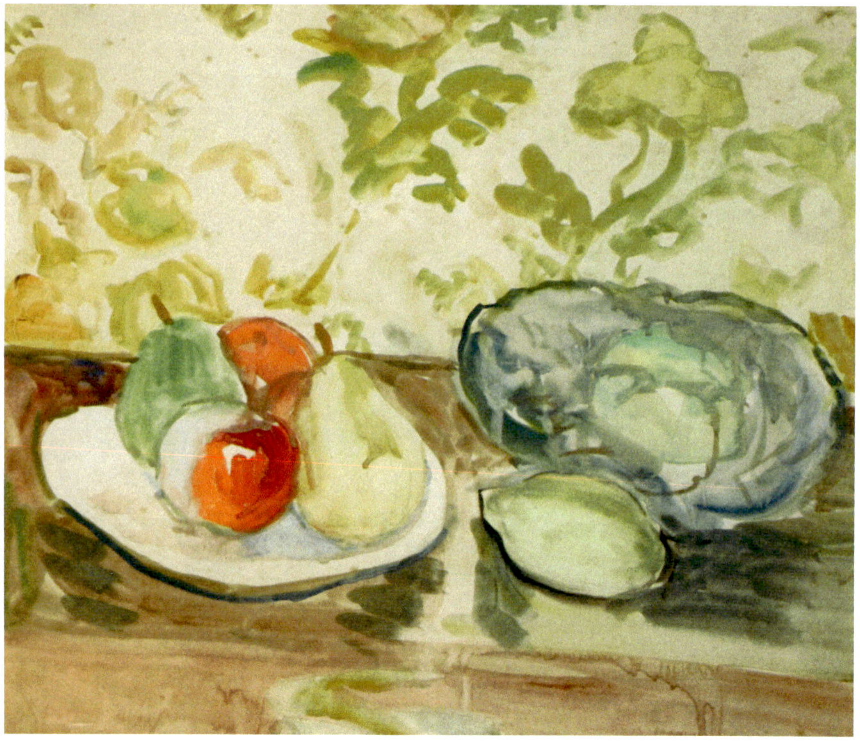

141 | Tulips
Oil on canvas, 1930
Private collection

142 | Still Life with Fruit and Oriental Screen
Watercolour, 1930
Private collection

such was Hunter's admiration for the Matisse that he would have been content to sit in front of the picture for hours.[8] It was one of the few paintings in Glasgow that had a significant energizing effect on Hunter. No doubt he fondly remembered his Paris trip with McInnes in 1925 when it was purchased. More important perhaps, it was almost the only link with a period of his life – three years in the south of France – that he had found so rewarding: meeting and working with artists in Matisse's circle.

Paying homage is one thing, but Hunter could never be a copyist. He would analyse what elements excited him and then adapt them to his own perception. In the case of the Matisse, it is the striking and fresh simplicity to which Hunter responded. There exist many still lifes of this period that demonstrate Hunter's affinity with Matisse. For instance *Fruit and Roses in Red Vase* (pl.140) is unmistakably by Hunter, yet in its simplicity and sense of order there is the same arresting quality that the Matisse still life displays. Hunter's picture is unusual in that he has completed it in watercolour. Its scale goes beyond that which would suggest it is merely a sketch for further reference, as was the case with many of his drawings. Similar in scale and presence, *Still Life with Fruit and Oriental Screen* (pl.142) embodies Hunter's inspired sense of pattern and decorative design. The confidence and depth of both works clearly demonstrate Hunter's mastery of still life.

143 | Interior with Piano and Screen
Brush with ink and watercolour, 1930
Private collection

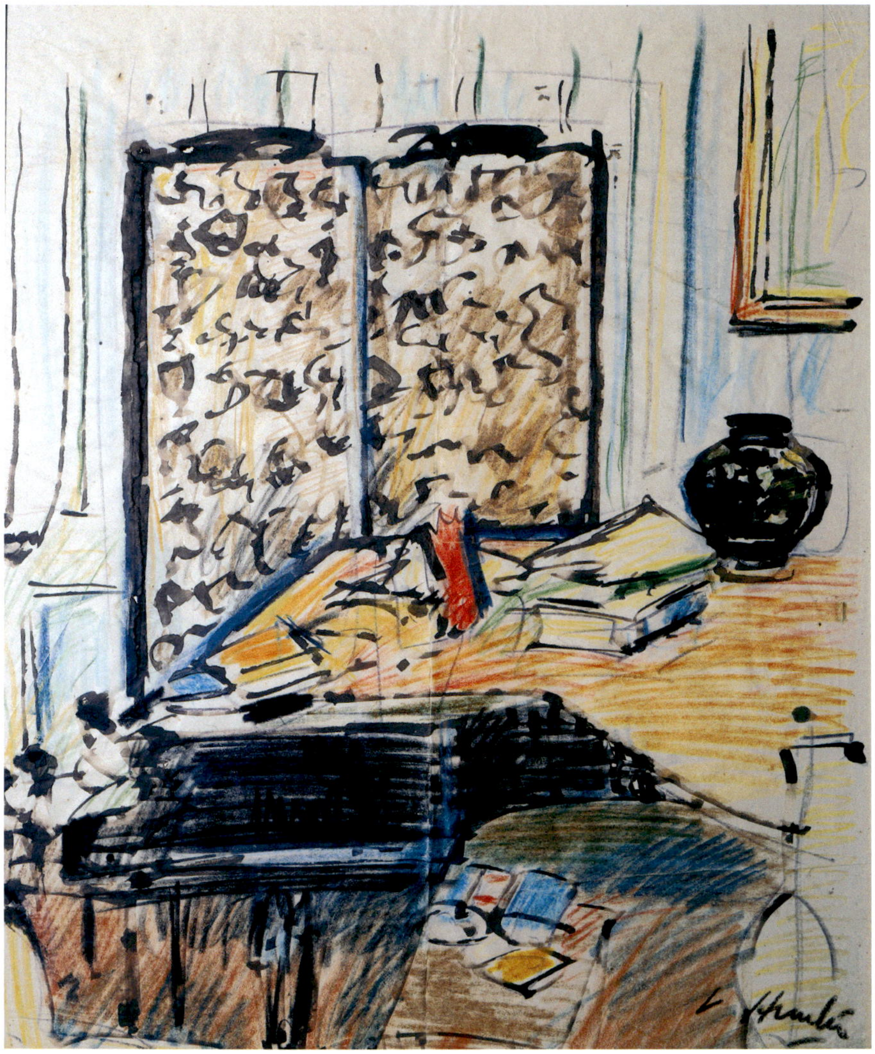

At first glance *Tulips* (pl.141) appears to have a far freer feel altogether, but its simplicity belies the extent of manipulation employed by Hunter. The paint is thin and flat, but he brings out the vitality of the flowers and beauty of the objects through his astute use of colour. Reduced almost to the quality of watercolour, Hunter's application of oil paint in *Still Life with Marguerites* (pl.144) achieves a wonderful luminous quality. His keen sense of pattern and colour allows individual elements to work together without jarring, resulting in a still life that glows with vitality. Similar paintings with such radiant qualities include *Still Life, Stocks* (pl.145) and *Marguerites*.

At his best Hunter's paintings are rich in variety as he exploits one quality over another, frequently to stunning effect. However Hunter was by no means perfect. It would be foolish to ignore other traits that go to make up his colourful personality and which have a bearing on his art. One facet of Hunter's personality that became particularly pronounced during the last two years of his life was his destructive habit, on returning to the studio late at night and seeing his latest canvas on the easel, of exorcising his perceived dissatisfaction with the picture by re-painting. This frequently proved a disaster. Instead of painting by natural light he was working in a distorting artificial light. In his tired

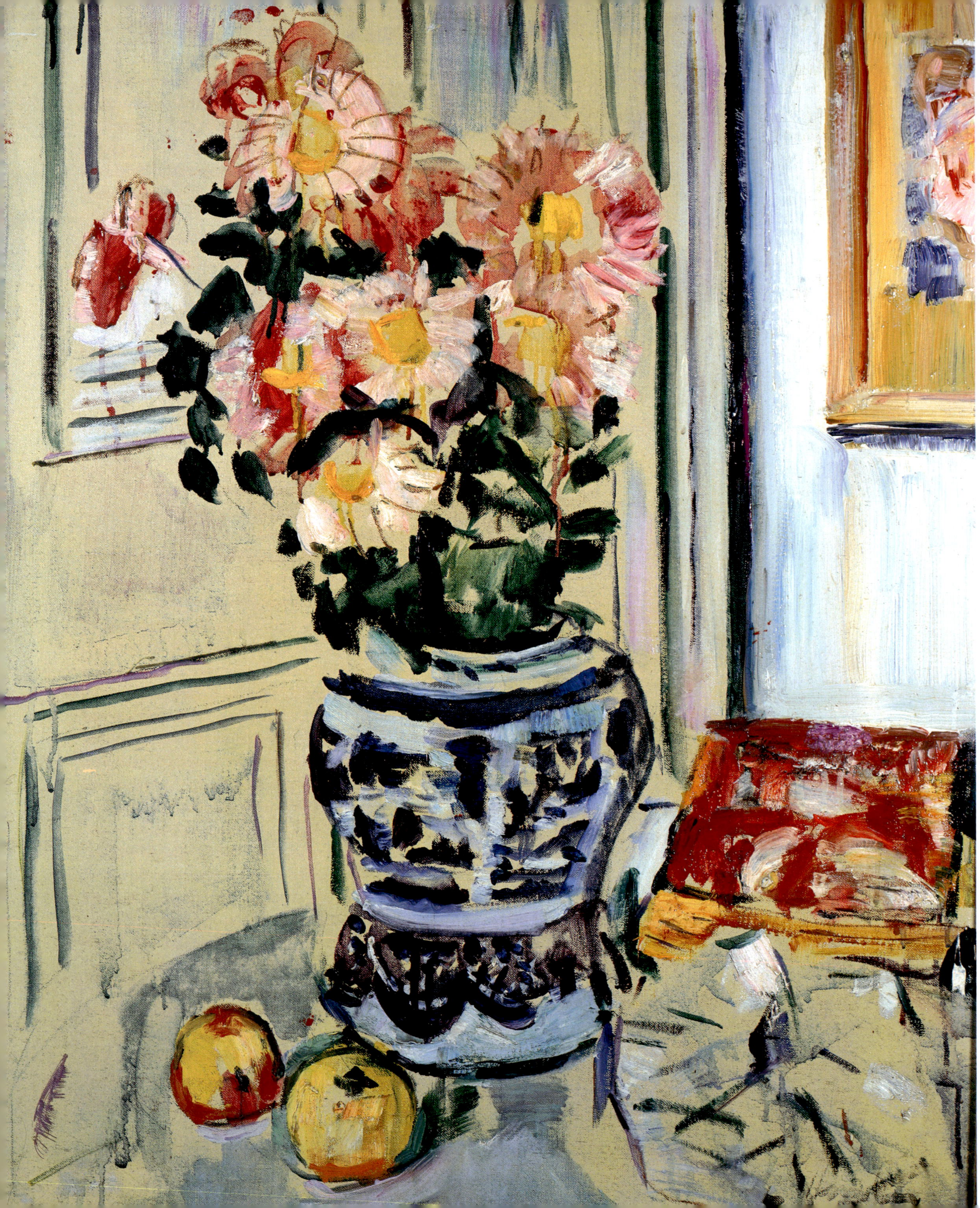

and often stressed state he would lose sight of what he had originally set out to achieve in the painting and end up spoiling it.

This compulsion to re-work canvases has led to the existence of paintings that, though obviously related to this series of still lifes, fall very short of his usual standards. Friends such as McInnes and Justice had long been aware of Hunter's potential during bouts of illness or stress to ruin pictures that had shown so much promise. Occasionally in the past they had been forced to 'rescue' the odd painting. However, following Hunter's return to Scotland towards the end of 1929 and an even more erratic lifestyle, the practice of his friends 'snatching' canvases from the easel became commonplace.

One such 'snatch', *Chrysanthemums* (pl.146), is a picture that illustrates unequivocally the enduring quality of Hunter's art and marks a specific stage in the development of that art. The purchaser recollected that the painting was still 'wet' when he bought it from Honeyman. The 1913 and 1922 series of chrysanthemum pictures epitomise stages in Hunter's artistic development. In 1930 he again embarked on a series of still life of the same motif. On this occasion, however, not only is the palette noticeably lighter, but the colour is quite deliberately applied with little reference to form. It is the exciting pattern of colour across the picture surface that provides a glorious vitality. Hunter's years of experiment and refinement were coming to fruition in a splendid manner.

However he did not want to confine himself solely to still life. Ambitiously Hunter envisaged completing a series of portraits. The reasons for this change of direction are not clear, but there are several interesting pointers. First, he was attending life classes run by Glasgow Art Club, which no doubt fuelled a desire to expand his *oeuvre*. Second, during his last year in St Paul de Vence Hunter had painted a series of portraits of women; now that he was well again, he may have wished to build on that experience. Third,

144 | Still Life with Marguerites
Oil on canvas, 1930
Private collection

145 | Still Life, Stocks
Oil on canvas, 1930
Scottish National Gallery of Modern Art

146 | Chrysanthemums
Oil on canvas, 1930
Private collection

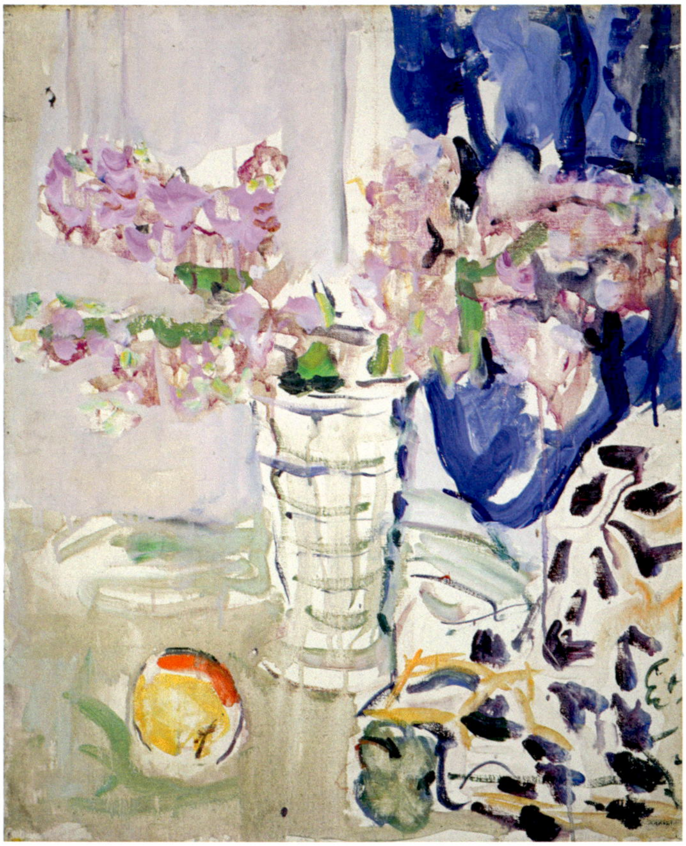

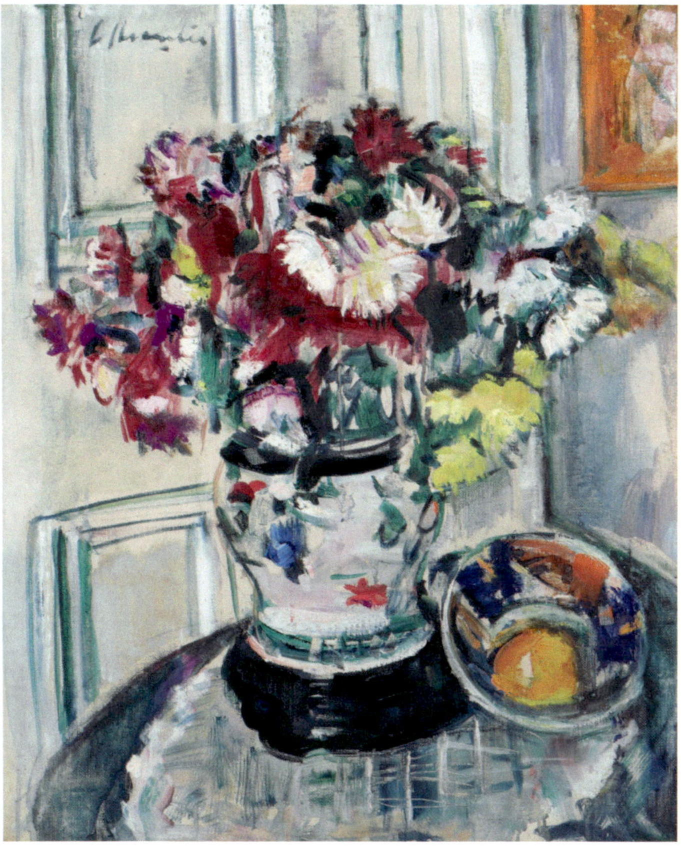

and perhaps most important, such was his confidence and belief in his painting that Hunter felt he could apply to portraiture the same principles and style he had achieved recently in his other work. It was a challenging concept and typical of Hunter's courage.

Before that could happen, however, there were several major problems to be overcome. Hunter's very haphazard way of working and his lack of personal care hardly rendered him likely to attract many commissions. Portraiture demands some commitment from the sitter in terms of time, and to have a sitter also endure the odd hours Hunter kept and the odours and discomfort of his miniscule studio seemed too much to ask. Help was at hand, however. Once Hunter's health and confidence had improved, he soon got back into the habit of meeting his friends during their morning coffee break. Going out for coffee during the morning and later for afternoon tea was then a way of life for the Glasgow businessman, which did not die out until the onset of the 1960s. Once the mail and dictation had been dealt with, the routine was to go out to places such as Miss Buick's, Gordons or Craigs for coffee, while letters were being typed back in the office. This afforded an opportunity to meet clients and colleagues, and to conduct any necessary business in a civilised manner.

Hunter's circle of friends regularly met for coffee in the 'Bon-Bon', which was situated in Glasgow's Central Station. The regulars included McInnes, McNair and Honeyman. Frequently they were joined by Ion Harrison, Matthew Dickie, Sam Warnock and R.C.Roy, and occasionally by Willie Gordon, who was on the staff of the *Evening News*. Hunter had a great ability to involve others in discussing art and, more intriguingly, the specific problem created by his latest artistic challenge. By and large this introduced a new breed of supporter and collector to Hunter's now depleted following; together they formed a sort of unofficial advisory committee. Such was their commitment to Hunter that when it came to the tricky question of whom he might paint, they rallied to the cause. It fell to the courageous Honeyman to come up with a plan, which was put to his business friends: *Hunter wants to paint portraits. Please swallow your modesty, give him some sittings, bring in your family: if you like the result you can purchase very cheaply, if you don't like it there is no harm done.*[9]

Evidently Honeyman was successful in his request, as he relates that despite the obvious drawbacks both artist and subjects had a lot of fun.[10] Nor did Honeyman draw the line at close friends; in his role as a partner in Reid & Lefevre, he approached some of the new enthusiasts for Hunter's art who ventured into his gallery. Considering the lack of understanding of Hunter's current style on the part of the majority of prospective sitters, a series of portraits was a dangerous gamble for both Hunter and Reid & Lefevre. The fact that such portraits

147 | Stocks in a White Vase
Oil on canvas, 1930–31
Private collection

148 | Dr James Harper
Oil on canvas, 1930
Private collection

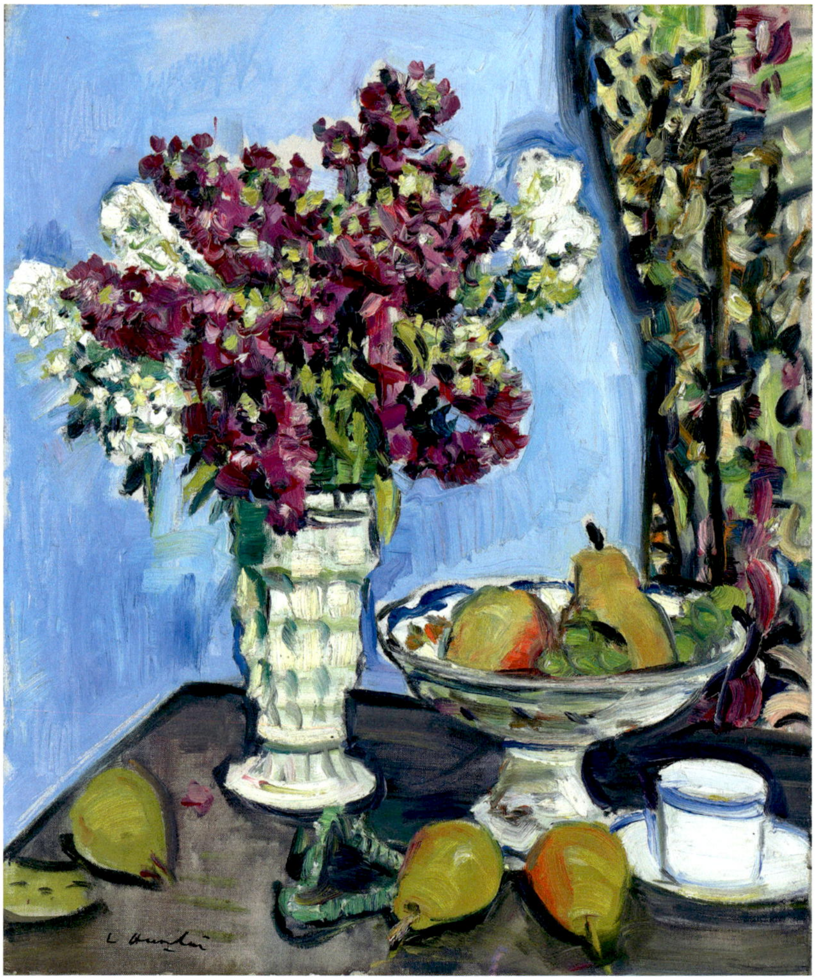

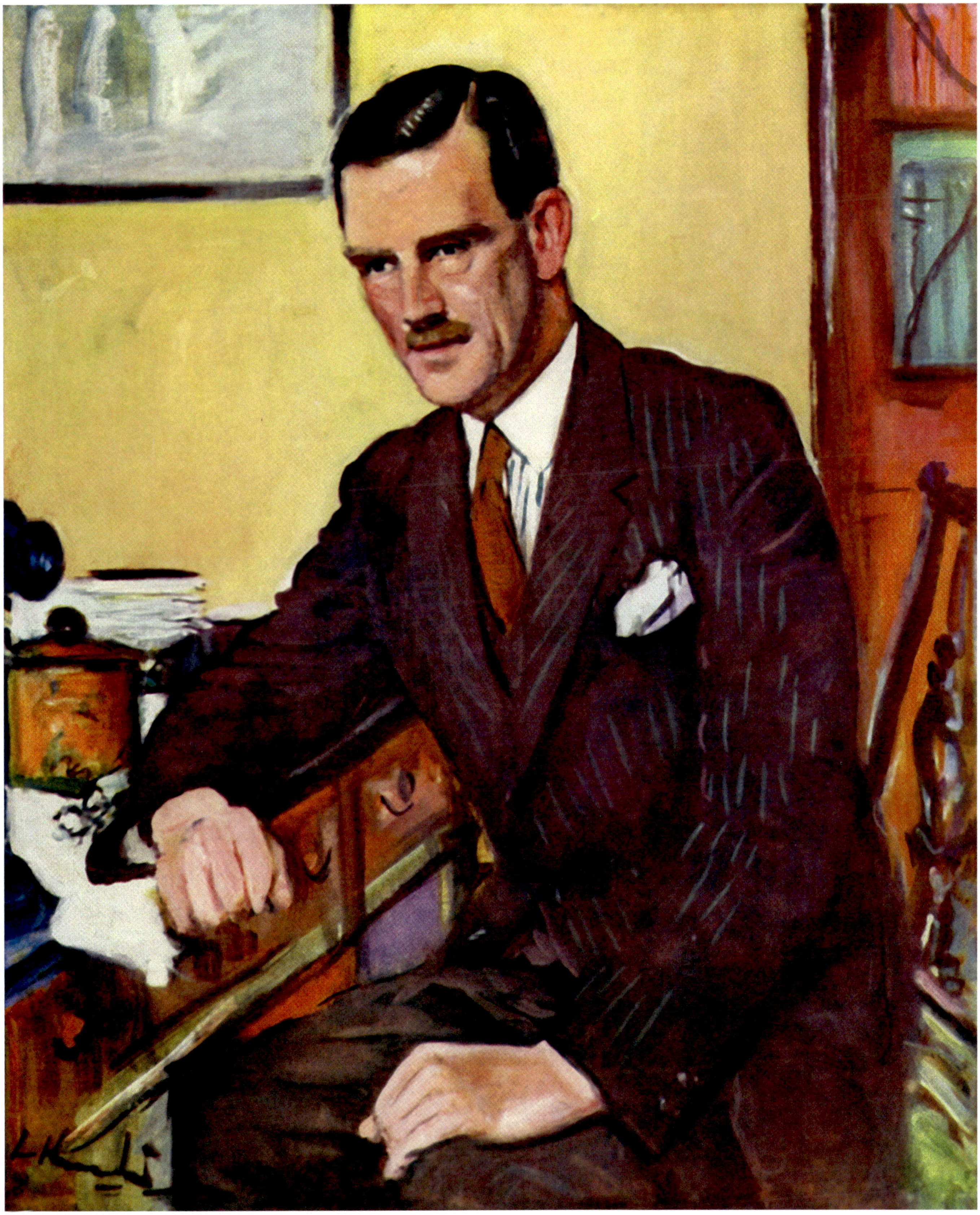

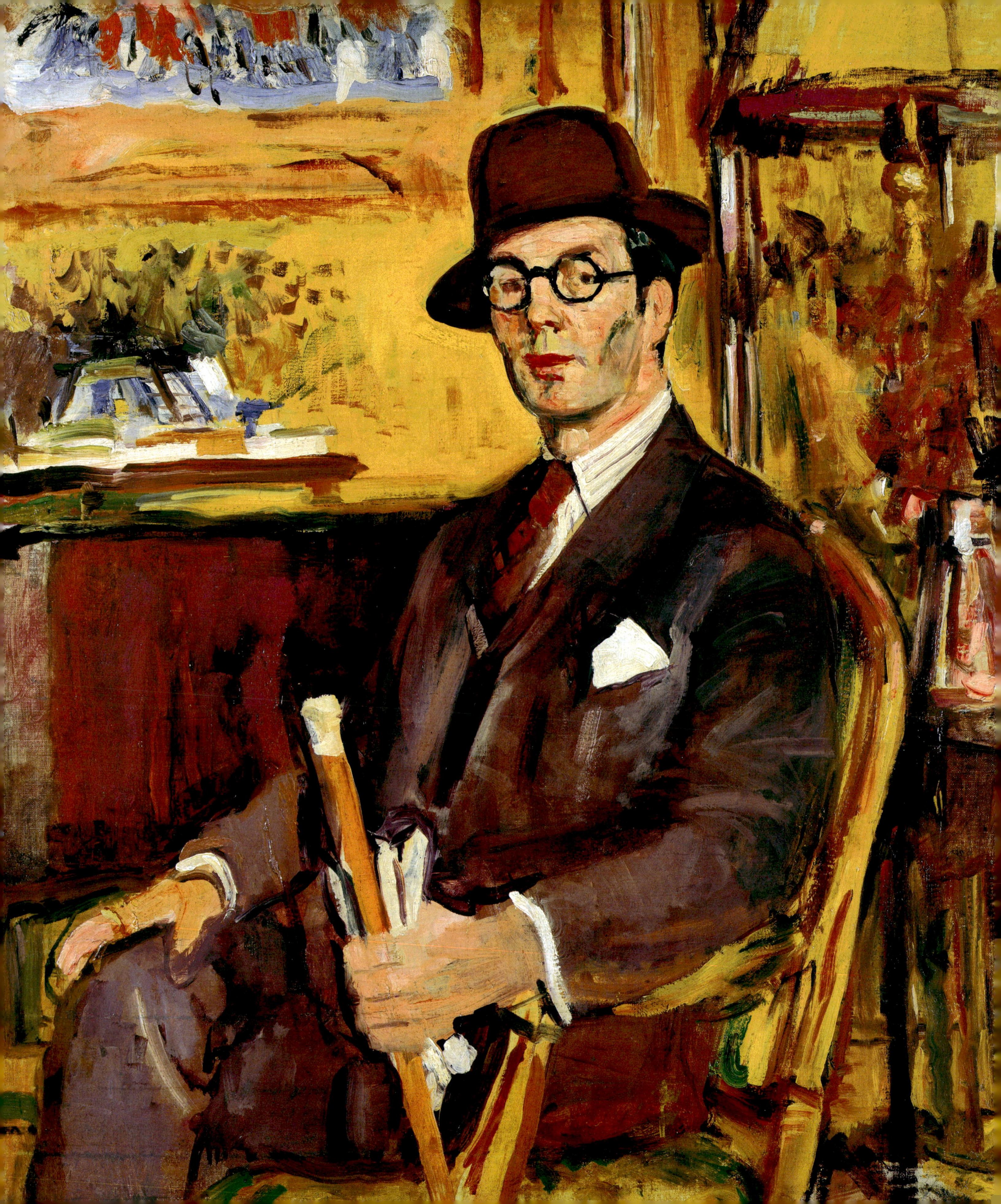

149 | The Malacca Cane, Duncan Macdonald
Oil on canvas, 1930
Private collection

would not be akin to a photographic likeness, the public's traditional impression of what a portrait should be, made the decision to proceed appear all the more courageous and innovative.

Using his own methods, Hunter produced a number of fine portraits. One of the best must be *Dr James Harper* (pl.148). Harper met Hunter completely by chance one day at Reid & Lefevre. After a general discussion on art, an intrigued Harper agreed in the spirit of adventure to sit for a portrait. Hunter's brief was perfectly simple – he wanted to paint a doctor. Following a number of discussions, Hunter eventually settled on posing Harper in his consulting room. Hunter's palette lifts the portrait well above the ordinary. Indeed it could have been a very dull picture, but he succeeds in recreating the depth and personality of the sitter solely through the use of strong colour. Dr Harper was an ear, nose and throat specialist, who in addition to his private practice ran two busy clinics at Glasgow hospitals. Hunter's forthright presentation leaves one in no doubt as to Dr Harper's professionalism and integrity, while his face embodies keen interest and genuine concern. Hunter's skill can be appreciated when it is realised he was not just painting what he saw. His creative mind visualised in bold colour the effect he wished to achieve. The sober suit is ingeniously enlivened through Hunter picking out the stripes in the same brilliant green he uses in the background. The elegant wood surface of the desk and bookcase are depicted in warm rust tones that also feature in Harper's tie. In fact the furniture in Harper's consulting rooms in Woodside Terrace was dark mahogany. The wall in the background was not yellow, yet Hunter cleverly employs such a strong colour as part of his overall scheme. In short Hunter brilliantly captures the essence of Harper's personality through his unique application of colour.

Hunter's manipulation of brilliant colour as a means of conveying the sitter's personality is unsurpassed in his unfinished portrait of Duncan Macdonald, known as *The Malacca Cane* (pl.149). As previously mentioned, Macdonald, the senior partner in Reid & Lefevre, had an extrovert personality and infinite flair. It was entirely appropriate for Hunter to have him seated on an elegant, ornate chair, holding gloves and a cane, the latter in particular being depicted as a flamboyant accessory. The whole effect at once conveys the artistic and sensitive nature expected of someone working within the fine art world of the 1920s and '30s. In total contrast to the solid control Hunter exercised in his portrayal of Harper, the lively brushwork and rich tone employed in the Macdonald portrait verge on the extravagant. Needless to say Hunter's desire to paint Macdonald, and indeed his wife, Lily, in London proved to be more than a little irksome for both parties. Macdonald writes to Honeyman:

He's been here all afternoon doing a full drawing of me and incensed Lily by making several ink stains on her best yellow satin couch and on the carpet. If his finished portrait is to be as weak it will do no good in Glasgow. However he's to try an oil and will hope for the best.[11]

The oil was started in Macdonald's flat in Bruton Street and good progress made until Hunter had to go back to Glasgow, leaving the hands and the lower part of the body only 'blocked in'. He told Macdonald that he would complete the portrait on his return, but that was not to be. Years after Hunter's death Reid & Lefevre's gallery in St James's Street was badly damaged in an air raid during the Second World War and the firm had to evacuate the unsafe building and move to New Bond Street. After the war ended Macdonald sent one of his young assistants to the bombed premises to see if he could find some account books in the attic. The youth 'returned with the books, and also with a roll of canvas under his arm which he had found in the beams in the Attic. Macdonald unrolled it, and was amazed to find it was his own portrait by Hunter', which, having been bombed out of both his gallery and his Bruton Street flat, Macdonald had forgotten about. Soon afterwards Ion Harrison called at the gallery and was shown the portrait by Macdonald. When he got back home to Glasgow, Harrison wrote to Macdonald:

Dear Macdonald,
If you will put a price on your head
And sell yourself I will willingly hang you.

Macdonald replied that he was too modest to put a price on his head, but he was willing to sell himself as he already had his portrait done by James McBey, Percy Wyndham Lewis and others, and suggested that Honeyman should fix the price. Thus Harrison added the portrait to his considerable collection.[12]

Of course Hunter was not always successful with his portraits. Regretfully he re-worked the portrait of Ion Harrison and of Mrs Cathy Honeyman, and for some reason he struggled with that of McInnes to little effect. Perhaps he was unable to stand back and sum up in paint the qualities in friends to whom he was closest. Honeyman amusingly relates how Hunter wished to paint a portrait of him in the style of Manet: 'I was persuaded ... to spend many a weary hour, clad in dress clothes for the black and white effect, while he expiated on the new technique he was evolving.' However the portrait was not working out to the satisfaction of either party, so Hunter never finished it. Such was its failure that apparently it attracted the amusing label *Seats still left at Eighteen-pence and Two Shillings*.[13] Subsequently Hunter relegated it to the reverse of a still life.

Having established his ideas and technique in regard to male sitters, Hunter turned his attention to painting a female portrait in his new style. He possessed a refreshing sensitivity when painting women, as he had displayed already in the portraits he executed in the south of France in 1929. One of his simplest, yet most arresting, is *Mrs R.C. Roy* (Carnegie Library, Ayr). Through his careful use of texture he reveals a thoughtful, serene and graceful woman. At their best Hunter's portraits are an important landmark in his career, because it was by an ingenious use of strong colour that he captured the character and personality of the sitter. It is noteworthy that no self-portraits have come to light. Probably Hunter never painted a formal portrait of himself.

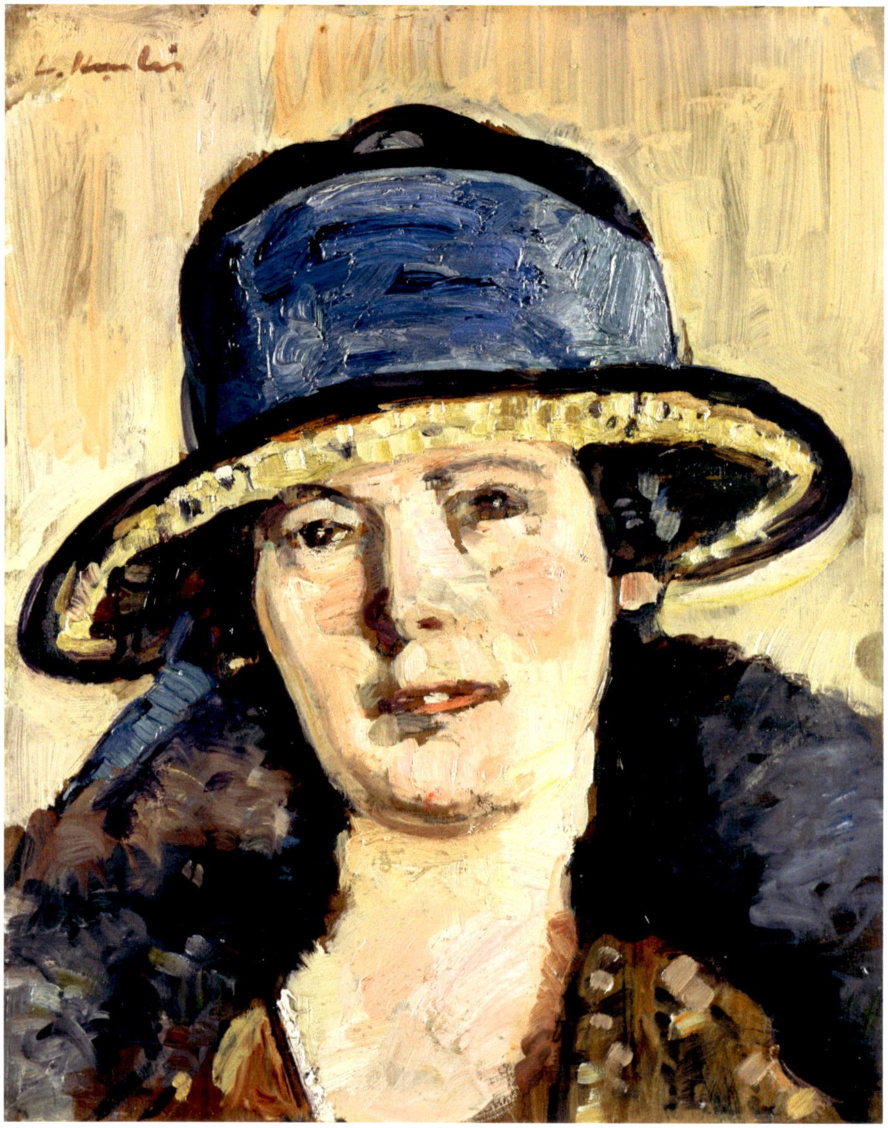

150 | Miss McNair
Oil on panel, 1931
University of Glasgow, Hunterian Art Gallery

Hunter spent the latter part of 1930 and the first few months of 1931 painting both still life and portraits. The quest for suitable 'victims' for portraiture was constant, and it was another chance encounter at Reid & Lefevre's Glasgow gallery that provided Hunter with an interesting artistic distraction. C.B.Cochran, the London impresario, had arrived in Glasgow to present his show, *Evergreen*, at the King's Theatre. Knowing of Cochran's interest in fine art, particularly French paintings, Honeyman invited Cochran to view what Reid & Lefevre had in stock. A still life of roses by Hunter caught Cochran's eye, the paint still wet, having been 'snatched' from Hunter's easel that very morning. Realising that he had never heard of the artist, Cochran's interest was aroused. Not only did Cochran buy the painting, but on being informed of Hunter's developing portrait series he was sufficiently impressed to lend his substantial support to Hunter's enterprise in the form of a portrait commission. Given Hunter's lifelong interest in the theatre and Cochran's growing interest in modern art, it is not hard to imagine the two men deep in discussion over the merits of both art forms.

Hunter decided to portray the maestro standing in the Grand Circle of the King's Theatre with his back to the stage. He also may have had it in mind to include a scene from the show taking place in the background. Unfortunately Cochran's other commitments made it impossible for him to pose long enough for Hunter, though Hunter did spend the considerable time in between sittings doing numerous sketches of the *Evergreen* production. At the end of the show's run in Glasgow Cochran returned to London. Understandably the portrait failed to materialise due to the continued absence of the sitter. Consequently Hunter went down to London early in 1931, where along with other pursuits, such as painting Duncan Macdonald and visiting friends and various galleries, he finally managed to arrange for Cochran to sit long enough for a second version to be tackled. Hunter writes to Honeyman:

... I got off the Cochran portrait all right on a fresh canvas. He came up to the office I have in the Palace [Theatre] *building, with his advertising man, at 11 p.m. one night, and with blue lights posed for about three-quarters of an hour. And I painted it all in making a likeness like a pen drawing. He is very pleased with it ...*

I am working on the Cochran sketches but am held up for the moment for some photographs that are

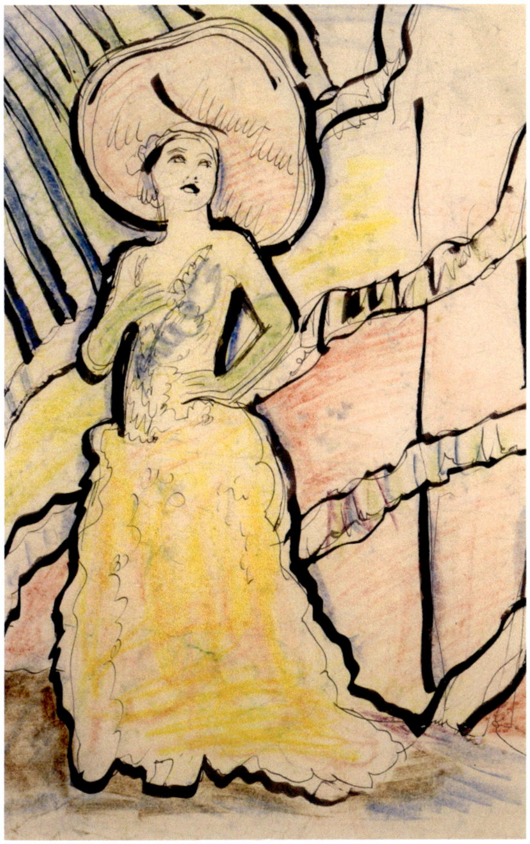

151 | Mabel Couper
Brush with ink and watercolour, 1930
Private collection

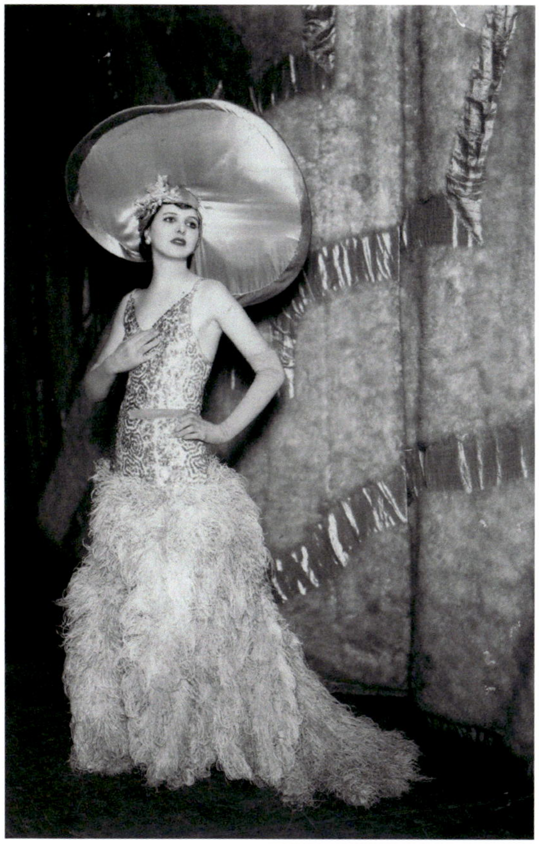

152 | Photograph of the actress Mabel Couper, who appeared in C.B.Cochran's *Evergreen* in Glasgow in 1930

coming. I am expecting to get back about the end of the week and get down to work again.[14]

The letter reveals that in addition to sketching *Evergreen* scenes *in situ*, Hunter also worked from publicity photographs, transforming the scene or figure by charging it with vitality in his sketch. This can be seen clearly in his ink sketch of *Mabel Couper* (pl.151) when compared with the corresponding photograph (pl.152). Through his bold line and keen sense of pattern, Hunter captures an excitement and theatrical presence which the photograph fails to convey.

Hunter's other sketches from *Evergreen* publicity photographs are executed in the form of rapid, spontaneous drawings, which one might be forgiven for thinking were done on the spot. Executing those sketches was a source of great enjoyment for Hunter, but in reality they were a diversion, displaying his talent for capturing the essence of what he was viewing rather than a genuinely deep feeling for the theatre. Over the years Hunter's interest in the theatre, whether it be in San Francisco's Chinatown, Largo's open-air theatre or Helen Vanel's tiny dance theatre in St Paul de Vence, was confined almost exclusively to the colour and spectacle, rather than the content. Interestingly Hunter made a sketch of Nikita Balieff with his company, *La Chauve Souris*, in Glasgow around this time (1931, private collection).

1931 was turning out to be a promising year for Hunter. Enjoying old and new friendships alike, he was in fine form. Although he did not manage to see Matthew Justice as often as he would have liked, Hunter still turned to him for help and advice, particularly relating to the supply of good quality canvas. It goes without saying that both Justice and Tattersall were on the 'victims' list for portraits, and Hunter intended to go to Dundee following the Paris group show in March. Hunter also struck up a friendship with the talented potter, Staite Murray, whom Reid & Lefevre was promoting then.

Undoubtedly the highlight of the year for Hunter was his inclusion in the important Paris exhibition, *Les Peintres Écossais* and he was anxious not to miss it. Honeyman on the other hand had other ideas, expressing to Macdonald his concern about Hunter (who was then in London) deciding on the spur of the moment to go to Paris for the opening of *Les Peintres Écossais* despite there being outstanding matters in Glasgow that required his immediate attention, such as his imminent portrait show. Some of the paintings were not finished and many still required framing, and this could not be done until Hunter's return to Glasgow, which he repeatedly postponed. A trip to Paris at that stage would further exacerbate Honeyman's already difficult schedule. Macdonald did his best to intervene, but admitting defeat he wrote to Honeyman:

Hunter I told you will only go his own way and insists on going to Paris. I don't think it would be of any use to write him an order of return. He'd set off to France just the same.[15]

Les Peintres Écossais at the Galeries Georges Petit, one of the oldest galleries in Paris, was a very grand affair. Reid & Lefevre had organised an impressive body of work by Peploe, Fergusson, Hunter, Cadell, Telfer Bear and R.O.Dunlop (included notwithstanding that Dunlop was born in Dublin). The exhibition was opened by the British Ambassador to France, and a letter of support by the Prime Minister, Ramsay Macdonald, was printed at the beginning of the catalogue. One can imagine the state

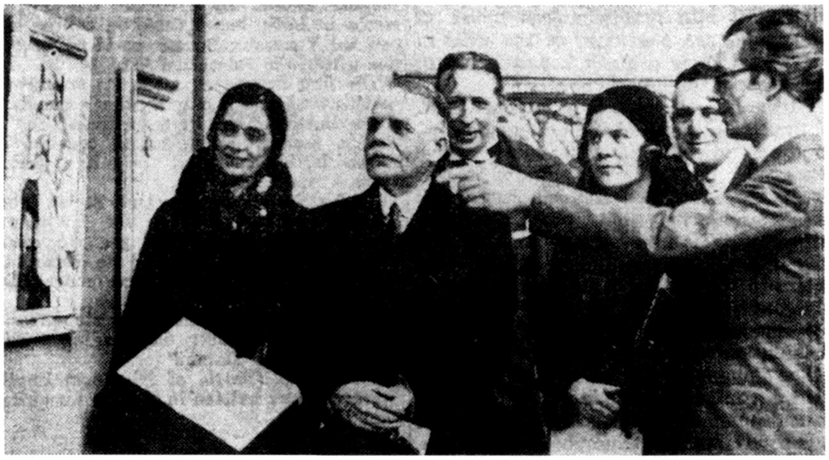

153 | The opening by the British Ambassador of the exhibition *Les Peintres écossais* at Galeries Georges Petit, Paris in March 1931. Leslie Hunter is immediately behind the ambassador in the centre of the photograph in *The Daily Sketch* on 2 March

154 | Loch Lomond
Oil on canvas, 1931
Private collection

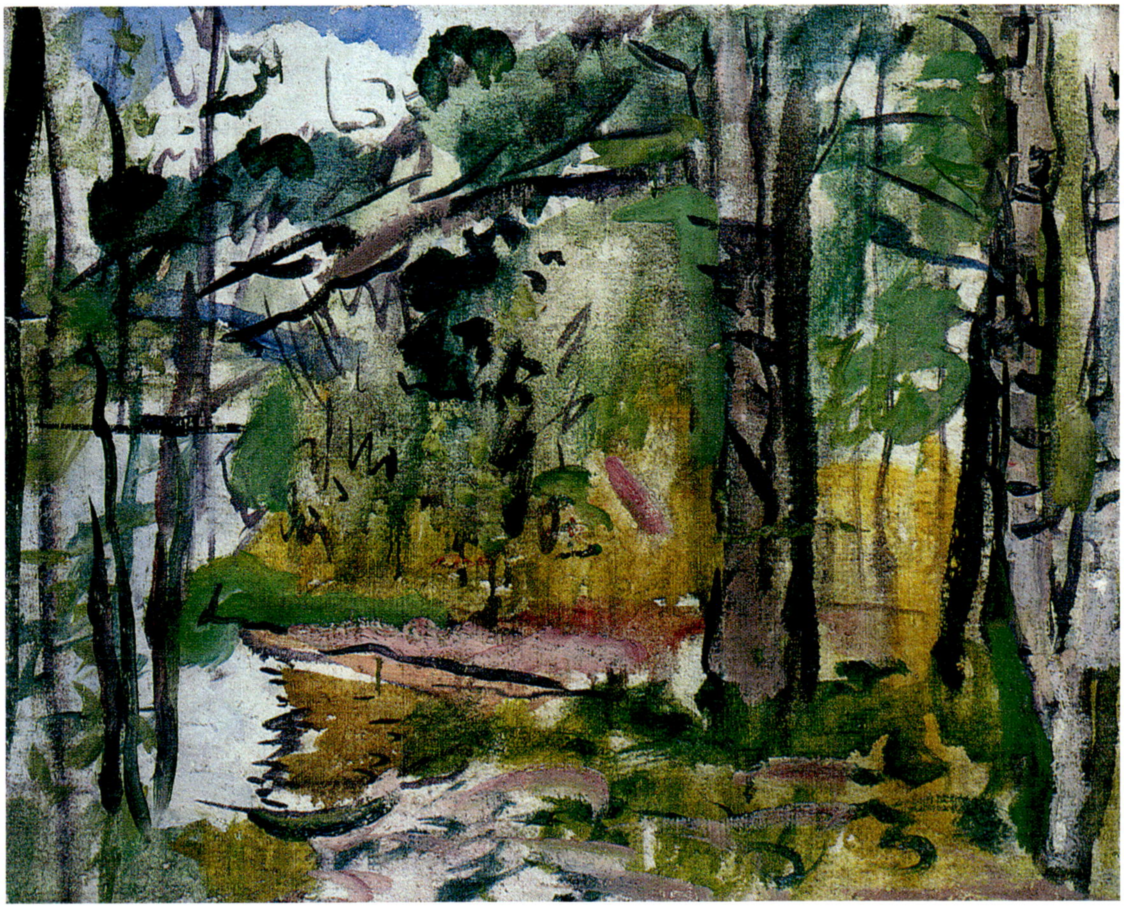

of Duncan Macdonald's nerves, knowing that Hunter was perfectly capable of turning up with non-matching shoes or having neglected to wear a well-pressed suit. It appears he did not let Reid & Lefevre down, however, judging from a press photograph (pl.153) showing Hunter lurking behind Lord Tyrell, the British Ambassador, who along with J.D.Fergusson and his partner, the dancer Margaret Morris, is listening attentively to Duncan Macdonald.

Macdonald and Reid had chosen a good cross-section of each artist's work. In Hunter's case they offered pictures dating back to his Fife years and included some of his stronger Loch Lomond paintings. The firm was amply rewarded when the French Government purchased *Houseboats, Loch Lomond* (1924) by Hunter, as well as a painting by Peploe and by Fergusson, a signal honour for all three artists.

André Salmon, the Paris correspondent of the arts magazine, *Apollo*, wrote in general praise:

... The Scottish artists appear to us to be painters of a very high standard, justly preoccupied by the new values introduced in art since the early years of the century, but they have never given up searching for this secret of communication.

On Hunter Salmon commented:

... His palette is very personal. He possesses the art of binding fundamental tones with light ones, notably yellows, prudently chosen and here and there pushed to a height almost harsh. It is a feature which deeply impressed the great number of artists present at the brilliant opening by the British Ambassador and French Ministers.[16]

At last Hunter's art was being recognised for what it was – an exploration in the modern use of colour.

No doubt Honeyman was pleased for Hunter and Reid & Lefevre that *Houseboats, Loch Lomond* had gone to such a prestigious home, effectively the national gallery of France, but he had rather more pressing matters on his mind, as a somewhat peeved Honeyman told Hunter in a letter dated 5 March:

I can only assume that you have had such a good time in London and Paris that you have forgotten all your Glasgow friends. We are all rather anxious to have news of you, and, more particularly, to have an idea when you are likely to return. For my part, I hope the return will not be long delayed, because there is much work waiting to be done and things are badly held up.

I hear the Paris Show opened with great éclat, and that a lot of nice things have been said about it. You certainly have had some publicity in Glasgow, but not nearly what it might have been if you had kept us posted – as we had hoped and thought.

Your studio has been tidied up, but I cannot lay my hands on some things I thought were there. Most of the stuff, however, is waiting for you to go over with me.

… The main object of this is to get news of you.

Your lady friends at the Bon Bon are growing grey-haired with anxiety … [17]

Hunter's response was hardly one of contrition:

I have just returned from Bray, where I spent a week-end with Staite Murray and enjoyed it very much. I had intended writing before leaving for Paris on Saturday morning, but a phone message asked me to come out to lunch and I had not time to write.

… It was a great opening and the French Government have bought the Loch Lomond picture for the Luxembourg. I believe they are going to hang all the foreign pictures in the Jeu de Paume. What about prophets without honour, etc.

I am taking your advice and my nerves are much better.

The letter also reveals how his plans for the rest of the year are developing:

I am certain that I should come to London for good. Ressich thinks so too. I don't think Glasgow is any good now and if Reid's give it up that will be the end of it. London is the place for you also. I am finishing some things here but I expect to be back again in about a week.

… When is the portrait show to open? I must finish one or two things for it. Then I must have another shot at Loch Lomond. Hyde Park is full of glorious material. It's a wonder nobody seems to have noticed it.

P.S. Have you a good cure for indigestion?[18]

Hunter's belief in his art was now unshakable. His letter to Honeyman contains the three main elements that dominate the last eight months of his life: an enthusiasm for trying his new technique at Loch Lomond; convinced he should move to London permanently, he already had the germ of an idea for a series of pictures based on Hyde Park; and the first real warning that all was not well with his health.

The exhibition of portraits opened on time in June, but, as anticipated, it proved somewhat controversial. Honeyman relates that 'the type of thing he [Hunter] had done was quite unlike anything hitherto seen in Glasgow, but Hunter did not feel called upon to make any apology and his friends were quite satisfied that the originality of his ideas, especially in the matter of backgrounds, would more than justify his departure from traditional methods'. Honeyman also mentioned how careful he had been 'to avoid everything in the nature of stunt publicity, although the novelty of it justified some advance propaganda'.[19]

Hunter took his experiment in portraiture very seriously. The ensuing – often passionate – debate his modern methods engendered at least demonstrates that others were taking an interest, where previously his work had not aroused the same degree of attention. As in the past, however, only a few people genuinely appreciated his new work. Wisely Honeyman had taken the opportunity to include a few still lifes and landscapes, which if sold might at least cover their costs.

Ironically, the most hostile critics turned out to be local artists, a few of whom went as far as to consider the exhibition as 'something in the nature of a joke and not in very good taste'. Some went as far as criticising Reid & Lefevre for mounting the show in the first place.[20] Hunter must have hit a nerve to have provoked such an extreme reaction. The press reaction certainly was lively, though overall the critics took a balanced but positive view. Under the headline 'Show that is causing Concern', the critic of the *Evening Citizen* poses the question: 'Should an artist attempt to reveal himself or his sitter?' and continues:

If, in some, Mr Hunter has permitted himself to subordinate the central figure to the scheme of decoration and pattern, in others he has certainly demonstrated that he possesses considerable powers of penetration and remarkable intuition.

... if an artist chooses as his convention to idealise his sitters by making them part of a design rather than in recording a doubtful nobility of expression, how can we insist that he has abused or exceeded the limits of his commission?[21]

The portrait exhibition behind him, Hunter turned his attention to the summer months he planned to spend at Loch Lomond. There were two reasons for his enthusiasm. The first was his desire to try out his new 'modern' style on territory he had recorded previously. The second concerned an affair of the heart. In the spring of 1931 Hunter had met a young woman called Marnie Scrafton. A former student of the Commercial College in Glasgow, Marnie was on the point of graduating from Jordanhill College as a teacher of special subjects, which included art and business studies, when she met Hunter. Born in Tain, Ross-shire in 1909, she was thirty-two years Hunter's junior. Honeyman describes how Hunter met her quite by chance in a Glasgow tearoom. She was one of a group of young undergraduates who were collecting on 'Charities Day'. Immediately Hunter was captivated by her face and costume and asked her if he could do a quick sketch.[22]

Marnie's memories of Hunter give an engaging insight into the last year of his life. Hunter had invited her to his studio, as she later recounted to Honeyman:

I went to his studio the following Saturday and he showed me some of his work and then we went out to lunch in what he called 'the only Continental Restaurant in Glasgow' and had a very 'Continental' meal with Chianti wine ... He talked to me about his early days in California and his running away from home at an early age.[23] *He talked to me of his laughing Celtic mother who sympathised with and understood him and his longings.*

We met often after that, and our friendship grew and grew. During the summer of that year [1931] *I used to go down to Loch Lomondside with him to paint, and we used to talk about everything under the sun. He painted my portrait for the exhibition of portraits in June.*

Time went on and soon he began to talk of moving to London. He went to London for a visit of a few weeks ... He wrote very enthusiastically about London and how happy he felt there, and that he had a new lease of life ... He felt that he was on the verge of a new spiritual era and the verge of success, as he was, I feel sure ...

... My impression of him was that he was a man of great simplicity of soul and great genius. He was a gay, laughing Bohemian with a wonderful knowledge of the world. At times he was a brilliant conversationalist. He was extremely sensitive which at times caused him unnecessary suffering.

... He cared for me and had great plans for the future when he made a success in London and would be able to marry me. Although he was so very much older than I in years, he was very young in mind and soul, and we had a great deal in common. I shall

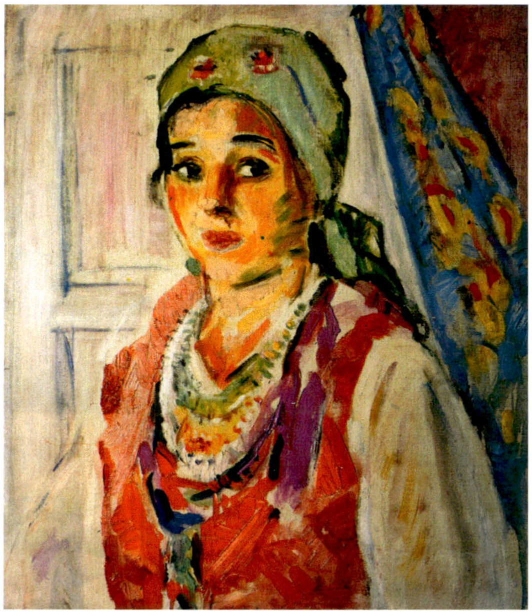

155 | Peasant Girl, St Paul.
This may be a portrait of Marnie Scrafton in peasant costume
Oil on canvas, 1931
Private collection

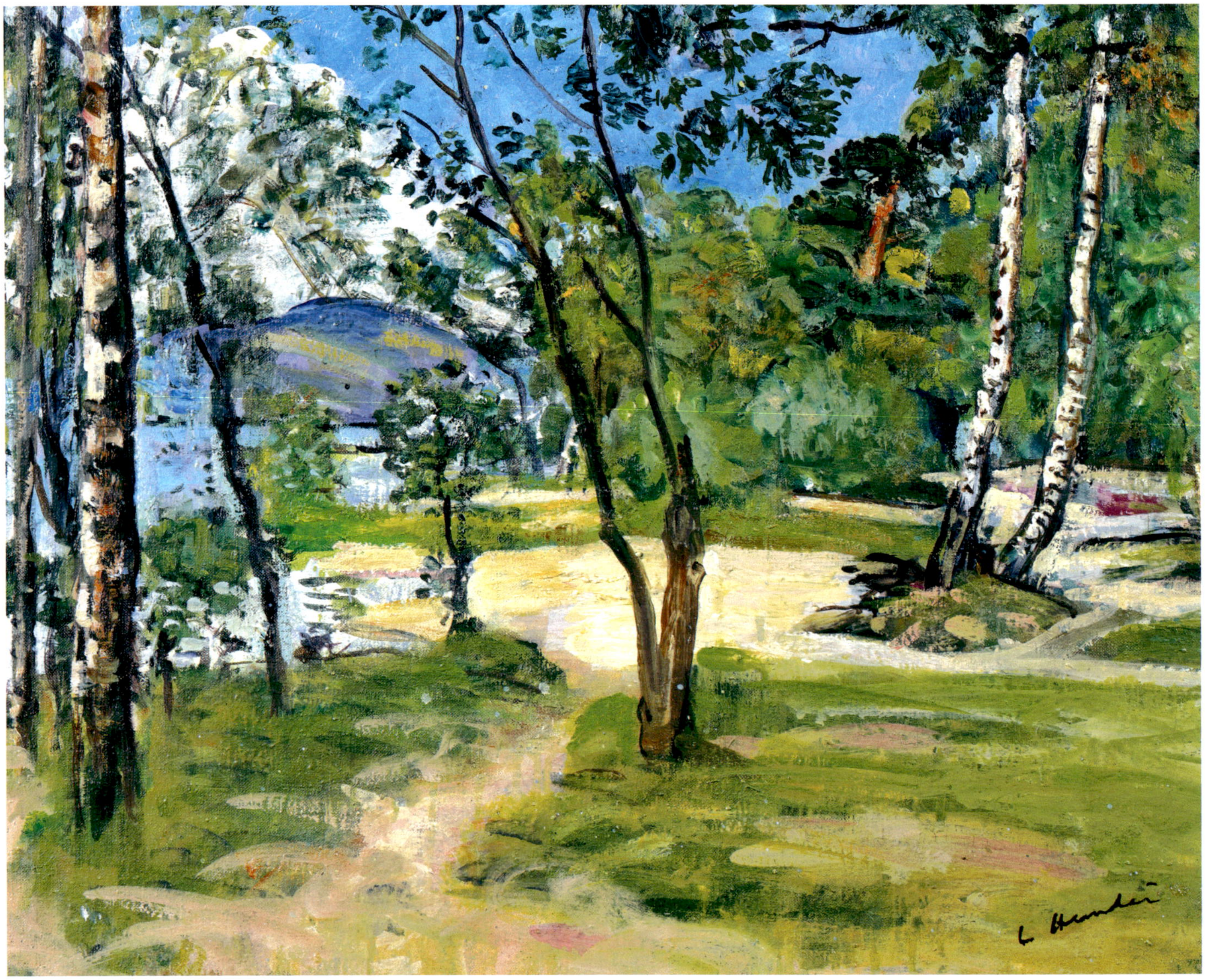

156 | Loch Lomond
Oil on canvas, 1931
The Fleming-Wyfold Art Foundation

always treasure his memory – a great artist and a great man.[24]

It would appear that Hunter had found true love at last. It is obvious that the considerable difference in age did not matter; both Marnie and he felt very happy in their relationship. Hunter was optimistic about the future. He had great plans for London and for their future together.

A houseboat at Loch Lomond had been rented for the summer. Hunter was happy, living life to the full, enjoying being with Marnie. He began in his usual fashion, completing numerous sketches, which naturally he kept on board the houseboat. According to Honeyman, he also enjoyed the company of a group of rather riotous young men. On one of the more boisterous evenings with his new friends, the houseboat was set on fire accidently.[25] Fortunately the drawings were saved, albeit with charred edges. From them Hunter created with a confidence rarely achieved in the past a number of stunning paintings, which rank among the finest of his career.

Several of these pictures are in the nature of a momentary glimpse, but at the same time exude an extraordinary timeless quality. *Loch Lomond*

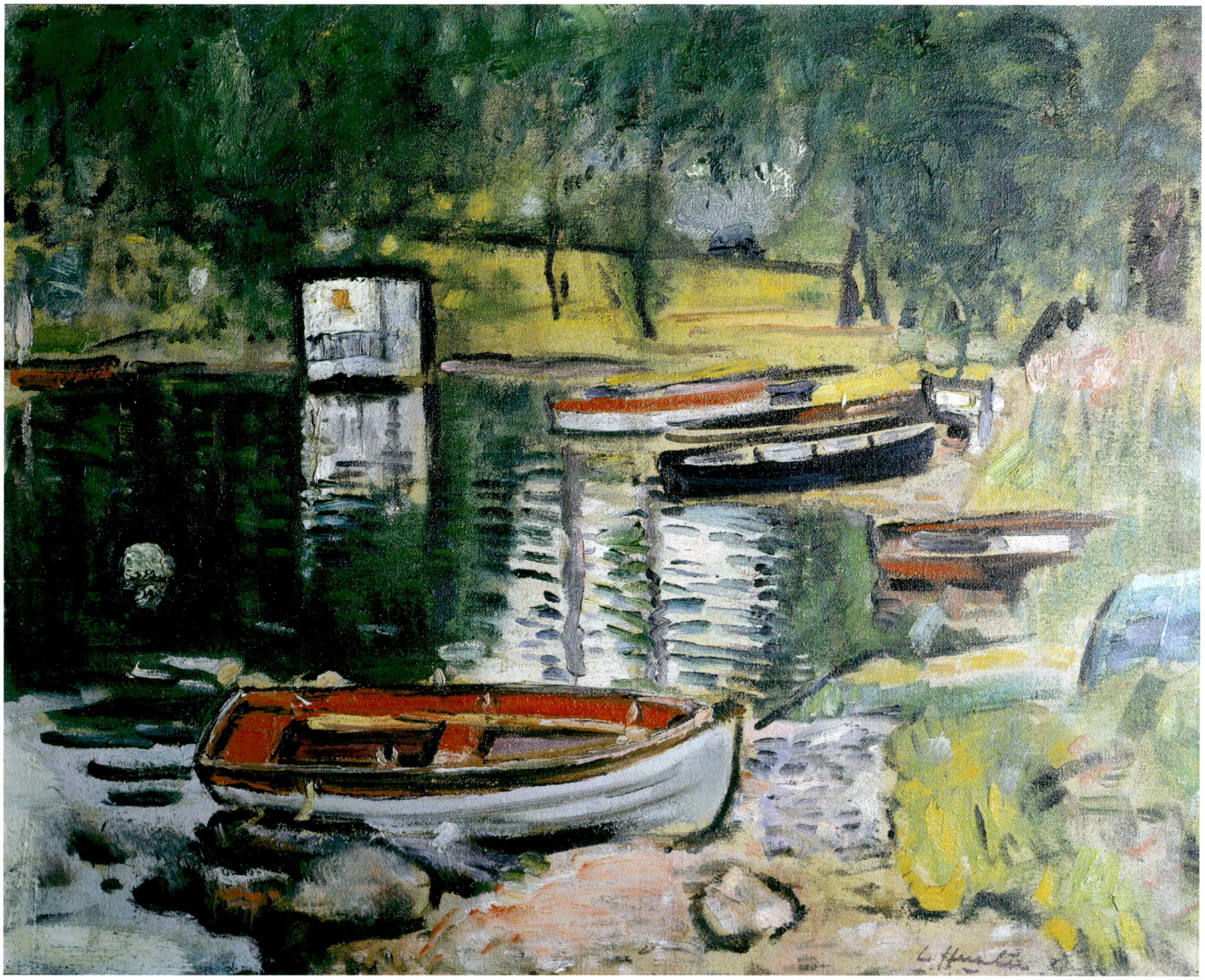

157 | Rowing Boats, Loch Lomond
Oil on canvas, 1931
Private collection

(pl.156) offers a fleeting look – the loch, distant mountain and partially-concealed cloud all revealed through dappled light filtering through bushes and birch trees. The contradiction lies in the painting's sense of permanence: well-balanced proportions in the overall design, while vigorous colour creates the spontaneous vitality that animates the whole composition.

On the Banks of Loch Lomond (pl.161) is treated in the same manner. The sinewy limbs and branches have an immediate impact, while the flattened perspective and texture bind together to achieve a compelling harmony.

One of Hunter's most stunning and enduring landscapes is *Reflections, Balloch* (pl.158). McInnes bought the painting in 1931 and two years later generously gifted it to the National Gallery of Scotland. All Hunter's skills as an artist seem to come together in this one painting. The colour is striking but never jarring, the scene is timeless, the effect is fresh and, quite simply, beautiful. It has an arresting quality that impresses at first sight and a masterful depth that increases every time one returns to it. *Moonlight, Loch Lomond* (pl.159) has many of these qualities too, but in this case Hunter exploits the different

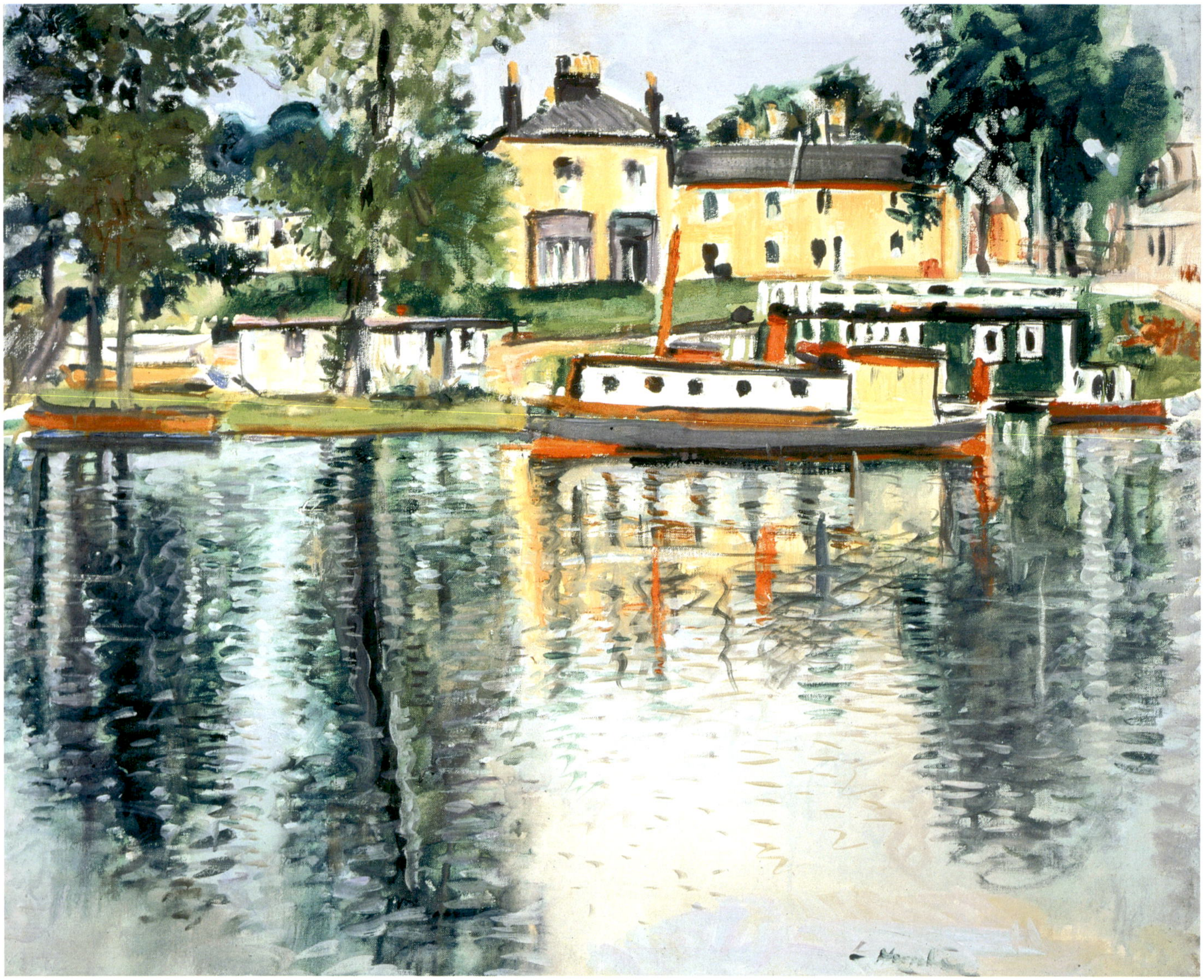

158 | Reflections, Balloch
Oil on canvas, 1931
Scottish National Gallery of Modern Art

natural and man-made elements in the view by subtly altering his technique. Perspective is still flattened, and thin paint is confidently applied, allowing Hunter to bring out the dramatic appeal of the moon with its strong reflection on the surface of the water. The bold yellow moon and reflection divide the composition into unequal parts, while the almost filigree form of the bush at the bottom right of the canvas redresses the balance by mirroring the form of tree branches and foliage at the top left and coherently binding the scene together. Had Hunter painted the water surface with the same rich tones and busy brushwork as in *Reflections, Balloch*, he would have negated the delicate harmonising effect of the bush. The contrasting sizes and colours of the various houseboats and buildings successfully counterbalance the potentially garish vivid yellow band of the moon's reflection, allowing the thinly-painted water surface to complement it rather than work against it.

Hunter's decision to return to Loch Lomond during the summer of 1931 resulted in some wonderful work. Throughout the autumn he continued to paint still life, characterised by a

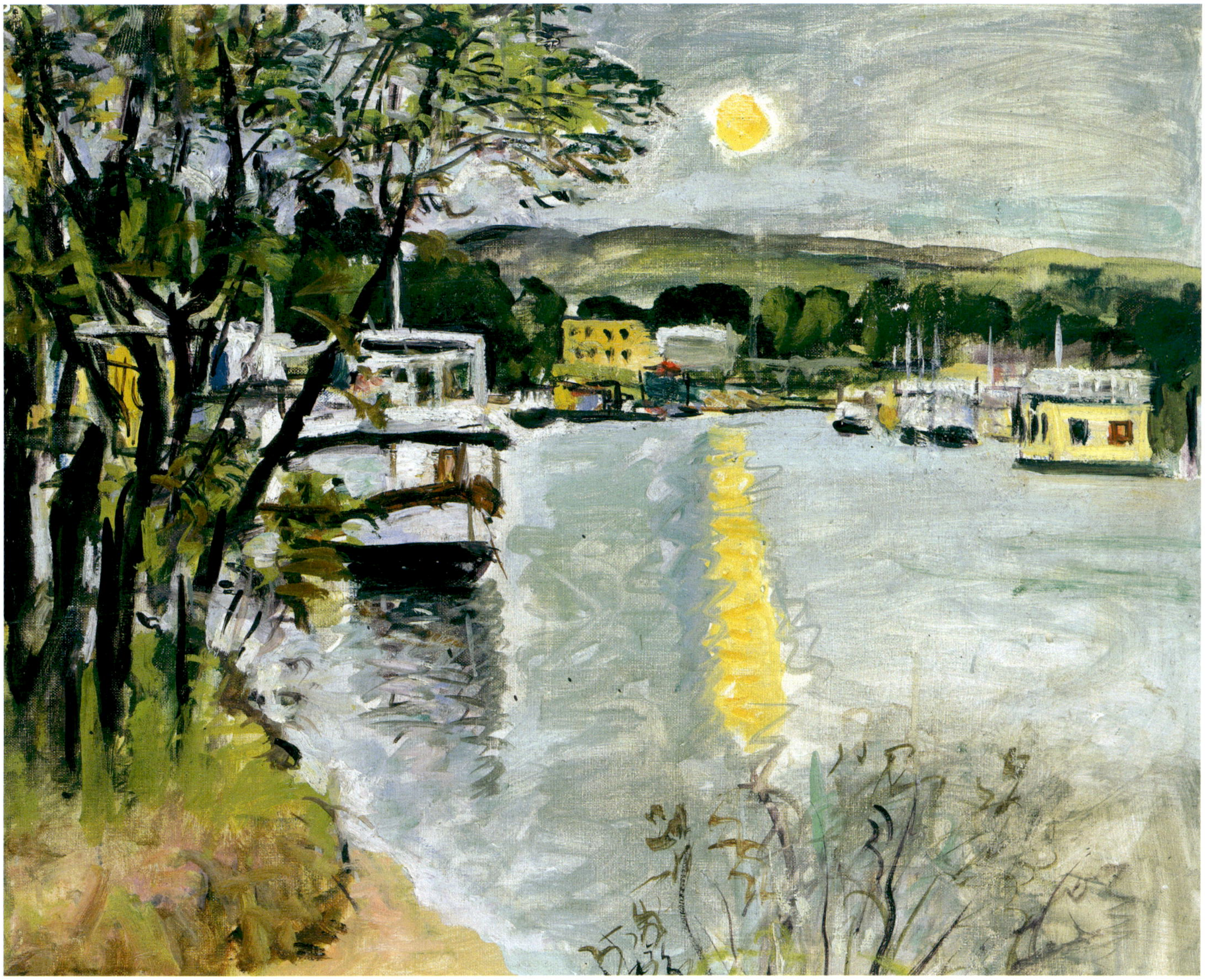

159 | Moonlight, Loch Lomond
Oil on canvas, 1931
Aberdeen Art Gallery & Museums Collections

simplification of design, colour and tone compared to the work he had produced earlier that year and during the previous year. The strong dark lines prevalent in the still lifes executed in the south of France are muted now to the point of unobtrusively blending into the whole design, allowing the colour to speak for itself. Hunter applied the same idea of spontaneity co-existing with timelessness that he adopted in his recent Loch Lomond landscapes.

By this time the economic recession was biting particularly severely in Scotland. Reid & Lefevre had come to the conclusion that the Glasgow gallery would have to close as it was no longer viable. Honeyman was preparing to move south to take up his post as co-director in London. Hunter too had sensed a deterioration in the Scottish economy and did not hold out much hope for immediate improvement. Believing that general acceptance of his work was almost around the corner and that London would offer him more opportunity, he put together plans to move there permanently.

In October Hunter went to London to find accommodation and a studio, staying on in the capital for several months and prompting a

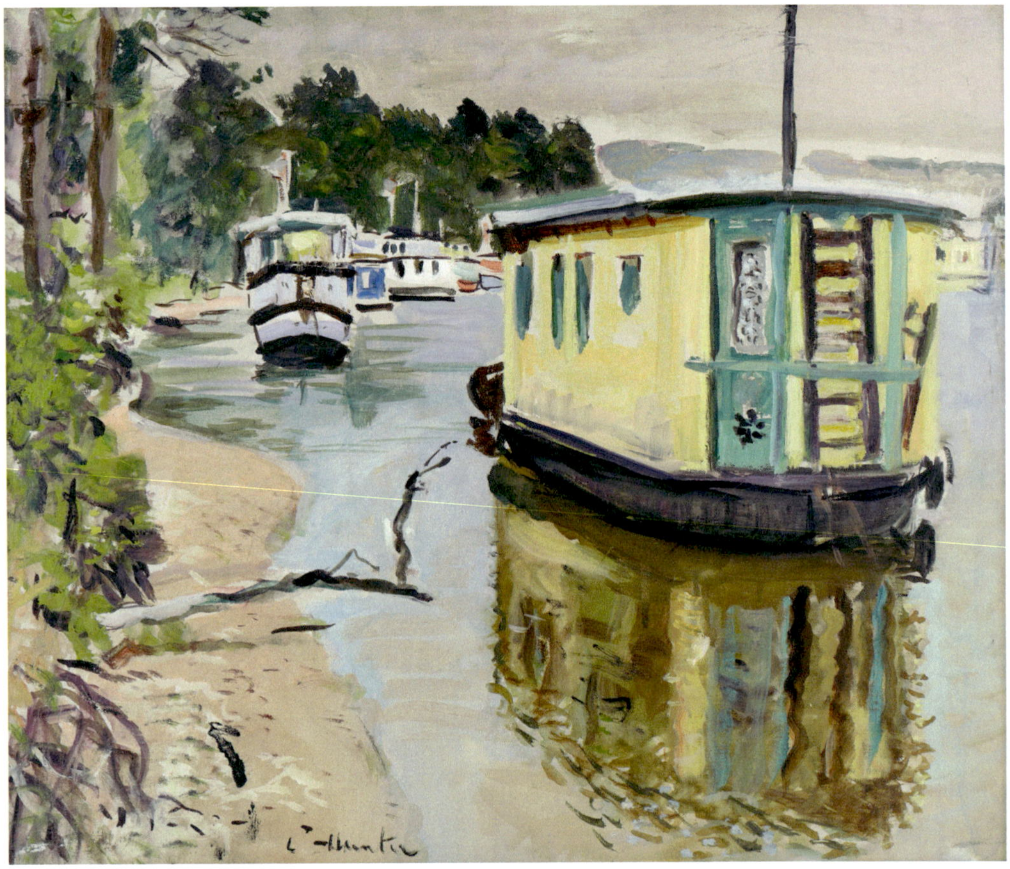

160 | Houseboats, Balloch
Oil on canvas, 1931
Private collection

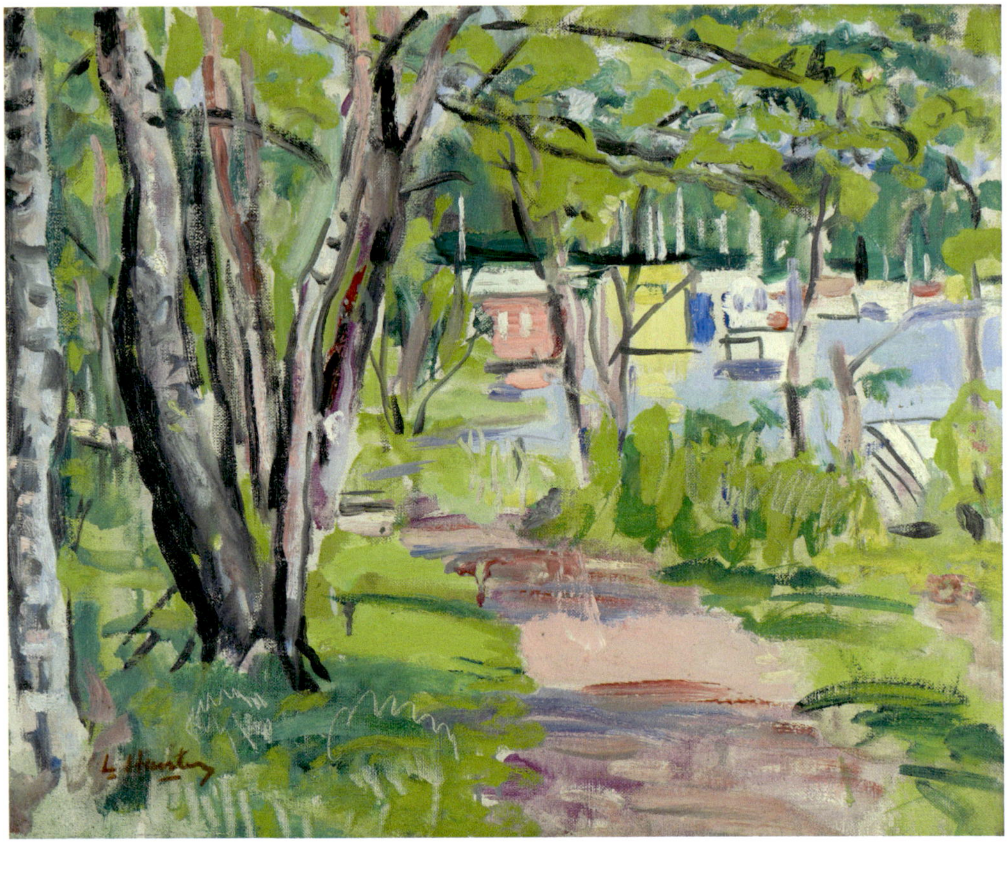

161 | On the Banks of Loch Lomond
Oil on canvas, 1931
Private collection

162 | Pathway, Loch Lomond
Oil on canvas, 1931
City Art Centre, Edinburgh

163 | House Boats, Loch Lomond
Oil on canvas, 1931
Private collection

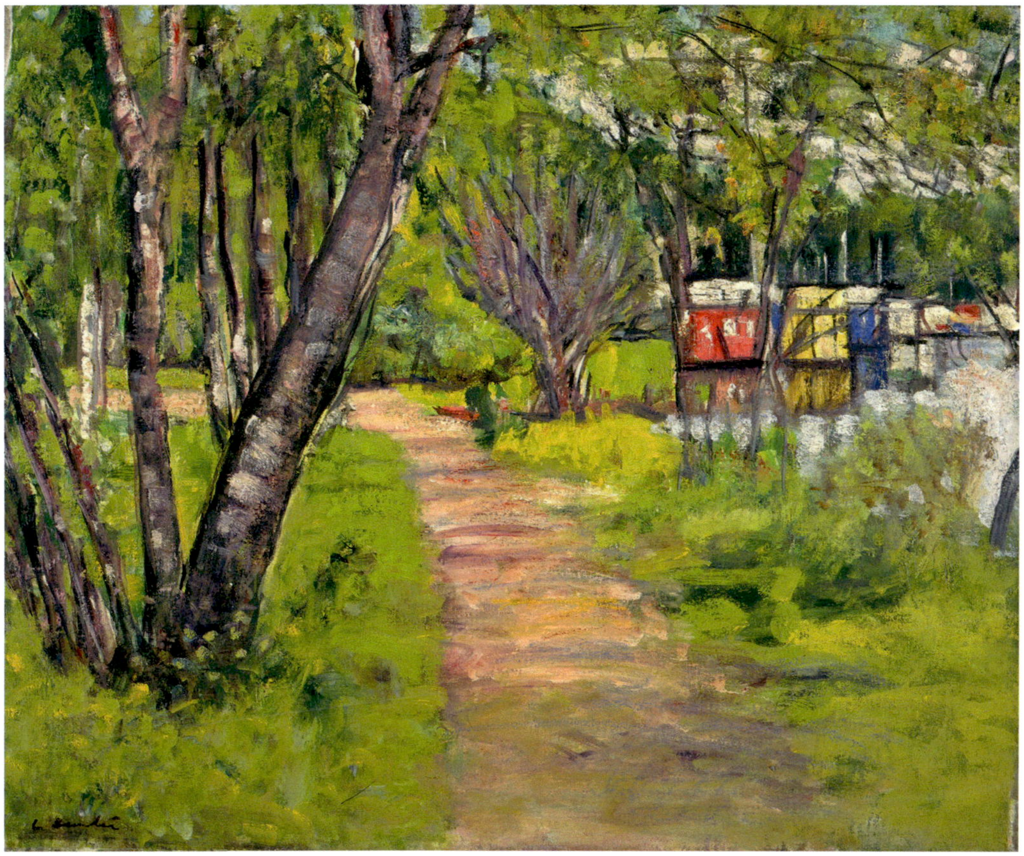

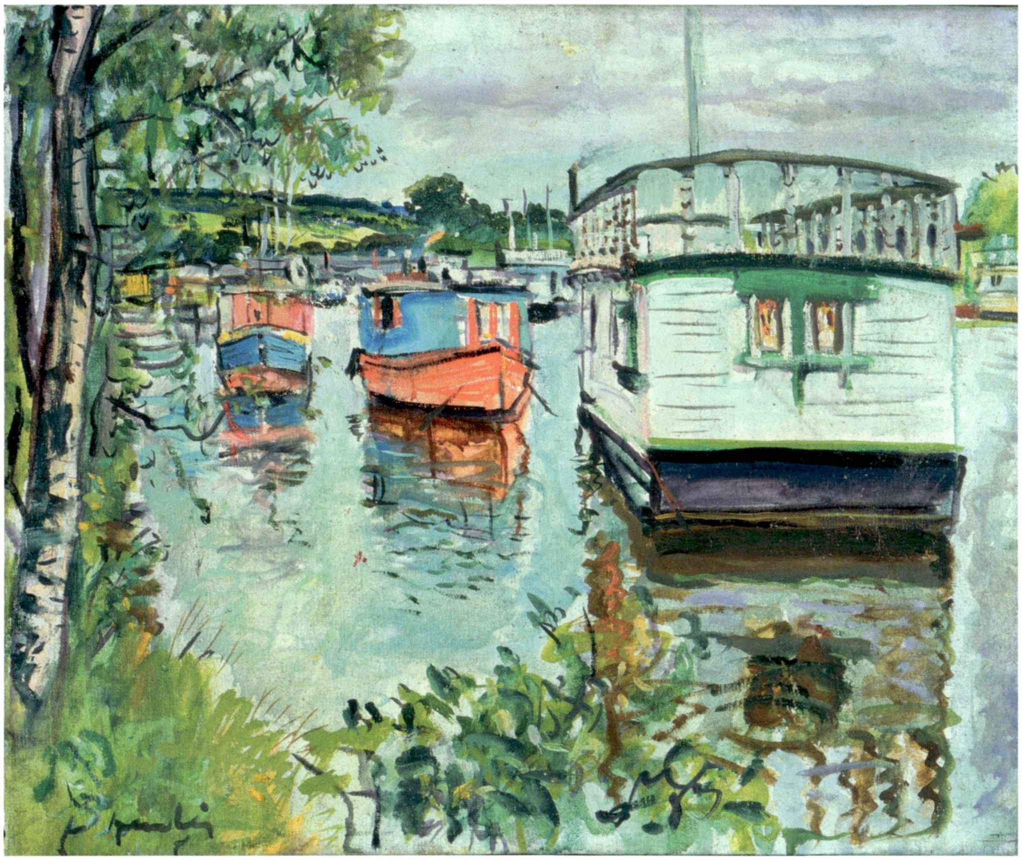

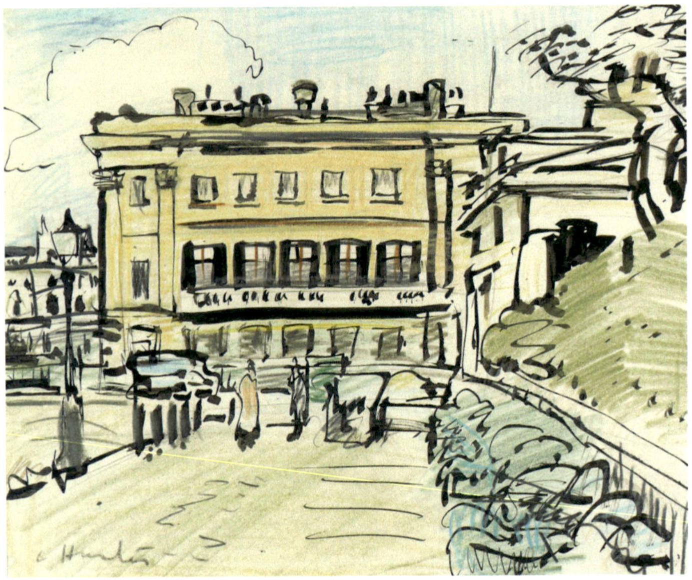

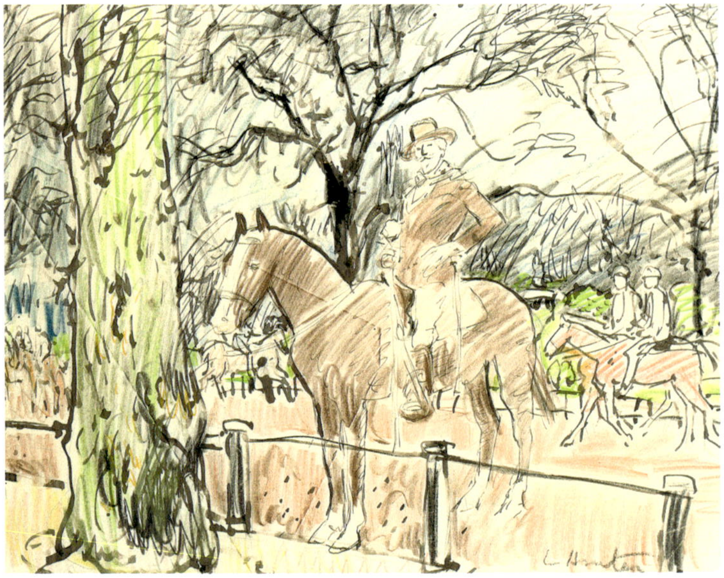

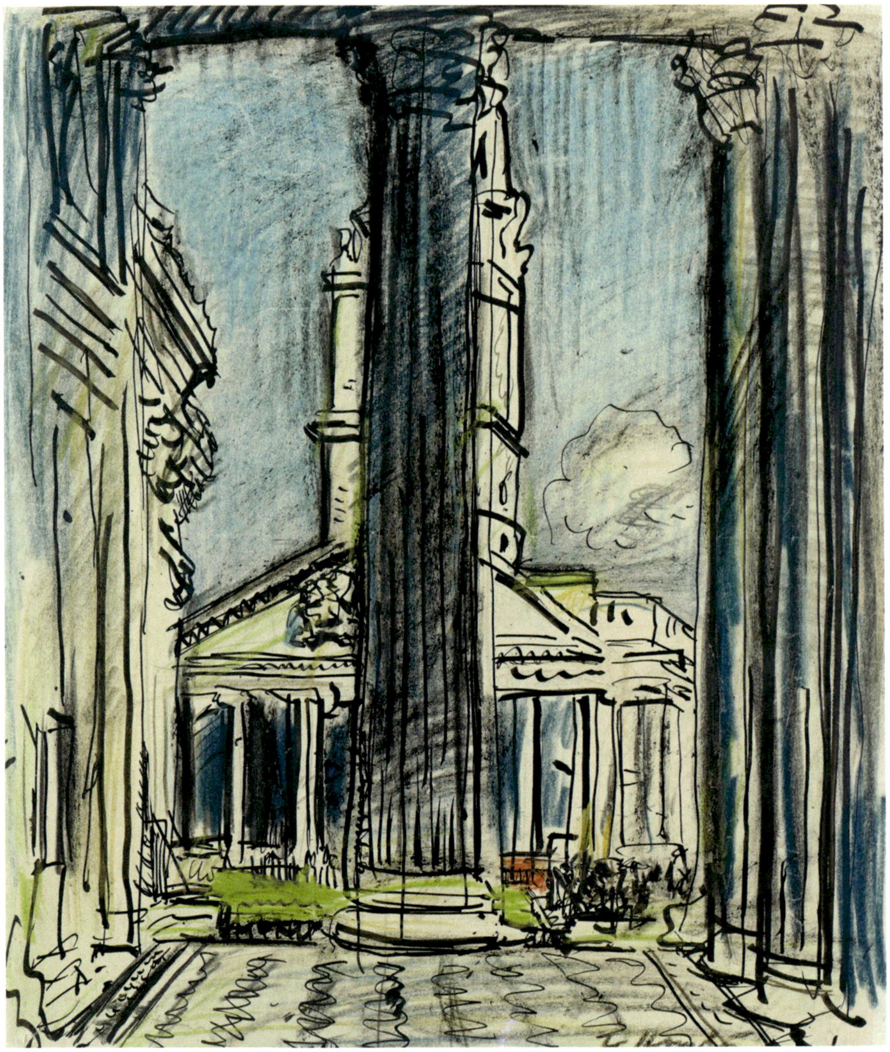

somewhat irritated Honeyman to write to him in February 1931:

I hope that your silence since you arrived in London really means that you are too busy to write ... Never mind your female friends, let us have some news of you ... I heard a rumour that you were anxious to go over to Paris, but unless there is any specific reason to take you there, I advise you not to go just now ... I would like you to keep in mind that there is plenty for you to do here [in Glasgow].[26]

While in London he began the preliminary sketches for his intended Hyde Park series. However it was not until the autumn of 1931 on a second visit to London that he got down to work in earnest. The choice of location probably came about through his contact with the Scottish writer, adventurer and Scottish Nationalist, R.B.Cunninghame Graham, affectionately known as 'Don Roberto', to whom Hunter was re-introduced by John Ressich.[27] Based in London, Cunninghame Graham went to the park every morning to ride along Rotten Row, and this may have prompted Hunter to go there in search of paintable material. Every now and then Cunninghame Graham would stop so that Hunter could include him in his sketches (pl.165).

Rotten Row (pl.167) is a lovely example of Hunter's sketches of Hyde Park. They show a

164 | St George's Hospital, Hyde Park Corner
Ink and coloured crayons, 1931
Private collection

165 | 'Don Roberto', Robert Bontine Cunninghame Graham
Watercolour, pastel and coloured crayons, 1931
Private collection

166 | St Martin's Church from the National Gallery
Ink and coloured crayons, 1931
Private collection

wonderful spontaneity and sense of activity. His enjoyment of the park is palpable. Moreover the vivid colour he injects into these sketches, while not being what the casual onlooker would register, confirms how Hunter's colour can convey the essential feel of this delightful oasis in central London. The verve with which Hunter captures the daily life of the park strongly suggests the promise of greater things to come.

Tragically it was not to be. Hunter found a London studio and returned to Glasgow to wind up his affairs there and prepare for the move south. The indigestion, about which he had asked Honeyman for advice in March, was troubling him increasingly. An anxious Staite Murray had told Honeyman how during several weekend visits to him at Bray, Hunter had had such dreadful attacks of pain that he was completely doubled up.[28] When they had passed, Hunter would pick up the conversation as if there had only been an insignificant minor interruption. This reaction was typical of Hunter's general attitude to life; art came first and anything else came a poor second.

Hunter was persuaded by Honeyman to see a specialist as soon as he could. However the gift of a magnificent bouquet of flowers distracted his attention and, inspired by the blooms, pressed on with a painting that he was forming in his mind. By evening he was in considerable pain and, uncharacteristically, was forced to return to his sister's house. The painting remained on his easel, becoming a final powerful testament to his lifelong love of colour. Despite being unfinished, *Flowers in a Chinese Vase* (pl.168) displays all the energy and verve of this rich, mature phase. One can only wonder what further achievements he might have attained.

Hunter's condition deteriorated rapidly and he was admitted to the Claremont Nursing Home. Operated upon immediately, it was discovered his gall bladder had ruptured. There was nothing that could be done. At 3.40 pm on 7 December 1931 Hunter died of cardiac failure, the result of the inevitable blood poisoning. He was 54 years old.

Honeyman and Hunter's other friends unfairly blamed themselves for not recognising earlier that his illness was far more serious than Hunter had made out. Had he sought medical advice earlier, he could very well have survived. However he was a man who lived for his art with such passion that all else was of small importance to him and that was to be his undoing. He left behind a huge gap in the affections of the people who loved and cared about him, not least a shocked Marnie Scrafton, who described what turned out to be her last contact with him:

It was just before the Art Club Ball and he was going to take me there. He said it would be our farewell to Glasgow before leaving finally for London ... On the Friday of the Art Club Ball I learned that he was ill and would have to stay in bed over the weekend. I did not think it was serious because he seemed very cheerful the night before when I left him. To my horror I read in the Monday morning papers of his death in a Nursing Home on the Sunday.[29]

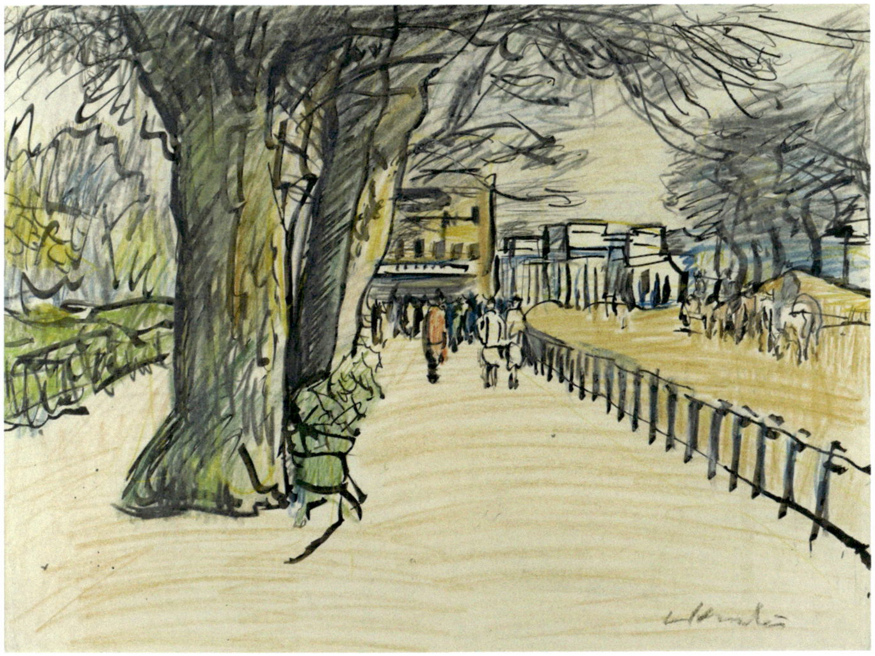

167 | Rotten Row, Hyde Park
Ink and coloured crayons
Private collection

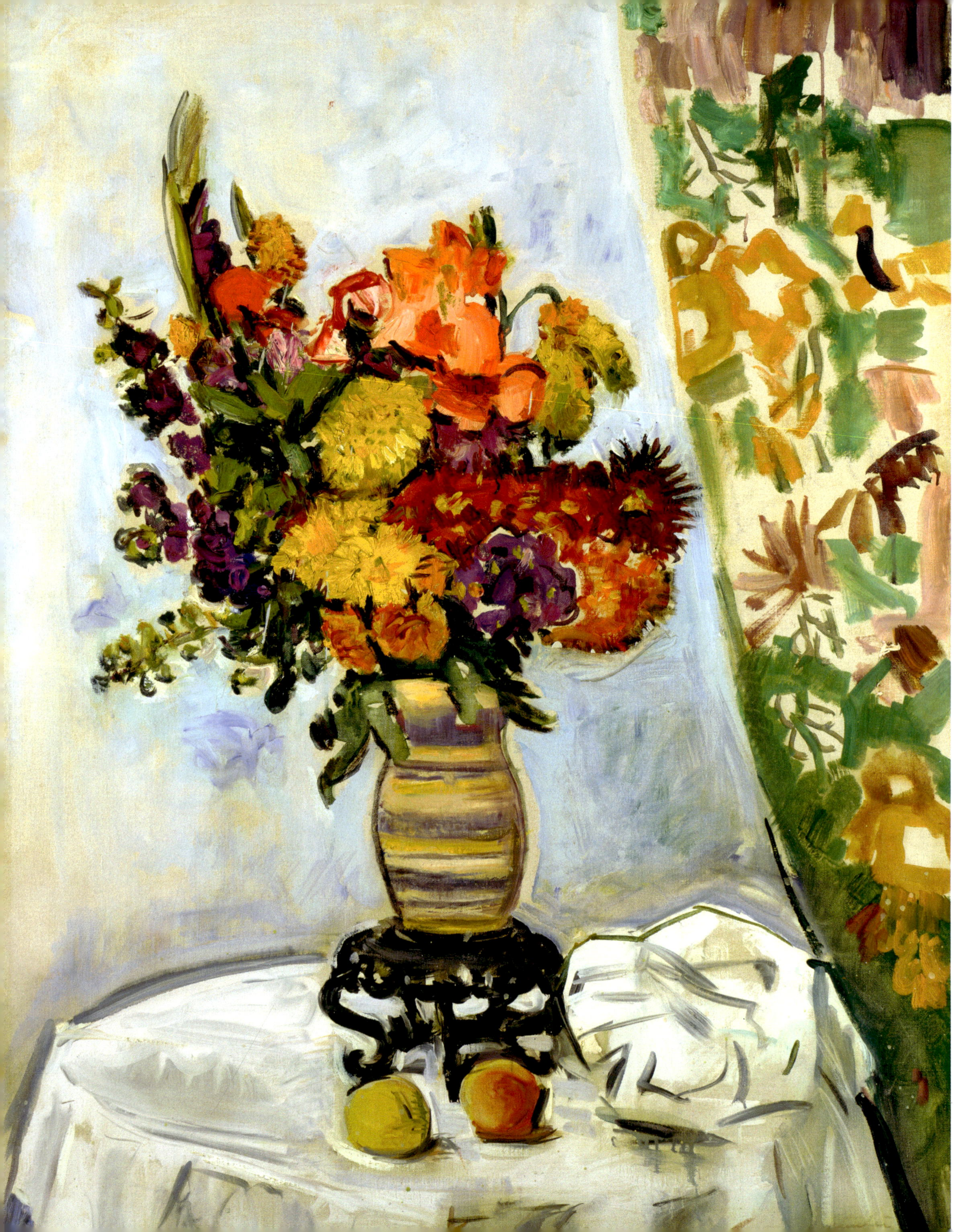

9 A Scottish Master

Scotland had lost one of her most creative sons. Honeyman's reaction to Hunter's death at the age of only 54 was eloquently expressed:

Contentment of mind and freedom from pain were the accompaniments of his passing, but the circumstances and the unfulfilled promise of his high hopes and aspirations makes his untimely death unutterably pitiful.[1]

Hunter's passing was indeed untimely. It is impossible to envision how his art would have developed had he lived longer. Certainly he felt that he was on the brink of a breakthrough in his painting, telling Marnie Scrafton shortly before his death: 'I have been kicking at the door so long, and at last it is beginning to open'.[2]

Hunter was an intelligent, sensitive, driven man, who lived for his art to the exclusion of almost everything else. Colour was unequivocally the guiding principle throughout his life. He had written in his notebook: 'Everyone must choose his own way, and mine will be the way of colour'.[3] Well-read in literature and philosophy, Hunter fully understood Schopenhauer's view that colour was the sensation in the eye, rather than the actual colour of an object. His painting developed gradually through exploration of the work of Manet, Van Gogh, Gauguin, Cézanne and Matisse – Matisse, the very artist whose work had profoundly shocked Hunter when he viewed it for the first time in the collection of Leo and Gertrude Stein in Paris in 1908.

The path Hunter trod was long and difficult in places, but Hunter persevered. Wholeheartedly he rose to the challenge of Cézanne's advanced theories on colour and form, applying them to his own end, as his Fife paintings of 1921–25 attest. When Hunter was further inspired by Matisse, his art moved in a different, but equally relevant direction. Who could have envisaged the beauty of Loch Lomond captured in such a bold and exciting manner? He also brought a new vibrancy to still life that is rarely equalled today, evolving his own fresh and inspired response through admiration for artists such as Kalf, Chardin, Manet, Cézanne and finally Matisse.

During his lifetime Hunter's art was thought to be too advanced, yet paradoxically more recent writers consider his work as being a generation behind the so-called *avant-garde*. At the time it was misunderstood by many, and laughed at by the majority of his contemporaries. With the exception of Peploe, Fergusson and a handful of others, few Scottish artists understood what Hunter was achieving. This shook him; how could they not see what he could see so clearly?

For Hunter the move to the south of France in 1926 came at a desperate point in his life. It provided him with the opportunity to meet and paint alongside friends and colleagues of Matisse, such as Dunoyer de Segonzac and Othon Friesz. Being among like-minded artists restored Hunter's faith in himself and what he was seeking to achieve. Such was the impression Hunter made on these artist friends that on a visit to London in 1937 Segonzac felt strongly enough to remark to Honeyman: 'You are a queer people. Here is one of your best artists

168 | Flowers in a Chinese Vase (unfinished)
Oil on canvas, 1931
Glasgow Museums

and nobody knows anything about him'.[4] It would be another forty years before Hunter's outstanding achievements in painting were fully recognized.

It is doubtful whether Hunter would have stayed the course without the support and encouragement of his small band of loyal friends in Dundee and Glasgow, particularly Justice, Tattersall, McInnes, McNair and Harrison. Hunter was fortunate indeed to have had such enlightened men as friends and supporters, but it is equally clear that he was a key element in their artistic endeavours also. Crucial too for Hunter's artistic survival were Alexander Reid, McNeill Reid, Duncan Macdonald and Honeyman. They had the vision and courage to promote modern art in Glasgow and London, providing important outlets for work that attracted knowledgeable and discerning collectors. Their role as Hunter's dealers cannot be underestimated in terms of their financial and moral support. And, as they discovered, Hunter on occasions could be a difficult, if not frustrating, person with whom to deal.

At his best Hunter has few equals in Scottish, if not British painting. Peploe's comment: 'That is Hunter at his best, and it is as fine as any Matisse', referring to *Houseboats, Loch Lomond*, the painting acquired by the French Government in 1931, can equally be applied to many works by Hunter.[5] However, his work is uneven, not so much because he was an uneven artist (though which painter is not?), but principally because, as mentioned, he had the destructive habit, on returning to the studio late at night, of 'improving' the canvas on his easel by re-painting in poor artificial light. There is no real evidence to suggest that another reason for Hunter's unevenness was that he was an alcoholic, a rumour that has persisted through the years and unfairly been accepted as fact. Certainly there is nothing to support this view in the recollections of either Marnie Scrafton or Joan Smith, both of whom knew Hunter as an artist and a friend.

Since his death there have been a number of exhibitions of Hunter's work, such as Reid & Lefevre's Memorial Exhibition in 1932 and a major retrospective in 1942 at Kelvingrove and the National Gallery of Scotland, as well as important Colourist exhibitions at the Royal Scottish Academy in 1949, the Thistle Foundation's 'Paintings from a Private Collection' in Edinburgh in 1951 and the National Gallery of Scotland in 2000. On each of those occasions the response has been one of astonishment at the beauty, diversity and depth revealed in Hunter's work.

Of Hunter himself, his unassuming attitude to life is well summed up by Joan Smith, a close friend from St Paul de Vence:

If one's intentions were good, one could enjoy the gift of life. Natural desires were not evil things or they would not be natural. The creative artist cannot help himself. He just happens in life. The trouble is that he so seldom knows when the important opportunity has reached him. And he destroys himself if he becomes too much of a critic of himself or if he is moved by the ignorant criticism of others. If people don't like or understand a man's work it cannot be helped. They will understand one day, when they discover the right way to look at it. There is too much talk about expressing one's emotions. His own pictures were expressed through his intellect – and he had a grip upon everything he was trying to do.[6]

Hunter's untimely death deprived him of the chance to fulfil the promise he displayed so gloriously. Of his special contribution to Scottish art, it is fitting that Matthew Justice should have the last word:

... to me it looks like as if the artist who gave us Nature as we see it is rightly deserving of recognition. At the same time the artist who gives us Nature as we've never seen but have often liked to see it, is bigger and better by far and deserves the 'acme totale' of our gratitude; that's the Real Master Art and our friend Hunter had a good slice of it in his make-up.

Never will I forget Hunter for many a time he was as a lamp lighting my way ... there are so many with nothing to say who shout so loud that the still small voice is picked out, heard and felt by the practised only.[7]

Notes and References

ABBREVIATIONS USED IN NOTES

NLS Honeyman Papers: National Library of Scotland, T.J.Honeyman Papers, Acc.9787, files 47–57

Honeyman 1937: T.J.Honeyman, ***Introducing Leslie Hunter*****, London, 1937**

Honeyman 1950: T.J.Honeyman, ***Three Scottish Colourists: Peploe, Cadell, Hunter*****, Edinburgh, 1950**

PREFACE · PAGES 7–9

1 Letter dated 25 September 1950 from Ion Harrison to T.C.Annan, private collection.

2 Honeyman 1937, p.139.

I · PASSAGE TO THE 'NEW WORLD' PAGES 11–17

1 Kevin Starr, *Americans and the California Dream 1850–1915*, New York, 1973, p.240.

2 National Records of Scotland: parish records, birth & marriage certificates, census for 1851, 1861, 1871 & 1881; Bute Museum, Rothesay.

3 Bute Museum, Rothesay; Graham Twaddle, *Old Bute*, Catrine, 2000, pp.3 & 7.

4 Bute Museum, Rothesay.

5 National Records of Scotland: census for 1891.

6 *Rothesay Chronicle*, 20 August 1892.

7 James Burnett Lawson, *Glimpses of Rothesay and its People Fifty Years Ago*, Glasgow, 1923, pp.80–83.

8 Brief manuscript biography prepared by Jeanie McFarlane (Hunter's sister) for T.J.Honeyman, undated [early 1930s], NLS Honeyman Papers.

9 A.M.Orr, *Rothesay Primary and Schools of Bute*, privately published, undated [*c.*1980], pp.24–26.

10 Brief manuscript biography prepared by Jeanie McFarlane.

11 Ibid.

12 Ibid.

13 National Records of Scotland: death certificates.

14 National Records of Scotland: census for 1891.

15 Starr, p.201.

16 *Rothesay Chronicle*, 20 August 1892.

17 Findmypast internet database of UK outgoing passengers in association with The National Archives, London.

18 Ancestry internet index to passenger ships; Ellis Island Foundation Inc internet database.

19 *The Works of Robert Louis Stevenson*, Tusitala Edition, vol.XVIII, 1924, *The Amateur Emigrant*.

20 Hunter family archives in California, courtesy of Jean Barnard.

21 *Lloyds List* 21 September 1892; *Glasgow Evening News* 28 September 1892.

22 Letter dated October 1892 from William Hunter (Hunter's brother) to Hilda Davidson (Hunter family archives in California).

23 Extensive research on websites of ancestry.com and US federal & state records.

24 United States Federal Census 1900.

25 Deduced from letter written in November 1892 by William Hunter to Hilda Davidson (Hunter family archives in California).

26 *The Works of Robert Louis Stevenson*, Tusitala Edition, vol.XVIII, 1924, *The Amateur Emigrant*.

27 Letter written in November 1892 by William Hunter to Hilda Davidson (Hunter family archives in California).

28 Letter dated 12 February 1892 from William Hunter to Hilda Davidson (Hunter family archives in California).

29 Email from Jean Barnard to Bill Smith dated 5 March 2012.

30 Letter from Jean Barnard to Derek Ogston dated 17 March 2001.

31 Brief manuscript biography prepared by Jeanie McFarlane.

32 Ibid.

33 Unpublished research by Douglas Harrison; letter from Jean Barnard to Derek Ogston dated 17 March 2001.

34 Letter dated 27 July 1893 from William Hunter to Hilda Davidson (Hunter family archives in California).

35 Letter dated September 1896 from William Hunter to Hilda Davidson (Derek Ogston/Hunter family archives in California).

36 Letters dated May 1896 & September 1896 from William Hunter to Hilda Davidson (Derek Ogston/Hunter family archives in California).

37 Letter dated April 1898 from William Hunter to Hilda Davidson (Derek Ogston/Hunter family archives in California).

38 Letter dated June 1898 from William Hunter to Hilda Davidson (Derek Ogston/Hunter family archives in California).

39 Letters from Jean Barnard to Derek Ogston and Bill Smith.

40 Ancestry internet database of UK incoming passengers in association with The National Archives, London (*Lloyds List* records *SS Scotsman* arriving at Liverpool on 24 May).

41 National Records of Scotland: marriage certificate.

42 National Records of Scotland: birth certificate.

43 Letter to Derek Ogston dated 17 March 2001 from Jean Barnard.

44 National Records of Scotland: death certificate.

45 National Records of Scotland: birth certificate.

46 Letter to Derek Ogston dated 17 March 2001 from Jean Barnard.

2 · THE BOHEMIAN LIFE PAGES 19–29

1 Letter dated 24 January 1899 from William Hunter to Hilda Davidson (Derek Ogston / Hunter family archives in California).

2 Gelett Burgess, *Bayside Bohemia: Fin de siècle San Francisco & its Little Magazines*, San Francisco, 1954, p.10.

3 Kevin Starr, *Americans and the California Dream 1850–1915*, New York, 1973, p.239.

4 Will Irwin, *The City That Was: A Requiem of Old San Francisco*, New York, 1906, p.7.

5 William Bronson, *The Earth Shook, The Sky Burned*, San Francisco, 1997, pp.13–14.

6 Irwin, p.15.

7 Irwin, p.22.

8 Irwin, p.43.

9 Honeyman 1937, p.50.

10 Birgitta Hjalmarson, *Artful Players: Artistic Life in Early San Francisco*, Glendale, 2000, pp.151–53.

11 Starr, pp.249–53.

12 Starr, pp.246, 253–54.

13 Irwin, p.38.

14 Irwin, pp.34–36.

15 Honeyman 1937, p.52.

16 Letter dated March 1899 from William Hunter to Hilda Davidson (Derek Ogston / Hunter family archives in California).

17 The authors have not been able to document the drawings that Hunter executed for the *San Francisco Examiner*, because back numbers of the newspaper have not been digitized (or indeed may have been destroyed in the fire following the 1906 earthquake).

18 Letter dated 30 June 1899 from Hunter to Hilda Davidson (Derek Ogston / Hunter family archives in California).

19 Scott A. Shields, *Eternal Light: Visions of Gottardo Piazzoni*, California Historical Society, 2001.

20 The authors are grateful to Douglas Harrison for this information.

21 *San Francisco Call*, 15 April 1900, p.30.

22 Will Irwin, *The Making of a Reporter*, 1942, pp.82–83.

23 Honeyman 1937, p.53.

24 Ibid.

25 Ibid., p.44.

26 Letter from T.J.Honeyman to William Hunter, responding to Hunter's letter to him, NLS Honeyman Papers.

27 Letter dated 30 June 1899 from Hunter to Hilda Davidson; Honeyman 1937, p.51.

28 Honeyman 1937, p.56.

29 Ibid.

30 See appendix for list of Hunter's known illustrations.

31 Do.

32 *San Francisco Call*, 17 February 1901, p.30.

33 *Overland Monthly*, *Bret Harte Memorial Number*, December 1902, pp.209–18.

34 Honeyman 1937, p.62.

35 Martin Hopkinson, *California, Scotland and Paris: the Prints of Leslie Hunter*, *Print Quarterly*, vol.XVI, 1999, p.264.

36 Donald J. Hagerty & Maynard Dixon, *Desert Dreams: the art and life of Maynard Dixon*, 1998, pp.30–31.

37 Honeyman 1937, pp.55–56.

38 Hagerty & Dixon, p.31.

39 Honeyman 1937, pp.55–56.

40 Hagerty & Dixon, p.31.

41 Hopkinson, p.264.

42 *San Francisco Call*, 2 May 1902, p.9.

43 *San Francisco Newsletter*, 26 April 1902, quoted in Hopkinson, p.258.

44 Honeyman 1937, p.55.

45 *San Francisco Call*, 29 December 1901, p.30.

46 *San Francisco Newsletter*, 10 May 1902, quoted in Hopkinson, p.258.

47 Honeyman, 1937, p.56.

3 · SCOTLAND AND PARIS PAGES 31–43

1 Patricia Junker, *Gottardo Piazzoni*, Grove Art Online, www.oxfordartonline.com.

2 Undated letter from Ralph Stackpole to Mireille Piazzoni Wood, Gottardo Piazzoni Papers, Archives of American Art, no.1902, fr.274.

3 There is no record of George Hunter (or G. Leslie Hunter) entering the United Kingdom in either 1902 or 1903 in the Ancestry internet database of UK incoming passengers (in association with The National Archives, London), and, although the absence of a record is not conclusive, it may suggest that he went first to France, for which no records appear to exist.

4 See appendix for list of Hunter's known illustrations.

5 *The British Journal of Nursing*, 28 November 1903, p.438.

6 The timing is based on the existence of a work by Hunter, Snow in London, exhibited at the San Francisco Artists' Society, 18–20 December 1905 (no.152).

7 Honeyman 1937, pp.56–57.

8 Hunter told Honeyman that Dr William Hunter was an ancestor, but so far no evidence has been uncovered to substantiate the claim.

9 See appendix for list of Hunter's known illustrations.

10 Hopkinson, p.264.

11 Honeyman in conversation with Tom Hunt, recounted in Honeyman, 1937, pp.61–62.

12 Ramón Balius Juli, *The Athlete as Model,* in *Art and Sport*, LA84 Foundation, pp.243–45.

13 Honeyman 1937, pp.58–59.

14 See appendix for list of Hunter's known etchings and monotypes.

15 Hopkinson, pp.250–51.

16 Antony Griffiths, *Prints and Printmaking,* second edition, British Museum Press, London, 1996, p.145.

17 Hopkinson, pp.260–61.

18 Ancestry internet database: New York Passenger Lists 1820–1957; Lloyds List, 28 November & 5 December 1904.

19 M. Sue Kendall, *Robert Henri*, Grove Art Online, www.oxfordartonline.com.

20 Werner Haftmann, *Painting in the Twentieth Century*, London, 1965, vol.1, pp.155–56.

21 M. Sue Kendall, *Ashcan school*, Grove Art Online, www.oxfordartonline.com; Haftmann, p.156.

22 Haftmann, pp.158–59.

23 Probably Thomas Lorraine Hunt (1882–1938), son of artist John Powell Hunt, born in London, Ontario, Canada, and moved to Southern California in 1924, where he died.

24 Hunt in conversation with T.J.Honeyman in the 1930s, Honeyman 1937, p.60.

25 Ibid., p.61.

26 See appendix for list of those illustrations.

27 Hunt in conversation with T.J.Honeyman in the 1930s, Honeyman 1937, p.62.

28 *San Francisco Call*, 28 May 1905, p.23.

29 *San Francisco Call*, 30 May 1905, p.8.

30 It seems unlikely that the newspaper was referring to the annual loan and sale exhibition of the San Francisco Artists' Society, which was not due to open until December 1905. Perhaps Hunter did plan a solo exhibition for summer 1905, but for one reason or another it had to be postponed.

31 See appendix for list of Hunter's known illustrations; Hopkinson, p.264.

32 Scott A. Shields, *Artists at Continent's End: The Monterey Peninsula Art Colony 1875–1907*, Crocker Art Museum, Sacramento, 2006, pp.179–80.

33 Hopkinson, p.264.

34 *San Francisco Call*, 24 December 1905, p.23.

35 *San Francisco Call*, 8 April 1906, p.23.

36 *San Francisco Call*, 11 April 1906, p.5.

37 Hopkinson, p.265.

38 Shields, p.180.

39 Gene Hailey (editor), *California Art Research* vol.14: *Ralph Stackpole, Jo Mora, Benjamino Bufano*, 1935, San Francisco, 1937, pp.6–7.

40 William Bronson, *The Earth Shook, The Sky Burned*: a photographic record of the 1906 San Francisco earthquake and fire, San Francisco, 1997.

41 Bronson, p.60.

42 Extract from Joaquin Miller's poem published in *Sunset*, June-July 1906, pp.11–12.

43 *San Francisco Call*, 10 June 1906, p.16.

44 Honeyman 1937, p.50.

45 Bronson, p.50.

46 Honeyman 1937, p.57.

47 Hailey, p.7.

48 Superior Court, San Francisco, 5 July 1905 (recorded in New York Passenger Lists 1820–1957, list of American citizens on board S.S. Transylvania from Glasgow, arriving New York 30 November 1928 – ancestry.com; the year of naturalisation is indistinct, either 1905 or 1906, but the former date is the more likely).

49 *San Francisco Call*, 4 July 1906, p.8.

50 *San Francisco Call*, 15 July 1906, p.24.

51 There is no record of George Hunter (or G. Leslie Hunter) entering the United Kingdom in 1906 in the Ancestry internet database of UK incoming passengers (in association with The National Archives, London), which suggests he entered the United Kingdom from the Continent.

52 Hailey, p.7.

53 Honeyman 1937, p.63.

54 NLS Honeyman Papers.

4 · RENEWAL · PAGES 45–69

1 Honeyman 1950, p.99.

2 James McFarlane and Jeanie Hunter were married in Cambuslang, Glasgow on 25 March 1915 in the presence of George Leslie Hunter and Irene Margaret S Hunter (niece), National Records of Scotland: marriage certificate; Honeyman 1950, p.99.

3 Letter dated 8 June 1907, quoted in Julie Heyneman, *Desert Cactus: The Portrait of a Sculptor*, London, 1934, p.122.

4 Honeyman, 1937, p.54.

5 Starr, pp.254 & 265.

6 Irwin, *The Making of a Reporter*, 1942, p.86.

7 Honeyman 1937, p.54.

8 Starr, p.254.

9 Letter from Ralph Stackpole to Hunter dated 9 September 1912, NLS Honeyman Papers.

10 Letter to Matthew Justice, quoted in Honeyman, 1937, p.90.

11 Gertrude Stein, *Paris France*, 1940, quoted in George Wickes, *Americans in Paris*, 1980, p.2.

12 Ibid., p.2.

13 Ibid., p.3.

14 Ibid.

15 Ibid., p.4.

16 Alice B. Toklas, *What is Remembered*, 1963, p.41.

17 Gelett Burgess, *Architectural Record*, 'The Wild Men of Paris: Matisse, Picasso and Les Fauves', May 1910.

18 Emily Braun, 'Saturday Evenings at the Steins', essay in exhibition catalogue *The Steins Collect*, San Francisco Museum of Modern Art in association with Yale University Press, 2011, p.58.

19 It is impossible to be precise about the year, but as Hunter was in Paris in 1907 only for the summer and Toklas was writing about something that occurred when Gertrude Stein was checking the final proofs of *Three Lives*, which was published in 1909, 1908 seems the probable year.

20 Braun, p.52.

21 Toklas, p.27.

22 San Francisco Museum of Modern Art, bequest of Elise S. Haase.

23 Museum of Modern Art, New York, The William S. Paley Collection.

24 A typical reaction was described by the critic, Lewis Hind, in his 1911 book on Post-Impressionism. Initially horrified by the Matisse canvases – 'that abortion of the female form so grotesquely naked' – he told his readers that after an hour he felt compelled to stay. '… I did feel a sense of excitement and stimulation. Here and there, as I waited and watched, an eccentricity seemed to start from the walls and say: I am alive. I am movement. I am rhythm. I exist.' [extract, Braun, p.55].

25 Braun, p.55.

26 Braun, p.49.

27 Kathleen married William Cockburn in Galashiels in 1953 and died in Selkirk in 1993, National Records of Scotland: marriage & death certificates; a birth certificate has not been located, which may mean she was not born in Scotland.

28 Honeyman, 1937, p.66.

29 See appendix for list of Hunter's known illustrations.

30 Letter dated 13 December 1936 from E.A.Taylor to Honeyman, NLS Honeyman Papers.

31 James Timothy Voorhies, *My Dear Stieglitz, Letters of Marsden Hartley and Alfred Stieglitz 1912–1915*, University of South Carolina Press, 2002, letter dated 20 June 1912, p.14.

32 Letter dated 13 December 1936 from E.A.Taylor to Honeyman, NLS Honeyman Papers.

33 Ibid.

34 See appendix for list of Hunter's known illustrations.

35 Undated letter from Hunter at that address to Matthew Justice (datable to June or July 1912), NLS Honeyman Papers.

36 See appendix for list of Hunter's known illustrations.

37 Honeyman, 1937, pp.68–69.

38 National Records of Scotland: death certificate; Jeanie Hunter's year of birth is not known, but it is thought to be 1840.

39 Frances Fowle, *Van Gogh's Twin: The Scottish Art Dealer Alexander Reid 1854–1928*, Edinburgh, 2010, p.114.

40 Honeyman, 1950, p.101.

41 Fowle, p.115.

42 *Glasgow Herald*, 7 November 1913.

43 Fowle, p.115.

44 Schopenhauer, *Aesthetics*, Volume 1, Book 3.

45 *Glasgow Herald*, 7 November 1913.

46 Fowle, p.97.

47 Letter dated 13 December 1936 from E.A.Taylor to Honeyman, NLS Honeyman Papers.

48 Ibid.

49 Honeyman, 1937, p.69.

50 Voorhies, letter dated 30 July 1912, p.22.

51 Letter dated 13 December 1936 from E.A.Taylor to Honeyman, NLS Honeyman Papers.

52 Ibid.

53 Ibid.

54 Ancestry.com: World War I Selective Service System Draft Registration Card 1917–1918.

55 Honeyman, 1937, p.109.

56 *The Bailie*, 26 March 1916.

57 Honeyman, 1937, pp.77–78.

58 Fowle, p.117.

59 Ibid, pp.117–18.

60 National Records of Scotland: census 1901 & 1911.

61 The authors are grateful to Douglas Harrison for this information, gained in the early 1980s from his interviews with individuals who remembered Hunter at Millburn Farm.

62 Honeyman, 1937, p.78.

63 Unpublished interviews by Douglas Harrison.

64 Unpublished notebook (Private Collection).

65 Ibid.

66 Ibid.

67 Ibid.

68 Honeyman, 1937, p.79.

69 Ibid.

70 Unpublished research by Douglas Harrison; unpublished transcript of taped interview by Jean Read, Larkhall Heritage Society, with Mrs Melville, a distant relative of Hunter, and Mrs Bower, who were children when Hunter was at Millburn Farm.

71 Unpublished interviews with individuals connected with Millburn Farm by Jill Marriner in 1990s.

72 Unpublished transcript of taped interview by Jean Read.

73 Letter dated 16 January 1936 from John McCrimmon to T.J.Honeyman, NLS Honeyman Papers.

5 · SEEKING THE WAY FORWARD PAGES 71–101

1 A postcard from Hunter at Millburn Farm to Alexander Reid in Glasgow is date-stamped 17 January 1919, indicating that Hunter did not move back to live in Glasgow until early that year, NLS Honeyman Papers.

2 The majority of Hunter's letters to Justice are held by the National Library of Scotland, T.J.Honeyman Papers, Acc.9787.

3 Unpublished research by Douglas Harrison in the early 1980s.

4 Fowle, p.136.

5 Justice letters: letter from Percy Moore Turner to Justice dated 3 October 1940, in which Turner laments that Boyd's love of modern French art had waned, resulting in Boyd disposing of the collection, whereas Turner had hoped the collection would be given to the Scottish nation, NLS Honeyman Papers.

6 Justice letters: letter from Hunter to Justice dated 2 January 1922, NLS Honeyman Papers.

7 *The Times*, 10 February 1951.

8 Ibid.

9 *The Burlington Magazine*, vol.36, 1920.

10 Unpublished notebook (Private Collection).

11 Letter dated 13 December 1936 from E. A. Taylor to Honeyman, NLS Honeyman Papers.

12 Hunter painted a similar version, now in Aberdeen Art Gallery.

13 Justice letters: letter from Hunter to Justice, May 1921, NLS Honeyman Papers.

14 Interview with Benno Schotz, unpublished research by Douglas Harrison.

15 Justice letters: letter from Hunter to Justice dated 8 December 1920, NLS Honeyman Papers.

16 *Scottish Art Review*, vol.9, no.2, 1963: article on John Quinton Pringle by Elizabeth Johnstone.

17 Unpublished research by Douglas Harrison.

18 Hunter's continued interest in Van Gogh is evidenced by Hunter sending a book on the artist to John Tattersall in 1920, and again in 1921, when Hunter wrote to Justice: 'I got "Van Gogh's" letter from McInnes and read again with much interest'.

19 Justice letters: letter from Hunter to Justice dated 8 December 1920, NLS Honeyman Papers.

20 Justice letters: letter from Hunter to Justice dateable to April-May 1921, NLS Honeyman Papers.

21 Justice letters: letter from Hunter to Justice dated 8 December 1920, NLS Honeyman Papers.

22 Ibid.

23 Justice letters: letter from Hunter to Justice dated 22 December 1920, NLS Honeyman Papers.

24 Justice letters: letter from Hunter to Justice dateable to 1920, NLS Honeyman Papers.

25 Justice letters: letters from Hunter to Justice dated 8 & 9 May 1921, NLS Honeyman Papers.

26 Justice letters: letter from Hunter to Tattersall dateable to April–May 1921, private collection.

27 Justice letters: letter from Hunter to Justice dateable to May 1921, private collection.

28 Ibid.

29 Justice letters: letter from Hunter to Justice dated 8 May 1921, NLS Honeyman Papers.

30 NLS Honeyman Papers.

31 See appendix of Hunter's monotypes and etchings.

32 Justice letters: letter from Hunter to Justice dateable to 1925–26, NLS Honeyman Papers.

33 Justice letters: letter from Hunter to Justice dated 8 December 1920, NLS Honeyman Papers.

34 *The Burlington Magazine*, vol.36, 1920.

35 Justice letters: letter from Hunter to Justice dateable to April-May 1921, NLS Honeyman Papers.

36 Ibid.

37 Fowle, p.121; Justice letters: letter from Hunter to Justice dated 8 December 1920, NLS Honeyman Papers.

38 Justice letters: letter from Hunter to Justice dated 22 December 1920, NLS Honeyman Papers.

39 Justice letters: letter from Hunter to Justice dateable to January 1921, NLS Honeyman Papers.

40 Ibid.

41 Justice letters: letter from Hunter to Justice dateable to May 1921, NLS Honeyman Papers.

42 Justice letters: letter from Hunter to Justice dated 25 December 1921, NLS Honeyman Papers.

43 Justice letters: letter from Hunter to Justice dateable to January 1921, NLS Honeyman Papers.

44 Justice letters: letter from Hunter to Justice dated 14 January 1922, NLS Honeyman Papers.

45 Letters from Hunter in Ceres to McNeill Reid dated 21 June & 3 July 1921, NLS Honeyman Papers.

46 *Dundee Advertiser*, 29 November 1921.

47 Hunter's notebook (private collection).

48 Justice letters: letter from Hunter to Justice, dated 14 January 1922, NLS Honeyman Papers.

49 Honeyman, 1937, p.82–83.

50 Ibid., p.86.

51 Ibid., p.84.

52 Ibid., p.85.

53 Justice letters: undated letter from Hunter to Justice, NLS Honeyman Papers.

54 Honeyman, 1937, p.84.

6 · STRUGGLE AND TRIUMPH PAGES 103–129

1 Fowle, p.123.

2 Ibid.

3 *The Times*, 6 January 1923; *Morning Post*, 16 January 1923.

4 *The Times*, 6 January 1923.

5 *Glasgow Herald*, 23 January 1923.

6 *Daily Mail*, 9 January 1923.

7 Alexander Reid's Glasgow Sales Journal, Tate Archives, TGA 200211, file 275.

8 Honeyman, 1937, pp.85–86.

9 *Glasgow Herald*, 2 March 1923.

10 Alexander Reid's Glasgow Sales Journal, Tate Archives, TGA 200211, file 275.

11 Honeyman, 1937, pp.86–87.

12 Justice letters: letter from Hunter in Settignano, Italy to Tattersall dateable to 1923, NLS Honeyman Papers.

13 Honeyman, 1937, p.90.

14 Ibid., pp.91–92.

15 Ibid., p.94.

16 Fowle, p.125.

17 Alexander Reid's Glasgow Sales Journal, Tate Archives, TGA 200211, file 275.

18 *Glasgow Herald*, 19 December 1923.

19 Honeyman, 1937, p.43.

20 Ibid., p.95.

21 *Glasgow Herald*, 23 January 1923.

22 Justice letters: letter from Hunter to Justice dated 26 April 1924, NLS Honeyman Papers.

23 Honeyman, 1937, p.93.

24 Ibid., p.97.

25 Ibid., p.97.

26 Ibid., pp.98–99; a copy of the agreement is held by National Library of Scotland, Aitken Dott Papers, Acc.10421/7.

27 Justice letters: letter from Hunter to Justice dateable to April 1924, NLS Honeyman Papers.

28 Honeyman, 1937, p.93.

29 William, his wife, Hilda, and their son, William Grant (born 7 April 1912), emigrated to America in September 1920, arriving at Port Huron, Michigan and staying with uncle at Sarnia, Canada, before moving to Los Angeles; William applied for US citizenship in February 1922. There is no mention of daughters, Irene (born 11 June 1900) and Hilda (born 17 April 1904) accompanying their parents (US Naturalization Records: ancestry.com).

30 Justice letters: letter from Hunter to Justice dated 26 April 1924, NLS Honeyman Papers.

31 National Archives UK: findmypast.co.uk

32 Honeyman, 1937, p.100.

33 National Archives UK, UK Incoming Passenger Lists 1878–1960.

34 Honeyman, 1937, p.101; Revue de Vrai et du Beau, 10 September 1924.

35 Honeyman, 1937, p.117.

36 Justice letters: letter from Hunter to Justice dateable to April 1924, NLS Honeyman Papers.

37 Honeyman, 1937, p.113.

38 Honeyman, 1937, p.114.

39 Ibid.

40 Justice letters: letter from Hunter to Justice dated 20 April 1925, NLS Honeyman Papers.

41 Justice letters: letter from Hunter to Justice dated 12 May 1925, NLS Honeyman Papers.

42 With the exception of several pictures bequeathed to family members, William McInnes generously left his entire collection of Impressionist and Post-Impressionist paintings to Glasgow's Kelvingrove Art Gallery.

43 Justice letters: letter from Hunter to Justice dated 10 July 1931, NLS Honeyman Papers.

44 Justice letters: letter from Hunter to Justice dateable to 1925, NLS Honeyman Papers.

45 *Glasgow Herald*, 17 December 1925.

46 Ibid.

47 Ibid.

48 Until this painting was acquired by The Fleming Collection it was known as 'Still Life with Fruit and Marigolds in a Chinese Vase', but during a viewing of the collection by a party from the Royal Horticultural Society the flowers were positively identified as peonies to Bill Smith, then Keeper of Art at the collection.

49 Honeyman, 1937, pp.18–19.

50 *Glasgow Herald*, 17 December 1925.

51 Honeyman, 1937, p.115.

52 Justice letters: letter from Hunter to Justice dateable to 1925, NLS Honeyman Papers.

53 Justice letters: letter from Hunter to Justice dated 6 March 1926, NLS Honeyman Papers.

54 Justice letters: letter from Hunter to Justice dated 26 April 1926, NLS Honeyman Papers.

55 Justice letters: letter from Hunter to Justice dateable to 1926, NLS Honeyman Papers.

56 Honeyman, 1937, p.116.

57 Stanley Cursiter, *Peploe*, Edinburgh, 1947, pp.57–58

7 · A BREATH OF FRESH AIR PAGES 131–157

1 Justice letters: letter from Hunter to Justice dateable to summer 1927, NLS Honeyman Papers.

2 Letter from Hunter to A.J.McNeill Reid dated 19 September 1927, NLS Honeyman Papers.

3 Private collection, France.

4 Justice letters: letter from Hunter to Justice dated 19 September 1927, NLS Honeyman Papers.

5 Honeyman, 1937, p.125.

6 Ibid., p.121.

7 Ibid., pp.120–21.

8 Ibid., pp.121–22.

9 Justice letters: letter from Hunter to Justice dateable to early 1928, NLS Honeyman Papers.

10 Letter from Hunter to Arthur Leyden in New York dated 15 January 1928, NLS Honeyman Papers.

11 Honeyman, 1937, pp.128–30.

12 Letter from Hunter to Arthur Leyden in New York dated 15 January 1928, NLS Honeyman Papers.

13 Justice letters: letter from Hunter to Justice dateable to 1928, NLS Honeyman Papers.

14 Honeyman, 1937, p.122.

15 Fowle, p.144.

16 Ibid., p.145.

17 Letter from Duncan Macdonald to T J Honeyman dated 3 June 1931, NLS Honeyman Papers.

18 Fowle, p.174, n.119.

19 Honeyman, 1937, pp.123–24.

20 Ibid., p.124.

21 Letter from Hunter to A J McNeill Reid dated 5 April 1928, NLS Honeyman Papers.

22 Letter from Hunter to A J McNeill Reid dateable to April 1928, NLS Honeyman Papers.

23 Honeyman, 1937, pp.125–26.

24 Letter from Hunter to A J McNeill Reid dateable to April 1928, NLS Honeyman Papers.

25 Letter from Hunter to A J McNeill Reid dated 18 August 1928, NLS Honeyman Papers.

26 Honeyman, 1937, p.86.

27 Ibid., p.126.

28 Ibid.

29 *The Times*, 27 October 1928.

30 *The Morning Post*, 31 October 1928.

31 *The Observer*, 4 November 1928.

32 *Art Weekly*, 6 November 1928.

33 G. Reitlinger, *The Economics of Taste*, vol.I, London, 1961, p.214.

34 NLS Honeyman Papers.

35 National Archives UK: Findmypast.co.uk; the Hunter relatives were David Hunter (42), an engineer, his wife, Grace (40), and their daughter, Helen (13).

36 Letter from T. J. Honeyman to Hunter dated 18 February 1929, NLS Honeyman Papers.

37 NLS Honeyman Papers.

38 *New York Herald*, 5 May 1929, NLS Honeyman Papers.

39 *New York Times*, 5 May 1929, NLS Honeyman Papers

40 *Brooklyn Daily Times*, 5 May 1929, NLS Honeyman Papers.

41 Honeyman, 1937, p.136.

42 Ibid.

43 National Archives UK: UK Incoming Passenger Lists 1878–1960.

44 Letter from Hunter to Arthur Leyden dated 10 July 1929, NLS Honeyman Papers.

45 Honeyman, 1937, p.136.

46 Ibid., p.147.

47 Ibid., pp.140–41.

8 · TRIUMPH AND TRAGEDY PAGES 159–183

1 Dreich [Scots], meaning in this context dreary, bleak.

2 Unpublished research by Douglas Harrison: interview with James Ferry.

3 Jack Webster, *from Dali to Burrell: the Tom Honeyman Story*, Edinburgh, 1997, pp.18, 39–40.

4 Ibid., p.49.

5 Letter from T.J.Honeyman to Hunter in New York dated 18 February 1929, NLS Honeyman Papers.

6 Honeyman, 1937, p.152.

7 Ibid., p.153.

8 Ibid., p.175.

9 Ibid., p.158.

10 Ibid.

11 Letter from Duncan Macdonald to T.J.Honeyman dated 21 February 1931, NLS Honeyman Papers.

12 Letter dated 25 September 1950 from Ion Harrison to T.C.Annan; the authors are grateful to Ronald Harrison for drawing their attention to this letter.

13 Honeyman, 1937, p.162.

14 Letter from Hunter to T.J.Honeyman dateable to 1931, NLS Honeyman Papers.

15 Letter from Duncan Macdonald to T.J.Honeyman dated 21 February 1931, NLS Honeyman Papers.

16 *Apollo*, April 1931.

17 Honeyman, 1937, pp.186–87.

18 Ibid., pp.187–88.

19 Ibid., p.191.

20 Ibid., pp.192–93.

21 *Evening Citizen*, 19 June 1931.

22 Honeyman, 1937, pp.196–97.

23 Hunter running away from home at an early age was not mentioned in the note on her brother prepared for Honeyman by Jeanie McFarlane in 1936, NLS Honeyman Papers.

24 Note for Honeyman by Marnie Scrafton, NLS Honeyman Papers.

25 Honeyman, 1937, p.169.

26 Letter from T.J.Honeyman to Hunter dated 6 February 1931 (NLS: Honeyman Papers)

27 In 1923 Cunninghame Graham met Hunter and subsequently wrote him a letter of encouragement (dated June 1923), particularly praising his paintings of Largo, NLS Honeyman Papers.

28 Honeyman, 1937, p.203.

29 Note for Honeyman by Marnie Scrafton, NLS Honeyman Papers.

9 · A VERITABLE SCOTTISH MASTER PAGES 185–186

1 Honeyman, 1937, p.208.

2 Note for Honeyman by Marnie Scrafton, NLS Honeyman Papers.

3 Honeyman, 1937, p.79.

4 Letter from T.J.Honeyman to Percy Moore Turner dated 10 August 1948, NLS Honeyman Papers.

5 Honeyman, 1937, p.139.

6 Ibid., p.147.

7 Letter from Matthew Justice to T.J.Honeyman dated 10 May 1942, NLS Honeyman Papers.

Leslie Hunter: a brief chronology

1877

Born at Rothesay, Isle of Bute, on 7 August

1892

Death of elder sister, Catherine, on 20 February, and oldest brother, James, on 9 March, probably both victims of the influenza pandemic in January

Family emigrate to California in September, acquiring orange grove 50 miles east of Los Angeles

1895

Family move to Los Angeles, acquiring fruit and grocery business whilst retaining the orange grove

1896

Hunter working in San Francisco 'painting house' for number of months

1899

When family returns to Scotland, Hunter stays in California and moves to San Francisco, making living as newspaper and magazine illustrator

1900

Father dies at Pitlochry on 20 December; family moves to Glasgow the following year

1901

Hunter exhibits his work for the first time

1902

Founding member of California Society of Artists

1903–04

Extended visit to Scotland and Paris

1904

Returns to America in December, spending a period in New York's Greenwich Village before going back to San Francisco

1906

Shortly before his first solo exhibition is due to open, Hunter's studio and all his work is destroyed in the San Francisco earthquake and fire

Becomes a naturalised US citizen

Decides to return to family in Glasgow

Visits Paris

1907

Spends summer working in Paris for the next two or three years

1908

Views the Stein collection of *avant-garde* paintings in Paris

1910

Birth of Katherine, Hunter's illegitimate daughter

Hunter moves to London, resuming work as an illustrator

Visits Paris on a number of occasions over the next five years

1912

Paints at Étaples in the Pas de Calais region of northern France over the next three years

Comes to the attention of Glasgow art dealer, Alexander Reid

1913

Mother dies in Glasgow on 15 March

First solo exhibition in November at Alex. Reid's gallery in Glasgow

1915

Exhibits for the first time at the Royal Scottish Academy

1916

Exhibits for the first time at the Royal Glasgow Institute of the Fine Arts

Solo exhibition at Alex. Reid, Glasgow in March

Moves from Glasgow to live with his cousin, Robert Hunter, at Millburn Farm, Dalserf near Larkhall, for the remainder of the First World War

1917

Elected artist member of Glasgow Art Club

1919

Returns from Millburn Farm to Glasgow in January

Discovers Fife as a painting ground, spending part of each spring and summer there up to 1926

Probably met Peploe for the first time

1921

Solo exhibition at Alex. Reid, Glasgow in April

Has solo exhibition in Dundee with James Foggie of Thomas Murray & Son in November

1922

Spends time in Paris, Rome, Venice and Florence

1923

Exhibition at The Leicester Galleries, London in January: paintings by S.J.Peploe, F.C.B.Cadell & Leslie Hunter

Visits Paris and goes on to spend time in Florence (with Ralph Stackpole), Venice and Settignano (where he visits Leo Stein); suffers mental breakdown in Italy and returns to Glasgow

Spends most of the summer working in Fife

Solo exhibition at Alex. Reid, Glasgow in December

1924

Solo exhibition at Aitken Dott & Son, Edinburgh in March

Spends six weeks in New York in May-June

Exhibition at Galerie Barbazanges, Paris in June: *Les Peintres de L'Écosse Moderne*: F.C.B.Cadell, J.D.Fergusson, Leslie Hunter & S.J.Peploe

Paints at Loch Lomond for the first time and in Fife

1925

Exhibition at The Leicester Galleries, London in January: paintings by S.J.Peploe, Leslie Hunter, F.C.B.Cadell & J.D.Fergusson

Solo exhibition at Alex. Reid, Glasgow in December

1927

Spends most of the year sketching in the south of France, latterly based at *La Colombe d'Or*, St Paul de Vence

Meets André Dunoyer de Segonzac, Othon Friesz and other artists in Matisse's circle in the south of France – possibly Matisse himself

1928

Solo exhibition at Alex. Reid & Lefevre, Glasgow in February

Spends much of the year painting in the south of France; paints with Peploe at Cassis

Solo exhibition at Alex. Reid & Lefevre, London in October-November

In November sails for America, spending 7 months in New York, mainly to organize an exhibition of his work there

1929

Solo exhibition at Ferargil Galleries, New York in April-May

Returns to paint in the south of France in July

Admitted to a clinic in Nice in September after mistakenly swallowing turpentine mixture stored in a wine bottle; three weeks later his sister, Jeanie, takes him back to Glasgow to recuperate

1930

Spends most of the year working from his Glasgow studio, concentrating on still life and latterly experimenting with portraiture

Solo exhibition at Alex. Reid & Lefevre, Glasgow in March

1931

Exhibition at Galeries Georges Petit, Paris in March: *Les Peintres écossais*, S.J.Peploe, J.D.Fergusson, Leslie Hunter, F.C.B.Cadell, Telfer Bear & R.O.Dunlop

Sketches in London and decides to move there permanently; arranges to rent a London studio

Solo exhibition, mainly of portraits, at Alex. Reid & Lefevre, Glasgow in June

Returns to Loch Lomond to paint

Solo exhibition at Alex. Reid & Lefevre, Glasgow in November

Health deteriorates and undergoes gall bladder operation; dies from cardiac failure on 7 December, aged 54

1932

Memorial Exhibition of Paintings and Drawings at Alex. Reid & Lefevre, Glasgow in February

Appendix 1 · Magazine & book illustrations by Hunter

Note: This should not be regarded as an exhaustive list of illustrations. Although the authors have scrutinized many publications likely to have commissioned illustrations from Leslie Hunter, it seems probable that more illustrations will be discovered over time.

Overland Monthly, vol.34
San Francisco, November 1899
Lizzie G. Wilcoxson: *A Pioneering Episode*
Three illustrations, pp.428, 430, 432

Overland Monthly, vol.36
San Francisco, December 1900
Cover illustration for Christmas Number [cowboy with guitar on his horse]
One illustration on front cover

Overland Monthly, vol.37
San Francisco, January 1901
Cover illustration [profile of a monk contemplating holding a small cross]
One illustration on front cover

Overland Monthly, vol.37
San Francisco
Title piece: Clara Spaulding Brown: *Picturesque Guanajuata*
One illustration on p.617

Overland Monthly, vol.37
San Francisco
Head piece: George Selwyn: *A Lawyer Poet's High Play at the National Capital*
One illustration on p.622

Overland Monthly, vol.37
San Francisco, February 1901
Jans Van Dusen: *Francesca, a Tale of Fisherman's Wharf*
Six illustrations, pp.658–59, 661, 663–65

Overland Monthly, vol.37
San Francisco
Waldon Allan Curtis: *The Princess Ronhilda and the Princess Laluaba*
Two illustrations, pp.676, 678

Overland Monthly, vol.37
San Francisco, March 1901
Cover illustration for 'Golden Gate Park' number [group of swans on a pond with tree foliage above]
One illustration on front cover

Overland Monthly, vol.37
San Francisco
Hester A. Benedict: *Kamako*
Four illustrations, pp.778, 782, 784–85

Overland Monthly, vol.37
San Francisco, April 1901
J. F. Rose-Soley: *The Girl from Noumea*
Three illustrations, pp.808, 811, 814

Overland Monthly, vol.37
San Francisco
R. B. Townsend: *The Big Yellow Stag*
Two illustrations, pp.825, 827

Overland Monthly, vol.37
San Francisco, May 1901
Jack London: *The Scorn of Women*
Three illustrations, pp.978, 982, 986

Overland Monthly, vol.37
San Francisco
Lucy Baker Jerome: *The Mad Patrol*
Five illustrations, pp.1019, 1021–23, 1025

Overland Monthly, vol.38
San Francisco, September 1901
A. J. Brown: *The Free Trader*
Three illustrations, pp.186, 189, 192

Overland Monthly, vol.38
San Francisco, December 1901
F. Bret Harte: *Lanty Foster's Mistake*
Two illustrations, pp.401, 405

Overland Monthly, vol.38
San Francisco
Leavenworth MacNab: *The Laugh of Fate*
Two illustrations, pp.446–47

Overland Monthly, vol.39
San Francisco, April 1902
Borders on double page spread for Francis A. Church's poem: *At Early Dawn*
Two illustrations, pp.758–59

Overland Monthly, vol.40
San Francisco, September 1902
F. Bret Harte: *The Outcasts of Poker Flat*
Six illustrations, pp.209–12, 215, 217

Sunset, The Pacific Monthly, vol.9
San Francisco, September 1902
Cecil Marrack: *A Knight of the Red Cross*
Two illustrations, pp.336–37

Sunset, The Pacific Monthly, vol.9
San Francisco, October 1902
Title piece for F. Bret Harte's poem: *The Angelus*
One illustration on p.349

Sunset, The Pacific Monthly, vol.9
San Francisco, November 1902
Title piece for V. Francis Duff: *Danby of San Pedro*
One illustration on p.388

Sunset, The Pacific Monthly, vol.10
San Francisco, November 1902
Flora Haines Loughead: *Mine Eyes unto the Hills Part I*
Four illustrations, pp.26, 28, 30–31

Sunset, The Pacific Monthly, vol.10
San Francisco, November 1902
Title piece for Arthur J. Burdick: *Anita's Sacrifice*
One illustration on p.44

Sunset, The Pacific Monthly, vol.10
San Francisco, December 1902
Flora Haines Loughead: *Mine Eyes unto the Hills*
Part II
Three illustrations, pp.107, 109, 112

Novel published by Thomas Nelson & Sons, London
1903
Charles R Kenyon: *Won in Warfare*
Two illustrations

Sunset, The Pacific Monthly, vol.10
San Francisco, January 1903
Flora Haines Loughead: *Mine Eyes unto the Hills*
Part III
Three illustrations, pp.191, 193, 196

Sunset, The Pacific Monthly, vol.10
San Francisco, February 1903
Flora Haines Loughead: *Mine Eyes unto the Hills*
Part IV
Two illustrations, pp.276, 280

Overland Monthly, vol.41
San Francisco, February 1903
Mrs E.M.Green: *The Chinese Theater*
illustrations, pp.118–25

Society Pictorial, vol.X
Glasgow, 4 April 1903
Street Flowers
One illustration on p.11

Society Pictorial, vol.X
Glasgow, 23 May 1903
Welcoming Their Majesties to Edinburgh
Welcoming Their Majesties to Glasgow
Two illustrations, pp.199, 207

Society Pictorial, vol.X
Glasgow, 13 June 1903
On a Clyde Steamer
One illustration on p.288

Society Pictorial, vol.X
Glasgow, 11 July 1903
A Garden Party
One illustration on p.384

Society Pictorial, vol.X
Glasgow, 12 September 1903
By the Sea – A Sketch at Portobello
One illustration on p.613

Society Pictorial, vol.X
Glasgow, 26 September 1903
An Impression of 'The Only Way'
One illustration on p.664

Society Pictorial, vol.XI
Glasgow, 10 October 1903
A Scene from 'Resurrection'
One illustration on p.32

Society Pictorial, vol.XI
Glasgow, 7 November 1903
Samaritan Fancy Dress Ball
One illustration on pp.146–47

Society Pictorial, vol.XI
Glasgow, 26 December 1903
The Barrier (dated Dec '03)
One illustration on p.372

The Idler, vol.24
1903–1904
Margaret Westrup: *Concerning a Proposal*
Three illustrations, pp.583, 589–90

Novel published by Collins, London
1904
Bessie Marchant: *The Girls of Wakenside – A Story for Girls*
Eight illustrations

The Idler, vol.25
1904
E. Burrowes: *The Wrentham Pearl*
Three illustrations, pp.191, 193, 195

Society Pictorial, vol.XI
Glasgow, 30 January 1904
A New Sport for Ladies
One illustration on p.524

Society Pictorial, vol.XII
Glasgow, 2 April 1904
Cartoon: *Artless Ethel and Artful Maud*
One illustration on p.165

Society Pictorial, vol.XII
Glasgow, 28 May 1904
In the Chapel of Holyrood
One illustration on p.416c

Society Pictorial, vol.XII
Glasgow, 4 June 1904
The Picture Season
One illustration on p.433

Society Pictorial, vol.XIII
Glasgow, 17 December 1904
Ready for the Ball (dated '04)
One illustration on p.581

The Idler, vol.26
1904–1905
J. S. Mackintosh: *An Object in Life*
Three illustrations, pp.19, 21, 23

The Idler, vol.27
1905
E. M. Hughes: *Twice Convicted*
Three illustrations, pp.519, 523–24

Life
23 March 1905
[Unknown]
One illustration on p.331

Society Pictorial, vol.XIV
Glasgow, 29 July 1905
The Garden Party
One illustration on p.9

Overland Monthly, vol.46
San Francisco, August 1905
Standalone illustration: *Viewing San Francisco from Sutro Forest*
One illustration on p.100

Overland Monthly, vol.46
San Francisco, August 1905
J. Gordon Smith: *The Outcast*
One illustration on p.99

Society Pictorial, vol.XIV
Glasgow, 19 August 1905
On a Clyde Steamer
One illustration on p.21

Overland Monthly, vol.46
San Francisco, September 1905
Della R. Neal: *A Strife in the Blood*
Two illustrations, pp.195, 198

Overland Monthly, vol.46
San Francisco date?
Mamie Buford Steele Harris: *A Memory*
One illustration between pp.186–187

Society Pictorial, vol.XIV
Glasgow, 2 September 1905
By the Sea – A Sketch at Portobello
One illustration on p.8

Overland Monthly, vol.46
San Francisco, October 1905
Fred A. Hunt: *Smoke*
One illustration between pp.290–291

Sunset, The Pacific Monthly, vol.16
San Francisco, February 1906
Charles Warren Stoddard: *Old Monterey* [poem]
Two illustrations, pp.358–59

Lady's Illustrated Weekly, vol.XVI
4 August 1906
By the Sea – A Sketch at Portobello
One illustration on p.9

Lady's Illustrated Weekly, vol.XVI
18 August 1906
On a Clyde Steamer
One illustration on p.11

Sunset, The Pacific Monthly, vol.17
San Francisco, September 1906
2 head pieces & 2 tail pieces for Amelia Woodward Truesdell's poem: *Francisca Reina*
Four illustrations, pp.256–57

Sunset, The Pacific Monthly, vol.17
San Francisco, October 1906
Eleanor Gates: *A Natural Vegetarian*
Two illustrations, pp.356, 358

Graphic London, vol.82
24 December 1910
The Cowboy's Christmas Eve [dated 1910]
One illustration on p.1035

Graphic London, vol.82 Christmas Supplement
24 December 1910
The Christmas Mail in a Canadian Mining Camp [dated 1910]
One illustration on p.37

The Strand Magazine, vol.41
February 1911
Morley Roberts: *Clever Mr. Painter*
Five illustrations, pp.222, 225, 226, 228, 231

Harper's Weekly, vol.55
15 July 1911
Herman Scheffauer: *Fire Child*
Three illustrations, pp.16–17

Graphic London, vol.84
11 November 1911
Abolishing their Badge of Servitude: Chinese having their Pigtails cut off [dated 1911]
One illustration on p.699

Graphic London, vol.84
25 November 1911
The Latest Craze of American Society: New Yorkers dining in a Chinese Restaurant
One illustration on p.791

Harper's Weekly, vol.55
23 December 1911
Herman Scheffauer: *Stolen Bride*
Three illustrations, pp.14–15

Pall Mall Magazine London
1913
Headpieces illustrating months April–October & December

Pall Mall Magazine London, vol.51
March 1913
Herman Scheffauer: *Twixt Dusk and Dawn in Paris*
Twelve illustrations

Pall Mall Magazine London
1914
Headpieces illustrating months January–August

Pall Mall Magazine London, vol.53
January 1914
Rosamond Napier: *The Sheepbells*
Three illustrations

Pall Mall Magazine London, vol.53
March 1914
Herman Scheffauer: *The City without Night, Berlin Twixt Dusk and Dawn*
Fourteen illustrations

Graphic London, vol.90
26 December 1914
The Christmas Goose in the Trenches
One illustration on p.877

Pearsons Magazine
1915
P.G. Wodehouse: *Crowned Heads*
Three illustrations, pp.394, 397, 403

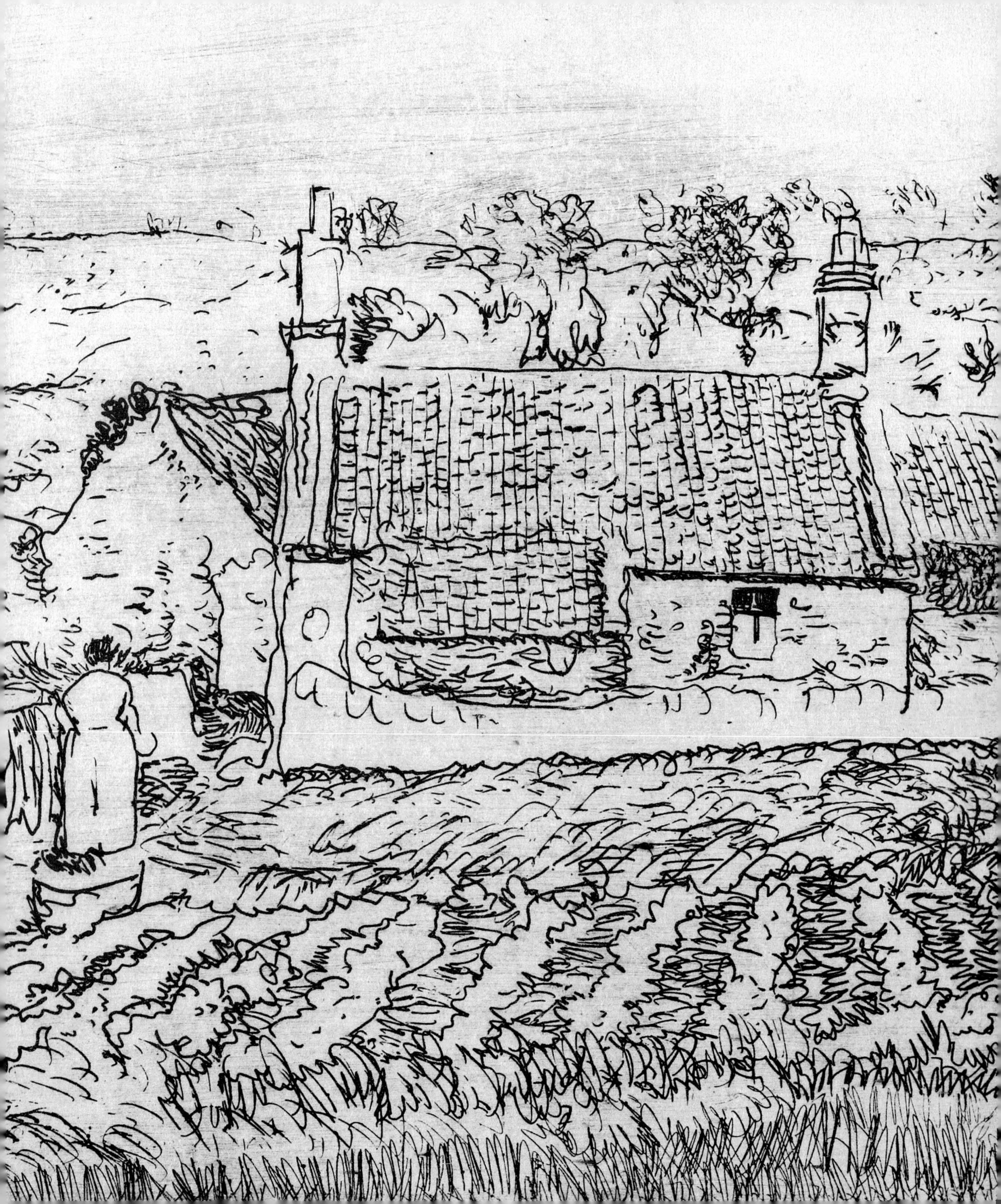

Appendix 2 · Prints by Hunter

Two labourers, *c.*1904
Colour monotype · 31.6 × 18.2 cm

Woman with a basket, *c.*1904
Colour monotype · 26 × 23.1 cm

Interior with a man gutting fish, *c.*1908
Colour monotype · 22 × 27.5 cm

Landscape with a white horse, *c.*1913
Colour monotype · 14.2 × 18.3 cm

Bearded gentleman wearing a ruff and a chain
Monotype · 21.5 × 20 cm

Still-life with apples
Etching touched in ink · 14.9 × 20 cm

Still-life with jug and apples, *c.*1919-20
Drypoint · 19.1 × 16.7 cm

Girl seated on a sofa, *c.*1920
Drypoint · 25 × 17.5 cm

Ceres Cottages, *c.*1920
Etching · 12.5 × 20 cm

Ceres, with two women in conversation, *c.*1920
Etching · 12.5 × 19.9 cm

Ceres, with three fishermen, *c.*1920
Etching · 12.7 × 14.9 cm

Ceres, *c.*1920
Etching & drypoint · 12.7 × 20.1 cm

Tree outside a Fife cottage with a paling, *c.*1920
Etching · 9.1 × 12.5 cm

Figure in a straw hat outside a Fife cottage, *c.*1920
Etching · 26.5 × 16.2 cm

Figure in a straw hat outside a Fife cottage (second version), *c.*1920
Etching · 22.5 × 14.9 cm

Cottage in a Fife fishing village (probably Largo), *c.*1920
Etching · 8.8 × 12.6 cm

Figure and cottages, Ceres, *c.*1920
Etching · 15 × 22.5 cm

Farmhouse, *c.*1920
Monotype · 26.5 × 32.3 cm

169 | Figure and Cottages, Ceres (detail)
Etching, *c.*1920 · see plate 64
Private collection

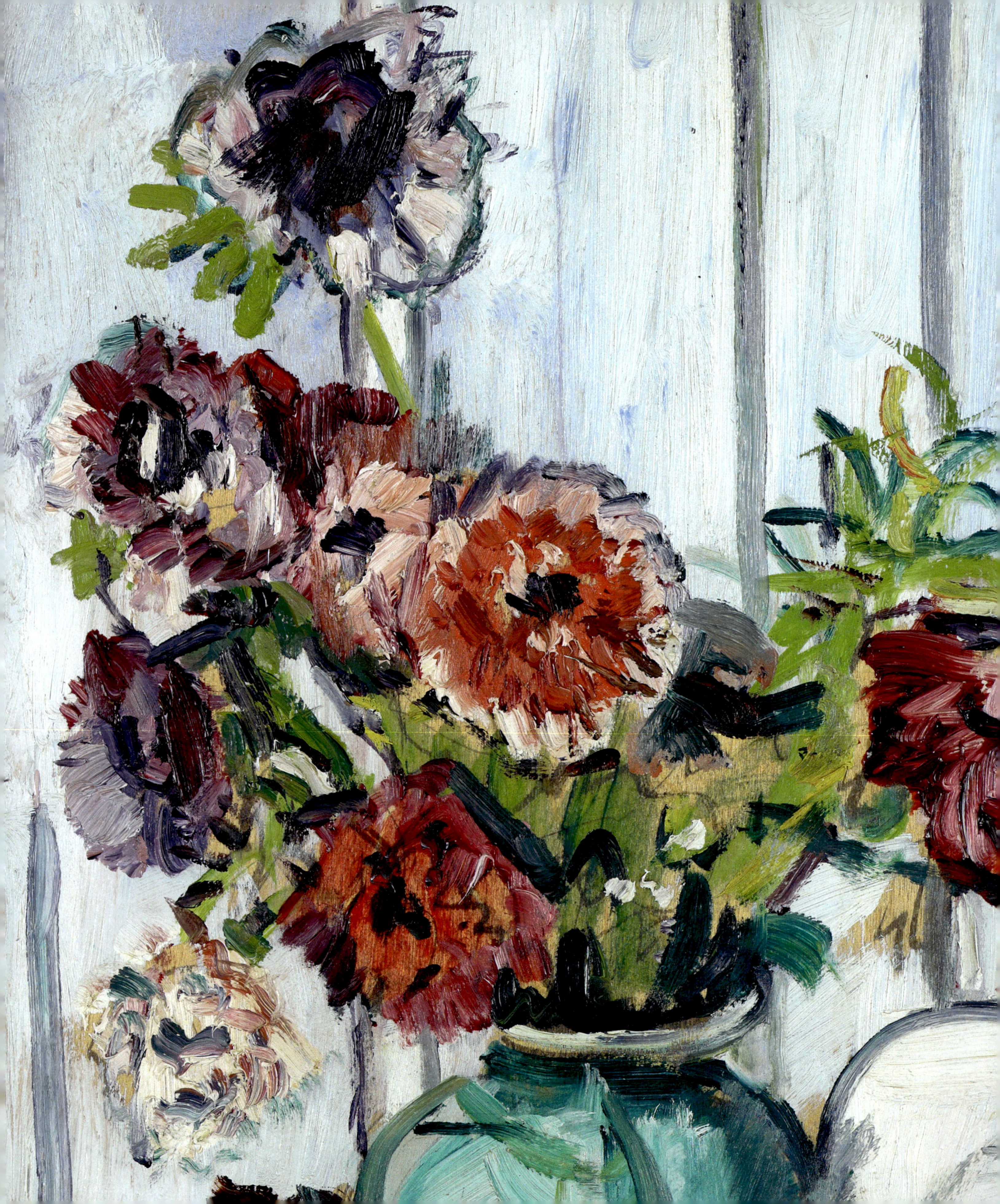

List of Plates

170 | Anemones in a Green Vase, Banana and Two Apples (detail)
Oil on panel, 1925–26 · see plate 88
Private collection

WORKS BY HUNTER

Listed in alphabetical order
Measurements are given in centimetres, height × width

OTHER ILLUSTRATIONS

Photographic Credits

References are to plate numbers

Aberdeen Art Gallery & Museums 16, 87, 118, 159

Jean Barnard, California 3, 5

Bonhams 35, 70

Bourne Fine Art, Edinburgh 54

The British Library 8, 9, 13, 20, 27

Christie's / Bridgeman Art Library 14, 109, 123, 134, 135, 149, 151, 163, 165

City Art Centre, Edinburgh 162

Duncan R Miller Fine Arts, London 6, 15, 22, 52, 98, 114, 120, 136, 154

Dundee Art Galleries & Museum 53

The Fine Art Society, London 42, 93

The Fine Art Society, London / Bridgeman Art Library 129

The Fleming-Wyfold Art Foundation / Bridgeman Art Library 67, 92, 104, 112, 156

Glasgow Museums 26, 41, 56, 68, 69, 83, 85, 95, 105, 137, 139, 168

Mark Medcalf Associates, Edinburgh 38

Museums Sheffield 74

National Library of Scotland 2, 4, 10, 28, 45, 138

Paisley Museum & Art Galleries 75

Portland Gallery, London 43, 91

Potteries Museum & Art Gallery, Stoke-on-Trent 103

Richard Green, London 73, 86

The Scottish Gallery, Edinburgh 77

Scottish National Gallery of Modern Art 30, 65, 106, 108, 111, 145, 158

Sotheby's 80, 99, 100, 124, 143, 146

Tate Britain 46

University of Edinburgh Fine Art Collection 90

University of Glasgow, Hunterian Art Gallery 11, 12, 17, 18, 19, 32, 48, 57, 58, 66, 96, 102, 150

Selected Bibliography

Scottish Art

HARDIE, William, *Scottish Painting: 1837 to the Present*, Studio Vista, London, 1990

MACDONALD, Murdo, *Scottish Art*, Thames & Hudson, London, 2000

MACMILLAN, Duncan, *Scottish Art 1460–2000*, Mainstream, Edinburgh, 2000

The Scottish Colourists

BILLCLIFFE, Roger, *The Scottish Colourists*, John Murray, London, 1996

FOWLE, Frances, 'Three Scottish Colourists: Early Patronage of Peploe, Hunter and Cadell', *Apollo*, October 2000

FOWLE, Frances, *Van Gogh's Twin: The Scottish Art Dealer Alexander Reid*, National Galleries of Scotland, Edinburgh, 2010

HEWLETT, Tom, & Duncan Macmillan, *F.C.B.Cadell: The Life and Works of a Scottish Colourist 1883–1937*, Lund Humphries, Farnham, 2011

HONEYMAN, T.J., *Three Scottish Colourists: Peploe, Cadell, Hunter*, Thomas Nelson, London, 1950

PEPLOE, Guy, *S.J.Peploe 1871—1935*, Mainstream, Edinburgh, 2000

SIMISTER, Kirsten, *Living Paint: J.D.Fergusson 1874–1961*, Mainstream, Edinburgh, 2001

Hunter

HJALMARSON, Birgitta, *Artful Players: Artistic Life in Early San Francisco*, Balcony Press, Los Angeles, 2000

HONEYMAN, T.J., *Introducing Leslie Hunter*, Faber & Faber, London, 1937

HOPKINSON, Martin, 'California, Scotland and Paris: The Prints of Leslie Hunter', *Print Quarterly* vol.xvi no.3, September 1999

OGSTON, Derek, *George Leslie Hunter 1877–1931*, Baillieknowe, Stichill, 2002

OGSTON, Derek, *Leslie Hunter: Paintings and Drawings of France and Italy*, Baillieknowe, Stichill, 2004

STARR, Kevin, *Americans and the California Dream 1850–1915*, Oxford University Press, New York, 1973

WICKES, George, *Americans in Paris*, Da Capo Press, New York, 1980

Exhibition catalogues

Memorial Exhibition of Paintings & Drawings by Leslie Hunter, Alex. Reid & Lefevre, Glasgow, 1932

Pictures from a Private Collection, The Thistle Foundation, Glasgow, 1951

Three Scottish Colourists: Peploe, Cadell, Hunter, Scottish Arts Council, Edinburgh, 1970

George Leslie Hunter 1877–1931, Duncan R. Miller Fine Arts, London, 1990

The Scottish Colourists 1900–1930, National Galleries of Scotland, Edinburgh, 2000

Intimate Friends: Scottish Colourists from the Hunterian Art Gallery and The Fleming Collection, The Fleming-Wyfold Art Foundation, London, 2003

Les Coloristes écossais de 1900 a 1935, Mona Bismarck Foundation, Paris, 2004

Index

Index of works by Hunter mentioned in the text